Where Marketing Theory Meets Practice:

Selected Papers from the Second Annual Conference of the Sport Marketing Association

Edited and Selected from the
SMA Conference,
November, 2004

Brenda G. Pitts, Editor
Vice President for Academic Affairs
Sport Marketing Association, 2003-2006
Professor, Director, Sport Management Masters Program
Georgia State University

Fitness Information Technology
A Division of the International
Center for Performance Excellence
262 Coliseum, WVU-PE, PO Box 6116
Morgantown, WV 26506-6116

Copyright ©2005 by Sport Marketing Association

ALL RIGHTS RESERVED

Reproduction or use of any portion of this publication by any mechanical, electronic, or other means is prohibited without the written permission of the publisher.

Library of Congress Card Catalog Number: 2005931191

ISBN: 1885693672

Cover design: Scribe, Inc.
Copyeditor: Corey Madsen
Proofreader: Matt Brann
Production Editor: Corey Madsen
Typeset by Scribe, Inc.
Printed by Publishers' Graphics
Printed in the United States of America

10 9 8 7 6 5 4 3 2 1

Fitness Information Technology
A Division of the International Center for Performance Excellence
262 Coliseum, WVU-PE, PO Box 6116
Morgantown, WV 26506-6116
800.477.4348 (toll free)
304.293.6888 (phone)
304.293.6658 (fax)
Email: icpe@mail.wvu.edu
Web Site: www.fitinfotech.com

Table of Contents

A Word From the Sport Marketing Association President
Richard Irwin
v

Introduction: Sport Marketing Research: Linkages Between
Academe and Practice & Who Can Use This Book
Brenda G. Pitts
vii

SECTION I
CONSUMER BEHAVIOR IN THE SPORT BUSINESS INDUSTRY

A New Stadium's Impact on Attendance in
Major League Baseball (MLB)
Stephen L. Baglione, Stewart Gillman, & Balbir Bal
3

The Spectators' Perceptions and Expectations on the
Quality of Competition and Services of the Arena at the
Corporate Basketball Games in the People's Republic of China
Steve Chen, Mark Zhang, & Ta-tsung Chiou
9

Sports Fan Involvement in New Zealand: The Case of
Cricket, Football (Soccer), and Rugby
Kathryn Dobie, James Grant, & James Zarick
19

Case Study: Sport Marketing Research for
Women's Athletics
Erin P. Hughes
27

A Cross-Cultural Study of Factors Explaining Action
Sports Fandom of Y Generation College Students in Korea,
Taiwan, and the USA
Sung-Bae Park, Soonhwan Lee, & Mei-Yen Chen
39

Consumer Complaint Behaviour in Sport Consumption
Michael Volkov, Melissa Johnson Morgan, & Jane Summers
49

The "Toughest Sport on Dirt": An Exploratory Study of
Market Demand Variables of Fans of the Professional
Bull Riders Inc.
Chia-ying (Doris) Lu, Brenda Pitts, Kevin Ayers, & Carol Lucas
65

Sports Event Spectators' Perceptions of Mobile Marketing.
    Empirical Evidence from Finland   73
Jari Salo, Heikki Karjaluoto, Manne Kesti, Timo Koivumäki,
Annu Ristola

SECTION II
MEDIA AND ITS MESSAGES: MANAGING FOR MARKETING

Framing Annika: An Analysis of Newspaper Columnist
    Writing About Annika Sorenstam Playing in the Colonial   89
John A. Fortunato & Eunyi Kim

Assessing the Impact of Sport Editorials and Cognitive
    Complexity on Social Behavior   101
Daniel C. Funk & Mark Pritchard

Sports Public Relations: The Strategic Application of
    Public Relations to the Business of Sport   117
Maria Hopwood

Rugby League: A Game in Crisis   131
Jane Summers, Melissa Johnson Morgan, & Michael Volkov

SECTION III
FINANCIAL MATTERS AND SPORT MARKETING

Zero-Based Sport Marketing Management:
    A Management and Budgeting Tool for Sport Managers   151
Dennis L. Bechtol

SECTION IV
SPONSORSHIP AND SPORT MARKETING

Fulfilling Sponsorship Goals: Evaluation of Major
    League Soccer Team Websites   163
Corey Braun, Vassilis Dalakas, Joe Fernandez, & Andrea Lansford

Utilizing Youth Sport Sponsorships to Break
    Through the Media Clutter   171
Eric J. Newman

Section V
Endorsement, Building Brand, and Promotional Strategies

Sports Celebrities as Endorsers: An Analysis of Tiger Woods   179
Dan Drane, Dennis Phillips, Alvin Williams, & Brian Crow

Branding Athletes: If the Athlete is the Brand, Does the
    Product Matter?   189
Ron Garland & Jan Charbonneau

Understanding and Adapting to Cultural Diversity in
    International Sport Marketing   197
Jaime Orejan

The Challenge of Building Brand Equity: A Look at
    Cases in North America and Europe   207
André Richelieu & Vincent Couvelaere

Case Study: How to Get a Minor League Promotion
    Major League Publicity   227
Authors: Douglas Blais & Eric C. Schwarz
Contributors: Jeff Eisenberg & Todd Marlin

Gender as a Determinant of the Relative Merits of
    Celebrity Sports Figures in Magazine Advertising   231
Melissa St. James & James E. Swartz

A Case Study of the SARS Epidemic and the
    Toronto Blue Jays   245
David Synowka, Scott Branvold, & Susan Hofacre

Editor Biography   253
Author Biographies   255

A WORD FROM THE SPORT MARKETING ASSOCIATION PRESIDENT

As SMA President and host of SMA II, the second annual SMA Conference, it gives me great pride to share this book with members of the Association as well as an extended readership base. The collection of outstanding papers contained within this manuscript is drawn from over 150 academic presentations delivered during the three day conference held in Memphis, Tennessee, November 18–20, 2004, attracting more than 300 sport marketing scholars, professionals, and students.

As a key scholarship initiative intended to fulfill the ambitious mission of the Association, this text represents a critical means of providing membership a medium for disseminating research on the sport industry's best practices in marketing. The breadth of topics addressed within clearly highlights the extensive research agendas and broad talents of those committed to the achievement of this mission.

Once again, SMA has been fortunate to have Dr. Brenda Pitts, Georgia State University professor and SMA Vice President for Academic Affairs, serve as this publication's editor. Similarly, I would like to take one last opportunity to thank the faculty and students at the University of Memphis for their diligent efforts to produce a truly magnificent conference. Most notably heartfelt gratitude goes out to Drs. Richard Southall and John Amis for their tireless efforts on the academic program, and Mr. John Mathers, SMA Business Manager, for his masterful organization of the conference.

Richard L. Irwin, President
Sport Marketing Association
Professor, University of Memphis

Introduction:
Sport Marketing Research:
Linkages Between
Academe and Practice

BRENDA G. PITTS

As we go to press with the second edition of the Sport Marketing Association's book of research papers from the second conference (held November 2004 in Memphis, Tennessee), I am excited about and impressed with the amount of work involved in conducting sport marketing research. For this second edition, there are 22 studies conducted and written by 56 authors from around the world who represent both sport management and/or sport marketing academe and industry. Like the first edition, this second edition provides a much-needed venue for publishing and disseminating sport marketing research. This book of papers adds significantly to the emerging field of sport marketing.

I am happy to report that this year there was an increase in the number of papers. In addition, there is one more section. For every reader of this book, I believe you will find something of interest.

Who Can Use This Book

This book is appropriate for use in industry and academe. Sport industry professionals working in any type of sport business will find the papers worth reading, and, moreover, that the information and strategies may be used for a variety of purposes.

Professors who teach sport marketing at both undergraduate and graduate levels may find the papers useful in a variety of ways. The papers may be used in class as case studies, as assigned reading, for critical analysis, or for encouraging progressive graduate research.

For students in sport management and sport marketing courses, this book provides contemporary sport marketing research on a number of industry segments utilizing a variety of research methods. Students may learn more about the industry and how research provides vital information for competitive strategy development.

SECTION I

CONSUMER BEHAVIOR IN THE SPORT BUSINESS INDUSTRY

A New Stadium's Impact on Attendance in Major League Baseball (MLB)

STEPHEN L. BAGLIONE
STEWART GILLMAN
BALBIR BAL

Abstract

Our paper quantifies the benefit to a Major League Baseball franchise for a new stadium. In our study, we examined data for the year 2002. Our results show that after controlling for differences in population, per capita income, ticket prices, and win-loss record through regression analysis, a new stadium increases attendance annually by 316,759 in the first five years and over 764,992 in years six to 10. Thus, the "novelty effect" of a new stadium appears to increase over time. Also, the study shows that the variables contributing the most to attendance are ticket prices and win-loss record.

Introduction

New stadiums in professional baseball, more than the other major sports where sellouts are common, boost short-term attendance (Depken, 2003; Noll, 1974). One study reported attendance increases of over 50% for new baseball stadiums, but little impact in basketball and football, although other sports may benefit from ticket price increases once a new stadium opens (Quirk & Fort, 1997). Another study suggests that the novelty effect "is strongest, and most persistent, in Major League Baseball, somewhat smaller and less persistent in the National Basketball Association, and relatively weak and short lived in the National Football League" (Coates & Humphreys, 2003, p. 17). This "novelty effect," or desire to experience a new venue, has been shown to extend up to 10 years (Quinn et al., 2003; Coates & Humphreys, 2001, 1999; Baade & Sanderson, 1997; Kahane & Schmanske, 1997; Coffin, 1996). Examining stadium age, not merely the novelty effect, Bruggink and Eaton (1996) found a negative effect for American League franchises but a positive effect for National League franchises. It is believed that this novelty effect in baseball may be declining after examining recent stadium openings in Pittsburgh, Detroit, and Milwaukee (Klein, 2002).

Public-Policy Implications

Whether attendance increases or not, clearly it has public-policy implications since almost all U.S. professional sports facilities receive some public subsidy (Coates & Humphreys, 2003), around 70% for NFL and MLB franchisees from taxpayers (Brown & Paul, 2002). And, it is estimated that about $10 billion will be spent on new sports facilities in the next decade (Brown & Paul, 2002).

Our paper does not attempt to justify the investment in local stadiums by municipalities. The academic literature is unequivocal: the cost of publicly financing stadiums exceeds the economic benefits to a community (Rappaport & Wilkerson, 2001; Noll & Zimbalist, 1997; Baade, 1996).

Methods

We use annual attendance data (2002) by MLB franchisees (home attendance only), common in the literature (Coates & Humphreys, 2003; Humphreys, 2002; Eckard, 2001). Thus, we assume that any novelty effect would continue over an entire year. We attempt to separate the impact of a new stadium on attendance through regression analysis from community size in population (Metropolitan Statistical Area [MSA] as defined by the U.S. Census Bureau), ticket price (weighted average), per capita income, and win-loss record (percentage). Other studies have used regression to control for other factors (Depken, 2003; Coates & Humphreys, 2003; Baade, 1996). Stadium age is converted into two dummy variables: zero to five years and six to 10 years, with the effect of stadiums older than 10 captured in the intercept. Ten years was chosen because the novelty effect has been shown to continue up to 10 years.

Data from the *SportsBusiness Journal* (2003) is used for stadium age, attendance, and ticket prices. Price is a weighted price for all tickets. (Note: A weighted ticket price did not exist for the Colorado Rockies.) Per capita income and population are from Rand McNally's *Commercial Atlas & Marketing Guide* (2003) and win-loss from MLB's website (www.mlb.com). Data for ticket price, win-loss, attendance, and population were for 2002, while per capita income was 2001, the last available year. For the two Canadian teams, per capita income and population figures are from 2001 (www.statcan.ca/start.html). Canadian per capita income was converted into United States' dollars (www.xe.com). Since we are examining a population instead of a sample, we do not use statistical techniques based on sampling. Our model is

Attendance (annual 2002) = a + ß1 population (2002) + ß2 per capita income (2001) + ß3 win-loss record (2002) + ß4 weighted ticket price (2002) + ß5 stadium age (0 to 5 years) + ß6 stadium age (6 to 10 years)

Hypotheses

Our focus is: Does the stadium provide a sustainable increase in attendance after controlling for differences in population, per capita income, ticket price, and win-loss record? One would expect that new stadiums would be a novelty for a few years, but what about five years or 10 years after completion? Also, among the regression variables, which one contributes the most to attendance? Since the variables are measured in different units, we examine standardized coefficients to determine variable contributions. ("Standardization is a method of removing the units of measure from each variable and placing all the predictors on the same scale" [Hair, Bush, & Ortinau, 2003, p. 576].)

H1: A new stadium, up to five years of age, will increase attendance.
H2: Stadiums from age six to 10 years will increase attendance.
H3: The increase in attendance for stadiums of up to five years of age will be greater than the increase in attendance of stadiums six to 10 years old.
H4: The most important variable, as measured by the standardized regression coefficients, will be a team's win-loss record.

Results

No significance tests were conducted since we examined a population. In our population, nine teams have stadiums five years old or less, and four have stadiums six to nine years old. Attendance ranges from 812,045 to 3,542,938. MSA populations range from 1,169,641 to 9,684,800. Per capita income ranges from $16,445 to $32,843. A franchise's win-loss record ranges from 34% to 64%. The weighted ticket price ranges from $8.99 to $41.94.

The regression model has an adjusted R^2 of 49% (Table 1). An increase in the MSA's population increases attendance by .06. That is, if the population increases by 100, attendance increases by six people. Per capita income increases attendance by 8.3; in other words, a one dollar increase in per capita income increases attendance by 8.3, while a 1% increase in a team's win-loss record increases attendance by 35,247. And, a one dollar increase in the weighted average ticket price increases attendance by 47,936. Having a stadium that is five years old or less increases attendance by 316,759. Stadiums 6 to 10 years of age increases attendance by 764,992. Hypotheses one and two are supported. Since 6 to 10 years is greater than 0 to 5 years in increasing attendance, hypothesis three is not supported. Using the standardized coefficients, the team's win-loss record has the greatest influence, followed very closely by the weighted ticket price, .43 and .40, respectively. That is, a one standard deviation change in the win-loss percentage causes a .43 standard deviation in the dependent variable, attendance (Pinkyck & Rubinfeld, 1998). This supports hypothesis four.

Table 1: Dependent variable: Annual Attendance by Franchise		
	Unstandardized Beta	Standardized Beta
Constant	-1,124,101	
Population (2002)	.057	.207
Per Capita Income (2001)	8.28	.037
Win-loss Record (2002)	3,524,740	.428
Weighted Ticket Price (2002)	47,936	.400
Stadium Five or Less Years (2002)	316,759	.195
Stadium Six to 10 Years (2002)	764,992	.311

$R^2 = .63$ *Adjusted R^2 = .49* $n = 30$

Conclusion

From our results, teams with older stadiums should examine the benefits of building a new stadium: new stadiums increase attendance substantially, with the greatest impact for stadiums between the ages of 6 to 10 years. We cannot say, however, that it increases revenue or profitability, although larger attendance should translate into greater parking and concession sales. According to Depken (2003), new baseball stadiums not only lead to higher attendance but also have an effect on winning percentage and concession revenue. Newly-built stadiums have become an important source of income for the clubs by providing luxury suites, souvenir shops, restaurants, and museums (Robinson, 1997). These added features help to sell more tickets and attract better corporate sponsorship deals, thus significantly increasing the income for the clubs. This is particularly important in the MLB stadiums, as clubs can keep all the income "from luxury suites, stadium-based sponsorships, naming rights, and food and parking concessions" (Robinson, 1997, p. 56).

Since prior research shows no economic benefit to communities that subsidize stadiums, our results only reinforce the argument that the economic benefits of a new stadium accrue to the franchisee. Increases in attendance—which we can hypothesize increases revenue—benefit the franchisee. As such, the franchise appears to be generating revenue. We do not estimate in our research how much of that revenue that could, and probably should be, used to pay for their own stadiums (Coates & Humphreys, 2003). With that said, weighted ticket prices and a team's win-loss record have the biggest impact on a team's attendance. We did rerun the regression, converting both attendance and weighted ticket price into logs to determine elasticity, which we found to be .61; this indicates inelastic demand. However, since this is a weighted ticket price, the weighted price itself could increase because there are more luxury boxes, while the lowest price ticket could decrease or increase less than inflation.

Limitations

Using dummy variables assumes that the effects of a new stadium are the same for all years that the dummy variable encompasses (i.e., five years); but since we examined only one year, there is not enough data to examine the effect of individual years (e.g., one-year old, two-years old). Our model does include other factors that have been used in the literature. Attendance may also be influenced by the previous year's win-loss record and whether the franchise made the playoffs the prior year (Depken, 2003). We did not control for team loyalty, although measuring team loyalty does create a problem for teams that have switched cities. For example, do you measure loyalty from the Dodgers' inception in Brooklyn or from their move to Los Angeles? One study's "crude measure" of team loyalty shows mixed results on attendance (Coates & Humphreys, 2003). Data for per capita income were for the previous year, not the study's year, due to non-availability of the data. Finally, and probably most importantly, we examined only one year of data.

Future Research

This research should be extended longitudinally, since only a cross-sectional study was completed. The study should be extended to other major professional sports, allowing us to compare across all professional sports.

References

Baade, R. A., & Sanderson, A. R. (1997). The employment effect of teams and sports facilities. In R. G. Noll & A. Zimbalist (Eds.). *Sports, jobs, and taxes: The economic impact of sports teams and stadiums.* Washington, DC: Brookings Institution Press, 92-118.

Baade, R. A. (1996). Professional sports and catalysts for metropolitan economic development. *Journal of Urban Affairs, 18*(1), 1-17.

Brown, C., & Paul, D. M. (2002). The political scorecard of professional sports facility referendums in the United States, 1984-2000. *Journal of Sport and Social Issues, 26*(3), 248-267.

Bruggink, T. H., & Eaton, J. W. (1996). Rebuilding attendance in Major League Baseball: The demand for individual games. In L. Hadley (Ed.), *Baseball economics: Current research.* Westport, CT: Praeger.

Coates, D., & Humphreys, B. R. (2003). Novelty effects of new facilities on attendance at professional sporting events. UMBC Economics Department Working Paper 03-101.

Coates, D., & Humphreys, B. R. (2001). The economic consequences of professional sports strikes and lockouts. *Southern Economic Journal, 67*(3), 737-747.

Coates, D., & Humphreys, B. R. (1999). The growth effects of sport franchises, stadia, and arenas. *Journal of Policy Analysis and Management, 18*(4), 601-624.

Coffin, D. A. (1996). If you build it will they come. In J. Fizel (Ed.), *Baseball economics: Current research.* Westport, CT: Praeger.

Commercial atlas and marketing guide (134th ed.). (2003). Skokie, IL: Rand McNally.

Depken, C. A. II. (2003). The novelty effect of a new stadium in Major League Baseball: Does it extend to concession prices? University of Texas, Arlington, Working Paper.

Eckard, E. W. (2001). Free agency, competitive balance, and diminishing returns to pennant contention. *Economic Inquiry, 39*(3), 430-443.

Hair, J. F., Bush, R. P., & Ortinau, D. J. (2003). *Marketing research: Within a changing information environment*. Boston: McGraw-Hill Irwin.

Humphreys, B. R. (2002). Alternative measures of competitive balance in sports leagues. *Journal of Sports Economics, 3*(2), 133-148.

Kahane, L., & Schmanske, S. (1997). Team roster turnover and attendance in Major League Baseball. *Applied Economics, 29*(4), 425-431.

Klein, F. C. (2002, 24 June). Build it, yet sometimes they don't come. *SportsBusiness Journal, 5*(32), 35-36.

Mark, S., Belkin, D., & Cortell, J. (2004). Double play: The economics and financing of stadiums for the Yankees and Mets. Retrieved July 2, 2004, from http://www.ibo.nyc.ny.us/iboreports/doubleplay.html.

Noll, R., & Zimblist, A. (1997). *Sports, jobs, and taxes: The economic impact of sports teams and stadiums*. Washington, DC: The Brookings Institution.

Noll, R. G. (1974). Attendance and price setting. In R. G. Noll (Ed.), *Government and the sports business*. Washington, DC: The Brookings Institution.

Pindyck, R. S., & Rubinfeld, D. L. (1998). *Econometric models and economic forecasts* (4th ed.). Boston, MA: Irwin McGraw-Hill.

Quinn, K. G., Bursik, P. B., Borick, C. P., & Raethz, L. (2003). Do new digs mean more wins? *Journal of Sports Economics, 4*(3), 167-182.

Quirk, J., & Fort, R. (1997). *Pay dirt: The business of professional team sports* (2nd ed.). Princeton, NJ: Princeton University Press.

Rappaport, J., & Wilkerson, C. (2001). What are the benefits of hosting a major league sports franchise? *Economic Review - Federal Reserve Bank of Kansas City, 86*(1), 55-87.

Robinson, E. (1997). It's where you play that counts. *Fortune, 136*(2), 54-57.

SportsBusiness Journal (2004). By the numbers. *5*(36), 89-97.

The Spectators' Perceptions and Expectations on the Quality of Competition and Services of the Arena at the Corporate Basketball Games in the People's Republic of China

STEVE CHEN
MARK ZHANG
TA-TSUNG CHIOU

Abstract

This study examined the perceptions and expectations of spectators on the quality of competition and services of the arena at the Corporate Basketball games in the People's Republic of China. A convenience sampling method was adopted to directly survey 194 spectators (male = 151; female = 43) at two Nangang Dragons' home games. A Chinese-version questionnaire was modified from Choo's (1998) survey questionnaire. It contained 21 questions which elicited information on participants' demographic characteristics, reasons for not attending the games, favorable choices on foods and souvenirs, willingness of purchasing the season ticket, preferences on entertaining activities, and perceptions and expectations on the quality of available services.

The results found that the participants were predominantly male in the age group of 20-39 years old, and many of them (92%) had income less than 450 USD per month. Three specific factors concerning the quality of the services were identified. Both male and female participants' perceptions and expectations on all three factors varied significantly ($p < .01$). Males also placed more value on the game itself than females did ($p < .05$). The less educated participants gave a higher score on the perceived service quality. Higher income individuals gave an inferior score toward physical entity and the intangible services. Both factors of physical entity and intangible services and the game itself are effective predictors of the overall satisfaction. Important service elements, such as the excitement of the game, lighting of the arena, and air conditioning were identified as critical and well served. In conclusion, suggestions and recommendations were provided for the purpose of maximizing the profits and improving the existing quality of services.

Introduction

Basketball is one of the most popular team sports in China. Basketball skills are taught in physical education classes at all levels. Intramural, interscholastic, and collegiate basketball games are the most commonly organized competitive activities among Chinese education institutions. At the corporate/professional level, basketball games are often used to promote teamwork, pride, and organizational spirit or culture. Since basketball was introduced to China in the early 20th century by YMCA missionaries, its popularity has grown consistently. Entering the 1990s, basketball fever in China greatly expanded with the booming popularity of the NBA and Michael Jordan. This hype reached a new height when the national hero, Yao Ming, became the number one draft pick of the Houston Rockets.

The first professional league, the China Basketball Association (CBA), was established in 1995. The CBA league was formed by 12 corporate-owned Division-I (Jia Ji) teams scattered in the east and middle-west major metropolitan cities. The league schedule and format are similar to the NBA's, in that it has home- and away-game, regular season and playoff systems to crown the champion. Spectators from all different regions are motivated by different reasons to attend the game. Finding out the spectators' expectations and satisfactions at different segments are critical in escalating customer loyalty. According to Lee's study (2002), developing successful team marketing strategies should consider fans of all levels, such as loyal fans, latent fans, spurious fans, and non-loyalty fans. A well-structured marketing plan will leverage the most basic league objective: increasing the ticket sale revenues. With a young league like the CBA, researching and collecting data from the spectators is very important.

Mullin, Hardy, and Stuton (2000) stated that the basic data for effective marketing decision-making are essential to any organization regardless of its size or scope. They explained that such data are especially crucial to sport organizations because the trends and consumption behaviors of spectators and fans appear to change rapidly. Pitts and Stotlar (2002) further state that, ideally, all of the marketing decisions should be made based on the information and knowledge obtained from research. After having some personal conversations with a few general managers of the CBA teams, the researchers found that marketing research was rarely conducted by the teams. By recognizing the importance of examining the needs of spectators, this study attempts to analyze the spectators' perceived satisfaction on the quality of competition and services of the arena in corporate basketball in P.R. China. The researcher would focus on the team operation and management of the Nangang Dragons, which is the runner-up of the 2004 CBA Championship. Services that are specifically examined would include the sales of season tickets, parking, concessions, marketing promotion, half-time entertainment, and licensing product sales. This study can be extremely valuable because it is the first case study on fan expectations and perceptions of the Nangang Dragons. The results of this research should enable the team management (a) to better serve the customer, (b) to analyze organizational strengths and weaknesses, (c) to identify the opportunities to maximize team profits, and (d) to create marketing strategies to cope with the foreseeable trends.

Review of Related Literature

Even with the existence of numerous gigantic TV contracts, the gate receipts and stadium revenues (e.g., luxury boxes, concessions, parking, venue advertising, and licensing and merchandising) are still important revenue sources for the National Basketball Association (Dick, 2000). Ticket sales do not just play a significant role in a team's overall revenue production; it may actually determine the fate of survival of many small minor league sports in either America or the Far East. In order to generate more ideas on how to promote game attendance and ticket sales, previous studies that examined spectator behavior in attending a sporting event had focused on variables in one or more of the following areas (Badde & Tiehen, 1990; Hansen & Gauthier, 1992; Noll, 1991; Zhang, Pease, Hui, & Michaud, 1995; Pease & Zhang, 2001):

> Game attractiveness—e.g., the level of playing skills, team records, competitiveness, and entertainment;
> Economic factors—e.g., ticket price, income, promotions, and competitions from entertainment business;
> Socio-demographic factors—e.g., population, age, gender, education, occupation, and ethnicity;
> Spectator preference—e.g., size, location, and quality of the facility, schedule, weather, and brand-equity; and furthermore
> Socio-motivational factors—e.g., fan identification, team image, salubrious attraction, and entertainment values.

Other than the aforementioned factors, the experts also identify that the spectators' satisfaction in stadium and venue services is another key in determining the rate of retention to the sport events (Madrigal, 1995). A research study on Japanese professional soccer game spectators by Matsuoka, Chelladurai, and Harada (2003) showed that both team identification and facets of satisfaction were significantly correlated to future game attendance. In Kang's study (1997) on the service quality of Korean baseball stadiums, it was found that the intention to return was most influenced by the variety of refreshments, palatability of refreshments, stadium and restroom cleanliness, and seasonal information. In Westerbeek's study (2000) on Australian football matches, he found that heavy users (serious fans) place importance on stadium characteristics (seating, venue, parking, and layout) and its environment that make them feel at home more than the light user. Significant differences were also found between older and younger spectators in those stadium characteristics. Gender seems to affect the spectators' perceptions and expectations. In a research examining the gender differences in satisfaction toward the venue services at the intercollegiate basketball games, Trail, Fink, and Anderson (2002) stated that male and female respondents clearly showed differences in satisfaction and perceived values toward the venue characteristics (i.e., overall venue cleanliness, concessions, parking, usher behavior, restrooms, audio experience).

A few studies have been conducted to examine the stadium services and the trend of game attendances for both Taiwan and Korean basketball. In Choo's study (1998), the findings indicated that the 600 Korean participants' expectations and perceptions on all 26 service items varied significantly. Interestingly, the satisfaction level of the Korean spectators was not significantly associated with factors like pre-game and half-time music and entertainment, parking availability, and the souvenir shop (Choi, 1999). Teng and Chen (2004) also found that the differences between the male and female perceptions of nine service items were significantly different. Their expectations on several items toward the quality of services and competitions (such as webpage information, security, and transportation) also varied significantly.

The researchers would like to compare the findings of this study to some of the results that were reported in the aforementioned studies, especially those studies that are done in Far East Asia. Due to a similarity in cultural backgrounds and the developmental trend of the basketball leagues among these Asian countries, the researchers expect to find some unique outcomes in advertising strategies, promotional ideas, entertainments, and preferences and expectations on stadium services compared to American basketball.

Methods

Subjects

One hundred ninety-four respondents (male = 151; female = 43) from two Jiangshu Nangang Dragons' 2003-04 regular season home games were invited to participate in the study. About 62% of the participants were in the age group of 20-39 years old, and 21% of the participants were under 20 years old. In terms of the participants' level of education, nearly 37% held a college degree or higher.

Instrument

A Chinese-version questionnaire was modified and translated based on Choo's (1998) and NBDL Mobile Revelers' survey questionnaire. The questionnaire contained two parts. The first part of the questionnaire included 19 fixed alternative questions and one open-ended question that elicited information on participants' demographic characteristics, reasons for not attending the games, favorable choices on foods and souvenirs, willingness of purchasing the season ticket, and preferences on entertaining activities. The second part contained two sets of 23 rating questions. The participants would rate the statements by using the five-point Likert scale, indicating their perceptions and expectations on the quality of available services of the facility and competition. The contents of the questionnaire have been examined by five Korean, five Taiwanese, and five American college professors who instructed in Sport Management. The participants' responses on two sets of the Likert Scale questions also yielded a high level of reliability (Cronbach a > .950).

Procedures

A convenience sampling method was used to directly survey the spectators of two Jiangshu Nangang Dragons' 2003-04 regular season home games. Six hundred questionnaires were distributed onsite at four entrances of the Nangang Arena on January 31 and February 7, 2004, by the teams' 15 student volunteer workers. One hundred ninety-four participants' completed responses (male = 151; female = 43) were collected and analyzed. The total attendance of those two games was estimated at 6,800. Other than the onsite questionnaire survey, an oral interview was conducted with the general manager of the Dragons, Mr. Wong, to further discuss the team's operational strategies. The interview focused on four areas: (1) pricing strategies and season ticket operation; (2) game day operation, including parking, concessions, and licensing product sale; (3) promotion/public relation, including broadcasting and community service; and (4) sponsorship.

Statistical Analysis

The data were analyzed by the 11.0 version of SPSS-Windows statistical package following a uniform coding scheme designed by the researcher. The descriptive percentage and frequency analysis were used to display the participants' demographic characteristics, preferences on souvenir items and entertainments, and perceived barriers for not attending games. The bivariate analysis and one-way analysis of variance (ANOVA) were used to compare the perceived satisfaction and expectation among different demographic and psychographic variables. The linear regression was used to identify the effective predictors for the overall satisfactory rating from the existing recognized service items.

Results

Demographic Information

Among the 194 surveyed participants, most were male (77.3%). About 59% of the participants purchased the 80-RMB ticket (10 US dollars) for the game. However, a high percentage of them (92%) had an income of less than 450 USD per month. Nearly 65% of the participants were comprised of two specific occupational groups: students (30.4%) and employees of the Nangang Steel Factory (34.5%). A majority of the participants (82%) had an educational level of high school or higher. Two-thirds of the participants (n = 102) came from an area within a four-mile radius of the arena. In general, a little more than half of the participants (54%) came to the game with one or two companions. Among those who came along with others (n = 127), only 17% came to the game with three or more companions. There were about 34.5% of the total participants who came to the game alone.

Surprisingly, 55% of the participants had attended a Dragons' home game more than six times in the 2003-04 season. Thirty percent of the total participants had actually shown up for 10 or more previous games. Further, nearly 80% of the participants indicated that they had followed the Nangang Dragons closely for more than three years.

More Descriptive Analyses

More descriptive analyses are completed to illustrate participants' preferences for sales items in the concessions as well as for half-time entertainment. In addition, the information related to the team's advertising strategies, the participants' satisfaction on various service items, and potential barriers for causing people not to attend the game are further elicited and presented. It was found that television (74%; n = 143) and newspapers (65%; n = 127) are identified as the two most important media for the participants to obtain information about the Nangang Dragons. This finding is similar to those obtained by Chen, Teng, and Teng (2004) in Taiwan. In addition, radio, word of mouth from friends and relatives, and Internet websites all received more than 32% of the vote for being recognized as important means to obtain team information.

At this point, the Nangang Dragons do not open any concession stand to sell foods or souvenirs to the spectators. According to the survey results, Coke (soft drink) and water/tea are the two most popular beverages that participants would like to purchase at the concessions. Each of the items receives 51.5% and 36.6% of the supportive vote, respectively. The participants tend to favor American snacks (30.4%) and fast food more than traditional Chinese snacks (17.0%). Only a small percentage of the participants (about 10%) favor the sale of beer. In terms of the participants' favorite souvenirs and team-associated merchandise, five items receive at least 30% of the popular vote. The most popular item is the T-shirt (37%). The rest of the four other items are key chains (36.6%), scarves (35.6%), sport jackets (32.5%), and caps (30.9%), which are listed in order according to their popularity. Dancing and cheerleading performances (56.7%) and musical concerts (45.3%) are identified as the two most popular half-time entertainment activities. In the meantime, raffle-drawing for prizes and fan-participation games also receive a considerable amount of votes (> 34.5%). Three major reasons for not attending home games include (a) no leisure time (40.2%), (b) tickets are hard to get (32.5%), and (c) tickets are too expensive (29.4%). They are by far more important than any other barriers, such as no transportation, not enough money, and inappropriate game schedule. Please refer to Table 1 for more information concerning the participants' choices on various service items.

Table 1: The Participants' Top 5 Choices on Various Services Items

Information Resource	Votes & Percentage	
TV	143	73.7%
Newspaper	127	65.5%
Radio	87	44.8%
Friends and Relatives	77	39.7%
Internet	63	32.5%
Foods and Drinks		
Coke and soft drink	100	51.5%
Water or Tea	71	36.6%
Western Snacks	59	30.4%
Western Fast Food Meal	34	17.5%
Chinese Snacks	33	17.0%
Souvenirs		
T-shirt	72	37.1%
Key Chain	71	36.6%
Scarf	69	35.6%
Sport Jacket	63	32.5%
Cap	60	30.9%
Half-Time Activity and Entertainment		
Dance and Cheer	110	56.7%
Concert	88	45.4%
Raffle Drawing	77	39.7%
Fan Participation	67	34.5%
Special Performance	59	30.4%
Potential Reasons for Not Attending Games		
No Time	78	40.2%
Tickets are Hard to Get	63	32.5%
Ticket is too Expensive	57	29.4%
No Transportation	36	18.6%
Not Enough Money	35	18.0%

Perceived Satisfaction Level and Expected Services

For those two sets of questions (22 items in each set) which survey the participants' perception and expectation on service quality, three major categories (factors) were identified by the factor analysis. They are (a) physical entity and intangible services, (b) the game itself, and (c) augmented services and entertainment. Please see Table 1 for the content of major factors related to perceived service items. The results of the study indicate that the participants' perceptions and expectations of those three factors actually vary significantly ($p < .01$). The mean score of the expected service quality in each of the factors, "physical entity and intangible services," "the game itself," and "augmented services and entertainment," is clearly greater than the mean score of perceived value (4.50 + .68 vs. 3.68 + .90; 4.49 + .72 vs. 3.72 + .93; 4.57 + .67 vs. 3.97 + .77). Table 2 lists the results of the factor analysis on both perceived and expected service items.

Table 2: The Analysis of Major Factors among Perceived Service Items

Major Factors & Cronbach's Mean Score	Number of Items	Percent of Variance	a	(M & SD)
Expectation				
Physical entity & intangible service	2-3, 4-12, 22	39.291	.964	4.51 ± .67
Augmented services	1, 13-21	33.794	.957	4.52 ± .70
Perception				
Physical entity & intangible service	1 & 4-10	26.594	.944	3.68 ± .9
Augmented services	15-22	26.032	.941	3.72 ± .93
The game itself	2-3 & 11-14	20.295	.901	3.97 ± .77

Table 3: Summary of Stepwise Regression Analysis of Overall Satisfaction in Perceived Service Quality

Variables	Unstandardized Coefficients Beta	Std. Error	Standardized Coefficients Beta	t
(Constant)	.978	.231		4.231**
The game itself	.488	.094	.446	5.178**
Physical entity	.286	.080	.307	3.568**

**$p < .01$

Among the 22 service items that are listed in the survey questionnaire, the excitement of the game (M = 4.05, SD = .85), lighting of the arena (M = 4.03, SD = .95), air conditioning (M = 4.00, SD = .97), game time schedule (M = 3.97, SD = .89), and safety of the arena (M = 3.97, SD = .97) were identified as the top five well-provided service items. The three worst served items that are recognized by the participants include the comfort of seats (M = 3.36, SD = .1.10), food/concessions (M = 3.46, SD = 1.22), and public transportation (M = 3.57, SD = 1.16). The participants also identified the excitement of the game (M = 4.62, SD = .74), lighting of the arena (M = 4.57, SD = .82), safety of the arena (M = 4.57, SD = .77), cleanliness of the facility (M = 4.56, SD = .75), and air conditioning (M = 4.55, SD = .76) as the top five most expected service items.

Some of the demographic variables have impacted the results of the participants' perceptions and expectations of the service items. Both male and female participants' perceptions and expectations of all three factors varied significantly ($p < .01$). Male participants valued more of the game itself than females [$t(181) = 2.104, p < .05$]. The participants who attend the game with one or more companions tend to have a higher expectation of the "augmented services and entertainment" than those who go to the game alone [$t(168) = 2.389, p < .05$].

The ANOVA results show the less-educated participants tended to give a higher score on the perceived service quality. The participants with a junior-high level of education have a significantly higher perceived satisfaction score on "physical entity and intangible services," "the game itself," and "augmented services and entertainment" than any other groups [$F(4,180) = 2.899, p < .05$; $F(4,179) = 2.666, p < .05$; $F(4,179) = 2.868, p < .05$]. The higher-income individuals (> 1,000 USD per month) would give an inferior score on physical entity and the intangible services than the others did. The participants who came from an area 4 to 6 miles away from the arena would rate their satisfaction higher than other groups on "physical entity and intangible services" and "augmented services and entertainment" [$F(4,180) = 4.278, p < .0$; $F(4,179) = 3.179, p < .05$].

The rating of overall satisfaction toward the provided services is between the range of "fair" and "good" ($M = 3.96$, $SD = .85$). Based on the results of the stepwise regression analysis, both factors of "physical entity and intangible services" and "the game itself" are effective predictors of the overall satisfaction of perceived service quality. If the mean scores of the two aforementioned factors are high, the perceived overall satisfaction will also be high. Table 3 reports the results of the regression analysis concerning overall satisfaction.

Discussions, Conclusions, & Recommendations

The results of descriptive analysis in demographic information show that the composition of the Chinese spectators seems to be quite different compared to the Taiwanese spectators. In this study, the majority of the participants are male students and steel workers. About 43% of the participants are older than the age of 30. In Taiwan, the majority of the spectators are female students with less than 10% who are 30 or older (Teng & Chen, 2004). In general, the Chinese spectators' educational level is a little lower than the level of Taiwanese spectators. However, these two groups of participants/spectators also share a couple similarities. More than 55% of either Chinese or Taiwanese spectators can be considered frequent viewers since they have attended the live games for more than five times within a year. Nearly 90% of the participants from both groups attend the game with other companions. It is found that Chinese participants who attend the game with other companions report a higher score on variables related to the game itself. Since a high rate of participants in this study (> 55%) is frequent spectators and loyal followers of the team, the authors believe that these people are the bread and butter of ticket sales. If the adage of 80-20% rule (Kotler, 2003) still holds true, then their needs and concerns must be highly valued for the purpose of retaining revenues. It is vital for the team to realize the importance of maintaining the existing core spectators' satisfaction.

Regarding the popular souvenirs/merchandise and food selections, there are two specific findings: (1) The Western soft drinks and snacks seem to be more popular than the traditional Chinese foods; (2) The popular team-associated merchandise items for the Chinese spectators also seem to be different from the Americans' common choices. Interestingly, the scarf is rated as the third most popular item that people would love to purchase. This phenomenon could be due to a strong influence of soccer tradition. Many Chinese soccer fans love to put on scarves during soccer matches. So far, the concession sale is a relatively new business at most of the arenas in China and Taiwan. By opening up more concessions to offer foods and souvenirs, this can be a wonderful opportunity for the Dragons to increase additional revenues and major sponsorships.

Although the "VIP service," "food/concession," and "mascot/cheerleading performance" do not make the top five list as highly expected service items, the participants still valued them as fairly important and well-expected service items. In fact, the participants have expected all of the 22 service items to be well provided. The least important service that is identified by the participants still receives a mean score greater than 4.39. Among the top five highly expected services items, four of them (the excitement of the game, lighting of the arena, air conditioning, and safety of the arena) also rank among the top five rating in actual perceived quality. It is nice to see the participants' expectations are being so well met.

It is found that the participants' overall satisfaction is effectively predicted by the factor of "the game itself." Many of the open-ended comments given as suggestions for improving the service deal with having a better record and hiring better coaches and foreign (American) players. This tends to show that Chinese fans have not directed much of their attention toward the "ancillary products," such as the entertainment programs and promotional activities. Unlike the Korean spectators in Choo's study (1998), the Chinese participants who have a higher level of income do not have high expectations of entertainment activities and food services like other income groups. The authors believe by adding more entertainment and performances to the game, the overall entertainment value of the game will increase. Professional basketball is an entertaining business. If the Chinese professional basketball league is expected to grow, the improvement of other "ancillary products" will be an inevitable process.

Based on their personal interview with the general manager of Nangang, Mr. Wong, the authors believe there is a great need for the team to build a new facility soon. The team nearly has a 100% capacity crowd for the average attendance. About a third of the participants indicated that home tickets are hard to come by. If a new facility is built, the team can implement more luxury boxes, club seating, and general seating for a variety of spectators. The high-income spectators tend to perceive the service of physical entity lower than other income groups. In order to draw more high-income spectators to attend the game, the authors believe that their expectations and needs must be well accommodated. Ideally, having a new arena would bring several benefits to many different spectator groups.

Many of the findings in demographic information and descriptive analyses would serve as the basic data needed for the Nangang Dragons to segment its market and differentiate its spectator/fan base. In order to improve the service quality and maximize ticket profits and concession sales, it would be practical for the Nangang Dragons to consider some of following recommendations.

- Improve the service of the physical entity, such as seating, bathroom, air conditioning, lighting, digital screen, and parking lots.
- Provide more entertainment activities, such as halftime dancing, cheerleading, and musical performances.
- Open up concession stands to sell popular souvenirs, soft drinks, and American snacks.
- Create more luxury boxes or club houses to attract corporate sponsors interested in becoming season ticket holders.
- Develop a user-friendly interactive website to provide general and ticket sale information.
- Offer the public transportation service by working with the city transportation bureau.
- Create strategies for playoff ticket sales.
- Negotiate the rights for televising and broadcasting the games with the regional broadcasting companies and radio stations.
- Evaluate the potential and plan to build a new facility for the team.

This study does not assess the participants' perception on the value of the ticket price and the services on ticket sales. It would be very beneficial for the team to include these elements in the future marketing research. The authors assume the study on service quality should be conducted in the other 11 arenas among teams in the Chinese Basketball Association (CBA). The obtained information certainly can further help the CBA teams enhance ticket sale revenues and provide better services and overall quality to the spectators.

References

Baade, R. A., & Tiehen, L. J. (1990). An analysis of Major League Baseball attendance, 1969-1987. *Journal of Sport and Social Issues, 14*(1), 14-32.

Chen, C. C., Teng, P. C., & Teng, P. Y. (2004). *The perceptions of basketball game spectators concerning sources of information, level of satisfaction, and impediments for attendance.* Paper presented at the annual conference of the University Physical Education, Taipei, Taiwan.

Choo, G. Y. (1998). *Service quality at corporate basketball games in the Republic of Korea.* Unpublished doctoral dissertation. United States Sports Academy, Daphne, Alabama.

Choi, H. A. (1999). *An analysis of spectators' satisfaction levels at professional basketball games in the Republic of Korea.* Unpublished doctoral dissertation. United States Sports Academy, Daphne, Alabama.

Dick, R. J. (2000). *Marketing techniques used by NBA franchises to increase home game attendance.* Unpublished doctoral dissertation, Temple University, Philadelphia.

Hansen, H., & Gauthier, R. (1992). Marketing objectives of professional and university sport organizations. *Journal of Sport Management, 6,* 27-37.

Kang, B. C. (1997). *Perceived and expected service quality by spectators at professional baseball games in the Republic of Korea.* Unpublished doctoral dissertation. United States Sports Academy, Daphne, Alabama.

Kotler, P. (2003). *Marketing management* (11th ed.). Upper Saddle River, NJ: Prentice Hall.

Lee, S. (2002). *A study of psychological, sociological environmental motivation, and loyalty of major and minor league baseball fans.* Unpublished doctoral dissertation. United States Sports Academy, Daphne, Alabama.

Madrigal, R. (1995). Cognitive and affective determinants of fan satisfaction with sporting event attendance. *Journal of Leisure Research, 27*(3), 205-227.

Matsuoka, H., Chelladurai, P., & Harada, M. (2003). Direct and interaction effects of team identification and satisfaction on intention to attend games. *Sport Marketing Quarterly, 12*(4), 244-263.

Mullin, B. J., Hardy, S., & Sutton, W. A. (2000). *Sport marketing* (2nd ed.). Champaign, IL: Human Kinetics.

Noll, R. G. (1991). Professional basketball: Economic and business perspectives. In R. D. Stadohar & J. A. Mangan (1999), *The business of professional sports* (pp. 18-47). Urbana, IL: University of Illinois.

Pease, D. G., & Zhang, J. J. (2001). Socio-motivational factors affecting spectator attendance at professional basketball games. *International Journal of Sport Management, 2*(1), 31-59.

Pitts, B. G., & Stotlar, D. K. (2002). *Foundation of sport marketing* (2nd Ed.). Morgantown, WV: Fitness Information Technology.

Teng, P. C., & Chen, S. (2004). *The perceptions of on-site spectators on service quality and expectations at corporate basketball games.* Paper presented at the annual conference of the University Physical Education, Taipei, Taiwan.

Trail, G. T., Fink, J. S., & Anderson, D. F. (2002). Examination of gender differences in importance of and satisfaction with venue factors at intercollegiate basketball games. *International Sports Journal, 6,* 33-62.

Westerbeek, H. M. (2000). The influence of frequency of attendance and age on "Place"-specific dimensions of service quality at Australian rules football matches. *Sport Marketing Quarterly, 9*(4), 194-216.

Zhang, J. J., Pease, D. G., Hui, S. C., & Michaud, T. J. (1995). Variables affecting the spectator decision to attend NBA game. *Sport Marketing Quarterly, 4*(4), 29-39.

Sports Fan Involvement in New Zealand: The Case of Cricket, Football (Soccer), and Rugby

KATHRYN DOBIE
JAMES GRANT
JAMES ZARICK

Abstract

The involvement of sports fans has important implications for the financial success of sport organizations. The sale not only of tickets but of sports regalia and souvenirs impacts the financial bottom line of a sport organization. It also has a spill-over effect on the economic impact of the sport venue in terms of retail sales of food, hotel accommodations, etc.

This research effort examines the involvement of sports fans in New Zealand. The particular sports under consideration are cricket, soccer, and rugby. The results of the study show that the level of involvement in the individual sports is dependent on a mix of history, media attention, and the number of people who participate in the sport.

Introduction

Attracting an actively involved fan base for any particular sport and the associated teams has important implications for the financial viability of the organization. These are the fans that are most likely to create the excitement and visibility that attract other less interested fans.

Sports have become an increasingly important part of society as evidenced by the increased popularity of spectator sports. There has been an associated increase in spending associated with spectator sports.

Spending for tickets, clothing, and other team-related paraphernalia is just the beginning. Communities benefit economically from spectator spending for food and hotel accommodations, and other activities that are not directly associated with the sporting event.

Television programming reflects the increased interest in sports viewing. Sports networks and increased sports coverage on the established channels further provides the sports fan with opportunities to immerse themselves in the spectator experience. ESPN was the fifth-highest ranked television network in terms of revenue, estimated at $2.1 billion. SKY Sport, a New Zealand television channel devoted to sports coverage, was introduced in the early 1990s. It has become so popular that two additional sports-only channels have been introduced.

Previous Research

Consumer involvement theory presents a method for understanding the psychology and behavior of the target audience. While other methods might be used, this is a simple and insightful way to investigate the motivation and loyalty that fans have in relation to their favorite sports and teams. Involvement refers to the amount of thought, time, and other resources that are devoted to the object of involvement. Consumer involvement has been widely researched as an explanatory theory of the benefits that sports fans receive. This research effort is focused on determining what differentiates New Zealand as a sporting and spectator nation.

"Grin from Gear to Gear" reads an ad designed to appeal to the emotional level of fan response. Ads such as this seek to reach the target fan base and promote excitement—and sales. There has been a significant increase in research efforts intended to explain fan involvement. Some efforts have focused on developing an understanding of fan motives. Motives such as increased self worth, escape from work and the routine aspects of life, excitement, entertainment, a sense of achievement , positive stress, group membership, and socialization have been identified (Sloan, 1979; Wann, Schrader, & Wilson, 1999; Zillman, Bryant, & Sapolsky, 1979).

For many sports spectators, watching a sporting event is "one of the most passionate and intense of human endeavors, utterly dominating affect and cognition for short periods of time" (Roese & Maniar, 1997, p. 1245). In fact, the avid or "extreme" sports fan is a well-recognized breed (Lieberman, 1991). Zillman, Bryant, and Sapolsky (1979) postulated that involvement as a sports fan can produce many of the same positive benefits that have been associated with sports participation.

There are others who do not share the same positive perspective. Some feel that watching sports events appeals to man's baser instincts and leads to aggression and violence (Smith, Patterson, Williams, & Hogg, 1981). Much of the social science research has focused on spectator violence (Wann & Branscombe, 1993). Other researchers have described sports as a pacifier for people who would otherwise be bored and unhappy with their lives (Smith et al., 1981).

Emotional impact has been the focus of another line of research designed to understand sports fan behavior. Sloan (1979) verified that the results of a sporting event—winning or losing—have a correlated effect on emotions. Winning efforts produced positive emotions while a losing effort produced negative emotions. Other researchers attributed the emotional responses of spectators to involvement (Bahk, 2000; Shank & Beasley, 1998). Involvement was measured by various aspects of fan participation in the spectator experience (Dietz-Uhler & Murrell, 1999; Fisher & Wakefield, 1998; Laverie & Arnett, 2000; Shank & Beasley, 1998; Wann & Branscombe, 1993; Wann & Schrader, 2000; Wann et. al., 1999). An extreme example of involvement was provided in a study by Eisler (1997) in which he studied the emotional involvement of the individual with his/her team. In this case, the fan's emotional balance hangs on the team's performance, with losses causing devastation and real emotional pain.

Sports in New Zealand

An important aspect of sports fans' involvement is in relation to "their" sports team. This relationship is reflected in the level of emotionality exhibited by the fan, behaviors which are often exhibited in positive or negative behaviors before, during, and after the individual events.

New Zealand prides itself on the variety of sports and other recreational activities that are available. The Hillary Commission was established to promote a wide range of sports opportunities for all New Zealanders. The government sets aside funding for this purpose. In fact, sports prowess is a source of great national identity and pride for New Zealanders.

Cricket

Cricket is considered to be New Zealand's summer game—much like baseball in the U.S. The sport is ranked second in terms of sports played by adult men (184,000) and fourth in boys and girls sporting activities (SPARC, 2002). The 2001-2002 season was considered a "landmark season." Total attendance at the National Bank One-Day Series exceeded expectations by 18%. Almost 100,000 people attended the five-match One-Day International series against England. In 2002, it was reported that 70% of the population was either very interested or fairly interested in cricket. Television ratings reflected the increased level of interest in cricket. SKY television coverage of the One-Day International series attracted 39% of the male audience. TV3 coverage of the final three One-Day International matches attracted between 33% and 53% of those 18-49 ("Cricinfo," 2002). The official website for New Zealand Cricket posted 6.8 million registered site visits during the first match of the One-Day International event. In addition to its attraction as a spectator sport, cricket remains a popular leisure activity in New Zealand.

Soccer

Soccer was first introduced into New Zealand in the 1870s. In 1982, the national team, the All Whites, qualified for the World Cup finals. This served to elevate soccer in the minds of New Zealanders. Soccer has been primarily a sport for juniors, with 120,000 participants. Women's and girls' soccer is gaining recognition. In 1999, New Zealand hosted the Under 17 World Championships. The professional side of soccer is in its infancy with the men's professional team being a mere four years old.

Rugby

Rugby has a long history in New Zealand. By the 1870s, matches were being played by various colleges and football clubs. Since 1893, New Zealand has sent teams to compete in numerous countries. New Zealand Rugby gained international attention with the introduction of the World Cup Tournament. This event has been held every four years since 1987.

New Zealand has a national men's rugby team, the All Blacks, and a national women's rugby team, the Black Ferns. These teams have a loyal following. The success of these teams has served to increase awareness and participation in the sport.

The increased interest in professional rugby is reflected in the proliferation of various television programming devoted to the sport. In addition to the televised matches, there are numerous related shows much like the pre-, half-, and post-game shows that are prevalent during the football season in the U.S.

The Study

The data for this study was gathered through the use of a personally administered research instrument. The rationale for this was that if there was any misunderstanding, the administrator would be able to explain the question further.

The Instrument

The initial step in the survey development process was to convene a focus group to generate ideas. As a result, it was decided to use a combination of quantitative and qualitative questions so that respondents would be encouraged to think about their past sporting history as they completed the survey.

After the survey had been produced, a pre-test sample was taken to ensure that question wording was not confusing. As a result, some questions were reworded to ensure that respondents would have a clear understanding of what was being asked.

The Sample

A sample of 100 surveys was collected. The sample consisted of 100 students and visitors to the campus of a major New Zealand University. The student body is composed of New Zealanders from both islands (Table 1).

Table 1: Demographic Characteristics of the Sample				
Age	10-20	21-30	31-40	41-50	over 50
	32%	45%	8%	9%	6%
Gender	Male		Female		
	64%		36%		
Income	$0-15,000	$15,001-30,000	$30,001-45,000		Over $45,000
	57%	18%	13%	12%	

Results

Respondents were initially asked when they first attended a sports match either as a spectator or as a participant. In general, sports exposure occurred between the ages of 4 and 6. As an indication of the level of importance placed on sports, 70% of the respondent indicated that sports involvement was considered to be important in their families. Respondents were then asked whether they had actually participated in sports activities either in the past or were presently involved (Figure 1).

Participation	%
Yes	65%
No	35%

Figure 1: Sports Participation

When asked regarding their level of involvement as a spectator, 82% of respondents indicated that they considered themselves to be sports fans. However, it is apparent that being a sports fan does not necessitate actual attendance, as 79% indicated that they actually attended sporting events. The rate of attendance varied according to the sport (Table 2).

Table 2: Frequency of Sports Event Attendance

	Never	Rarely	Sometimes	Often	Always
Rugby	11%	22%	26%	32%	09%
Cricket	36%	25%	24%	14%	01%
Soccer	59%	28%	05%	02%	06%

The results indicated that many of the respondents did not attend games, yet they had indicated that they considered themselves to be sports fans. Therefore, they were asked what method they used to follow sports. Respondents indicated that 45% would prefer to attend the game while 48% would prefer to watch it on television. However, while many indicated that they would have preferred to go to the game, only 5% reported actually attending a game. Instead, 82% reported that they watched the games on television.

Considering the large number of respondents who had indicated that they were sports fans via television, the question might be raised as to just how loyal these fans considered themselves to be (Table 3).

Table 3: Level of Fan Loyalty (Self Reported)

	Low						High
	1	2	3	4	5	6	7
Cricket	8%	5%	6%	14%	20%	25%	22%
Rugby	17%	16%	7%	17%	24%	14%	5%
Soccer	39%	19%	14%	9%	6%	6%	7%

Data Analysis

Data obtained from the completed surveys was analyzed to determine the extent of relationships between attendance and loyalty to a specific sport and relationships between a family "sports culture" and loyalty to a specific sport using Pearson's Correlations (Table 4).

Table 4: Sport Loyalty

Attendance/Loyalty		Pearson's Correlation	P-value
	Rugby	0.620	0.000
	Cricket	0.673	0.000
	Soccer	0.752	0.000
Family Sports Culture/Loyalty			
	Rugby	0.624	0.000
	Cricket	0.429	0.000
	Soccer	0.194	0.053

The results of this analysis showed that there is a significant relationship between the self-reported loyalty of a sports fan and their game attendance. Similarly, the sports orientation of the family strongly influences the level of self-reported fan loyalty.

Discussion

Sports fans exhibit highly involved behavior patterns when it comes to sports in general, and especially to their team or specific sport of interest. New Zealanders in particular possess a sporting culture where great interest is focused on the national teams. Rugby (All Blacks) is the leading sport, most likely due to the international success of the team. But all the other New Zealand teams—America's Cup (sailing), the Tall Blacks (basketball), the All Whites (soccer), the Black Socks (softball), Black Caps (cricket), Black Ferns (women's rugby), Silver Ferns (net ball), and the Black Sticks (hockey)— have an avid following. This may be due to the fact that the team is the national representative for the chosen sport.

Due to the national character of the teams, there are situational factors which must be considered when using attendance as the main loyalty measure. Away games are played in other countries. Tickets to an international game, including air fare and accommodations, might easily reach $3,000. The SKY Sports Channel is $90 a month. Many avid fans therefore watch the games on television rather than personally attending the game.

Loyal fans are most likely to demonstrate that loyalty through the purchase of sports apparel and equipment. Stores that sell New Zealand national team apparel exclusively are present in every city of any size. When fans are able to attend a game, they are likely to sport the team attire (60%) and especially avid fans are likely to paint their faces in the team colors.

Results of the study did show that there was a positive link between fan loyalty to a sport and the fact that they had played this sport in the past. This may be due to the fact that they know the rules of the sport and have an understanding and respect for the level of skill that is required to play on a national team. However, for some of those who described themselves as sports fans, they could be better described as fans of sport as opposed to being an avid follower of a particular sport.

Conclusions

As ticket prices climb and sales fall, it is important for sports marketers to gain a better understanding of the factors which contribute to the likelihood that fans will attend games. Gaining a more complete picture of the factors comprising team loyalty will enable marketers to target the appropriate "hot buttons" to generate enthusiasm and promote the sale of team paraphernalia as well as the tickets themselves.

Results of the research on fan loyalty in New Zealand serve to underscore the environmental differences that may be encountered between sports, countries, and levels of play. One size does not fit all. Marketers are responsible for identifying the differences and designing a marketing strategy that appeals to the established fan base and also reaches out to new fans to the sport and to new generations of fans. Sports marketers are challenged to meet the needs of the sport and the fans.

References

Bahk, C. M. (2000). Sex differences in sport spectator involvement. *Perceptual and Motor Skills, 91,* 79-83.

Cricinfo (2002). Cricinfo homepage. Retrieved October 1, 2002, from http://www.cricinfo.co.nz.

Dietz-Uhler, B., & Murrell, A. (1999). Examining fan reactions to game outcomes: A longitudinal study of social identity. *Journal of Sport Behavior, 22*(1), 15-27.

Eisler, P. (1997, March 27). When your team takes a tumble: Guys go awry over losing. *USA Today,* p. 1D.

Fisher, R. J., & Wakefield, K. (1998). Factors leading to group identification: A field study of winners and losers. *Psychology and Marketing*, *15*(1), 23-40.

SPARC (2002). *Investing in sport*. Retrieved September 1, 2002, from http://www.sparc.org.

Laverie, D. A., & Arnett, D. B. (2000). Factors affecting fan attendance: The influence of identity salience and satisfaction. *Journal of Leisure Research*, *32*(2), 225-246.

Lieberman, S. (1991). The popular culture: Sports in America: A look at the avid sports fan. *The Public Perspective: A Roper Center Review of Public Opinion and Polling*, *2*(6), 28-29.

Roese, N. J., & Maniar, S. D. (1997). Perceptions of purple, counterfactual and hindsight judgments at Northwestern Wildcats football games. *Personality and Social Psychology Bulletin*, *23*(12), 1245-1253.

Shank, M. D., & Beasley, F. M. (1998). Fan or fanatic: Refining a measure of sports involvement. *Journal of Sport Behavior*, *21*(4), 435-443.

Sloan, L. R. (1979). The function and impact of sports for fans: A review of theory and contemporary research. In J. H. Goldstein (Ed.), *Sports, games, and play: Social and psychological viewpoints* (pp. 219-262). Hillsdale, NJ: John Wiley & Sons Inc.

Smith, G. J., Patterson, B., Williams, T., & Hogg, J. (1981). A profile of the deeply committed sports fan. *Arena Review*, *5*(2), 26-44.

Wann, D. L., & Branscombe, N. R. (1993). Sports fans: Measuring the degree of identification with their teams. *International Journal of Sports Psychology*, *24*, 1-17.

Wann, D. L., & Schrader, M. P. (2000). Controllability and stability in the self-serving attributions of sports spectators. *The Journal of Social Psychology*, *140*(2), 160-168.

Wann, D. L., Schrader, M. P., & Wilson, A. M. (1999). Sport fan motivation: Questionnaire validation, comparisons by sport, and relationship to athletic motivation. *Journal of Sport Behavior*, *22*(1), 114-139.

Zillman, D., Bryant, J., & Sapolsky, S. (1979). The enjoyment of watching sports contests. In J. H. Goldstein (Ed.), *Sports, games, and play: Social and psychological viewpoints* (pp. 293-335). Hillsdale, NJ: John Wiley & Sons Inc.

Case Study: Sport Marketing Research for Women's Athletics

ERIN P. HUGHES

Abstract

The University of Arkansas is one of only four universities nationwide not receiving funding from the state legislature to support athletic programming. This requires Arkansas women's athletics to be self-sufficient, generating additional funding to improve opportunities and resources for the program. In the past, women's athletics has utilized data from men's athletics for market analysis. There is a need for current statistics showing variations in demographics of women's athletics patrons from sport to sport, and statistics indicating the target market for women's athletics as a whole. In addition, data useful for enhancing corporate sponsorships and commercial involvement is needed to facilitate strategic marketing for the program. The study surveyed 363 women's athletics patrons attending all 10 types of women's sporting events during the 2003-2004 seasons. A set of descriptive statistics was compiled for each sport indicating the demographic target market, media recall, purchasing behavior, and patron association with the sport. A discriminate analysis was then run to identify the factors creating the demographic discrepancy among sports. The results showed each sport to be a separate target market with varying levels of patron income, age, and purchasing behavior. There was a significant relationship between age and type of sporting event, showing older groups attending basketball and volleyball, and younger groups attending gymnastics and soccer. In addition, the results indicated the most successful form of media varied by sport. The significance of this study is the identification of specific target markets, as well as correlating factors affecting patron brand choice and recognition.

Introduction

As a result of Title IX, many college and university athletic departments are increasing the number of women's sports. As women's sports gain in popularity, marketing research gleaned from men's sports may not be a reliable indicator of the demographics and buying patterns of women's sports patrons.

The purpose of this study was to determine if women's sports patrons are the same patrons that attend men's sports events. It also explores variations in women's athletic patrons from sport to sport, as well as collects descriptive data indicating the target market for women's athletics as a whole. In addition, data useful for enhancing corporate sponsorships and commercial involvement was gathered. Though not included in this article, this data included feedback on product usage, corporate name and product association, and patron reaction to corporate sponsorships. Though this article is a case study of Women's Athletics for the University of Arkansas, the issues are similar across most institutions of higher education.

Review of Literature

Intercollegiate athletics have been in existence since 1852, almost as long as higher education itself (Gerdy, 1997). Athletic programs serve to generate revenue and increase media attention for the university. This media attention allows the program to recruit talented athletes who will, in turn, create a winning team and yield higher revenues for the institution. Both athletic departments and the educational institution benefit from the increased visibility a successful athletic team brings (Henderson, 1995).

Intercollegiate athletics remains the surest way of enlisting donations, sponsorships, and funding, as well as attracting national media attention for the university. According to Chu,

> While the need for resources has remained an ever-pressing imperative throughout the history of higher education in this country, it was only at the turn of the century, with the invention of mass sports in America and the complex of factors that affected the university's internal and external constituencies, the resource acquisition through athletics became a possibility. A sports-hungry populace consumed athletic entertainment with increasing gusto as the tempo of industrialization, urbanization, leisure time, and accumulation of expendable capital quickened. The large land-grant schools saw a means of acquiring increased support from the legislature and the people. (1989, p.33)

Collegiate athletics is big business. As Paul "Bear" Bryant, the University of Alabama head football coach, allegedly said, "Fifty thousand people don't come to watch English class" (cited in Grahm, Goldblatt, & Delpy, 1995, p. 36). It seems as if there is lots of money to be made in the college athletics "industry." Back in 1990, corporate America was already spending $23.5 billion on sports marketing, and more recently a seven-year, $1.7 billion contract was signed with CBS for NCAA Division I basketball rights (Grahm et al., 1995).

However, the majority of the Division I college athletic programs lose money. According to an NCAA-sponsored report, only 28 percent of Division I programs generate more revenues than they expend. Furthermore, only 46 percent of the 89 Division I-A schools reporting generated a profit (Gerdy, 1997, p. 47).

Most collegiate athletic departments depend on additional state funds or money from the institution to keep them going. The Chronicle of Higher Education reported that Division I-A and I-AA schools spent $4.2 million on football alone in 2001-2002 (Suggs, 2003). In many cases, the state legislature supports college athletics by including them as a line-item on the state budget. Presently these additional funds are not always available, as the institutions themselves struggle for funding because of state and national budgets cuts. Many athletic programs are being forced to drop their low- or no-profit teams just to stay within budget (Gerdy, 1997).

The University of Arkansas is one of only four universities nationwide who is not receiving funding from the state legislature to support athletic programs. The athletic program is financially independent from the academic sector, relying on sponsorships, alumni funding, and donations to make up what incoming revenue does not cover. The athletic program has been quite successful in recent years; in 2000-2001, the men's and women's athletic departments reported total expenses of $26,847,362 and incoming revenues totaling $79,575,384 (Gender Equity in College Sports, 2002).

Unlike most college athletic programs, the University of Arkansas Men's and Women's Athletic Departments are two discrete entities, each with its own administration and budget (University of Arkansas Women's Athletics, 2003). While the men's program is totally self-supporting, a majority of the financial support for the women's program comes from sales of the Razorback trademark, which is owned by the men's department. This money is supplemented with funding from donations and corporate sponsorships and yields a total operating budget of $8,088,366 for women's sports, a number not comparable to the men's total operating budget that totaled $22,853,599 in 2001-2002 (Gender Equity in College Sports, 2002).

As women's sport continues to grow on the University of Arkansas campus, the need to develop a larger funding base grows as well. Women's Athletics must be self-sufficient. Additional funding must be generated from fan support and corporate sponsorship in order to improve opportunities and resources for the Lady'Back program.

Growth of Women's Sport

The rapid growth in women's sport at the University of Arkansas and across the nation is due in part to the Title IX legislation and changes in societal trends. This has sparked growth in women's athletics not only in the intercollegiate sector, but in women of all ages and socioeconomic classes (Gender Equity in College Sports, 2002).

Title IX of the Education Amendments of 1972 was the first comprehensive legislation to protect students from discrimination on the basis of sex. It states that "no person in the United States shall, on the basis of sex, be excluded from participation in, be denied the benefits of, or be subjected to discrimination under any education program or activity receiving Federal financial assistance" (Title IX and Sex Discrimination, 1998). Since its implementation in 1975, Title IX has been controversial. Affecting more than 2,700 post-secondary institutions, this amendment affects discrimination on the basis of sex in admissions, treatment of students, employment, and athletics. In regard to athletic programs, Title IX states that if separated teams are offered, the institution may not discriminate on the basis of sex in the provision of the necessary equipment or supplies or in any other way (Oglesby, 1978). Factors in athletic programs that are affected by Title IX include supplies and equipment; game and practice schedules; travel and per diem allowances; coaching and academic tutoring opportunities; locker room, practice, and competitive facilities; medical and training services; housing and dining; pay and publicity. Compliance with Title IX led to the upsurge in women's intercollegiate athletic teams during the years of 1975-1978 (Morse, 1992). Many more have been added since that time in order to keep the numbers of women's and men's teams relatively equal on college campuses. The most recent study on Gender Equity in College Sports by the Chronicle of Higher Education in 2002 noted that

> The only purely numerical section of federal guidelines issued under Title IX of the Education Amendments of 1972 covers scholarship funds allocated to female athletes. The U.S. Department of Education's Office for Civil Rights has specified that, absent nondiscriminatory circumstances, colleges must award the same proportion of aid (within one percentage point) to female athletes as there are women participating in varsity sports. Athletes who compete in more than one sport are not counted two or more times (p. 23).

By increasing the number of women's sports the University offers, the scholarship percentages will also increase, thereby drawing more athletes to women's programs.

Changing societal trends has perhaps been the largest factor in the growth of women's sport. The reluctance of society to accept a female athlete is waning as sports are no longer considered specifically an agent of masculine orientation. Highly visible female athletes and role models have commanded the acceptance and encouragement of women's participation in sport. An article by Susan Morse in *CQ Researcher* recently observed that the increased levels of national interest in women's college athletics were due in large part to a growth in female participation in high school athletics. The article reported that "between 1972 and 1985 women's participation in High School sports increased almost 500%" (Morse, 1992 p. 185). This early involvement in athletics has yielded increased female participation in intercollegiate and intramural sports. The fitness movement of the 1970s and 1980s had a distinct impact on the future of athletics as well. During this period, millions of American women took up walking, jogging, aerobics, and other team and individual sports for better mental and physical health. This movement, combined with the impact of the media's portrayal of fit, hard bodies helped lead to the acceptance of athletics as a means to reach physical fitness goals (Oglesby, 1978).

Plainly, an increase in funding is necessary as women's sport continues to grow nationally, as well as on the University of Arkansas campus. This growth in funding would enable the Women's Athletics program to expand in order to meet the needs of both athletes and patrons. An increase in sponsor dollars would assist Women's Athletics in advertising and increasing awareness about events and the program as a whole, thus increasing attendance. In addition, it would provide better fan experiences and game atmosphere through giveaways and contests. This additional funding would allow Women's Athletics to provide the best possible program for their athletes.

Expansion of Funding

In order to reach these goals and increase funding for women's athletics, an increase in both the fan base and the sponsorship base must occur. Increasing the fan base will draw larger crowds to women's sporting events, and increase ticket and merchandise sales as well as team and name recognition. By enhancing the sponsorship base, the Women's Athletics department will be able to provide better program amenities, and meet many of their expansion goals. By targeting the advertising and monetary goals of both parties, the University of Arkansas Athletics department will be able to maximize sales and profits in their program. However, in order to increase the fan and sponsorship bases, further research and data collection regarding these target markets is needed.

Market Research

Marketing research is information that can identify opportunities and problems, and that can evaluate the actions and performance of an organization (Boone & Kurtz, 1992). According to Boone and Kurtz's Contemporary Marketing, "Marketing research specifies the information required to address these issues; designs the method for collecting information, manages and implements the data collection process; analyzes the results and communicates the findings and their implications" (Boone & Kurtz, 1992, p. 158). In short, research into target markets helps to clarify decision making by providing useful facts about the marketer and the marketplace.

The variables usually used in market research are typically divided into demographics, market segmentation, and consumer behavior. In researching the target population for women's athletics, information that describes the lives of athletic patrons is needed. The demographic data needed will include household income, gender, marital status, age, and residential zip code. This allows marketers to identify segments within their market of patrons to be targeted.

Market segmentation divides the market into groups with similar interests or characteristics to serve the specific needs of each section more efficiently (Boone & Kurtz, 1992). By identifying interest groups such as season ticket holders or family groups, an athletic department can provide specific incentives enticing to each group.

Finally, data regarding consumer behavior should be collected and analyzed. These variables include ticket purchasing, event attendance, corporate sponsor recognition, relationship to team, and spending during athletic events. Data on several other consumer spending habits such as frequency of soda consumption, attendance at cultural events, subscription to media, etc. was collected to aid in the continuation and development of corporate sponsorships. Target markets can be matched with specific corporate sponsors and media outlets to yield the most productive partnerships for all parties.

Methodology

The Women's Athletics Department at the University of Arkansas currently offers 10 sports as compared to the seven sports offered by the men's program. This variance in numbers creates a need to address the possible differences in fan base between women's and men's sporting events. The University of Arkansas added six women's sports during the years of 1976-1986 and three sports during the 1990s. As the new women's sports gain popularity, demographic changes in patrons have been observed. As an example, the addition of Lady'Back gymnastics to women's sports has drawn groups of families and younger supporters to enjoy these athletic events.

For this study each women's sport was classified as an independent variable. The non-ticketed events— cross country, golf, tennis, swimming, and track and field—did not provide a large enough sample size to generate results that could be generalized. Thus, they are not included in the discussion of findings.

Table 1 lists the dependant variables, which include demographics, media effectiveness, ticket purchasing behavior, and corporate sponsorships. The dependant variables were measured by surveying randomly selected Lady'Back patrons.

Table 1: Dependent Variables	
Variables	**Measure**
Demographic Characteristics	Age
	Income
	Gender
	Marital status
	Residential location
Ticket Purchasing	Media recall
	Travel
	Relationship to team
	Relationship to other attendees
Consumer Behavior	Credit card use
	Sport merchandise expenditures
	Fitness
	Ownership of residence
	Product use
Corporate Sponsorships	

A set of descriptive statistics for each sport was gained by compiling the results of this survey. A random survey method was utilized, and was administered during randomly chosen events for each sport. Each sport was considered to be a unique population, and data was thus gathered separately at each sporting event.

Subjects

The subjects for this study include selected Lady Razorback patrons who were in attendance at the sporting events on the day the instrument was administered, and who agreed to participate. Patrons were chosen by calculating the average attendance for each sport. Every patron was approached for sports with average attendance of 100 patrons or less. At sports with 100 patrons or more, every fifth patron was approached. Participation was voluntary; if a patron declined when asked to participate, the next entrant was approached and asked to complete the instrument.

Instrument

The instrument was adapted from the 1999-2000 NCAA Championship Patron Questionnaires, and focused on areas including patron demographics; event media recall, ticket purchase, and corporate partner identification; and purchasing behavior (Irwin, 1995). Patron feedback provides information necessary to create market segments within the population. Data on the purchasing behavior of patrons will be used to market more effectively as well as to match corporate sponsors with target sporting events. Event media recall and attendance decision making allows the marketing department to publicize more effectively. Finally, brand association and corporate partner identification allows Women's Athletics to better understand their market and match corporate sponsors with sporting events or teams. This partnership yields better results for all involved. The businesses targeted by the instrument have been or are current program sponsors/contributors for the Lady Razorbacks. Responses to these segments of the instrument were analyzed and helped to generate data reflecting the general buying patterns of women's athletics patrons, as well as the population for each sport.

Procedures

Game dates to administer the instrument were based off the 2002-2003 schedules for each sport, as number of games and dates will not vary significantly between years. Game-days on which to administer the survey were randomly selected.

Permission was secured from Women's Athletics to set up a table at the main entrances to sports arenas for volleyball, gymnastics, and basketball one hour prior to the start of the event on the selected date. At all other events, workers met at the main entrance or gate one hour prior to the start of the event. Volunteers were equipped with clipboards, instruments, identification, and pens. Instruments were administered to subjects who were chosen to participate in the survey and were willing to do so. The surveys were self-administered by patrons on-site and took approximately five to ten minutes to complete. The surveys were then returned to a data collection team member by each respondent and were labeled with an ID number, the sport, and the date collected.

An incentive of a free soft drink coupon upon completion of the survey was offered to the participants. Names were in no way related to data gathered and privacy was assured for all respondents.

For most events, four workers were needed to administer the instrument. Volunteers were given written instructions prior to and on the day of the event to ensure surveys were administered uniformly. At each event, volunteers were assigned to gain the attention of the chosen patron upon entrance, explain the purpose of the study, and request that they complete the instrument. This procedure was repeated for each of the randomly selected dates for each sport. Three hundred and sixty three (363) useable surveys were completed and returned by event patrons. Only three instruments were deemed unusable, as the respondents were under the age of 18. A limited amount of rejections were given by patrons approached to complete the survey.

Analysis of Data

The dependant variables for this study included the demographic characteristics, ticket purchasing behavior, and consumer behavior of women's athletics patrons. Each of the ten women's sports was classified as an independent variable.

The study looked to achieve four general objectives:

1. To develop a demographic profile of UA women's athletic patrons.
2. To analyze media effectiveness.
3. To analyze ticket purchasing behaviors of patrons.
4. To collect data useful for enhancing corporate sponsorships.

The following analyses summarize the information collected from the University of Arkansas Lady'Back 2003-2004 season.

Results

The data collected was analyzed using the SAS statistical package (Version 6.12) (SAS Institute, Inc., 1999). Default settings were used unless otherwise specified. Although games at each of the 10 women's athletic events were surveyed and data collected, this analysis focuses only on ticketed events of basketball, volleyball, gymnastics, and softball. These sports were chosen due to the size of the population, as well as the popularity of these events. Women's cross country and track and field events were not chosen as their meets are not held separately from men's. This creates a mixed population; the data gathered is not specific to women's sport. Data collection at golf and tennis events found that these sports have too small a population to ensure that results can be generalized. It was found that the majority of soccer and swimming fans are relatives of participating players. This population should be analyzed separately as their marketing patterns will be significantly different from all other events. The results of this study do not reflect patrons under the age of 18 attending these events, as it was expected that fans over this age would best represent those with decision-making powers.

Patron Demographic Profiles

The following analysis is based on a compiled profile of all surveyed patrons from the 2003-2004 season. This summary indicates that the primary market for UA Women's Athletics is married patrons of either gender with an annual household income ranging from $25,000-$49,999. According to the 2000 census, the average household income of Arkansas residents is $32,182 (US Census Bureau, 2004). However, volleyball patrons appear to have a higher income level ($50,000-$74,000) than those attending other sports. Gymnastics patrons appear to have one of the lower income levels with 25% reporting their income to be less than $25,000.

There seem to be two target age ranges for these patrons, those 18-28 and those 40-50, with an average age of 43. Again, some variations occur within sport. Over half of all volleyball respondents were ages 40-61, while 48% of basketball patrons are 18-39.

Several demographic trends were consistent throughout all four sports. The analysis showed no significant difference in the number of male patrons versus female patrons at any women's event. In addition, the majority of patrons attend all women's events with zero to three companions: primarily their spouse, children, and friends. The majority of attendees who noted a relationship to the team were relatives or friends of participating players, or UA students and alumni.

The vast majority of respondents (93.6%) live within the state of Arkansas. Of these patrons, just under half live within the 20 mile radius of the statistical metropolitan area of the university.

Basketball Profile

The target market for basketball consists of individuals 18-39 years of age with an annual income in the $25,000-$49,999 range. A slight majority of these patrons are male (59%) and single (55%). Basketball patrons attending the event with companions came primarily with their spouse and with friends. Those who noted a relationship to the team were mainly UA employees and UA alumni. One of the surveyed basketball games was UA Employee Night, which may factor into the high number of employee responses received.

Volleyball Profile

Most volleyball patrons are married, 40-61-year-olds attending the event with their spouse and children. There are an equal number of men and women attendees, with primary affiliations as UA Booster Club and UA Alumni members. Many respondents (36%) have an annual household income of $60,000-$74,999. Volleyball patrons tend to be an older and wealthier group of patrons when compared to the other sports analyzed.

Gymnastics Profile

A slight majority of gymnastics patrons are married (64%) females (63%) who attend events with their spouse, children, and friends. The mean age of these patrons is 39 years; however, two distinct target age groups are visible. Patrons aged 18-28 and those 40-50 are primary attendees. The annual household income of gymnastics fans is under $49,999. Fans attending gymnastics are younger and part of a lower income bracket than attendees at other sporting events.

Softball Profile

The primary market for softball points to married individuals between the ages of 29 and 50 with an annual household income level of $25,000-$49,999. Patrons attend most softball events with their spouse and children, and are primarily relatives of participating players. A slight majority (60%) of fans is male, and the crowd appears to be a bit younger than volleyball and basketball crowds.

Media Effectiveness

The most frequently cited sources of media for women's events are word of mouth and prior attendance. Although these sources are indeed the most effective, they are also difficult to utilize as a part of a successful advertising campaign. In order to gain a better understanding of the most effective advertising tools for women's athletics, these two sources of information were omitted in the overall analysis. The primary sources for overall event information are newspaper, internet, and collegiate schedules (see Figure 1).

Ticket Purchasing Behavior

Almost half of all Lady Razorback fans make their decision to attend sporting events 31 days or more prior to the event (see Figure 2). However, most actual ticket purchases occur within 24 hours of the event, with the majority occurring at the door upon patron arrival. A small percentage of patrons (19%) reported that their ticket was given to them for the event. Approximately 21% of respondents reported that their ticket had been obtained in ways other than those listed (see Figure 3). When asked to explain, most of these patrons reported that they gained admission via the team pass list. Overall ticket prices were reported as being either very low (35%) or moderate (36%). At non-ticketed events, respondents noted that they would be willing to spend $0-$5 on a ticket.

Consumption Patterns

Patrons of women's athletics chose basketball, volleyball, gymnastics, and softball as the sports they are most likely to attend overall. The majority of these fans do not attend men's events, and are almost exclusive to the

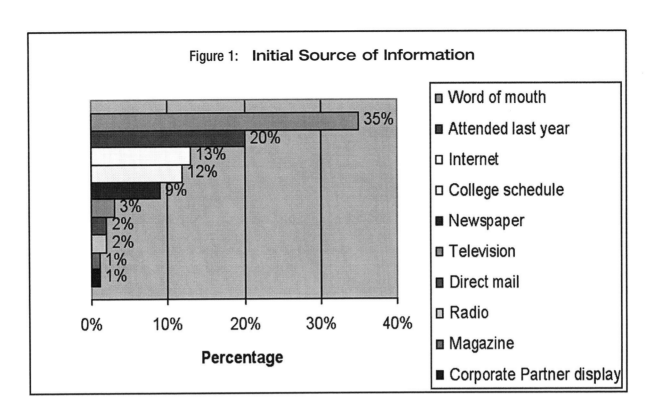

Figure 1: Initial Source of Information

Legend:
- Word of mouth
- Attended last year
- Internet
- College schedule
- Newspaper
- Television
- Direct mail
- Radio
- Magazine
- Corporate Partner display

Values: 35%, 20%, 13%, 12%, 9%, 3%, 2%, 2%, 1%, 1%

Percentage

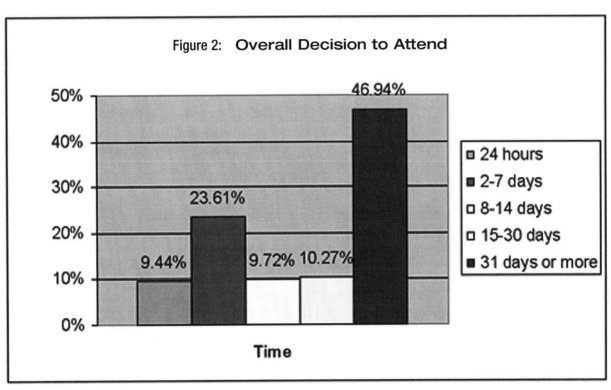

Figure 2: Overall Decision to Attend

Legend:
- 24 hours
- 2-7 days
- 8-14 days
- 15-30 days
- 31 days or more

Values: 9.44%, 23.61%, 9.72%, 10.27%, 46.94%

Time

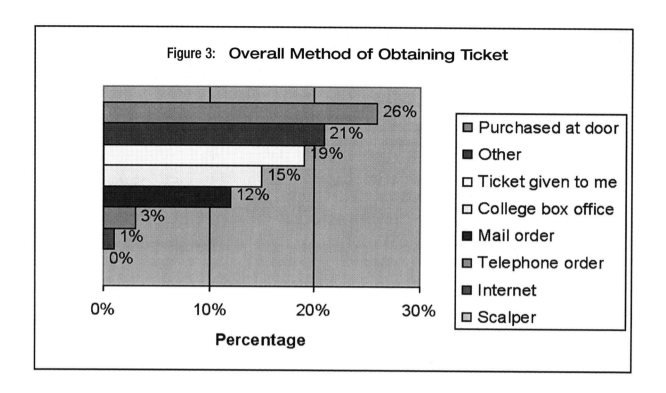

Figure 3: Overall Method of Obtaining Ticket

- Purchased at door 26%
- Other 21%
- Ticket given to me 19%
- College box office 15%
- Mail order 12%
- Telephone order 3%
- Internet 1%
- Scalper 0%

Lady'Backs. Almost all fans are from a 30-mile radius of Fayetteville, and therefore do not create a significant economic impact on the community. The top choices for consumer products and services for all women's athletic patrons were ownership of a cellular phone, ownership of a home computer with internet, and traveling out of town at least once per year for pleasure (see Figure 4). This information can be used to acquire corporate sponsorships and increase funding for Women's Athletics.

Conclusions and Recommendations

The need for Women's Athletics to have current demographic and patron trend data has been demonstrated with the findings of this study. Current marketing, ticketing, and promotional techniques may be changed to incorporate this new information. The following recommendations have been made to enhance the UA Women's Athletic program through use of the data collected in this study.

Media Communications

Newspaper, internet, television, and radio are the most effective sources for event information. The primary advertising area is within the state of Arkansas, and within a 200-mile radius of Fayetteville. The most effective marketing techniques will be long term, or more than one month prior to the event, and again the week of the event. Most ticket sales are accomplished within 24 hours of the event, primarily at the door. This is another good time for promotional items to be sold and publicity for alternate events presented.

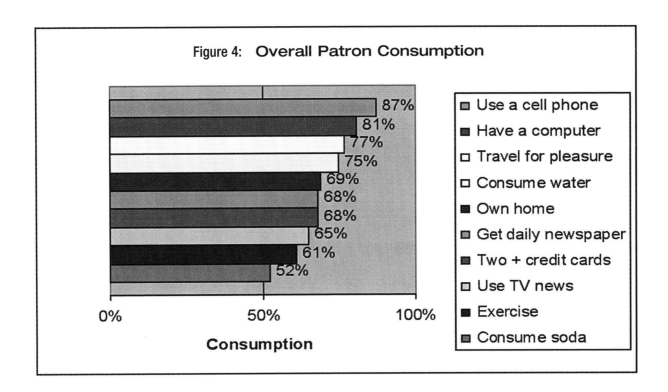

Figure 4: Overall Patron Consumption

- Use a cell phone — 87%
- Have a computer — 81%
- Travel for pleasure — 77%
- Consume water — 75%
- Own home — 69%
- Get daily newspaper — 68%
- Two + credit cards — 68%
- Use TV news — 65%
- Exercise — 61%
- Consume soda — 52%

As most basketball patrons picked gymnastics and volleyball as their alternate sports of choice, upcoming events should be advertised at basketball games. In addition to publicity, incentives for repeat attendance could be offered.

Ticket Sales

Patrons attend most events with immediate family (spouse and children) or friends. Ticket packages could be created to entice families to purchase tickets for multiple events, or even season tickets. Family nights at events such as volleyball and gymnastics are an excellent way to bring these groups in. To attract larger groups of friends, a discount on ticket prices could be offered for groups of four or more.

Ticket sales were ranked as moderate by most respondents. Rather than raising overall ticket prices, a correlation should be run to identify which groups found prices to be low or high. This would enable the athletic department to ticket for each market segment. The non-ticketed events are attended primarily by family and friends of the players. Although creating an admission fee for these types of events is not feasible, merchandise sales specific to the event and to the player may generate additional revenue.

Sponsorship Enhancement

Corporate sponsorships are an excellent source of funding, and if matched with the correct patron set, are as equally beneficial for the sponsor. The majority of women's patrons use a mobile phone service. This is a good opportunity for an overall sponsorship, but volleyball patrons are a great target market for this service. Travel services are also widely used among patrons, and could possibly be included in a promotion or giveaway. Consumption of both water and soda ranked high on product lists, as did ownership of two or more credit cards. This type of information cannot only be used to entice future sponsors, but also to identify patron's interests and product choices.

Recommendation for Future Research

It is recommended that patron analysis be completed every five years to best serve the target market for these events. Future analyses should be split between ticketed and non-ticketed events, and include a larger population. Due to patron fatigue, the corporate sponsorship recognition and interest section of the instrument should be distributed as a stand-alone study to produce more reliable results. It would be interesting to perform this study on men's athletic events as well. This could provide insight on the difference in patrons, marketing strategies, and target markets between the two sports.

References

Boone, L., & Kurtz, D. (1992). *Contemporary marketing*. Fort Worth, TX: Dryden Press.

Chu, D. (1989). *The character of American higher education and intercollegiate sport*. Albany, NY: State University of New York Press.

Gender equity in college sports. University of Arkansas, Fayetteville. (2002). Chronicle of Higher Education. Retrieved June 18, 2003, from http://chronicle.com/stats/genderequity/.

Gerdy, J. R. (1997). *The successful college athletic program*. Westport, CT: American Council on Education/Oryx Press.

Grahm, S., Goldblatt, J. J., & Delpy, L. (1995) *The ultimate guide to sport event management and marketing*. Chicago, IL: Irwin.

Henderson, K. A. (1995). *Evaluating leisure services*. State College, PA: Venture Publishing, Inc.

Irwin, R. L. (1995). *1995 NCAA Championship patron analysis summary report*. Unpublished manuscript, University of Memphis Bureau of Sport & Leisure Commerce.

Morse, S. C. (1992, March). Women and sport: The issues. *CQ Researcher*, *2*(9).

Oglesby, C. A. (1978). *Women in sport: From myth to reality*. Philadelphia, PA: Lea & Febiger.

SAS Institute Inc. (1999). Proprietary Software Release 6.12. Cary, N.C.

Suggs, W. (2003, June). Information published under the Equity in Athletics Disclosure Act of 1994. *The Chronicle of Higher Education*, Vol. XLIX, 39.

Title IX & Sex Discrimination (1998). Retrieved August 3, 2003, from http://www.ed.gov/offices/OCR/docs/tix_dis.html.

US Census Bureau (2004). *Arkansas Quick Facts*. Retrieved April 12, 2004, from http://quickfacts.census.gov/qfd/states/05000.html.

A Cross-Cultural Study of Factors Explaining Action Sports Fandom of Y Generation College Students in Korea, Taiwan, and the USA

SUNG-BAE PARK
SOONHWAN LEE
MEI-YEN CHEN

Introduction

Participation in action sports has been increasing immensely over the past few years (DesMarteau, 2004; Petrecca, 2000; Yin, 2001). Inline skaters, skateboarders, and BMX riders are estimated at 150 million worldwide, and these main three sports have shown a 700% increase in growth over the past 12 years, with a 30% growth in participants each year (LG Electronics, 2003). Professional action sports athletes are estimated at about 30,000 people all over the world (Liberman, 2004). A 10-year trend in the participation of youths (ages 7-17) showed an especially interesting pattern. Several traditional activities suffered large declines in participation from 1992 to 2002: volleyball (-48.3%), tennis (-36.7%), bicycle riding (-24.2%), and softball (-29%); while three new sports exploded in popularity: snowboarding (355.5%), inline skating (93.9%), and skateboarding (75%) (Sports Participation Trends, 2003).

According to DesMarteau (2004), the average skateboarder's age is 13.6 years and skateboarding participation went up 80.8% from 1998 to 2002. An increase in number of frequent boarders, who skateboarded 52-plus days annually, was 173% from 1998 to 2002, and skateboarding has become the fastest-growing extreme sport from 1998 to 2002. An increase in the number of female skateboard riders from 1998 to 2002 was 132%, which explains why almost 24% of skateboarders in 2002 were female.

Snowboarding participation increased 269.5% from 1990 to 2003 (1.7% increase from 2002 to 2003). Finally, surfing participation has also increased 43% from 1987 to 2003 (11.1% from 2002 to 2003).

Yin (2001) reported that snowboarding skyrocketed to 7 million participants in 2000, expanding 51% between 1999 and 2000. Skateboarding increased by 49% to 12 million enthusiasts, far outpacing tackle football, which has grown by only 15% to 6 million players in 2000. Wakeboarding, snowmobiling, and artificial wall climbing also increased 32%, 28%, and 27% from 1999 to 2000, respectively. In contrast, traditional sports such as beach volleyball, racquetball, and baseball decreased 8%, 9%, and 10% from 1999 to 2000, respectively (Yin, 2001).

Importance of Understanding a Cross-Cultural Study in Action Sports

A number of studies support the notion that culture has a critical psychological impact on the pattern of individual thought and behavior. Yi and Park (2003) showed that people with the different cultural backgrounds are likely to have different attitudes and styles of decision making in negotiation, bargaining processes, and problem solving in various social settings because they have different value systems in societies. Stevenson and Stigler (1992) showed, for instance, that there was a far greater belief in malleable intelligence and in the importance of effort among those in the Asian culture than the American culture when they compared the achievement beliefs of Asian and American school children and their parents. Bracken and Barona (1991) mentioned that obvious cultural influences include beliefs, customs, values, the degree of acculturation of assimilation, and generational status of the individual. Furnham, McClelland, and Omer (2003) examined whether the ratings of attractiveness and related attributes are indeed pan-cultural, as evolutionary psychologists have suggested, or cultural-specific as some studies have suggested (Furnham & Alibhai, 1983; Furnham & Baguma, 1994; Zebrowitz et al., 1993).

From the business perspective, a cross-cultural study still greatly contributes to the understanding of an international or multinational business market. Luo, Hoek, and Roos (2001) explained how the ability to effectively manage logistics in a cross-cultural context has become one of the crucial success factors in today's business world in the face of ever-increasing globalization. In addition, they insisted that cross-cultural logistics research could have the benefit of applying the experience learned in cross-cultural research in general, and through cross-cultural research in management and marketing, through international or multinational business.

Despite the fact that more and more researchers and marketers all over the world have become interested in a cross-cultural study, relatively few cross-cultural studies have been done so far. Kriska (2000) studied the ethnic and cultural issues in assessing physical activity and explained that there were substantial differences in the distribution of both chronic diseases and inactivity among the various segments of the population. *The Economist* (1998, June 6) showed that people in different regions also enjoy different categories of sports while explaining the worldwide popularity of sporting events and estimating the television audience for the FIFA World Cup in 1998, the 2000 Sydney Olympic Games, the Rugby World Cup, two Formula One automobile-racing seasons, and American football. Therefore, it is worth examining the relationship among action sports familiarity, popularity, advancement, media preference, and action sports fandom.

Review of Literature

Collectivism and Individualism Theory

One way to explain the cultural difference between Korea and the United States is *collectivism and individualism theory*. Markus and Kitayama (1991) dichotomized two opposite cultures as an interdependent and independent self, and they hypothesized that people in collectivist (Asian) cultures would be less likely to explain people's behavior in terms of context-free personality traits than would people in the individualist (American) culture. Research (Miller, 1984; Morris & Peng, 1994; Shweder & Bourne, 1984) supports that individuals in Eastern or Asian cultures do produce fewer personality traits or internal attributions and more context-situated attributions when describing people and explaining their behavior than do their Americans counterparts. In other words, it can be said that the Korean people are more likely to be collectivists while Americans tend to be individualists. Thus, collectivism and individualism theory can be used to explain the phenomena of action sports across Korea and the United States, as it explores the motivation factors across these two countries.

Emic-Etic Theory

Emic and etic theory can also be a useful approach to conduct a cross-cultural study. The contextual nature of *emic* measurement means that each concept derived in a given culture will be specific to the context of that culture, while the *etic* approach to measurement is based on universality (Brislin, 1986; Kluckhohn, 1953). In emic measurement, a behavior is observed in its social context and its meaning is inferred. In contrast, etic measurement begins with a concept and specifies an observable indicator of the concept's meaning (Bell et al., 2004). Therefore, the meanings that the investigator seeks in a given culture may be meanings external to the culture, assuming that there is some commonality across human cultures. All cultures are made up of humans with a common biology and, to some extent, a common social psychology, so that at least some patterns of thought and behavior must apply to all cultures, according to this approach (Bell et al., 2004).

Therefore, with regard to the action sports phenomenon that exists in both Korea and the United States, emic or etic theory may also be an efficient approach to identify cultural differences. It is unknown whether or not etic theory can explain the worldwide boom in action sports. If it can, it may be because of the fact that all cultures are made of humans with a common biology and a common social psychology (Bell et al., 2004).

> **Research Hypothesis 1:** Korean and the American college students will have different levels of perceptions on action sports fandom, action sports familiarity, popularity, advancement, and media preference.

Increased Popularity of Generation Y

Generation Y has received a great amount of attention from marketers mainly due to its large size of 78 million (Hochman, 1999; Hollingsworth, 2000; Stapinski, 1999). The generation is three times the size of its Generation X predecessor (Lim & Turco, 1999). Because of this, the youth generation, including college students (also described as Generation Y), have easily become a target group of action sports and have been spotlighted by many sport marketers (Bennett & Henson, 2003; Bennett et al., 2003). Two motivation theories associated with youth sport are competence motivation theory (Harter, 1981) and achievement goal theory (Nicholls, 1984, 1989), which are theories that have made a significant contribution toward our understanding of the psychological processes. There are several applications for these theories which deal with sport participation in youth sports.

Klint and Weiss (1987) found that gymnasts, who were higher in perceptions of social competence, rated friends and team atmosphere as more important motives for participation versus those who were lower. Ebbeck and Becker (1994) examined potential predictors of goal orientations with youth soccer players. They revealed that self-esteem, perceived soccer competence, perceived mastery climate, and perceived parent task orientation scores would be positively related to player task orientation scores. And they also investigated that the lower self-esteem scores, as well as higher perceived performance climate and perceived parent ego orientation scores, would be related to a higher level of player ego orientation. Youth sport participants frequently report social reasons, such as wanting to be part of a team or to be with friends, and social sources of positive and negative affect, such as social recognition and parental pressure, for their involvement in sport. And social interactions with parents, coaches, and peers have all been associated with the quality of young people's sport experience (Brustad, 1993; Duncan, 1993; Wylleman, 2000).

> **Research Hypothesis 2**: Gender affects the level of action sports fandom, familiarity, popularity, advancement, and media preference for college students across the countries of Korea, Taiwan, and the USA.

> **Research Hypothesis 3**: Action sports popularity, advancement, familiarity, and media preference will explain the high proportion of variances among action sports fandom levels for college students in Korea, Taiwan, and the USA after controlling the personal characteristics (i.e., gender, age, and nationality).

Methods

One hundred forty-four university/college students (49% male and 51.4% female; mean age = 21.07 years, SD = 2.57 years) from a Korea university (N = 34), a Taiwan college (N = 59), and a northeastern college in the United States (N = 50) responded to the survey questionnaires in classes and one questionnaire was eliminated due to the data availability.

The Action Sports Questionnaire (ASQ) (Bennett & Henson, 2003), and the Sport Fandom Questionniare (SFQ) (Wann, 2002) were used as the research instrument. All instruments were partially modified and translated into Korean and Taiwanese versions for the participants. And the bilingual and committee approach was used to keep the test content identical to the original version (Brislin, 1980). Basically, all these methods are aimed at putting the same test in different languages while preserving the same ideas across the linguistic boundaries (Hui & Triandis, 1985). The modified research instruments included 5-item for action sports familiarity; 2-item action sports advancement; 6-item action sports popularity; 5-item media preference; 5-item action sports fandom; and several demographic questions. The internal consistency estimated by Cronbach's alpha of familiarity, popularity, advancement, media preference, and action sports fandom were .81, .84, .81, 078, and .93, respectively.

Results

T-test and ANOVA were utilized to test if action sports familiarity, action sports popularity, action sports advancement, media preference, and action sports fandom can be explained by gender and nationality. Additionally, a hierarchical multiple regression analysis was executed to examine if action sports familiarity, action sports popularity, action sports advancement, and media preference account for a significant proportion of the variance in action sports fandom for college students in a Korean university, a Taiwan college, and a northeastern university in the USA after controlling personal characteristics (i.e., gender, age, and nationality).

Based on the results of the t-test, action sports popularity ($p<.001$), action sports advancement ($p<.01$), and media preference ($p<.05$) levels were significantly different between male and female college students (see Table 1). According to the ANOVA and Tukey HSD, Taiwanese college students have statistically significant levels on all the variables (i.e., action sports familiarity, action sports popularity, action sports advancement, media preference, and action sports fandom) over Korean and American college students (see Table 2).

In addition, there is a significant difference on the action sports familiarity, action sports popularity, action sports advancement, media preference, and action sport fandom among Korean, Taiwanese, and American college students, $F(2,139)=17.153$, $F(2,140)=20.197$, $F(2,140)=20.092$, $F(2,139)=40.984$, and $F(2,138)=16.232$, respectively, $ps=.000$.

Table 1: T-test Summary of the Difference on Familiarity, Popularity, Advancement, Media Preference, and Action Sports Fandom by Gender (N=143)

Variable	Gender	N	M	STD	t
Familiarity	Male (Female)	69(73)	15.04(14.15)	4.69(3.99)	1.224
Popularity	Male (Female)	69(74)	12.33(14.43)	3.95(3.69)	3.287***
Advancement	Male (Female)	69(74)	5.87(6.85)	2.05(1.72)	3.112**
Media	Male (Female)	69(73)	11.10(12.85)	4.66(4.55)	-2.262*
Fandom	Male (Female)	69(72)	10.45(10.17)	4.88(3.74)	378

*$p<.05$, **$p<.01$, ***$p<.001$

Table 2: ANOVA and Tukey HSD Summary of the Difference on Action Sports Familiarity, Popularity, Advancement, Media Preference, and Action Sports Fandom by Nationality (N=143)

Variable	Nationality	N	M	STD	F	Tukey HSD
Familiarity	Korea	34	11.147	2.664		
	USA	50	15.680	5.235	17.153***	Taiwan>USA>Korea
	Taiwan	58	15.655	3.143		
Popularity	Korea	34	10.265	2.895		
	USA	50	13.660	3.983	20.197***	Taiwan>USA>Korea
	Taiwan	59	15.034	3.378		
Advancement	Korea		34	5.177	2.249	
	USA	50	5.980	1.835	59.725***	Taiwan>USA>Korea
	Taiwan	59	7.401	1.205		
Media	Korea	34	7.618	3.806		
	USA	50	11.640	4.256	40.984***	Taiwan>USA>Korea
	Taiwan	58	14.879	3.159		
Fandom	Korea	34	7.265	3.527		
	USA	50	10.200	4.589	16.232***	Taiwan>USA>Korea
Taiwan	57	12.210	4.424			

***$p<.001$

Based on the results of hierarchical regression analysis, age, gender, and nationality explained a significant proportion of the variance for action sports fandom, $R2$change = .106, F change $(3,136)$ = 5.361, $p<.05$. In addition, age and nationality contributed significantly to explaining action sports fandom, $t(136)$ = -2.973 and $t(136)$ = 2.714, $ps<.05$. Furthermore, familiarity, popularity, advancement, and media preference explained a significant proportion of the variance of college students' action sports fandom, above and beyond what age, gender, and nationality explained, $R2$change = .500, F change $(4,132)$ = 41.901, $p<.05$.

Table 3: The Intercorrelations among the Continuous Variables (N = 140)					
Variables	1	2	3	4	5
1. Action Sports Fandom	-	.674***	.550***	.455***	.644***
2. Familiarity		.520***	.405***	.541***	
3. Popularity			-	.469***	.573***
4. Advancement			-		.422***
5. Media Preference			-		

*p<.05, **p<.01, ***p<.001

In addition, action sports familiarity, action sports popularity, and media preference contributed significantly to explaining action sports fandom for college students in a Korean university, a Taiwan college, and a northeastern college in the USA, $ts(132)$ = 4.827, 2.091, and 4,305, respectively, $ps<.05$. Finally, the total proportion of the variance of college students' action sports fandom by the variables of personal characteristics (i.e., age, gender, and nationality), familiarity, popularity, advancement, and media preference was 60.6% (see Table 4).

Table 4: Summary of Hierarchical Regression Analysis for Variables Explaining the Action Sports Fandom among Korean, American, and Taiwan Students (N = 143)					
Variable	B	SE	b	R² change	F change
Step 1					
Gender	-1.493	.767	-.170		
Age	-.434	.146	-.225**		
Nationality	1.133	.418	.225**		
				,106	5.361**
Step 2					
Familiarity	.365	.076	.363***		
Popularity	.175	.984	.156*		
Advancement	.275	.154	.122		
Media Preference	.316	.073	.333***		
				.500	41.901***

*p<.05, **p<.01, ***p<.001

Discussion

The findings of the study included the following: (a) Action sports are more popular to male students than female students, and male students also expect that action sports will be more developed in the future, becoming an Olympic sports program. This explains that action sports has been dominated by males than females so far, even though DesMarteau (2004) mentioned that an increase in number of female skateboard riders from 1998 to 2002 was 132%, explaining that almost 24% of skateboarders in 2002 were females. It shows that the number of female athletes, who participate in summer X-Games, has continually decreased. However, it supports the trend of female action sports athletes in summer X-Games from 1995 to 2003. As you look at Table 5, the number of female action sports athletes in the summer X-Games decreased steadily from 1997 to 2002, although this number turns slightly positive in 2003. (b) Male college students are more likely to watch action sports on various media channels. When generalizing this finding, one should be cautious, because the media opportunities in terms of number and quality of the program, and number of channels and hours of the broadcasting, are not the same in these three countries. However, it can be concluded that male college students in each country of Korea, Taiwan, and the USA are likely to watch action sports programs than the counterparts in each country. (c) Taiwanese college students are more familiar with action sports than Korean and American college students in the sample. (d) Action sports are more popular to Taiwanese students than Korean and American college students.

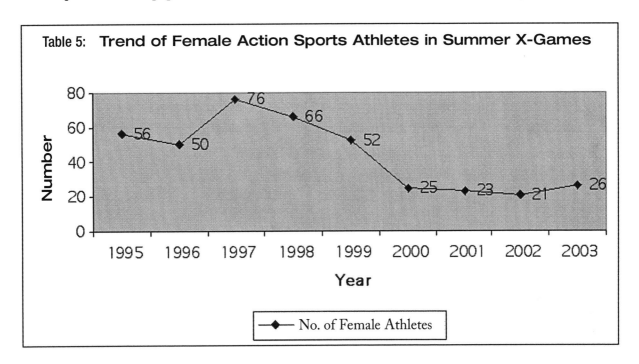

Table 5: Trend of Female Action Sports Athletes in Summer X-Games

The results of this study are interesting because action sports have been regarded as individualistic rather than team-oriented. Markus and Kitayama (1991) dichotomized two opposite cultures as an interdependent and independent self, and they hypothesized that people in collectivist (Asian) cultures would be less likely to explain people's behavior in terms of context-free personality traits than would people in the individualist (American) culture. Research (Miller, 1984; Morris & Peng, 1994; Shweder & Bourne, 1984) supports that individuals in Eastern or Asian cultures produce fewer personality traits or internal attributions and more context-situated attributions when describing people and explaining their behavior than do their American counterparts. In other words, it can be said that the Korean and Taiwanese college students are more likely to be collectivists while the American people to be individualists. On the basis of collectivism and individualism theory, it was expected that the Korean and Taiwanese college students would have similar levels of familiarity over their American counterparts in the sample, since the two Asian college students have a similar culture of collectivism while the American college students have a culture of individualism. However, this result doesn't support this hypothesis, but instead implies that action sports familiarity may be affected by specific cultural variables, or maybe better yet explained by the action sports boom itself, which can be considered a universal phenomena attributable to Generation Y college students.

Finally, gender, nationality, action sports familiarity, action sports popularity, and media preference were significant factors in explaining action sports fandom of college students in a Korean university, a Taiwan college, and a northeastern college in the USA. As far as the nationality, it is supported by emic theory, which means that each concept derived in a given culture will be specific to the context of that culture, rather than etic theory (Brislin, 1986; Kluckhohn, 1953). In other words, the behavior toward the action sports fandom can be observed in its social context of Korea, Taiwan, and the USA.

Limitations and Recommendations

A cross-cultural study can be useful as a basic approach to examine a worldwide phenomenon such as the action sports boom. A two or three country comparison has been shown in this study, and more countries or more diversified cultural factors can also be applied. At the same time, a larger sample size is desirable for a cross-cultural study, and it would be safer to generalize the results. Second, further research can be focused on generations younger than college students—it will be interesting to see if there are any differences among generation Y of middle, high school, and college students.

Although the literature is replete with examples of tests translated from English into other languages, the procedures for engaging in these activities are still in their infancy, and many of the better procedures are not widely practiced (Geisinger, 1994). In some instances, however, adaptations of assessment instruments are needed even when the language remains the same, because the culture or life experiences of those speaking the same language differ. Therefore, the present study needs to be duplicated in different cultures and nations.

References

Bell, L. G., Dendo, H., Nakata, Y., Bell, D. C., Munakata, T., & Nakamura, S. I. (2004). The experience of family in Japan and the United States: Working with the constraints inherent in cross-cultural research. *Journal of Comparative Family Studies, 35*(3), 351-373.

Bennett, G., & Henson, R. K. (2003). Perceived status of the action sports segment among college students. *International Sports Journal, 7*(1), 124-138.

Bennett, G., Henson, R. K., & Zhang, J. (2003). Generation Y's perceptions of the action sports industry segment. *Journal of Sport Management, 17*, 95-115.

Ben-Porath, Y. S. (1990). Cross-cultural assessment of personality: The case for replicatory factor analysis. In J. N. Butcher & C. D. Spielberger (Eds.), *Advances in personality assessment* (Vol. 8, pp. 1-26). Hillsdale, NJ: Erlbaum.

Bracken, B. A., & Barona, A. (1991). State of the art procedures for translating, validating and using psychoeducational tests in cross-cultural assessment. *School Psychology International, 12*, 119-132.

Brislin, R. W. (1980). Translation and content analysis of oral and written materials. In H. C. Triandis & H. W. Berry (Eds.), *Handbook of cross-cultural psychology* (Vol. 2, pp. 389-444), Boston: Allyn & Bacon.

Brislin, R. W. (1986). The wording and translation of research instruments. In W. J. Lonner and J. W. Berry (Eds.), *Field methods in cross-cultural research* (pp. 137-164). Beverly Hills, CA: Sage.

DesMarteau, K. (2004, June). Action sports success: Total immersion required. *Apparel Magazine, 45*(10), 12-13.

Economist (1998, June 6). Not just a game. *Economist, 347*(8071), 5-6.

Florenthal, B., & Shoham, A. (2000). Value differences between risky sports participants and nonparticipants. *Sport Marketing Quarterly, 9*(1), 26-33.

Furnham, A., & Alibhai, N. (1983). Cross-cultural differences in the perception of female body shapes. *Psychological Medicine, 13*, 829-837.

Furnham, A., & Baguma, P. (1994). Gender and locus of control correlates of body image dissatisfaction. *European Journal of Personality, 8*, 183-200.

Furnham, A., McClelland, A., & Omer, L. (2003). A cross-cultural comparison of ratings of perceived fecundity and sexual attractiveness as a function of body weight and waist-to-hip ratio. *Psychology, Health & Medicine, 8*(2), 219-230.

Geisinger, K. F. (1994). Cross-cultural normative assessment: Translation and adaptation issues influencing the normative interpretation of assessment instruments. *Psychological Assessment, 6*(4), 304-312.

Hui, C. H., & Traindis, H. C. (1985). Measurement in cross-cultural psychology: A review and comparison of strategies. *Journal of Cross-Cultural Psychology, 16*(2), 131-152.

Kluckhome, C. (1953). Universal categories of culture. In A. L. Kroeber (Ed.), *Anthropology today: An encyclopedic inventory* (pp. 507-523). Chicago: University of Chicago Press.

Kriska, A. (2000). Ethnic and cultural issues in assessing physical activity. *Research Quarterly for Exercise & Sport, 71*(2), 47-53.

Liberman, N. (2004, 26 January -1 February). New alt-sports group wants to sign up athletes and fans. *SportsBusiness Journal, 7.*

LG Electronics, Corp. (2003). *LG Action Sports Championship Report.*

Luo, W., Hoek, R. I., & Roos, H. H. (2001). Cross-cultural logistics research: A literature review and propositions. *International Journal of Logistics: Research and Applications, 4*(1), 57-78.

Markus, H. R., & Kitayama, S. (1991). Culture and the self: Implications for cognition, emotion, and motivation. *Psychological Review, 98*, 224-253.

Michener, H. A., & DeLamater, J. D. (1998). *Social psychology.* Belmont, CA: Thomson Learning, Inc., 101-29.

Miller, J. G. (1984). Culture and the development of everyday psychological explanation. *Journal of Personality and Social Psychology, 46*, 961-978.

Morris, M., & Peng, K. (1994). Culture and cause: American and Chinese attributions for social and physical events. *Journal of Personality and Social Psychology, 67*, 949-971.

Petrecca, L. (1999, October 11). Going to extremes. *Advertising Age, 70*(42), 36-40.

Poortinga, Y. H. (1989). Equivalence of cross-cultural data: An overview of basic issues. *International Journal of Psychology, 24*, 737-756.

Shweder, R. A., & Bourne, E. J. (1984). Does the concept of the person vary cross-culturally? In R. A. Shweder & R. A. LeVine (Eds.), *Culture theory: Essays on mind, self, and emotion* (pp. 1-24). Cambridge, UK: Cambridge University Press.

Smith, P. B., Dugan, S., Peterson, M., & Leung, K. (1998). Individualism: Collectivism and the handling of disagreement. A 23 country study. *International Journal of Intercultural Relations, 22*, 351-367.

Stevenson, H. W., & Stigler, J. W. (1992). *The learning gap: Why our schools are failing and what we can learn from Japanese and Chinese education.* New York: Summit.

Taylor, S. E., & Crocker, J. (1981). Schematic bases of social information processing. *Social Congnition: The Ontario Symposium* (Vol. 1). Hillsdale, NJ: Erlbaum.

Yi, J. S., & Park, S. (2003). Cross-cultural differences in decision-making styles: A study of college students in five countries. *Social Behavior and Personality, 31*(1), 35-48.

Yin, S (2001, June). Going to extremes. *American Demographics, 23*(6), 26.

Zebrowitz, L. A., Montepare, J. M., & Lee, H. K. (1993). They don't all look alike: Individuated impressions of other racial groups. *Journal of Personal and Social Psychology, 65*, 85-101.

Consumer Complaint Behaviour in Sport Consumption

MICHAEL VOLKOV
MELISSA JOHNSON MORGAN
JANE SUMMERS

Abstract

While consumer complaint behaviour, and specifically voicing, has been extensively investigated from the perspective of goods (see Volkov et al., 2003, for a review), there have been fewer studies investigating consumer voicing with regard to services (Andreasen, 1984, 1985; Singh, 1988, 1990; Zeithaml, Berry, & Parasuraman, 1996). Further, no research can be identified in the extant literature with respect to experiential consumer voicing. This research proposes an examination of voicing behaviour of consumers in an experiential consumption setting and uses sport consumption as the context. A review of literature in the area is presented and a proposal for experiential research is offered.

In experiential consumption settings, consumers are more likely to experience emotional reactions to, and be actively involved in, the experience than in traditional consumption episodes (Addis & Holbrook, 2001; Hoffman, Kumar, & Novak, 2003; Lofman, 1991). Further, experiential consumption episodes involve greater emotional processing, more activity, more evaluation, but less overall cognitive processing than traditional episodes (Lofman, 1991), which in turn is likely to result in different consumer behaviour in these experiential settings.

In this study, traditional consumer complaint behaviours are re-examined in an experiential context; specifically, consumption of live sport. It is proposed that these behaviours are not motivated by the traditional antecedents of anger and involvement and, further, that they are not enacted with the purpose of reducing dissonance. Instead, it would appear that traditional complaint behaviour concepts such as voicing, overt aggression, and assignment of blame take on a more functional role in the sport consumption experience. The possibility exists that for some spectators these complaining behaviours that have traditionally been classified as negative, actually contribute to overall enjoyment of, and satisfaction with, a sport consumption experience.

Introduction

Managing the complaint behaviour of consumers is vital for businesses (Tax, Brown, & Chandrashekaran, 1998) regardless of industry type or structure. Current research has found that identification and management of consumer complaint behaviour improves consumer retention rates, negates the diffusion of negative word-of-mouth, and minimizes firm and consumer disadvantages (Kim et al., 2003). Further, the existence of consumer complaints indicates that an economic system may be performing unsatisfactorily. They provide feedback to firms and they assist in planning consumer programs and activities (Best & Andreasen, 1977; Chiu, Tsang, & Yang, 1987; Day 1977; Fornell & Didow, 1980). Thus, understanding consumer complaints is necessary for both organisations and for business researchers.

While consumer complaint behaviour has been extensively investigated from the perspective of goods (see Volkov, Harker, & Harker, 2003, for a review), there have been relatively few studies investigating consumer complaint behaviour with regard to services (Andreasen, 1984, 1985; Singh, 1988, 1990; Zeithaml, Berry, & Parasuraman, 1996). Further, no research can be identified in the extant literature with respect to experiential consumer complaint behaviour. This research heeds the call to stimulate discourse between consumer behaviour and sport marketing researchers (Kates, 1998) by investigating how consumer complaint behaviour differs in the experiential consumption of sport.

This paper has four objectives: first, to briefly review established research in the field of consumer complaint responses; second, to contextualise this research in the area of experiential consumption, specifically sport consumption; and third, to present a conceptual model based on the reviewed literature. The roles of mood, identification, emotion, and involvement in particular will be considered. This model will be based on the proposition that there are generalizable differences between consumer complaint behaviour in experiential consumption settings as compared to "traditional" consumption models. Finally, this paper will conclude with a proposal for experiential research.

In experiential consumption settings, consumers are more likely to experience emotional reactions to and be actively involved in the experience than they are in traditional consumption episodes (Addis & Holbrook, 2001; Hoffman, Kumar, & Novak, 2003; Lofman, 1991). Further, experiential consumption episodes involve greater emotional processing, more activity, more evaluation, but less overall cognitive processing than more traditional consumption episodes (Lofman, 1991). Given the special nature of experiential consumption, behaviour of consumers in this realm is also likely to differ (Cooper-Martin, 1992; Lofman, 1991). This research focuses on sport as the consumption experience due to its wide appeal to a large range of consumers (as evidenced by global consumption of sport). Other experiential consumption experience episodes that could have been considered were the arts or wine consumption (Cooper-Martin, 1992); however, these were rejected due to their more constrained and limited consumer appeal.

Consumer Complaint Behaviour in Experiential Consumption

This research can be justified with regard to both theoretical and practical applications. This research will make four contributions in theoretical areas, firstly by enabling the analysis of how involvement, mood, emotion, and identification affect the consumption experience. Second, this analysis will enable the identification of individual differences in experience within the same product class. This research differs from the existing literature in that it places the consumers in a "real-world" situation rather than using the recall-based methods of traditional consumer complaint behaviour research literature.

Third, no previous study has investigated consumer complaint behaviour in the context of an experiential consumption episode, and, given the special nature of experiential goods and services, it is argued that consumer behaviour differs from that exhibited during consumption of other types of goods and services (Cooper-Martin, 1992; Dube & Mukherejee, 2003; Hirschman & Holbrook, 1982; Hoffman, Kumar, & Novak, 2003; Holbrook & Hirschman, 1982).

Fourth, research has identified that the management of consumer complaint behaviour is vital to improve consumer retention rates, negate the diffusion of negative word-of-mouth, and minimize firm and consumer disadvantages (Kim et al., 2003). This research will extend theoretical knowledge regarding the effective identification and management of consumer complaint behaviour.

In terms of marketing practice, this research and its outcomes will contribute to the practice of sport marketing in areas such as the provision of a valid and empirically tested model for sport consumer complaint behaviour, which will afford sport marketers a more detailed and thorough understanding of the sport consumer. Practitioners will be able to more effectively position their sport product on the basis of experiences and marry the distribution channels selected with the experiences elicited. In addition, this research has important implications for sport marketers, particularly as a segmentation tool. Marketers may leverage this information to develop the best product, distribution, and message mixes to more effectively reach and communicate with this consumer base. This will permit organisations to formulate "best practice" strategies regarding seeking out potential, actual or repeat complainants, and to better direct their efforts in resolving failed consumption episodes. This is important to future revenue, the projection of positive organisational image, and the creation of positive consumer perception. Finally, this research presents sport marketers with guidelines for policy formation and training in areas including customer service, stadium management, human resource management, and the like. We will begin this paper with a general discussion of consumer complaint behaviour.

Consumer Complaint Behaviour

Consumer complaint behaviour involves the set of multiple, active behavioural responses to dissatisfaction during or following a consumption episode (Volkov, 2003; Volkov, Harker, & Harker, 2002, 2003). Consumer complaint responses can been described as the set of all behavioural responses portrayed by consumers which involve the communication of negative perceptions relating to a consumption episode and triggered by dissatisfaction and mediated by anger with that episode (Bougie, Pieters, & Zeelenberg, 2003; Day, 1984; Rogers & Williams, 1990; Singh & Howell, 1985; Volkov, Harker, & Harker, 2002). It can be argued that this implies that consumer complaint responses are influenced by a multitude of situational, product, and personal variables unrelated to, but triggered by, the intensity of the consumer's dissatisfaction and anger with the consumption episode. The extant literature therefore provides a path with which to analyse the consumer complaint process, commencing with an explanation of consumer complaint behaviour.

Consumer complaints occur due to a variety of scenarios with the majority being made by consumers who are dissatisfied with a product they are or have been using (Jacoby & Jaccard, 1981). Yet complaints may also originate from satisfied consumers of a product, non-users of a product, and non-purchasers of a product (Jacoby & Jaccard, 1981). Consumer complaints have been defined as an action taken by an individual whereby they communicate something negative regarding a product or service to either the firm manufacturing or marketing the particular product or service, to family, to friends, or to some third-party entity (Jacoby & Jaccard, 1981; Landon, 1980; Rogers & Williams, 1990; Singh & Howell, 1985). However, not all complainants seek redress (Alicke et al., 1992; Jacoby & Jaccard, 1981; Nyer, 2000; Owens & Hausknecht, 1999; Rogers & Williams, 1990; Singh, 1988).

Within this definition of a consumer complaint, the term *individual* refers to a person acting on their own behalf (or on behalf of their family unit) and can be purchasers, non-purchasers, users, or non-users of the product (Jacoby & Jaccard, 1981). To limit the scope of this specific research, this particular term excludes organisational entities and third parties. *Communication* refers to expressions made either in writing or orally but excludes informal word-of-mouth communication (again, this step has been taken to limit the scope of this research). *Product or service* refers to something offered for sale to consumers. *Third party* refers to formally constituted entities such as governments, special-interest groups, and other sanctioned bodies. These complaints may focus on either the functional (performance-related) or non-functional (the package, price, and the like) components of the consumption process. This section has reviewed what consumer complaint behaviour is. The following section will explore why consumers choose to complain.

Why Consumers Complain

Prior literature suggests that a dissatisfying consumption experience serves as the primary input into the consumer complaint behaviour process (Day, 1984; Stephens & Gwinner, 1998). That is, those consumption experiences in which consumers' performance perceptions compare negatively to some standard (such as their previous expectations), and therefore are evaluated as dissatisfying, serves as the stressful event that is cognitively evaluated by the consumer and leads to the complaint behaviour (Stephens & Gwinner, 1998). Included in the daily, stress-causing issues that people face are the many problems consumers experience in the marketplace (Stephens & Gwinner, 1998). The dissatisfying marketplace experience has the potential to cause stress in one's daily life (Stephens & Gwinner, 1998). Further, when consumers suppress their feelings of distress, they dwell on the cause(s) of their dissatisfaction, which then results in heightened levels of dissatisfaction (Kowalski, 1996; Kowalski & Erickson, 1997; Nyer, 2000).

Consumers' perceptions regarding the functional performance of a product or service are based on their evaluation of the product or service in relation to their expectations prior to usage and any first-hand experience acquired from that usage (Day & Landon, 1977; Jacoby & Jaccard, 1981). These consumer usage experiences either exceed, match, or fall below the consumers' prior expectations, with dissatisfaction occurring if the performance of the product or service falls below those expectations (Day & Landon, 1977; Granbois, Summers, & Frazier, 1977; Jacoby & Jaccard, 1981). However, it must be noted that at times the consumers' expectations prior to usage or first-hand experience are unreasonable, and the consumer is without the necessary skills to properly evaluate the performance (Jacoby & Jaccard, 1981). Regardless, dissatisfaction alone is not sufficient for the production of a consumer complaint (Jacoby & Jaccard, 1981).

Other factors, such as the individual consumer themselves and the situation, also impact the propensity of consumer complaint behaviour occurring and the level of consumer dissatisfaction (Bolfing, 1989; Jacoby & Jaccard, 1981). Further, the consumer's anger with the consumption experience has been shown to have a moderating effect, and it further influences that complaining propensity (Bougie, Pieters, & Zeelenberg, 2003).

Related to the consumers themselves, individual factors affecting their propensity to complain include their personality, their attitudes, their motives, perceived value of time, the information levels, and their sociodemographics (Bolfing, 1989; Jacoby & Jaccard, 1981; Moyer, 1984; Volkov, 2003; Volkov, Harker, & Harker, 2002, 2003). That is, consumer complainants are not characterized by a cross-section of society because complaining propensities and abilities are stronger in some societal groups than in others (for example, those community members that are of a higher socio-economic status tend to complain more than those community members that have lower status). Further, consumer complaint behaviour is a complex function of many variables including those intrinsic to the consumer themselves.

The literature suggests that there are differences between those consumers who complain and those who do not. Such findings indicate that complainants tend to be older, have attained higher levels of educational qualifications, earn a higher gross weekly income, possess greater degrees of wealth, and have higher participant levels of local community involvement. Further, in general terms, complainants have more resources in terms of intrinsic abilities (for example, self-confidence, feelings of self-worth) and external resources (for example, time, money, qualifications) to avail themselves when dissatisfied (Kolodinsky & Aelong, 1990; Volkov, Harker, & Harker, 2003).

The importance of the situation to the consumer and the prevailing social climate (relating to societal norms) are also stimulants to complaints from a situational perspective (Jacoby & Jaccard, 1981). The importance of the situation does not necessarily relate to the cost of the product or service, but rather relates to the magnitude of the perceived loss (Bolfing, 1989; Granbois, Summers, & Frazier, 1977; Prakash, 1991; Singh & Widing, 1991) and its essential nature for daily living (Day & Landon, 1977). Specifically, through development of ideals such as consumerism, consumer rights, and the alteration of social norms, it is now more acceptable for consumers to complain (Jacoby & Jaccard, 1981; Landon, 1977), and thus complaint behaviour is increasing.

Therefore, complainants display a variety of attributes that set them apart from other members of the population and also possess specific attitudes that provide the motivation for them to exhibit complaint behaviour. The following section will review the behaviours consumers exhibit when complaining.

Consumer Complaint Behaviour

Complaint responses have been categorised in two ways: behavioural and non-behavioural (Singh, 1988). Behavioural responses constitute any or all consumer actions that openly express dissatisfaction (Day, 1984; Landon, 1980; Singh, 1988). These responses include those directed towards the seller, manufacturer, retailer, service provider, third parties, family, friends, and others (Andreasen & Manning, 1990; Day, 1984; Richins, 1983; Singh, 1988, 1990). Non-behavioural responses are viewed as those situations when the consumer takes no action at all (Singh, 1988). That is, the consumer forgets about or ignores the dissatisfying experience and does nothing about it. Although some researchers view non-behavioural complaint responses as elements to research (Day et al., 1981), the fact that these responses entail no behaviour indicates that this category falls outside the scope of this specific research into consumer complaint behaviour.

A review of the consumer complaint behaviour literature indicates that researchers appear unified in their understanding of the classification of consumer complaint behavioural responses (Day & Landon, 1977; Singh, 1988; Volkov, 2003; Volkov, Harker, & Harker, 2002, 2003). That is, with respect to behavioural responses, consumers have three basic options: private responses, direct voicing, and amplified voicing (Day & Landon, 1977; Singh, 1988). Private responses are consumer complaint behaviours that are directed towards family, friends, acquaintances, and the like through word-of-mouth communication. These responses are directed towards actors that are within the complainant's social network, but these actors are not directly involved in the dissatisfying consumption experience.

Direct voicing is consumer complaint behaviour directed towards the seller, manufacturer, retailer, service provider, and/or any other parties involved in the production and delivery of the product. Direct voicing is usually directed towards actors that are not within the complainant's social network (this is not always necessarily so) and who are directly involved with the dissatisfying consumption experience. In contrast, amplified voicing is consumer complaint behaviours that are directed towards third parties such as regulatory bodies, journalists, and legal representatives. Amplified voicing is directed towards actors that are neither within the complainant's social network, nor are they directly involved with the dissatisfying consumption experience. Therefore, the network position of the actors and their involvement with the consumption experience are used to categorise consumer complaint behavioural responses into the three categories of this taxonomy.

When considering consumers' post-purchase alternatives for action in a complaint situation, alternatives within the sport context can be explained as follows: A *private response* would involve the consumer communicating a dissatisfactory experience concerning the league, team, player, stadium, etc. to family, friends, or acquaintances to identify to them that the consumption experience led to the dissatisfaction and anger. *Voicing* would occur when a private response would not yield appropriately perceived restitution in the opinion of the individual consumer. *Direct voicing* would be represented by the consumer complaining directly to the league, team management, stadium manager, etc. *Amplified voicing* would occur when the consumer enlists the support of third parties such as broadcast or print journalists, consumer protection agencies, or industry regulatory or self-regulatory bodies to act on her or his behalf.

These behavioural responses are goal directed (Bagozzi & Warshaw, 1990; Singh & Wilkes, 1996). This indicates that consumer complainants perceive their behaviours as aiming to achieve a particular goal, rather than as an end in and of themselves (Singh & Wilkes, 1996). These complaint behaviours increase the probability of achieving goals but do not guarantee success in that goal attainment. Specific goal attainment through consumer complaint behaviour is difficult due to lack of control on behalf of the dissatisfied consumer, scarcity of resources available to the consumer, and other environmental contingencies (Singh & Wilkes, 1996). Further, consumer complaint behaviour is multifaceted. That is, consumers may engage in one or all of the diverse options—private responses, direct voicing, and amplified voicing (Day, 1984;

Richins, 1983; Singh & Wilkes, 1996). Importantly, these behaviours are independent—a consumer may undertake one, two, or all three of these behaviours in response to a consumption experience (Liu, Watkins, & Yi, 1997; Richins, 1987).

Although extant literature has mentioned mere dissatisfaction as the antecedent feeling that consumers experience prior to expressing complaint behaviour (Singh, 1988, 1990), Bougie, Pieters, and Zeelenberg (2003) identify that anger must be felt for consumers to enact behavioural complaint responses. Further, alternate research investigating consumer complaint behaviour finds that consumers tend to remain passive rather than complain when they are merely dissatisfied (Best & Andreasen, 1977; Chiu, Tsang, & Yang, 1987; Oliver, 1996; Stephens & Gwinner, 1998). Contrasting literature from disciplines such as anthropology, social psychology, sociology ,and marketing explain that complaint behaviour is a common response when consumers are angry (Bougie, Pieters, & Zeelenberg, 2003; Roseman, Wiest, & Swartz, 1994; Shaver et al., 1987). Therefore, the current literature suggests that both dissatisfaction and anger are required for consumer complaint behaviour to be evidenced, with anger being a mediator of the effect of dissatisfaction on consumer behavioural responses (Bougie, Pieters, & Zeelenberg, 2003) . This relationship is illustrated in Figure 1.

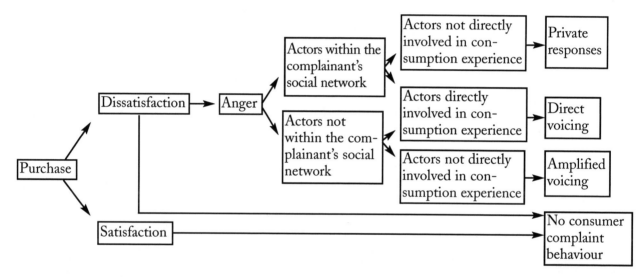

Source: Developed for this research from Bougie, Pieters, & Zeelenberg, 2003; Day, 1984; Day & Landon, 1977; Jacoby & Jaccard, 1981; Lando, 1980; Singh, 1988, 1990; Volkov, Harker, & Harker 2002.

Figure 1:   Taxonomy of CCB behavioural responses

This research specifically investigates the consumer voicing aspect of consumer complaint behaviour, and, thus, consumer voicing will now be specifically addressed.

The voicing of complaints may have limited ability to affect the outcome of the critical incident; however, it can provide a cathartic, satisfying interaction through which to air grievances. This process can be enough to encourage further consumer voicing and a return to the consumption experience through alleviating consumer dissatisfaction and anger. It is therefore evident that consumer voicing is a relevant area for investigation from practitioner, organisational, and theoretical perspectives within the consumer complaint literature in that it provides indications of market and firm performance; allows analysis of consumer behaviours; adds direction to strategy and policy formulation; provides meaningful communication between the stakeholders; and identifies social concerns. To contextualise this research of consumer voicing in the field of sport spectator consumption, experiential consumption is now addressed.

Experiential Consumption

There has been an important shift in the attention of researchers towards the experiential aspects of consumption (Holbrook et al., 1984; Hopkinson & Pujari, 1999) in an attempt to understand consumer behaviour in a more holistic sense (Addis & Holbrook, 2001; Holbrook et al., 1984; Lofman, 1991). Within the broad discipline of consumer behaviour, experiential consumption deals with goods and services that consumers choose, buy, and use purely to experience and enjoy (Cooper-Martin, 1992). Sport consumption, therefore, constitutes a relevant area of research, as the consumption of sport is an end in itself and serves as the primary benefit in use (Holbrook et al., 1984) and constitutes an area that requires further attention (Addis & Holbrook, 2001; Hirschman & Holbrook, 1982; Holbrook et al., 1984; Hopkinson & Pujari, 1999). As such, this research heeds the call to stimulate discourse between consumer behaviour and sport marketing researchers (Kates, 1998) by investigating how consumer complaint behaviour differs in the experiential consumption of sport.

Since the late 1970s, researchers have identified that consumer behaviour involves more than mere information processing in order to reach a purchase decision or to solve a particular problem (Olshavsky & Granbois, 1979; Sheth, 1979). Research has identified that elements including fantasy, fun, imagination, feelings, pleasure, emotions, and the like also have a role in some consumption experiences (Addis & Holbrook, 2001; Hirschman & Holbrook, 1982; Holbrook & Hirschman, 1982; Holbrook et al., 1984). This extension of consumer behaviour theory indicates that research should not always assume that consumers will behave as rational decision makers and that marketers need to understand this phenomenon in order to more fully understand their consumers (Addis & Holbrook, 2001).

With regard to experiential consumption, the core function of the product as a good or service takes on less relevance, while the product's role in symbolism increases (Addis & Holbrook, 2001). When considering a product in the experiential consumption realm, the relative weight of the objective features of the product is lower than one would expect if considering the process from a more rational or utilitarian framework (Addis & Holbrook, 2001). As such, consumer decisions and behaviours rely on fast, intuitive consideration of the relevant information and how that makes them feel (Dube & Mukherejee, 2003). Far from being purely rational decision makers, consumers in the experiential realm rely on their intuitions and emotions associated with prior experience of the situation (Dube & Mukherejee, 2003).

An example of such a product is sport. The differences between the utilitarian and experiential views of consumption assist in rationalising the need to adopt two different views of consumer behaviour (Addis & Holbrook, 2001). The experiential perspective indicates that in a sport consumption experience, consumers consume in order to create feelings, experiences, and emotions rather than merely to solve a problem (Mowen, 1988). The consumption of sport as a spectator (and therefore the viewing of sport) results in the emotion related components of the consumption experience predominating. That is, these facets of consumer behaviour relate to the multisensory aspects of the consumer experience (Addis & Holbrook, 2001; Hirschman & Holbrook, 1982).

Given the special nature of experiential consumption, the behaviour of consumers is likely to be different due to the relatively greater emotional processing, more activity and evaluation, but relatively less cognitive processing (Cooper-Martin, 1992; Lofman, 1991). The differences arise due to the understanding that consumers in an experiential consumption setting do not act as rational decision makers as they have been portrayed in "traditional" product and service consumption settings, and, as such, their behaviours (including complaint behaviour) are unlikely to fit with the extant view (Addis & Holbrook, 2001; Hoffman, Kumar, & Novak, 2003).

Sport consumption is subject to a high degree of consumer subjectivity, and therefore uncertainty, which leads to an inability of researchers to rationally analyse this consumption episode utilising existing models (Addis & Holbrook, 2001; Hoffman, Kumar, & Novak, 2003; Mizerski & White, 1986). Further, as experiential consumption relies on rich, sensory input, it requires different measures than those developed for utilitarian or functional products to ascertain consumer dissatisfaction, anger, and complaint behaviour (Minor et al., 2004). Through analysis of the published consumption literature, it is clear that the existing "traditional" and typical consumer behaviour models do not explain consumer complaint behaviour in real-life experiential consumption settings.

Specifically, these models do not allow for the influence of emotion, mood, and involvement, all of which have been shown to be relevant and critical constructs in sport research. Further, traditional models do not consider a priori and experiential emotion, mood, and involvement, where sport consumption research has shown that in these experiential settings, these constructs vary prior to and following an experiential incident or experience. Figure 2 shows the experiential consumer complaint behaviour model as we believe it operates.

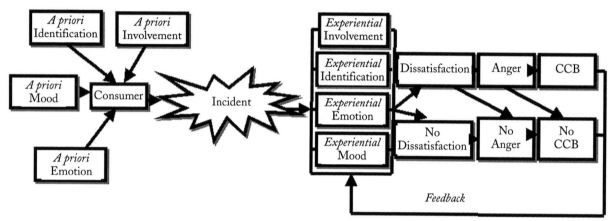

Source: Literature reviewed for this study.

Figure 2: Experiential consumer complaint behaviour model

The research question posited in this study is

How does consumer complaint behaviour occur in the experiential consumption of sport?

Consumer behaviour and service literature have shown mood, emotion, identification, and involvement to be important predictive variables. However, if we consider the inherently variable nature of services and events, traditional measures of mood and involvement appear inadequate. If emotion, identification, mood, and involvement are indeed variable during the time of the consumption experience, marketers would have unique opportunities to influence this fluctuation or react to variations in the construction of the encounter.

We propose that fans bring an existing mood state, emotion level, level of identification with the actors involved in the sporting contest itself, and level of involvement into the sport consumption experience, which we term *"a priori mood," "a priori emotion," "a priori identification,"* and *"a priori involvement."* We further propose that this mood state, emotion level, level of identification with the actors involved in the sporting contest itself, and level of involvement is likely to then vary constantly during the consumption experience, which we term to be *"experiential mood," "experiential emotion," "experiential identification,"* and *"experiential involvement."* Therefore we propose that in sport consumption settings, mood, emotion, identification, and involvement will be dynamic constructs operating both on a priori and on experiential levels.

Mood

Mood is considered to be a dimension of experiential sport consumption with research identifying that optimal experience is in part defined by mood (Chalip et al., 1984; Johnson Morgan & Summers, 2003).

Further, Chalip et al. (1984) state that conditions conducive to optimal experience are accompanied by states of high positive moods. Following such research, it has been identified that consumers regulate their expectations, satisfaction, and verbalisation aspects of a consumption experience depending on their mood before and during the experience (Johnson Morgan & Summers, 2003).

Due to the sport consumption experience being so unpredictable because of the uncontrollable elements of competition, mood has been identified as a dynamic, mediating factor in the sport consumption experience (Johnson Morgan & Summers, 2003).

Emotion

Emotion is an important component of consumer response (Holdbrook, Chestnut, Oliva, & Greenleaf, 1984; Oliver, 1994; Schultz, Kleine, & Kernan, 1989; Havlena & Holbrook, 1993; Mano & Oliver, 1993; Westbrook & Oliver, 1991). The extreme emotions and violence displayed by some sport fans at sports events is testimony to the passion of the spectator and the power of the sport (Strychacz, 1994). Building on the previous depiction of the conceptual model provided for this study, the addition of emotion is necessary as it may be a mediating factor on the variables of anger and identification and ultimately on consumers' complaint behaviour. Similar to the other mediating constructs in the model, emotion is believed to have an a priori and experiential state where the emotion brought to the experience by the fan may in fact vary during the sport experience.

The "experiential view" is based on the premise of hedonic consumption as described by Hirschman and Holbrook (1982):

> "Hedonic consumption designates those facets of consumer behavior that relate to the multi-sensory, fantasy and emotive aspects of one's experience . . ." (p. 92).

Indeed, Hirschman and Holbrook (1982, p. 98), specifically cite the watching of a football game as an example of an experience which could be laden with fluctuating emotions.

Emotion is defined here as more than just pleasant or happy feelings. In contrast to low involvement activities such as brushing one's teeth or doing the dishes, watching a sporting event is more intense, more involving, and potentially more important in the life of a consumer (Maslow, 1968). Therefore, sport spectating as a form of intrinsically motivated consumption could be expected to evoke more than just unidimensional emotional responses, such as positive or negative, happy or sad, particularly with people who are enthusiastic about sports.

Involvement

Experiential consumption researchers have long advocated a shift in focus from the "degree of involvement" (low versus high) to the "type of involvement" (Holbrook & Hirschman, 1982), which will allow researchers to consider involvement in terms of the degree of activation or arousal during the experience (Johnson Morgan & Summers, 2003). This approach would suggest that there is potential for involvement to change during an experience to moderate the effect of other factors (Johnson Morgan & Summers, 2003).

In order to discover more about the operation of the mood, emotion, identification, and involvement constructs in relation to voicing, a series of existential-phenomenology focus groups is proposed. In this method, participants will be encouraged to describe their experiences with sport consumption. There will be an emphasis on letting the participants naturally describe only those factors of prior experiences that they considered relevant, avoiding the use of "why?" questions at all times (Dale, 1996; Johnson Morgan & Summers, 2003).

Identification

Anger

Traditional consumer complaint behaviour models identify that anger is an important element in models exploring or predicting consumer complaint behaviour. Research that has considered the behaviours of sport fans has also highlighted that anger and yelling abuse (such as yelling at the referee for a bad decision) are socially sanctioned as part of the sporting experience (Wann, Carlson, & Schrader, 1999a; Wann et al., 1999a). In fact, some research has indicated that the greater the level of affiliation felt by the fans with the respective sporting combatants, the greater the levels of aggression and the more vocal the fans will be (Wann, Carlson, & Schrader, 1999a; Wann et al., 1999a). This affiliation, or identification, with the fan's chosen team enhances the feeling of solidarity amongst groups of supporters and is a key preoccupation of the individual's self concept, with the team's values marrying with those more established foci of fan support (Giulianotti, 2002). The team, however, reciprocates in the relationship by providing a complex and evolving representation of the fan's public identity (Giulianotti, 2002). Such a relationship provides the fan with a strong, obligatory, collaborative motive to support her/his chosen team. Thus, it would appear that a mediating role of aggression in the decision to "voice" in a sport consumption setting would still be prevalent.

Prior research has identified that the greater the level of identification that fans feel for a team, the more aggressive they are on behalf of that team (Wann, Carlson, & Schrader, 1999b; Wann et al., 1999b). Sociology theorists indicate that this is due to this identification being a central component of the fans' identity, and any competition that their team is involved in will hold great relevance for their own, personal self-worth (Wann et al., 1999a).

Through fan association in a crowd, as is common in sporting stadia, "fanatical" excitement can lead to significant arousal, including increased heart rate, whereby fans may actually exert as much energy and effort as the sporting participants themselves (Corbin, 1973; Sloan, 1979). Excitement, such as that experienced by fans, can produce unacceptable complaint behaviour outcomes in terms of legalities and other social issues, including destructive violence and hooliganism. However, excitement can contribute to the growth of personal aggression amongst fans that has outcomes that are possibly more socially acceptable (e.g., raucous applause) (Bromberger, Hayot, & Mariottini, 1993; Fiske, 1992; Redden & Steiner, 2000; Sloan, 1979).

Emotionally, two types of aggression can be differentiated: hostile and instrumental (Conroy et al., 2001). Hostile aggression is classed as behaviour that is designed to harm a specific target and the reinforcement sought by the fan is solely from injuring the targeted victim or seeing that target injured (e.g., injurious hooliganism) (Husman & Silva, 1984). Alternatively, if the reinforcement sought from the aggressive act is designed purely to present the fan with an action that will allow her/him some sort of advantage without causing injury, this is classed as instrumental aggression (e.g., yelling cheers when their team performs well) (Husman & Silva, 1984). Research investigating aggression portrayed by sportspeople, and fan opinion of this aggression, identified that consumers perceive that aggression is increasingly acceptable when the actor, or athlete, is competing at a higher level of sporting contest (Conroy et al., 2001). Following this assertion, it can be said that fans would perceive their own aggression as more acceptable if directed towards a higher-level sporting competition.

A Methodology for Experiential Consumption Research

Some of the phenomenological focus groups will be carried out before and during a televised broadcast of a live national football league game. Conducting the focus groups during an actual experience of the type being investigated is required to conform to the phenomenological method of first-degree information collection (Johnson Morgan & Summers, 2003). This method also differentiates the current research from the recall-based methods of traditional consumer complaint behaviour research literature, in that it places the respondents in a real-world situation.

Phenomenological focus groups are considered a particularly appropriate choice for those wishing to explore consumer experience (Calder, 1977), as they provide a systematic description in terms of first-degree constructs of the consumption-relevant intersubjectivity of the target segment (Johnson Morgan & Summers, 2003). Phenomenological focus groups require the participants and the researcher to share participatively (Calder, 1977; Johnson Morgan & Summers, 2003). This means that the researcher should immerse themselves in the experience, with the subjects, in order to collect data from the respondents about the experience (Johnson Morgan & Summers, 2003). Another important reason for conducting the focus groups during an actual sport consumption experience is to document which characteristics of the game elicit responses, changes in mood, discussion among participants, emotion displayed, and the like (Johnson Morgan & Summers, 2003).

Phenomenological focus groups require homogeneous participants in a natural setting (Calder, 1977; Johnson Morgan & Summers, 2003). For this reason, participants will be recruited using the snowball sampling technique. The groups will be made up of friends and associates who normally watch football together.

This paper has achieved the three objectives set: first, to bring together established research in the field of consumer complaint responses; second, to contextualise this research into the general area of experiential consumption, specifically sport; and third, to present a conceptual model based on the reviewed literature espousing the proposition posited by authors that there are generalisable differences between consumer complaint behaviour in experiential consumption when compared to "traditional" consumption models. As such, an exciting and revolutionary program of research was presented.

References

Addis, M., & Holbrook, M. B. (2001). On the conceptual dink between mass customisation and experiential consumption: An explosion of subjectivity. *Journal of Consumer Behaviour, 1*(1), 50-66.

Alicke, M. D., Braun, J. C., Glor, J. E., Klotz, M. L., Magee, J., Sederholm, H., & Siegel, R. (1992). Complaining behavior in social interaction. *Personality and Social Psychology Bulletin, 18*(3), 286-95.

Andreasen, A. R. (1984). Consumer satisfaction in loose monopolies: The case of medical care. *Journal of Public Policy and Marketing, 2*, 122-35.

Andreasen, A. R. (1985). Consumer responses to dissatisfaction in loose monopolies. *Journal of Consumer Research, 12*, 135-41.

Andreasen, A. R., & Manning, J. (1990). The dissatisfaction and complaining behaviour of vulnerable consumers. *Journal of Consumer Satisfaction, Dissatisfaction and Complaining Behaviour, 3*, 12-20.

Bagozzi, R. P., & Warshaw, P. R. (1990). Trying to consume. *Journal of Consumer Research, 17*, 127-40.

Best, A., & Andreasen, A. R. (1977). Consumer response to unsatisfactory purchases: A survey of perceiving defects, voicing complaints and obtaining redress. *Law and Society Review, 11*, 701-42.

Bolfing, C. P. (1989, Spring). How do consumers express dissatisfaction and what can service marketers do about it? *Journal of Services Marketing, 3*, 5-23.

Bougie, R., Pieters, R., & Zeelenberg, M. (2003). Angry customers don't come back, they get back: The experience and behavioural implications of anger and dissatisfaction in services. *Journal of the Academy of Marketing Science, 31*(4), 377-93.

Bromberger, C., Hayot, A., & Mariottini, J. (1993). Allez l'O.M., forza Juve': The passion for football in Marseille and Turin'. In S. Redhead (Ed.), *The passion and the fashion. Football fandom in the New Europe.* Sydney, AU: Avebury.

Calder, B. J. (1977). Focus groups and the nature of qualitative marketing research. *Journal of Marketing Research, 14*, 353-64.

Chalip, L., Csikszentmihalyi, M., Kleiber, D., & Larson, R. (1984). Variation of experience in formal and informal sport. *Research Quarterly for Exercise and Sport, 55*(2), 109-16.

Chiu, C-Y., Tsang, S-C., & Yang, C-F. (1987). The role of face situation and attitudinal antecedents in Chinese consumer complaint behaviour. *The Journal of Social Psychology, 128*(2), 173-80.

Cialdini, R., Borden, R. J., Thorne, A., & Sloan, L. R. (1976). Basking in reflected glory: Three (football) field studies. *Journal of Personality and Social Psychology, 34*(3), 366-75.

Conroy, D. E., Silva, J. M., Newcomer, R. R., Walker, B. W., & Johnson, M. S. (2001). Personal and participatory socializers of the perceived legitimacy of aggressive behaviour in sport. *Aggressive Behaviour, 27,* 405-18.

Cooper-Martin, E. (1992). Consumers and movies: Information sources for experiential products. *Advances in Consumer Research, 19,* 756-61.

Corbin, C. B. (1973). Among spectators "trait" anxiety and coronary risk. *Physician and Sports Medicine, 1*(2), 55-8.

Dale, G. (1996). Existential phenomenology: Emphasizing the experience of the athlete in sport psychology research. *The Sport Psychologist, 10,* 307-21.

Day, R. L. (1977). Extending the concept of consumer satisfaction. *Advances in Consumer Research, 4,* 149-54.

Day, R. L. (1984). Modelling choices among alternative responses to dissatisfaction. In T. C. Kinnear (Ed.), *Advances in consumer research, 2* (pp. 496-499). Duluth, MN: Association for Consumer Research.

Day, R. L., & Landon, E. L. (1977). Toward a theory of consumer complaining behaviour. In A. G. Woodside, J. N. Sheth, & P. D. Bennett (Eds.), *Consumer and industrial buying behaviour* (pp. 425-437). New York: Elsevier.

Day, R. L., Grabricke, K., Schaetzle, T., & Stavbach, F. (1981). The hidden agenda of consumer complaining, *Journal of Retailing, 57,* 86-106.

Dube, L., & Mukherejee, A. (2003). The relationship between rational and experiential processing: Conflict, complicity, or independence? *Advances in Consumer Research,* p. 30.

Fiske, J. (1992). The cultural economy of fandom. In L. A. Lewis (Ed.), *The adoring audience: Fan culture and popular media.* New York: Routledge.

Fornell, C., & Didow, N. M. (1980). Economic constraints on consumer complaint behavior. *Advances in Consumer Research, 7,* 318-23.

Fornell, C., & Wernerfelt, B. (1987). Defensive marketing strategy by customer complaint management: A theoretical analysis. *Journal of Marketing Research, 24,* 337-46.

Giulianotti, R. (2002). Supporters, followers, fans, and flaneurs. *Journal of Sport and Social Issues, 26*(1), 25-46.

Granbois, D. J., Summers, J. O., & Frazier, G. (1977). Correlates of consumer expectations and complaining behavior. In R. L. Day (Ed.), *Consumer satisfaction, dissatisfaction and complaining behavior* (pp. 18-25). Bloomington, IN: Indiana University Press.

Havlena, W. J., & Holbrook, M. B. (1986, December). The varieties of consumption experience: Comparing two typologies of emotions in consumer behavior. *Journal of Consumer Research, 13,* 394-404.

Hirschman, A. O. (1970). Exit, voice and loyalty: *Responses to decline in firms, organisations and states.* Cambridge, MA: Harvard University Press.

Hirschman, E. C., & Holbrook, M. A. (1982). Hedonic consumption: Emerging concepts, methods and propositions. *Journal of Marketing, 46,* 92-101.

Hoffman, D., Kumar, P., & Novak, T. (2003). How processing modes influence consumers' cognitive representations of product perceptions formed from similarity judgments. *Advances in Consumer Research,* p. 30.

Holbrook, M. A., & Hirschman, E. C. (1982). The experiential aspects of consumption: Consumer fantasies, feelings and fun. *Journal of Consumer Research, 9,* 132-40.

Holbrook, M. B., Chestnut, R. W., Oliva, T. A., & Greenleaf, E. A. (1984). Play as a consumption experience: The roles of emotions, performance, and personality in the enjoyment of games. *Journal of Consumer Research, 11,* 728-39.

Hopkinson, G. C., & Pujari, D. (1999). A factory analytic study of the sources of meaning in hedonic consumption. *European Journal of Marketing, 33*(3/4), 273-90.

Hunt, K. A., Bristol, T., & Bashaw, R. E. (1999). A conceptual approach to classifying sports fans. *Journal of Services Marketing, 13*(6), 439-52.

Husman, B., & Silva, J. (1984). Aggression: Definitional considerations. In R. S. Weinberg (Ed.), *Psychological foundations of sport*. Champaign, IL: Human Kinetics.

Jacoby, J., & Jaccard, J. J. (1981, Fall). The sources, meaning and validity of consumer complaint behaviour: A psychological analysis. *Journal of Retailing, 57*, 4-24.

Johnson Morgan, M., & Summers, J. (2003). Sport consumption: Exploring the duality of constructs in experiential research. In B. G. Pitts (Ed.), *Sharing best practices in sport marketing: The Sport Marketing Association's inaugural book of papers* (pp. 23-34). Morgantown, WV: Fitness Information Technology.

Jones, I. (1997). A further examination of the factors influencing current identification with a sports team, a response to Wann et al. (1996). *Perceptual and Motor Skills, 85*, 257-8.

Kasouf, C. J., Celuch, K. G., & Strieter, J. C. (1995). Consumer complaints as market intelligence: Orienting context and conceptual framework. *Journal of Consumer Satisfaction, Dissatisfaction and Complaining Behavior, 8*, 59-68.

Kates, S. M. (1998). Consumer research and sport marketing: Starting the conversation between two different academic discourses. *Sport Marketing Quarterly, 7*(2), 24-31.

Kim, C., Kim, S., Im, S., & Shin, C. (2003). The effect of attitude and perception on consumer complaint intentions. *Journal of Consumer Marketing, 20*(4), 352-71.

Kolodinsky, J., & Aelong, J. (1990). An integrated model of consumer complaint action applied to services: A pilot study. *Journal of Consumer Satisfaction, Dissatisfaction and Complaining Behaviour, 5*, 36-44.

Kowalski, R. M. (1996). Complaints and complaining: Functions, antecedents and consequences. *Psychological Bulletin, 199*(2), 179-96.

Kowalski, R. M., & Erickson, J. R. (1997). Complaining: What's all the fuss about? In R. M. Kowalski (Ed.), *Adverse interpersonal behaviors* (pp. 91-100). New York: Plenum Press.

Landon, E. L. (1977). A model of consumer complaint behaviour. In R. L. Day (Ed.), *Consumer satisfaction, dissatisfaction and complaining behavior* (pp. 31-35). Bloomington, IN: Indiana University Press.

Landon, E. L. (1980). The direction of consumer complaint research. In C. Olsen (Ed.), *Advances in consumer research* (pp. 335-338). Ann Arbor, MI: Association for Consumer Research.

Liu, R. R., Watkins, H. S., & Yi, Y. (1997). Taxonomy of consumer complaint behaviour: Replication and extension. *Journal of Consumer Satisfaction, Dissatisfaction and Complaining Behaviour, 10*, 92-103.

Lofman, B. (1991). Elements of experiential consumption: An exploratory study. *Advances in Consumer Research, 18*, 729-735.

Mano, H., & Oliver, R. L. (1993). Assessing the dimensionality and structure of the consumption experience: Evaluation, feeling, and satisfaction. *Journal of Consumer Research, 20*, 451-461.

Minor, M. S., Wagner, T., Brewerton, F. J., & Hausman, A. (2004). Rock on! An elementary model of customer satisfaction with musical performances. *Journal of Services Marketing, 18*(1), 7-18.

Mizerski, R. W., & White, J. D. (1986). Understanding and using emotions in advertising. *Journal of Consumer Marketing, 3*(4), 57-69.

Mowen, J. C. (1988). Beyond consumer decision making. *Journal of Consumer Marketing, 5*(1), 15-25.

Moyer, M. S. (1984). Characteristics of consumer complainants: Implications for marketing and public policy. *Journal of Public Policy and Marketing, 3*, 67-84.

Nyer, P. U. (2000). An investigation into whether complaining can cause increased consumer satisfaction. *Journal of Consumer Marketing, 17*(1), 9-17.

Oliver, R. L. (1993). Cognitive, affective, and attribute bases of the satisfaction response. *Journal of Consumer Research, 20*, 418-430.

Oliver, R. L. (1996). *Satisfaction: A behavioural perspective on the consumer*. New York: McGraw-Hill.

Olshavsky, R. W., & Granbois, D. H. (1979). Consumer decision making—fact or fiction? *Journal of Consumer Research, 6*, 93-100.

Owens, D. L., & Hausknecht, D. R. (1999). The effect of simplifying the complaint process: A field experiment with the Better Business Bureau. *Journal of Consumer, Satisfaction, Dissatisfaction and Complaining Behavior, 12*, 35-43.

Prakash, V. (1991). Intensity of dissatisfaction and consumer complaint behaviors. *Journal of Consumer Satisfaction, Dissatisfaction and Complaining Behavior, 4*, 110-22.

Real, M. R., & Mechikoff, R. A. (1992). Deep fan: Mythic identification, technology and advertising in spectator sport. *Sociology of Sport Journal, 9*, 323-339.

Redden, J., & Steiner, C. J. (2000). Fanatical consumers: Towards a framework for research. *Journal of Consumer Marketing, 17*(4), 322-37.

Richins, M. L. (1983). An analysis of consumer interaction styles in the marketplace. *Journal of Consumer Research, 10*, 73-82.

Richins, M. L. (1987). A multivariate analysis of responses to dissatisfaction. *Journal of the Academy of Marketing Science, 15*, 24-31.

Rogers, J. C., & Williams, T. G. (1990). Consumer personal values as antecedents to dyadic and third party public consumer complaining behaviour: An exploratory study. *Journal of Consumer Satisfaction, Dissatisfaction and Complaining Behaviour, 3*, 71-81.

Roseman, I. J., Wiest, C. M. S., & Swartz, T. S. (1994). Phenomenology, behaviours and goals differentiate discrete emotions. *Journal of Personality and Social Psychology, 67*, 206-11.

Schaff, D. (1995). *Sports marketing: It's not just a game anymore.* Amherst, NY: Prometheus Books.

Schibrowsky, J. A., & Lapidus, R. S. (1994). Gaining competitive advantage by analyzing aggregate complaints. *Journal of Consumer Marketing, 11*(1), 15-26.

Schultz, S. E., Kleine, R. E., & Kernan, J. B. (1989). "These are a few of my favorite things": Toward an explication of attachment as a consumer behavior construct. In T. K. Srull (Ed.), *Advances in consumer research, 16* (pp. 359-366). Provo, UT: Association for Consumer Research.

Shaver, P., Schwartz, J., Kirson, D., & O'Connor, C. (1987). Emotion knowledge: Further exploration of the prototype approach. *Journal of Personality and Social Psychology, 52*, 1061-86.

Sheth, J. N. (1979). The surpluses and shortages in consumer behavior theory and research. *Journal of the Academy of Marketing Science, 7*, 414-27.

Singh, J. (1988). Consumer complaint intentions and behaviour: Definitional and taxonomical issues. *Journal of Marketing, 52*, 93-107.

Singh, J. (1990). A typology of consumer dissatisfaction response styles. *Journal of Retailing, 66*, 57-99.

Singh, J., & Howell, R. D. (1985). Consumer complaining behaviour: A review and prospectus. *Journal of Consumer Satisfaction, Dissatisfaction and Complaining Behaviour*, pp. 41-9.

Singh, J., & Widing, R. E. (1991). What occurs once consumers complain? A theoretical model for understanding satisfaction/dissatisfaction outcomes of complaint responses. *European Journal of Marketing, 25*(5), 30-46.

Singh, J., & Wilkes, R. E. (1996). When consumers complain: A path analysis of the key triggers of consumer complaint response estimates. *Journal of the Academy of Marketing Science, 24*(4), 350-65.

Sloan, L. R. (1979). The function and impact of sports for fans: A review of theory and contemporary research. In J. H Goldstein (Ed.), *Sports games and play: Social and psychological viewpoints.* New York: John Wiley & Sons.

Snyder, E., Lassegard, M., & Ford, C. E. (1983). Distancing after group success and failure: Basking in reflected glory and cutting off reflected failure. *Journal of Personality and Social Psychology, 51*(2), 382-8.

Stephens, N., & Gwinner, K. P. (1998). Why don't some people complain? A cognitive emotive process model of consumer complaint behaviour. *Journal of the Academy of Marketing Science, 26*(3), 172-89.

Strychacz, T. (1994, April) American sports writers and "unruly rooters": The significance of orderly spectating. *Journal of American Studies, 28*(1), 84-90.

TARP (1986). Consumer complaint handling in America: An update study. Technical Assistance Research Program Institute for member agencies of the Consumer Affairs Council, United States Office of Consumer Affairs, Washington, DC.

Tax, S. S., Brown, S. W., & Chandrashekaran, M. (1998). Customer evaluations of service complaint experiences: Implications for relationship marketing. *Journal of Marketing, 62*(2), 60-76.

Volkov, M. (2003). Consumer complaint actions: A conceptual model based on complainants about advertising in Australia. *Journal of New Business Ideas and Trends, 1*(1), 50-60.

Volkov, M., Harker, D., & Harker, M. (2002). Complaint behaviour: A study of the differences between complainants about advertising in Australia and the population at large. *Journal of Consumer Marketing, 19*(4), 319-32.

Volkov, M., Harker, M., & Harker, D. (2003, February). Who are they? A profile of complainants about advertising in Australia. Paper presented to 2003 AMA Marketing Educators' Conference, Orlando, Florida.

Wann, D. L., Carlson, J. D., & Schrader, M. P. (1999). The impact of team identification on the hostile and instrumental verbal aggression of sport spectators. *Journal of Social Behavior & Personality, 14*(2), 279-86.

Wann, D. L., Peterson, R. R., Cothran, C., & Dykes, M. (1999). Sport fan aggression and anonymity: The importance of team identification. *Social Behavior and Personality, 27*(6), 597-602.

Westbrook, R. A., & Oliver, R. L. (1991, June). The dimensionality of consumption emotion patterns and consumer satisfaction. *Journal of Consumer Research, 18*, 84-91.

Zeithaml, V. A., Berry, L. L., & Parasuraman, A. (1996). The behavioral consequences of service quality. *Journal of Marketing, 60*, 31-46.

The "Toughest Sport on Dirt": An Exploratory Study of Market Demand Variables of Fans of the Professional Bull Riders Inc.

CHIA-YING (DORIS) LU
BRENDA PITTS
KEVIN AYERS
CAROL LUCAS

Introduction

With a television viewership of 90 million, a multi-network contract, a world championship ending in Las Vegas, large corporation sponsorship, and a growing fan base, the sport of bull riding has come a long way since its professional start a mere 10 years ago. From a socially accepted stereotype of the poor, lonely cowboy, cowboys and cowgirls today can reap hundreds of thousands—and even millions—of dollars in professional rodeo circuits. The professional rodeo industry even has the attention of ESPN and NBC Sports. Within the industry, one of the most popular events, the bull riding event, has become a stand alone professional league—the Professional Bull Riders Inc. Started in 1992 by 20 accomplished bull riders who each invested $1,000, the PBR is very popular, with each event bringing in 20,000 to 30,000 spectators and winnings beginning to hit the million dollar mark.

Unfortunately, the sport management academic world has ignored this industry. Current researchers were unable to locate any studies involving professional rodeo in the sport management literature.

Literature Review

The Sport Industry

The sport business industry has experienced phenomenal growth in a short period of time (Pitts & Stotlar, 2002). Pitts and Stotlar indicated that studies have been conducted in an attempt to place a dollar value or economic impact number on the sport business industry, with each study focused on similar segments of the industry.

Although methodologies in the studies were not exactly the same and did not include the same factors, they at least provided an estimate of the size of the industry and the various segments from which the industry is composed since 1986 (Pitts & Stotlar, 2002). Some of the studies included spectator spending, which is a sign of the popularity of sports events as entertainment.

The most current study, conducted by and published in *The Street & Smith's SportsBusiness Journal*, included spectator spending information. That study reported that the size of the sport business industry (with a specific focus on spectator sports) was $213 billion and that gate receipts alone accounted for $10.47 billion of that total (The Answer, 1999).

In another study also reported by the *SportsBusiness Journal*, spectator spending for sports events had increased to $26.17 billion dollars in 2001—a 16% increase from 1999. Of this, $11.74 billion were ticket sales, $10.70 billion was spent on concessions, parking, and on-site merchandise sales, and $3.73 billion was spent on premium seating (King, Sweet, Lefton, Cameron, Broughton, Lombardo, & Lee, 2002).

The ticket sales alone increased 12.1% from 1999. In addition, King et al. (2002) also declared that not only the revenue from premium seating contributed to increased spectator spending, but also spending throughout the modern sports venue had been streamlined by the advent of fan-loyalty programs and the growing number of shops where merchandise and concessions are available.

Professional Bull Riding

The modern extreme sport has become the fastest growing segment of sport spending at the beginning of the new millennium. These sports appear to be in the newly emergent "alternative, extreme, or lifestyle" sports, which are highly individualistic, free-spirited, adrenaline-rush activities (Howard & Crompton, 2004). Those include such sports as in-line skating, skateboarding, snowboarding, whitewater kayaking and rafting, bungee jumping, BMX biking, windsurfing, surfing, and several others. Bull riding can also be considered one of America's original extreme sports. Bull riding is a fierce, rough, and grueling sport with roots deep in American culture. Bull riding has turned into a "captivating, dangerous, on-the-edge-of-your-seat, stunt-like sporting event" (All About . . . , 2004).

The Professional Bull Riders Inc. (PBR) was created in Colorado Springs in 1992. A group of 20 bull riders broke away from the traditional rodeo scene and decided to start a circuit for bull riders only. Currently there are more than 800 bull riders from the U.S., Canada, Brazil, and Australia holding PBR memberships. They compete in more than 100 bull riding events per year on either the elite tour, the Built Ford Tough Series (BFTS), or the two minor league tours, U.S. Smokeless Tobacco Company Challenger Tour and the Humps n' Horns Tour. They accumulate the ranking for a chance to qualify for the PBR World Finals in Las Vegas and win the coveted title of PBR World Champion (All about..., 2004). In addition, riders compete across the circuit to accumulate points to win a $1 million dollar bonus at the end of the season (Built Ford Tough Million Dollar Bonus, 2004).

Corporate sponsors of the PBR include well known brands such as Ford, Bud Light, Wrangler, Jack Daniel's, Mossy Oak, U.S. Smokeless Tobacco Company, and the city of Las Vegas. Annual prize money has increased from $660,000 dollars in 1994 to over $9.5 million dollars in 2003 (Professional Bull Riding

Competition, 2004). With increasing sponsorship interests, more television networks have carried the events as well. The number of fans watching the events on television has gained momentum—television viewership has grown from 12 million to over 90 million. In 2003, seven Built Ford Tough Series (BFTS) events were aired on NBC. All 29 events aired on the Outdoor Life Network (OLN) and a few even aired on the Spanish station Telemundo. OLN has provided fans with over 188 hours of original PBR events. And more and more people attend PBR tournaments. An Atlanta Invitational held in the Georgia Dome had a record-breaking attendance of 33,000 fans (Professional Bull Riders on TV, 2004).

Obviously, professional bull riding is a growing sport and there is growing interest from the fans. The event we examined was the first of three to be held in Atlanta, Georgia. This current study is also the first of three in which we hope to examine thoroughly this sport and its fans.

Sports Event Attendance Factors

Many sport marketing researchers (Green, 1995; Greenstein & Marcum, 1981; Hansen & Gauthier, 1989; Lu, 2001; Lu & Pitts, 2003; Schofield, 1983; Zhang, Pease, Hui, & Michaud, 1995a; Zhang, Smith, Pease, & Jambor, 1997b; Zhang, Smith, Pease, & Lam, 1998) have concluded that the factors that affect spectator sports event attendance fall into four broad categories: (a) game attractiveness factors (individual player skills, team records, league standing, record-breaking performance, closeness of competition, special events, and entertainment), (b) economic and spending factors (ticket price, substitute forms of entertainment, television effect), (c) sociodemographic factors (population factors, age, gender, ethnicity, occupation, education, geography), and (d) audience preference factors (event schedule, convenience, weather, stadium quality, team history in the community).

Game attractiveness factors have been found to be positively related to game attendance (Demmert, 1973; Zhang, Smith, Pease, & Mahar, 1996). Game day promotions, for instance, have been associated with a discernible increase in attendance (Marcum & Greenstein, 1985; McDonald & Rascher, 2000; Pruegger, 2003) and sales, or price, promotions have traditionally been in the form of price or nonprice promotions in professional sport (McDonald & Rascher, 2000; Mullin, Hardy, & Sutton, 2000; Pitts & Stotlar, 2002). Other game attractiveness factors such as a strong rivalry between teams, a possible record-breaking performance, and the chance to see outstanding athletes positively affect attendance (Fillingham, 1977; Green, 1995; Noll, 1974).

Economic and visitor spending factors can affect a consumer's decision to attend a sports event. Some of these factors include the cost of the ticket, the cost of other amenities, availability of substitute forms of entertainment or activities, if the event will be on television, and the choice to attend other sports events in the area. It is reported in the literature that these factors tend to have a more negative effect on the decision to attend an event (Green, 1995; Hansen & Gauthier, 1989; Jones, 1984; Zhang et al., 1995; Zhang et al., 1996). For example, a person on a tight budget may forego the opportunity to attend an event based on the fact that the price is too high for their budget.

Sociodemographic factors include such basic demographical and sociocultural characteristics as age, gender, ethnicity, income, education, occupation, and household status, as well as geographical factors such as distance to the park and type of transportation (Green, 1995; Hansen & Gauthier, 1989; Kasky, 1994). In addition, some research shows that a new stadium can positively affect attendance (Hill, Madura, & Zuber, 1982).

Audience preference factors include such factors as game schedule, stadium quality, weather, convenience, food, parking, accommodation availability, and the history of the team in that community (Green, 1995; Hansen & Gauthier, 1989; Pitts, Lu, Ayers, & Lucas, 2004; Zhang et al., 1996). A certain level of comfort is expected when attending an event. Many fans prefer a clean facility, well-behaved crowds, good food and drink, and reasonable parking.

Purpose of the Study

The PBR and the world of professional bull riding are receiving an increasing amount of media attention. Further, bull riding can certainly be considered an extreme sport. With no research (that the authors could find) for the sport management literature, the current researchers believed that both the profession of bull riding and the academic literature could benefit from research into this sport. In addition, understanding the fans of this emerging sport can be very helpful to the sport marketers and managers in the sport. Therefore, the purpose of this study was to explore the fans of the Professional Bull Riders Inc.

Methods

Subjects

One PBR event in Georgia was identified for a first study merely based on its close proximity and convenience to the researchers in an attempt to explore sociodemographics, market demand variables, and fan interest in the PBR event. Subjects were 54 spectators who attended this PBR event.

Survey Instrument

Four major categories of variables affecting spectator decision making on game attendance identified in prior research were examined: (a) game attractiveness, (b) economic, (c) sociodemographic, and (d) audience preference (Green, 1995; Greenstein & Marcum, 1981; Hansen & Gauthier, 1989; Hart, Hutton, & Sharot, 1975; Lu, 2001; Schofield, 1983; Zhang, Pease, Hui, & Michaud, 1995). The questionnaire used in this study was developed with the use of those used by Green (1995), Hansen and Gauthier (1989), Kasky (1994), Schofiled (1983), Zhang et al. (1995), Lu (2001), and subsequently modified by the researchers. An influencing rating was translated as follows: 1 (no influence) to 5 (strong influence), NA=Not Applicable. After analyzing by Cronbach's Alpha, the reliability of the questionnaire was .75.

Analysis of Data

First, because this study was exploratory, descriptive statistics of the composite scores were calculated for each factor. Second, the data were analyzed by using regression to determine if there were major factors that would contribute to attendance factors.

Results and Discussion

Subjects were 54 spectators who attended this PBR event. They averaged 30 years of age, 50% were females, 56% had some form of college education, most were Caucasians (72.5%), reported a household income average of $72,000, and 51% of subjects reported to be single. A large majority—96%—were from the local area, and 81% of them had attended PBR events before (see Table 1). In addition, the average age of these PBR spectators was younger compared to spectators who attended other professional sport games (averaged around 40 years old) (Green, 1995; Lu, 2001).

While previous studies suggested that promotions of the game, rivalry, closeness of the competition, record-breaking performances, schedule, access, and cleanness of the facility have positive impact on attendance (Green, 1995; Greenstein & Marcum, 1981; Hansen & Gauthier, 1989; Hart, Hutton, & Sharot, 1975; Lu, 2001; Schofield, 1983; Zhang, Pease, Hui, & Michaud, 1995), none were found in this study.

Table 1: Descriptive Statistics for the Demographic Variables (n = 54)

Variables	Category	n	%	Cumulative %
Gender				
	Female	27	50	50.0
	Male	27	50	100.0
Age				
	Under 18	5	9.4	9.4
	18-24	15	28.3	37.7
	25-34	14	26.5	64.2
	35-44	14	26.4	90.6
	45-54	3	5.6	96.2
	55-plus	2	3.8	100.0
Marital/Household Status				
	Single	27	50.9	50.9
	Married	23	43.4	94.3
	Divorced	0	0	94.3
	Living with a partner	3	5.7	100.0
	Other	0	0	100.0
Highest Education Level				
	Some High School	2	3.8	3.8
	High School Graduated	20	38.5	42.3
	Vocational/Technical School	1	1.9	44.2
	Some College	3	5.8	50.0
	College Degree	23	44.2	94.2
	Some Post-Graduate Studies	0	0.0	94.2
	Master's Degree	2	3.8	98.1
	Doctoral Degree	1	1.9	100.0
Ethnicity				
	African American/Black	13	25.5	25.5
	Caucasian	37	72.5	98.0
	Asian/Pacific Islander	0	0.0	98.0
	Hispanic/Latino	0	0.0	98.0
	Others	1	2.0	100.0
Annual Household Income				
	$10,000 and under	0	0.0	0.0
	$10,001-$29,999	5	11.9	11.9
	$30,000-$49,999	11	26.2	38.1
	$50,000-$69,999	4	9.5	47.6
	$70,000-$89,999	5	11.9	59.5
	$90,000-$109,999	10	23.8	83.3
	$110,000-$129,999	4	11.9	95.2
	$130,000-$149,999	1	2.4	97.6
	$150,000 or more	1	2.4	100.0

Table 1: Descriptive Statistics for the Demographic Variables (n = 54) (continued)

Variables	Category	n	%	Cumulative %
Numbers of children in the house (under 18)				
	0	15	36.6	36.6
	1	7	17.1	53.7
	2	11	26.8	80.5
	3	6	14.6	95.1
	4	2	4.9	100.0
Companion				
	Family only	12	22.6	22.6
	Partner only	8	15.1	37.7
	Friends only	19	35.8	73.5
	Alone	1	1.9	75.4
	Family, friends, and partner	12	22.7	98.1
	Others	1	1.9	100.0
People in the party				
	1	1	2.6	2.6
	2	12	30.8	33.3
	3	4	10.3	43.6
	4	5	12.8	56.4
	5	4	10.3	66.7
	6	7	17.9	84.6
	7	4	10.3	94.9
	8 and plus	2	15.5	100.0
Previously attended				
	Yes	43	81.1	81.1
	No	10	18.9	100.0
Zip code				
	Georgia area	50	96.0	96.0
	Other	2	4.0	100.0
How did you find out?				
	Radio	24	34.8	34.8
	Newspapers	4	5.80	40.6
	TV	12	17.4	58.0
	Friends	17	24.6	82.6
	Website	3	4.3	87.0
	Mail	1	1.4	88.4
	Local sports organization	1	1.4	89.9
	Other	7	10.1	100.0

Although subjects perceived highly on several factors that influenced their attendance, such as price of ticket, chance to attend a new sport, and a chance to see a star rider, regression analysis (R square = .121) and ANOVA (p > .05) showed that there were no major factors that influenced spectators' attendance in the categories of demographic, audience preference, economics, and game attractiveness. Further, the three major league standings of the bull riders (Challenger Tour Standings, Built Ford Tough Standings, and Qualified Standings) were listed only as somewhat important when people made decisions to go to this event.

One anecdotal finding in this study revealed a seating mistake made by the Georgia Dome. Fans in two seating locations found themselves behind the stage and others found themselves sitting behind television cameras. As a result, these fans could not see the event. The results of this study helped the Georgia Dome event management group to develop a different seating arrangement and event configuration in the facility for the next year's event (this was the first year of a three-year event contract between the Dome and the PBR).

Summary

The Georgia Dome staff have benefited from this research. There were follow-up meetings in which strategic decisions were made to enhance the event for its second scheduled date the following year. Follow-up studies are planned and will be conducted at each of the second and third event. The results of those studies will be used for comparison against the first.

Sport management faculty and students may also benefit from this research. For instance, this study reports information regarding a sport that is typically not studied and, thus, has yet to be included in sport management literature. Students can learn about this professional sport and might consider a career in it. Finally, it is hoped that this study will encourage sport management academics to conduct more research into the variety of sport businesses in the industry. Future research will involve follow-up studies at the annual event for comparison to the results in the current study.

In addition, this study contributes to the small but growing literature on fans and factors that affect their attendance at sports events in a number of ways. First, this study involved a sport that has yet to be included in the sport marketing literature. The authors hope that inclusion of previously ignored sports will encourage more research involving sports and sports events in order to enhance the literature.

References

Demmert, H. G. (1973). *The economics of professional team sports.* Lexington, MA: D.C. Health.

Fillingham, E. J. (1977). *Major league hockey: An industry study.* Master's thesis, University of Alberta, Alberta, Canada.

Green, F. E. (1995). *An examination of factors related to consumer behavior influencing attendance at professional sporting events.* Unpublished doctoral dissertation, Florida State University, Tallahassee.

Greenstein, T. N., & Marcum, J. P. (1981). Factors affecting attendance of Major League Baseball: Team performance. *Review of Sport and Leisure, 6*(2), 21-33.

Hansen, H., & Gauthier, R. (1989). Factors affecting attendance at professional sport event. *Journal of Sport Management, 3*(1), 15-32.

Hart, R., Hutton, J., & Sharot, T. (1975). A statistical analysis of association football attendance. *Applied Statistics, 24*(1), 17.

Hill, J. R., Madura, J., & Zuber, R. A. (1982). The short run demand for Major League Baseball. *Atlantic Economic Journal, 10*(2), 31-35.

Howard, D. R., & Crompton, J. L. (2004). *Financing sport.* Morgantown, WV: Fitness Information Technology.

Jones, J. C. H. (1984). Winners, losers and hosers: Demand and survival in the National Hockey League. *Atlantic Economic Journal, 12*(3), 54-63.

Kasky, J. (1994, October). Money's sports value rankings. *Money, 10,* 158-170.

King, B., Sweet, D., Lefton, T., Cameron, S., Broughton, D., Lombardo, J., & Lee, J (2002). Dollars in sports: Passion that can't be counted puts billions of dollars in play. *Street & Smith's SportsBusiness Journal, 4*(47), 25-39.

Lu, D. (2001, May). *Factors affecting spectator attendance in professional baseball: A pilot study.* Paper presented at the 16th annual conference of the North America Society for Sport Management, Virginia Beach, VA.

Lu, D., & Pitts, B. G. (2004). Culture and other market demand variables: An exploration with professional baseball in the USA and Taiwan. In B. G. Pitts (Ed.), *Sharing best practices in sport marketing.* Morgantown, WV: Fitness Information Technology, pp. 141–166.

Marcum, J. P., & Greenstein, T. N. (1985). Factors affecting attendance of Major League Baseball: II. A within-season analysis. *Sociology of Sport Journal, 2*(4), 314-322.

McDonald, M., & Rascher, D. (2000). Does bat day make cents? The effect of promotions on the demand for Major League Baseball. *Journal of Sport Management, 14*(1), 8-27.

Mullin, B. J., Hardy, S., & Sutton, W. A. (2000). *Sport marketing* (2nd ed.). Champaign, IL: Human Kinetics.

Noll, R. G. (1974). Attendance and price setting. In R. G. Noll (Ed.), *Government and the sports business* (pp.115-157). Washington, DC: The Bookings Institute.

Pitts, B. G., & Stotlar, D. K. (2002). *Fundamentals of sport marketing* (2nd ed.). Morgantown, WV: Fitness Information Technology.

Professional Bull Riders (2004). *All about bull riding.* Retrieved June 30, 2004, from http://www.pbrnow.com/about/sportinfo.

Professional Bull Riders (2004). *Built Ford tough million dollar bonus.* Retrieved June 12, 2004, from http://www.pbrnow.com/BFTS.million.cfm.

Professional Bull Riders. (2004). *Professional bull riders on TV.* Retrieved June 2, 2004, from http://www.pbrnow.com/media/tv/.

Schofield, J. A. (1983). Performance and attendance at professional team sports. *Journal of Sport Behavior, 6*(4), 196-206.

The answer: $213 billion. (1999, December 20-26). *SportsBusiness Journal.*

Zhang, J. J., Pease, D. G., Hui, S. C., & Michaud, T. J. (1995). Variables affecting the spectator decision to attend NBA games. *Sport Marketing Quarterly, 4*(4), 29-39.

Zhang, J. J., & Smith, D. W., Pease, D. G., & Jambor, E. A. (1997). Negative influence of market competitors on the attendance of professional sport games: The case of a minor league hockey team. *Sport Marketing Quarterly, 6*(3), 31-40.

Zhang, J. J., Smith, D. W., Pease, D. G., & Lam, E. T. C. (1998). Dimensions of spectator satisfaction toward support programs of professional hockey games. *International Sports Journal, 12*(2), 1-17.

Zhang, J. J., Smith, D. W., Pease, D. G., & Mahar, M. T. (1996). Spectator knowledge of hockey as a significant predictor of game attendance. *Sport Marketing Quarterly, 5*(3), 41-48.

Sports Event Spectators' Perceptions of Mobile Marketing. Empirical Evidence from Finland

JARI SALO
HEIKKI KARJALUOTO
MANNE KESTI
TIMO KOIVUMÄKI
ANNU RISTOLA

Abstract

This paper studies sport event spectators perceptions of m-marketing campaigns in a series of ice hockey playoff games in Finland during spring 2004. M-marketing is in this paper understood as pull type of mobile services that spectators can download during the game to their mobile phones or PDAs equipped with Bluetooth, WLAN, or GPRS technology. Theoretically our study breaks new ground by dealing with sports marketing conducted with m-marketing campaigns. Data for this study comes from two studies conducted with spectators of the Kärpät ice hockey team. Study 1 is comprised of 20 in-depth interviews and observations with spectators, and study 2 of 645 online survey responses. The preliminary findings of the studies indicate that pull type of m-marketing services have the potential to enhance spectator experience positively, especially among technology savvy users. The test users regarded downloads of video material and statistics from the ongoing game as the most valuable services, whereas video clips from audience, cheerleader cards, and opposing team and coach cards had little value. Moreover, m-marketing seems to have a more positive effect on spectators with some prior experience in using mobile services and devices. Some of the inexperienced test users found the service even distracting while more advanced users saw the service more as an added value service. The findings gained from the survey show support for the conclusions drawn from the interviews. On this basis m-marketing services might increase the price/quality ratio of ice hockey games and strengthen the team brand. Finally, the paper provides both theoretical and managerial implications and suggests areas for future research in this emerging field.

Introduction

This paper deepens our understanding of mobile marketing (m-marketing) and how sport event spectators perceive the novel marketing and communications channel. The purpose of this study is to provide much needed insights for sport event organizers, managers, and sport academics who are trying to grasp the new wireless reality. We are trying to answer this by building a preliminary theoretical framework which is then used to shed light on empirical phenomena consisting of pilot study 1 (comprised of 20 in-depth interviews), and pilot study 2 (comprised of 645 online survey responses). Given that the economic impact of the sports industry only in New York City has been approximately $6.9 billion, and the sport industry in general is growing at a rapid pace with a value of over $500 billion globally (Graham, Goldblatt, & Neirotti, 2001), we find it vital to grasp the issues from the m-marketing viewpoint. In addition, according to Jupiter Research, the mobile commerce (m-commerce) industry is expected to be US $22 billion globally (cited in Kini & Somboon, 2004; see also Durclacher, 2000; Siemens, 2001). The future of m-marketing is perceived to be bright by Siemens (2001), as they estimate that the earnings in this sector will triplicate in Europe until 2010.

It should be noted here that both theoretical and empirical research into m-marketing is scarce. We can only find studies that illustrate m-marketing in another context (Barwise & Strong, 2002; Pura, 2002; Tsang, Ho, & Liang, 2004; Salo & Tähtinen, 2005) or focus theoretically on m-marketing (Barnes & Scornavacca, 2004; Leppäniemi & Karjaluoto, 2004; Leppäniemi, Karjaluoto, & Salo, 2004). A noteworthy practical exception is the first NHL wireless service launched by the Carolina Hurricanes (Swartz, 2001).

Next, we will provide an overview of m-marketing and consumer perceptions of it. We then move to illustrate our employed methodology. Finally, results and conclusions of the study are presented together with limitations and future research areas.

Mobile Marketing

Lets us first consider concepts that are often misunderstood and overlooked in m-marketing research. To begin with, m-marketing is in this paper seen as a subset of m-commerce since it is defined as "any form of marketing, advertising or sales promotion activity aimed at consumers" (MMA, 2003). In other words, m-marketing can be seen as a way to sell and distribute retailers' digital products or services to customers through a mobile device (see Choi, Stahl, & Whinston, 1997). Clarke III (2001, p. 134) points out that mobile devices such as mobile phones, smart phones, personal digital assistants (PDAs), and hybrid devices are the fastest adopted consumer products of all time. Consumers by now use mobile devices for traditional phone calls and message handling (Kalakota & Robinson, 2002; Mort & Drennan, 2002). Increasingly, the value added by these devices is escalating due to the fact that they provide useful functions and their capacity to provide entertainment, enhance communication, and enable transactions is constantly boosted.

Second, the term mobile advertising is seen as a part of m-marketing, since m-advertising refers to advertisements sent to and received on mobile devices (see Tähtinen & Salo, 2004). It should be pointed out that m-advertising in this study does not refer to advertisements that move from place to place—i.e., buses, trucks, trains, trams, and taxis (Goldsborough, 1995; Hume, 1988). Thus, m-marketing encompasses transactions, advertising, and marketing elements as building blocks of a m-marketing concept that is depicted in Figure 1 below.

Figure 1 illuminates relationships between m-commerce, m-marketing, and m-advertising. It can be easily seen that m-marketing is composed of both sending mobile ads and distribution of mobile services (m-services) in addition to commerce over mobile channels. The combination of rapidly developing mobile technology—i.e., processing and transmitting capacity—and high uptake rates of mobile devices presents

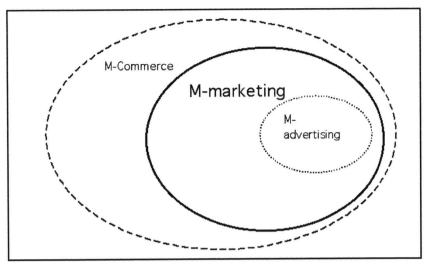

Figure 1: Relationship between used mobile concepts

vast potential for delivery of m-services through mobile devices (Bitner, Brown, & Meuter, 2000). M-services encompass a wide variety of types, including the ability to send and receive text, pictures, music, and video clips, to trade stock, to book airline or movie tickets online, and receive personalized shopping alerts (see Tähtinen & Salo, 2004).

To continue, the context specificity of m-marketing allows sport event organizers and managers to send targeted and personalized m-services and mobile advertisements (m-ads) to consumers on the move within sport event areas. Hence an alternative term, *location based commerce* (Turban, King, Lee, Warkentin, & Chung, 2002), has been suggested for m-commerce. M-marketing enables not only the sending of unique, personalized, and customized content (Turban et al., 2002) but also enables consumers' interaction with the sender of the message. As with other forms of electronic marketing, m-marketing incorporates interactivity and transcends traditional communication, allowing for one-to-one, mass communication, and many-to-many models (see Barwise, Elberse, & Hammond, 2002; Hoffman & Novak, 1996; Jee & Lee, 2002).

Because of the special features, m-marketing can and should be used to deliver m-services and m-ads that differ from the traditional advertisements employed in other media (see Pieters & Wedel, 2004). In implementing m-marketing in the sport event context it is important to make the m-service interactive, given the nature of mobile phones, context dependent, and real time. Figure 2 illuminates the relations between key factors of m-marketing in relation to a sport event.

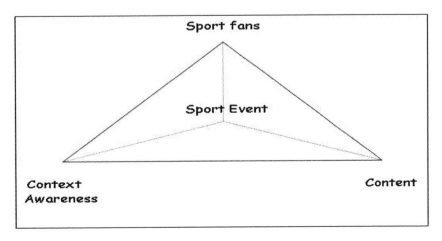

Figure 2: M-marketing of a sport event

Figure 2 depicts how m-marketing of a sport event is dependent on the context of the sport event as well as the fans. In addition, the m-marketing content/m-service offering should be taken into consideration while planning m-marketing of a sport event.

Moreover, the special features of m-marketing influence the type of content that permission based m-marketing should offer to the consumer in order to be perceived as valuable and/or entertaining. Thus, it is no surprise that m-advertising is predicted to become the second largest form of m-commerce by the year 2005, reaching more than US $6 billion in Europe alone (Durlacher, 2000), globally up to US $16-23 billion (IMAP, 2002; Ovum, 2002), and to US $17.2 billion by 2007 (Nokia, 2003).

Although the importance of m-marketing is obvious, academic research into this emerging, novel topic is scarce, and, more importantly, empirical research of context aware m-marketing in real life settings presents a challenge. First of all, the technology has to be easily available, and, second, the consumers have to be familiar with mobile devices and services. In the city of Oulu, Finland, the above mentioned prerequisites are in place (see www.rotuaari.net/?lang=en). In Finland, consumers' mobile phone subscriptions reached 84 percent in 2002 (Ministry of Transport and Communications Finland, 2003). In addition, more than 30 percent of users younger than 35 years have received m-advertising in the form of an SMS, and over 20 percent of all users have made mobile payments (www.opas.net/suora/).

Although the technology is available and used, Finnish legislation restricts m-advertising to some extent, as it allows only permission-based m-advertising. Without consumers' permission, only information that is related to the administration of the customer relationship (e.g., the customer's flight to Memphis is late) can be sent to mobile devices. Therefore, this empirical research is limited to pull type of m-services (see Paavilainen, 2001). To clarify, in the pull m-marketing the customer wants to perform something with the mobile device—i.e., download video clips or other provided content related to sport events.

Mobile Marketing

There has been a debate going on whether or not consumers are willing to accept m-marketing and m-advertising. On one hand, there is evidence that consumers are willing to receive m-marketing to their mobile devices (Enpocket, 2003), mainly to subside the cost of other mobile services, such as e-mail and news services (Lewis, 2001), and to get discounts into brick-and-mortar stores (Nikulainen, 2002; Nokia, 2002; Saunders, 2003). On the other hand, studies have found that mobile phone users are not willing to receive m-adverting due to small screen size and the personal nature of the phone (Lewis, 2001), as well as due to technical constraints referring to the device's ability to receive different forms of marketing information, slow download times, and different standards, which together make it hard to standardize and regulate m-marketing (Yunos, Gao, & Shim, 2003).

The so-called critical factors affecting the success of m-marketing have first been outlined in an extensive survey of m-marketing professionals conducted by Mobile Marketing Association (in *Marketing Week*, 2001). According to the study, m-marketing has the potential to become an important communication channel if m-marketing has the ability to target audiences precisely and its effectiveness can be measured and tracked. Moreover, the respondents valued the availability of specialist expertise in agency/content/service provider and wanted case studies on m-advertising from relevant actors. Additionally, the survey found that the development of m-marketing is driven by various factors such as the possibility to personalize the messages, allowing opt-in, giving immediate response, and location specific. In light of the above, an ice hockey stadium context has the potential to fulfil these expectations related to m-marketing. Figure 3 illuminates some of the suggested impacts of pull type m-marketing on technology savvy and technophobe spectators' reactions and the outcome of those impacts.

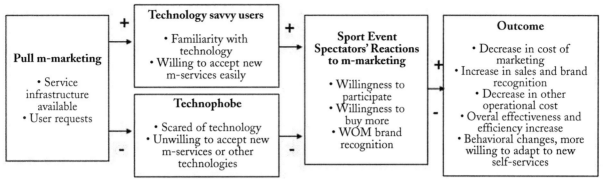

Figure 3: Pull m-marketing impacts on spectators

Methodology

This research is part of the Rotuaari project, which is a research project in the University of Oulu, focusing on the development and testing of technologies and business models for mobile multimedia services of the future. In this particular field test, the first task was to find out what kind of services should be offered in order for people interested in ice hockey to be satisfied users after using the m-services that were to be tested in the upcoming ice hockey playoffs. An internet questionnaire was set up to find out fan opinions of the local hockey team. This research had its basis in the "real" world in the sense that there was interest from certain factions to implement this kind of service; thus, more information about the likes and dislikes of the audience was needed. Before the online questionnaire (study 2), a preliminary qualitative study (study 1) was conducted that tried to find out what is important for the spectators when it comes to watching a hockey game and how it would be possible to make the game experience more fascinating by using the mobile device as a beneficent tool. There were 20 in-depth interviews done altogether, which is a satisfactory amount when looking for such profound information. The main purpose of this qualitative study was to find out the necessary information for the questionnaire that was to be posted on the internet. It gave valuable information for creating a rational internet questionnaire for the hockey fans.

The data for finding out the expectations and reactions people have on the m-services in an ice hockey context was collected using a questionnaire on the internet. The online survey method was justifiable in this context, because it was easy to execute quickly and a cost-effective way to reach hockey fans. A link to the questionnaire was placed on the homepage of the local ice hockey team's website two weeks before the playoffs were to begin. Seven-point scales were used for content questions, with 1 being the negative end of the scale and 7 being the positive end of the scale. Other questions were implemented in a way that respondents were able to pick the suitable answers for them. The scales to measure beliefs and attitudes have been used before and are well-tried (Fishbein & Ajzen, 1975; Chae, Kim, Kim, & Ryu, 2002).

The general demographic questions asked basic information of respondents. The people who answered this online questionnaire were most likely young local team hockey fans with some interest in technology. The results, however, cannot be called biased, since these are the people that we set out to find with this questionnaire, being the most likely people to use the m-services about to be launched. Thus, the interests they have are very relevant to study.

The hobbyism questions were intended to determine how big of a hockey fan each respondent was. This was relevant information for various reasons. We asked how the respondents usually looked for information concerning ice hockey. Basically our aim in posing this question was to gauge the enthusiasm of using new sources for finding information. After that the more detailed question of visiting the team's website was asked. Our aim was to find out what kind of information people look for on this particular site. The third part of measuring the hobbyism was to sort out how often respondents attended real games.

The basic mobile device questions were primarily designed to determine what kind of mobile devices respondents have and whether or not they know the features they have on their phones. This question was essential for future field trials where actual mobile services are to be tested with people's own mobile phones.

The questions concerning the content of the hockey mobile service were designed to describe in detail what kind of information people want to have on their mobile phone when talking about the subject they are interested in. There were 34 different information packages for which the respondents were able to estimate importance. Then a confirmatory factor analysis was conducted on wanted information.

The questions about factors affecting the willingness to use the new mobile services were designed to plot the importance and priority of, for example, technical usability, price, and ease of use.

Results

The preliminary study 1 was made by interviewing 21- to 55-year-old males and females with different educational and work backgrounds. The main purpose was to clarify the thoughts and expectations toward new m-services in an ice hockey context. Based on the results gained from this study, study 2 was created on the internet. It seems that there are different kinds of spectators among ice hockey fans. Some fans follow intensely every game, and some only visit the game occasionally, even though it is an important hobby for them. The actual game is the most important as such, and between the periods respondents "grab a snack" and browse through the game program. Only a few of the respondents had tried some m-services before. The respondents value different things when concerning the game—e.g., enthusiastic audience, easy arriving, good seats, or supplementary services—but for all of them the game itself is the most important reason for coming to the stadium. When inquiring about possible improvements to be made to make the game experience even better, there were a lot of suggestions—e.g., the big screen, WLAN, warm stadium, and more program between the periods.

If the respondents would try new m-services, those would need to be low cost, fast, and content should be of high quality, service should be easy to use, and it should be useful. Ease of use and price seemed to be the most important factors when the respondents were asked to consider the factors themselves. When given alternatives, the order of the answers was costs, content quality, ease of use, and technical quality. When inquiring more deeply about the wanted content for their own mobile device, the most wanted content was statistics, slow-motions, and background information, which are basically quite the same information that can be acquired from the program leaflet that is available at the games. Almost all of the respondents also wanted some added value, like video clips. When given the alternatives, the three most interesting services seemed to be video clips and slow motions of goals, statistics, and league scores.

According to the results, content is good if it is understandable and clear, informative, easy to use and browse, professional, and value adding. Content quality alone is not enough; technical quality also should be in good condition (e.g., functionality and quickness). Respondents were willing to pay a small amount for the services. All of the respondents were ready to try the new m-services in the future if there were a chance.

Study 2 was made on the internet after analyzing the data gathered from study 1. The questionnaire was filled out by a total of 645 people, of which most (496) were men, probably due to the subject and venue at hand. The age distribution reveals a rather young group of sports fans; 84.3 % of the people who answered were less than 34 years old consisting of different educational and occupational backgrounds. Table 1 depicts an accurate profile of the respondents.

Table 1: Profile of the respondents				
	Frequency	Percent	Valid Percent	Cumulative Percent
TV	217	33.6	33.7	33.7
Radio	4	.6	.6	34.3
Newspaper	53	8.2	2.2	42.5
Hockey team's www-site	165	25.6	25.6	68.2
SM-league www-site	34	20.8	20.8	89
Other	71	11	11	100
Total	644	99.8	100	
Missing	1	.2		
Total	645	100		

When designing the m-service for a specific group interested in a particular hobby, it is interesting to find out the level of hobbyism. This was studied first by finding out the source where respondents find the hockey information most frequently. It seems that the most visited sources are television (33.6 percent), hockey team's website (25.6 percent), and national league's website (20.8 percent). The result that getting information from the internet is so popular is a very positive one, considering the idea of launching a new kind of information source. It is natural that people watch news and get their information from TV almost effortlessly. But seeking the information from the internet reveals that people want to find acute information and are willing to use new kinds of technology to get it. These are illuminated further in Table 2 below.

The other aspect of hobbyism to explore is the content that interests respondents on hockey teams' websites. It seems that the most wanted content is clearly news (79.2 percent) and the information concerning the games (70.9 percent). Also, content that can be seen as a bit interesting for respondents is information concerning the local hockey team (31.2 percent) and information concerning other teams

Table 2: Sources of ice hockey related information			
	N	Mean	Std. Deviation
Real-time statistics of current match	591	2.99	1.874
Real-time information and statistics of other ongoing matches	596	5.19	1.919
Video clips and slow motions of goals and situation of current match	597	5.09	2.056
Team composition and lists of current match	592	5.07	1.883
League scores	596	5.03	1.857
Advance ticketing to next match by mobile device	591	5.02	2.005
Gossips and latest news	588	4.95	1.898
Information about your hockey team	591	4.89	1.913
Statistics	593	4.84	1.813
Team related material, e.g., ringing tones, wallpapers, logos	588	4.84	1.937
Merchandise offers or other offers	590	4.79	1.998
Top-5 goals and saves	593	4.79	2.108
Information about players	589	4.74	1.884
The Finnish ice-hockey league score situation of own players	591	4.54	2.089
Online betting, e.g., first who scores	590	4.52	2.046
Real-time betting information	589	4.43	2.059
Pictures and video clips of other matches	594	4.37	1.967
Video clips of commenting coach and interviews	594	4.34	1.908
Team cards	590	4.31	1.949
On-line player voting	591	4.22	1.993
Video summary of previous game	591	4.20	1.965
Information of the opposing team	591	4.16	1.773
Shooting maps	593	4.09	1.978
Changes to team lists	590	3.83	1.910
Fan Club IRC	5.87	3.82	1.976
Referee cards, statistics, etc.	591	3.77	1.919
Advertisements of current sport event merchandise	588	3.77	2.068
Ice-hockey slang vocabulary	589	3.73	2.122
Instant messaging through mobile devices with other spectators	589	3.65	2.014
Novice guide book	589	3.62	2.058
Coach cards	589	3.61	1.878
Opposing team cards	588	3.60	1.885
Cheerleader cards	589	3.54	2.215
Video clips of audience	592	3.14	2.065

(32.1 percent). In addition, it seems that respondents are interested in having the conversation possibility with other people (34.0 percent). Content that respondents are not interested in are history (6.8 percent), information concerning juniors (10.7 percent), and cheerleaders (12.6 percent).

To put this together, it seems that content which includes real information and hard facts are the most valuable for the respondents interested in ice hockey. The leisure content is not so popular. Of course it is possible that even though the "fan part" is not admitted to be so important, if it was lacking the fans would probably be annoyed.

The third aspect of measuring hobbyism was studied by asking how often respondents go to the game. Only around 7 percent of respondents went to every game, around 19 percent of respondents visited most of the games, and a majority of the respondents (61.2 percent) visited games occasionally. This information is valuable for different reference groups, such as for the hockey team itself, service providers, and marketers. If games would be more interesting and it would be possible to get some added value, there is large potential for these occasional visitors to become regular spectators to the game.

Respondents were asked what kind of m-devices they have and if they knew the features they have on their phones. This information was of particular interest because forthcoming services work only in some particular phones. Also it was interesting to explore the extent to which people know what their phones are capable of. As expected in Finland, the most common phone was Nokia. The unfortunate news was that more than half of the models were so old that forthcoming services would not work on those devices. Mobile devices had to have bluetooth and GPRS connection that were required to use the service. Over half of the respondents (52 percent) had the old model, 24 percent had the series 40 model phone, and only 3.5 percent of the respondents had the series 60 model that allows the use of the m-services. Slightly over half (53 percent) knew they had GPRS connection on their phone. Around 20 percent of the respondents knew they had the Bluetooth feature on their phone. It is worthy to note that only 17 percent of the respondents knew what Bluetooth was, which indicates that people are not aware of this feature and in that way they might be hindered from trying services that works with Bluetooth.

When people come to ice hockey games they do not want any disturbance and irrelevant data sent to their phones. The game is the most important thing and other services just add some value to it. If the mobile services are offered, the content has to be the kind that it does not require special attention. It just offers something other than paper brochures, or at least it offers the content that interests spectators and has a close connection to the game. Based on the in-depth interviews, the different kinds of contents were gathered together and respondents had to estimate those on a seven-point Likert-type of scales (ranging from 1 "Strongly disagree" to 7 "Strongly agree"). Although none of the means of these factors were over six, the expectations toward mobile services content can be said to be high. The results can be seen in Table 3.

The most wanted content in ice hockey m-service were the ones with real-time information and statistics from the current match (mean 5.29) and other ongoing matches (mean 5.19). Also video clips (mean 5.09) and getting tickets to the next game using the mobile device (mean 5.02) were the kinds of service that aroused high levels of interest among the respondents. This was quite a natural outcome, because the local ice hockey stadium does not have a screen that can display videos. This kind of real-time information would be useful and would provide something different from existing services like brochures and announcements. League scores (mean 5.03), information about the home hockey team (mean 4.89), and top-5 goals and saves (mean 4.79) seem to be the information that should be offered to spectators, since it seems to be the content that is necessary to most hockey game spectators.

When inquiring about feelings toward commercial content, response was surprisingly positive. For example, for material related to the hockey team (e.g., ringing tones and logos), the mean of the answers was 4.84. Also respondents seem to take quite a positive attitude toward merchandise and other offers (mean 4.79). On the other hand, ads concerning the products that are offered in the hockey stadium were not the kind of things respondents wanted on their phones (mean 3.77). According to these results, mobile service providers should understand that there could be a need for some commercial marketing, but it has to be related to the context.

In an ice hockey context, it is quite natural that online betting is of relative importance among game spectators. For example, online betting (mean 4.52), real-time betting information (4.43), and online player

	1	2	3	4	5
Table 3: Wanted content of mobile services in ice hockey content					
Coach cards	.864				
Referee cards, statistics, etc.	.850				
Opposing team cards	.822				
Changes to team lists	.757				
Information of the opposing team	.746				
Shooting maps	.736				
Team cards	.727				
Novice guide book	.711				
Video clips of audience	.660				
Cheerleader cards	.643				
Instant messaging through mobile devices with other spectators	.636				
Fan Club IRC	.625				
Real-time information and statistics of other ongoing matches in the Finnish ice hockey league		.715			
League scores		.707			
Team composition and lists of current match		.689			
Information about your hockey team		.683			
Information about players		.641			
Statistics		.601			
Video clips and slow motions of goals and situations of current match			.864		
Pictures and video clips of other matches			.828		
Video summary of previous game			.815		
Top-5 goals and saves			.785		
Video clips of commenting coach and interviews			.705		
The Finnish ice hockey league score situation of own players			.620		
Real-time betting information				.921	
Online betting, e.g., first who scores				.921	
On-line player voting				.725	
Merchandise offers or other offers					.845
Team related material, e.g., ringing tones, wallpapers, logos					.813
Ice hockey slang vocabulary					.775
Advertisements of current sport event merchandise					.770

Extraction Method: Principal Component Analysis
Rotation Method: Oblimin with Kaiser Normalization

voting (mean 4.22) seem to be fascinating services. This kind of real time betting service could be just the right sort of addition for games that come with very little extras.

With certainty there are some limits that have to be put to every service. Everything cannot be offered and everyone cannot be pleased. Results we got reveal that information that is not tightly connected to the game itself is not so important to the respondents. For instance, video clips from the audience (mean 3.14), cheerleader cards (mean 3.60), opposing team cards (mean 3.60), and coach cards (mean 3.61) are the ones that get lowest support from the respondents. This kind of content is nice to know, but has little value to the ongoing game.

Factor Analysis

An exploratory factor analysis was conducted on the items that are connected to ice hockey. The factor analysis was conducted using principal component analysis with varimax rotation as an extraction method (for details, see Hair, Anderson, Tatham, & Black, 1998). Three variables from the original variable list did not fit into the factor model. The Bartlett's Test of Sphericity confirmed that the variables within factors are correlated. The Kaiser-Meyer-Olkin (KMO) measure of sampling adequacy indicated a practical level of common variance (KMO = 0.945). Thereby, the factor analysis was appropriate. The identified factors (Table 4) represent 60.4 percent of the variance of the variables. The first factor, information package for active visitors, consists of 12 variables (alpha = .864). For basic research, Cronbach's alpha should be higher than 0.7-0.8. For example, Peterson (1994) points out that the acceptable value of Cronbach's alpha can vary between 0.5 and 0.95 depending on the type of research. The second factor, the information package for occasional visitors, is loaded with six variables (alpha = .715). The third factor, video content, contained six variables (alpha = .864). The fourth factor, betting, exhibits loadings for three variables (alpha = .921). The fifth factor refers to ancillary information and was loaded with four variables (alpha =.845). The overall reliability of the factor analysis was 0.89.

It seems that there are content packages that can be distinguished from each other. It is expected that people who visit most of the games anticipate different information compared to occasional visitors. For active visitors, there should be more profound information and they might also be interested in entertainment services. For occasional visitors, the basic information concerning the game and the team would be the best content for their mobile device. The content that comprises real time information like video clips and interviews seems to be the kind that interests all visitors. The fourth factor shows that online betting information could be one kind of content package for the audience. After all, betting has long been associated with sport events, and it would be natural to offer that kind of mobile service for hockey spectators. The fifth factor refers to the commercial services that could be offered to hockey fans. All the customary services that people are already used to, when talking about mobile services (e.g., ring tones) could be offered.

It seems that m-marketing services are seen as value adding facilitates in an ice hockey context. The information quality wanted in m-services is high but not unattainable. When actually using the m-service in some special context, the importance of content arises. To make users satisfied, the content should be relevant for users by providing some extra value to them. The importance of context is self-evident in an ice hockey context. The information users want in that situation should be related to ice hockey. The sport spectator values easy interaction with the mobile device, but the content has to be the kind that interests him or her and is related to the context.

Figure 4 shows the results when asking what factors most affect one's willingness to use the new m-service. The respondents were asked to pick the three most important factors. Results show that quality of the content (68.2 percent), ease of use (60.5 percent), and the price of using the service (55.8 percent) are the most significant factors. According to the results, pressure from friends and ads are not affecting factors.

Conclusions

The objective of this paper was to investigate sport event spectators' perceptions of m-marketing and m-services in a series of ice hockey playoff games in Finland during spring 2004. The main findings of the study indicate that pull type of m-marketing services have the potential to enhance spectator experience positively, especially among technology savvy users. Specifically, downloads of video material and statistics from the ongoing game were regarded as the most valuable information during the game, whereas video clips from the audience, cheerleader cards, or information concerning the opposite team and coaches were not found so valuable. Our study further shows that m-marketing services seem to have a more positive effect on spectators with some prior experience in using mobile services and devices.

	1	2	3	4	5
Table 4: Factor analysis					
Coach cards	.864				
Referee cards, statistics, etc.	.850				
Opposing team cards	.822				
Changes to team lists	.757				
Information of the opposing team	.746				
Shooting maps	.736				
Team cards	.727				
Novice guide book	.711				
Video clips of audience	.660				
Cheerleader cards	.643				
Instant messaging through mobile devices with other spectators	.636				
Fan Club IRC	.625				
Real-time information and statistics of other ongoing matches in the Finnish ice hockey league		.715			
League scores		.707			
Team composition and lists of current match		.689			
Information about your hockey team		.683			
Information about players		.641			
Statistics		.601			
Video clips and slow motions of goals and situations of current match			.864		
Pictures and video clips of other matches			.828		
Video summary of previous game			.815		
Top-5 goals and saves			.785		
Video clips of commenting coach and interviews			.705		
The Finnish ice hockey league score situation of own players				.620	
Real-time betting information				.921	
Online betting, e.g., first who scores				.921	
On-line player voting				.725	
Merchandise offers or other offers					.845
Team related material, e.g., ringing tones, wallpapers, logos					.813
Ice hockey slang vocabulary					.775
Advertisements of current sport event merchandise					.770

Extraction Method: Principal Component Analysis
Rotation Method: Oblimin with Kaiser Normalization

It seems that while fans attending sports events receive benefits by using provided m-marketing material, the greatest benefit is probably received by sport lovers not attending the sport events. Thus, m-marketing potential is harnessed by providing sport lovers scores and video clips of goals to their mobile terminals.

Still, the biggest challenge of m-marketing is to present the m-service or m-ads in a way that makes the customers want to satisfy their needs with that particular content, thereby making money for the company who offered the experiences needed by the consumer (Kotler, 2000). Figure 5 draws together some preliminary factors impacting the m-marketing of a sport event.

Figure 5 depicts that antecedents of a sport event (e.g., positive publicity) might have a positive impact on the success of m-marketing campaigns.

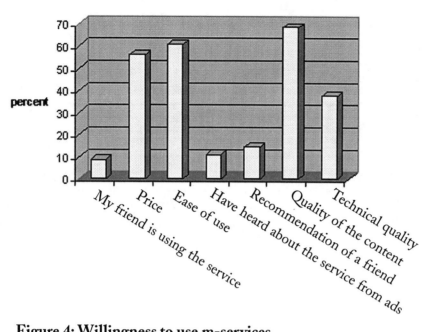

Figure 4: Willingness to use m-services

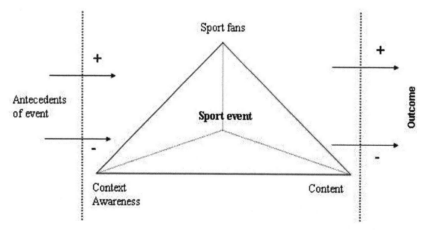

Figure 5. Empirically grounded framework for m-marketing of a sport event

The empirical studies presented here were later used to design the m-marketing service infrastructure for the hockey team in question. This was well accepted and after playoffs the technological innovation made by the academic research project was commercialized by companies involved in the research project.

Given the early stage of the m-marketing utilization in a sports context, it is difficult to draw strong conclusions about how m-marketing might evolve. However, we believe that m-marketing will step-by-step play an increasingly important role in sports events. M-marketing might and probably will provide something extra to lure consumers in our hectic attention economy. This said, more research is needed to develop the framework presented and further investigate m-marketing services in a sports marketing context.

Acknowledgments

The financial support of the National Technology Agency of Finland is gratefully acknowledged. The authors also wish to thank all the study participants.

References

Barnes, S. J., & Scornavacca, E. (2004). Mobile marketing: The role of permission and acceptance. *International Journal of Mobile Communication 2*(2), 128–139.

Barwise, P., & Strong, C. (2002). Permission-based mobile advertising. *Journal of Interactive Marketing, 16*(1), 14-24.

Barwise, P., Elberse, A., & Hammond, K. (2002). *Marketing and the Internet: A research review*. Retrieved March 15, 2002, from http://www.london.edu/marketing/Future/future _media_research_ projects/Untitled/internet/MATI_1.3.pdf.

Bitner, M. J., Brown, S. W., & Meuter, M. L. (2000). Technology infusion in service encounters. *Journal of the Academy of Marketing Science, 28*(1), 138-149.

System News (2004). Carolina Hurricanes launch first NHL wireless service. Retrieved July 27, 2004, from http://sun.systemnews.com/articles/59/4/feature/8563.

Chae, M., Kim, J., Kim, H., & Ryu, H. (2002). Information quality for mobile Internet services: A theoretical model with empirical validation. *Electronic Markets, 12*(1), 38-46.

Choi, S. Y., Stahl, D. O., & Whinston, A. B. (1997). *The economics of electronic commerce*. Indianapolis, IN: Macmillan Technical Publishing.

Clarke III, I. (2001). Emerging value propositions for m-commerce. *Journal of Business Strategy, 18*(2), 133-148.

Durclacher Research Ltd. (2000). *UMTS report an investment perspective*. Retrieved October 5, 2002, from http://www.durlacher.com.

Enpocket (2003, February). The response performance of SMS advertising. *Research Report 3*. Retrieved November 12, 2003, from http://www.enpocket.com.

Fishbein, M., & Ajzen, I. (1975). *Belief, attitude, intention and behavior: An introduction to theory and research*. Reading, MA: Addison-Wesley.

Goldsborough, R. (1995, 8 May 8). Hong Kong trams keep ads rolling. *Advertising Age, Midwest region edition, 66*, 36.

Graham, S., Goldblatt J. J., & Neirotti, L. D. (2001). *The ultimate guide to sports marketing, 2ⁿᵈ edition*. New York: McGraw-Hill.

Hair, J. F., Anderson, R. E., Tatham, R. L., & Black, W. C. (1998). *Multivariate data analysis* (5ᵗʰ ed.). Upper Saddle River, NJ: Prentice-Hall.

Hoffman, D. L., & Novak, T. P. (1996, July). Marketing in hypermedia computer-mediated environments: Conceptual foundations. *Journal of Marketing, 60*, 50-68.

Hume, S. (1988, 11 April). New medium is semi success. *Advertising Age, Midwest region edition, 59*, 22-24.

IMAP (innovative Interactive Mobile Advertising Platform) Project (2002). Analysis of user requirements. *Research Report*. Retrieved September 17, 2002, from http://www.imapproject.org/imap-project/hmain.jsp.

Jee, J., & Lee, W. N. (2002). Antecedents and consequences of perceived interactivity: An exploratory study. *Journal of Interactive Advertising, 3*(1).

Kalakota, R., & Robinson, M. (2002). *M-business. The race to mobility*. New York: McGraw-Hill.

Kini, R. B., & Somboon, T. (2004). Mobile commerce and electronic commerce in Thailand: A value space analysis. *International Journal of Mobile Communication, 2*(1), 22–37.

Kotler, P. (2000). *Marketing management* (Millenium ed.). Upper Saddle River, NJ: Prentice-Hall.

Leppäniemi, M., & Karjaluoto, H. (in press). Factors influencing consumer willingness to accept mobile advertising. A conceptual model. *International Journal of Mobile Communications*.

Leppäniemi, M., Karjaluoto, H., & Salo, J. (2004). The success factors of mobile advertising value chain. *E-Business Review, 4*, 93-97.

Lewis, S. (2001, January). M-commerce: Ads in the ether. *Asian Business, 37*, 1, 31.

Ministry of Transport and Communications Finland (2003). *Ensimmäisen aallon harjalla. Tekstiviesti-, WAP- ja MMS-palveluiden markkinat 2000–2004.* [On the first wave]. Publication of the Ministry of Transport and Communications Finland. Retrieved November 13, 2003, from http://www.mintc.fi/www/sivut/dokumentit/julkaisu/julkaisusarja/2003/al192003.pdf.

Mobile adds industry survey (2001, June). *Marketing Week* (UK), *24*, 33.

Mobile Marketing Association, MMA (2003). MMA code for responsible mobile marketing. Retrieved July 27, 2004, from http//www.mmaglobal.co.uk/.

Nikulainen, K. (2002). Kuluttajat suhtautuvat mobiilimainontaan myönteisesti [Consumers perceive mobile advertising as positive], *Digitoday.* Retrieved April 11, 2002, from http://www.digitoday.fi.

Nokia (2002). New Nokia research shows consumers ready for m-marketing via mobile handsets. HPI Research Group, *Research Report* (January). Retrieved October 10, 2002, from http://press.nokia.com/PR/200201/846567_5.html.

Nokia (2003). Java MIDP business opportunities. Presentation by Frederik Westring, *Software Goes Mobile Seminar*, 6 February, Seoul, Korea. Retrieved October 10, 2002, from http://www.forum.nokia.com/seap/events/mobile_software/mobile_material.

Ovum (2002, February). Ovum forecasts: Global wireless markets 2002-2006, *Research Report.*

Paavilainen, J. (2001). *Mobile commerce strategies.* Helsinki: IT Press.

Peterson, R. A. (1994, September). A meta-analysis of Cronbach's Coefficient Alpha. *Journal of Consumer Research, 21*, 381-91.

Pieters, R., & Wedel, M. (2004, April). Attention capture and transfer in advertising: Brand, pictorial, and text-size effects. *Journal of Marketing, 68*, 36-50.

Pura, M. (2002). Case study: The role of mobile advertising in building a brand. In B. E. Mennecke & T. J. Strader (Eds.), *Mobile commerce: Technology, theory and applications* (pp. 291-308). Hershey, PA: Idea Group Publishing.

Salo, J., & Tähtinen, J. (in press). Retailer use of permission-based mobile advertising. In I. Clarke III & T. B. Flaherty (eds.) *Advances in electronic marketing.* Hershey, PA: Idea Group Publishing.

Saunders, C. (2003, November). Studies: Mobile ad market to grow, amid risks. *Internet Advertising Report, 1.* Retrieved November 1, 2003, from http://www.internetnews.com/IAR/article.php/915121.

Siemens (2001). *Siemens end-user survey Europe.* München: Siemens AG.

Mort, G. S., & Drennan, J. (2002). Mobile digital technology: Emerging issues for marketing. *The Journal of Database Marketing, 10*(1), 9-23.

Swartz, N. (2001, January). Selling wireless advertising. *Wireless Review, 1.* Retrieved July 27, 2004, from http://wirelessreview.com/ar/wireless_selling_wireless_advertising/.

Tsang, M. M., Ho, S. C., & Liang, T. P. (2004). Consumer attitudes toward mobile advertising: An empirical study. *International Journal of Electronic Commerce, 8*(3), 65-78.

Turban, E., King, D., Lee, J., Warkentin, M., & Chung, H. M. (2002). *Electronic commerce: A managerial perspective.* Upper Saddle River, NJ: Prentice-Hall.

Tähtinen, J., & Salo, J. (2004, 18-21 May). Special features of mobile advertising and their utilization EMAC (European Marketing Academy) 33rd conference. *Proceedings (CD-ROM) of the 33rd EMAC conference*, Murcia, Spain.

Yunos, H. M., Gao, J. Z., & Shim, S. (2003). Wireless advertising's challenges and opportunities. *IEEE Computer, 36*(5), 30-37.

Section II

Media and Its Messages: Managing for Marketing

Framing Annika: An Analysis of Newspaper Columnist Writing About Annika Sorenstam Playing in the Colonial

JOHN A. FORTUNATO
EUNYI KIM

Abstract

On May 22, 2003, Annika Sorenstam became the first woman to compete in a men's Professional Golf Association (PGA) Tour event since 1945 by accepting an invitation to participate in the Colonial. Her playing in the tournament caused much controversy and intrigue. Although Sorenstam failed to make the cut, the reaction of what determined a success for Sorenstam and the social implications of her playing was varied. Sports events occur and even though the public often watches them live on television, they still look for expert analysis to place the event in some meaningful context. It is the various newspaper sports columnists who select certain highlights and quotes from the athletes to analyze, interpret, and write the stories that have that responsibility. Communication literature on the concept of framing lends insight into the activities of the newspaper columnist. The purpose of this paper is to examine newspaper media coverage of Annika Sorenstam's playing in the Colonial, posing the central research question of how was her playing analyzed or framed by print sports columnists?

Introduction

On May 22, 2003, Annika Sorenstam became the first woman to compete in a men's Professional Golf Association (PGA) Tour event since 1945 (when Babe Didrikson Zaharias competed in the Los Angeles Open) by accepting an invitation to participate in the Colonial. Sorenstam received one of eight sponsor's exemptions to play the 7,080-yard, par-70 course in Fort Worth, Texas. Her playing in the event caused much controversy and intrigue. The golf tournament became such a national story that even President George W. Bush offered a comment, stating, "I hope she makes the cut. I'm pulling for her, and I hope I'll be watching her Saturday and Sunday" (cited in Mariotti, 2003c, p. 134). Sorenstam failed to make the cut and continued playing on the weekend after shooting rounds of 71 and 74. Her two-day total of 145, five over par, missed the cut by four strokes.

The reaction of what would determine a success for Sorenstam and the social implications of her playing was varied. It is the many newspaper sports columnists around the country who not only describe events, but select certain highlights and quotes from athletes to analyze, interpret, and write the stories that help place events into some meaningful context. Brennan (2003d) even commented on the job of a newspaper columnist, stating it is "to examine the larger picture" (p. 13c). Sorenstam's participation in the Colonial was instantly intriguing because it dealt with gender involvement in sports. Writing about events involving issues of gender can be complicated. Lopresti (2003a) described the challenge, commenting, "the risk in taking sides against Sorenstam playing next week is that it invariably comes off belittling a great champion. Either that, or woman-bashing. Or both" ("Male golfers opposed").

Communication literature on the concept of framing lends insight into the activities of the newspaper columnist. Framing indicates that journalists select and emphasize some facts or highlights and make them more prominent in their presentation of a story. Through their analysis, the calling of attention to some facts and ignoring others could lead to an audience interpretation reflective of the presented frame. The purpose of this paper is therefore to examine media coverage of Annika Sorenstam's playing in the Colonial, posing the central research question of how was her playing in the Colonial analyzed or framed by newspaper sports columnists?

Literature Review

Sports events compete with each other for media attention and the opportunity to have their events appear on the various sports television programs or their stories grace the sports sections of newspapers and sports magazines. In this sense, sports events are not all that different from other organizations that are trying to receive coverage or be the topic of discussion in the mass media. Selection is a necessary condition of the mass media decision-making process, as mass media organizations are limited by the available time and space to present events. The idea of selection was introduced by Lippmann (1922), who pointed out that reporters could not report all of the happenings of the world; therefore, a selection process is necessary. It is through this characteristic of selection that people or events have the opportunity to be exposed to the audience, with other neglected topics having almost no opportunity to reach a wide-scale audience. Fishman (1997) simply states, "Some happenings in the world become public events. Others are condemned to obscurity as the personal experience of a handful of people. The mass media, and in particular news organizations, make all the difference" (p. 210).

Although the PGA and LPGA do not generally receive the same extensive coverage as some team sports (notably football, baseball, and basketball), one of the aspects that Annika Sorenstam's participation in the Colonial immediately contained was that, because of the gender angle, the story was definitely going to be covered, or selected, in great depth by many mass media organizations. The critical question thus becomes how would her participation be analyzed or framed?

In addition to story selection alone, the audience relies on the media to describe and explain the importance of each story. Just as some stories will not be covered at all, the time and space restrictions of the media do not permit even the issues that are covered to be done so with the same standard. Entman (1993) explains that "to frame is to select some aspects of a perceived reality and make them more salient in a communicating text, in such a way as to promote a particular problem definition, causal interpretation, moral evaluation, and/or treatment recommendation for the item described" (p. 52). He also claims that frames "call attention to some aspects of reality while obscuring other elements, which might lead audiences to have different reactions" (p. 55). Jamieson and Waldman (2003) point out that "just as there are countless events reporters could write about each day, there are many more pieces of information than could possibly fit into a single story. The metaphor of a frame—a fixed border that includes some things and excludes others—describes the way information is arranged and packaged in news stories. The story's frame determines what information is included and what is ignored" (p. xiii).

For every event, there are multiple frames that can be focused on, as different reporters offer different analysis of events (Gamson & Modigliani, 1989; Jamieson & Waldman, 2003; Reese, 2001). Gamson (2001) simply points out that, "two independent investigators will inevitably slice up the discourse in different ways" (p. x). The reporter has to make critical, often instantaneous decisions about what the emphasized frame will be. It is the reporter who is going to the scene of the event and is getting paid for his or her ability to provide an account of what is occurring. The reporter is responsible for asking questions of the proper people at the scene and organizing the facts into a coherent, enlightening, and understandable story. The columnist has a slightly different mandate from that of the reporter, in that in addition to providing an objective description of the event, he or she gets to offer an analysis of the facts and happenings at an event. The columnist is getting paid for his or her eye and ear, interpretive ability, and adeptness at putting events into a meaningful context. The columnist helps the audience "understand" what occurred and provides an explanation for what the event means, even though in many instances the event was probably viewed by many of the sports fans.

The potentially multiple frames center around storylines. A storyline is the theme that will be focused on in the story (Fortunato, 2001). Every sports event has some storyline that is presented to attract the audience that explains why this particular game or event is important and why fans should watch. One of the storylines for a sports event is always how the star player will perform (i.e., Tiger Woods performance is always a notable storyline for every tournament he participates in, even if he does not play well). As soon as Sorenstam accepted an invitation to play in the Colonial, who would win the tournament was no longer the major storyline, and how Sorenstam would perform became the focus. The storylines are promoted by sports reporters and then, no matter how the athlete or team performs, the reporter has an interesting story of either success or failure.

What clearly made Sorenstam's playing in the Colonial so intriguing and able to generate such media and audience attention is the gender storyline. Women's sports have received far less coverage than men's in both print and electronic media (Rintala & Birrell, 1984; Tuggle, 1997). The reasoning for this is largely because women's sports do not attract the audiences that men's sports do. The mass media organizations that cover sports are also trying to attract an audience to absorb their content and naturally focus on the sports that fans are most interested in. There is even a hierarchy of coverage within men's sports, as the National Football League certainly receives substantially more coverage than the National Hockey League or boxing.

A more pivotal issue might be the framing that women's sports receive when they are covered. The skills and strengths of women athletes are often undervalued in comparison to male athletic excellence. The coverage is often framed within stereotypes that pertain more to appearance and attractiveness than to athletic skill (Duncan, Jensen, & Messner, 1993; Kane & Greendorfer, 1994). For example, the media often present female athletes as cardboard, uni-dimensional individuals rather than representing them as the diverse individuals that they are (Kane & Greendorfer, 1994).

In a study that compared the verbal descriptors applied to men and women athletes, Duncan, Jensen, and Messner (1993) found that men were framed as active subjects, women as reactive objects. Male athletes were more often described in terms of strengths rather than weaknesses, successes rather than failures. Because women do not typically compete directly with men in the sports world, sex-segregated settings in sports invite biological comparisons between men and women. Biological differences can be translated into differences in performance, disparity in prize money, and dissimilar media coverage. Crosset

(1995) comments that "when talent is used to describe women, it takes on the meaning of deviance or biological abnormality" (p. 224).

The importance of both selection and framing is the potential influence it has on how the issue might be perceived by the audience. Just as the selection of issues can potentially influence the perception of a story by an audience, so too can its framing (Gandy, 2001; Jamieson & Waldman, 2003; Kaneva & Lenert, 2003; McCombs & Reynolds, 2002). For example, the language that is used in the framing process can be pivotal in the actual frame that is presented to the audience and what might be interpreted by the audience (Garcia & Stark, 1991; Scheufele, 2000; Yioutas & Servic, 2003). Nelson, Clawson, and Oxley (1997) comment that "frames influence opinions by stressing specific values, facts, and other considerations, endowing them with greater apparent relevance to the issue than they might appear to have under an alternative frame" (p. 569).

The audience relies on the media to describe and explain the importance of the story. Kaneva and Lenert (2003) state that "individuals routinely turn to major news outlets, such as local and national newspapers, for information on issues of immediate concern and tips on what action can and should be taken in response to certain events" (pp. 149-150). It is more than simply facts that people are interested in; they seek out analysis of events. This is why people read the editorials of their favorite columnists, listen to talk radio, or watch commentary on television.

Jamieson and Waldman (2003) summarize:

> Journalists help mold public understanding and opinion by deciding what is important and what may be ignored, what is subject to debate and what is beyond question, and what is true and false. In order to make those judgments, they have to navigate an often confusing thicket of information and assertions. "Facts" can be difficult to discern and relate to the public, particularly in a context in which the news is driven by politicians and other interested parties who selectively offer some pieces of information while suppressing others. (p. xiii)

Story selection is inevitable, so too is framing. Some frames will result from the work of the reporter. The frame is the product of what is actually presented to the audience. The audience does not see the alternative frames that were not ultimately selected in the presentation of the story, at least at that time, through that medium. This selection elevates the status of the presented frame as more relevant in comparison to the frames that are ignored.

Method

To examine how Annika Sorenstam's playing in the Colonial was covered, the writing of several notable sports columnists is used. The facts of what occurred on two days in Fort Worth, Texas, cannot change and cannot be disputed—Annika Sorenstam had a two-day total of 145 at the Colonial, finished five-over-par, and missed the cut by four strokes. It is the meaning of this performance from a standpoint of individual athletic achievement and even larger social achievement that can be debated and provides a desire to examine newspaper columnist framing of this event.

Recently, the sports columnist has attained more national notoriety. Appearances on television programs such as ESPN's "The Sports Reporters," "Pardon the Interruption," and "Around the Horn" have made the sports columnist known beyond the area of the local newspaper. All of the columnists articles used for this paper have frequently appeared on those television programs and have national notoriety. The columnists are Dave Anderson (New York Times), Tom Boswell (Washington Post), Christine Brennan (USA Today), Tim Cowlishaw (Dallas Morning News), Sally Jenkins (Washington Post), Mike Lupica (New York Daily News), Jackie MacMullan (Boston Globe), and Jay Mariotti (Chicago Sun-Times). This paper examines what they wrote, demonstrates how their framing of the story evolved throughout the event, and, in some instances, presents analysis of how these writers even interpreted statements made by Sorenstam herself. It is important to note that the timing of the Colonial (late May) did not allow every notable columnist to be at the event, as many columnists could have been covering the NBA or NHL playoffs, or the MLB season.

Results

Many consistent themes emerged through the various newspaper columnists' articles. These themes centered on a few central questions: What was Sorenstam's motivation for playing in the Colonial? Should she have been invited to play? What was the magnitude of the event because of her playing? What was expected of Sorenstam's performance? What would constitute a successful performance? And, how was her actual performance analyzed?

What Was Sorenstam's Motivation For Playing Frame

There can be many plausible theories as to why Annika Sorenstam accepted an invitation to play in the Colonial, but as soon as she decided to participate, there was instant intrigue because of the gender angle. The most prominent frame centered on the gender competition that was created. Since men do not compete with women in sports, when they do, it immediately transcends sports and becomes a larger social story. Prior to playing, Sorenstam appeared in many non-sports, mainstream media outlets, including "60 Minutes" and "The Today Show." In explaining the heightened interest, Brennan (2003b) simply commented, "There is no rivalry that is simpler to understand in sports, and throughout our culture, than the boys versus the girls" (p. 7c). The storyline of the Colonial immediately became not who would win the tournament, but how Sorenstam would perform, and, whether she succeeded or failed, it was going to be an interesting sports and human interest story. Jenkins (2003a) stated, "What we've really come to the Colonial Invitational to find out is whether she'll finish last. It's an old axiom: The worst male player is still better than the best female" (p. 1).

What was at stake in terms of overall perceptions of women in sports was posed by several columnists. Jenkins (2003a) pointed out that athletics present a tremendous opportunity for women to demonstrate some form of equality, or at least acceptance. She stated, "A good performance can erode stereotypical assumptions about the range of female athletic ability and acceptable female conduct. Whether you like it or not, athletic performance confers a credibility that can't be earned in any other arena. When women show they can play from the tips, they prove a physical and emotional competence to men, and that results in acceptance and belonging" (Jenkins, 2003a, p. 1). Mariotti (2003a) commented, "A[n] historic battle of genders encompasses more than what happens on the course. It also is a test of dignity, perspective and manners" (p. 110).

The gender angle was enhanced through the recognition of Sorenstam's talent and her superiority on the LPGA Tour. The event featured the best female player that was attempting to play in a men's tournament. It was Sorenstam's already well-established skill that added to the curiosity and interest of how she would compete. Prior to the Colonial on the LPGA Tour, Sorenstam had won 53 tournaments worldwide (including 13 in 2002), had earned over $11 million in winnings, and was named the LPGA player of the year five times. Her credentials also include a round of 59 in an event in Phoenix in 2001.

For every frame that was pursued, largely through the reporters' questioning of Sorenstam at the many press conferences that were conducted and subsequently presented in newspaper columns, Sorenstam offered her own perspective. Instead of mainly focusing on the gender angle and that her rationale for playing was to advance women's sports, Sorenstam attempted to frame the story as an athlete testing her skills. She explained, "I'm testing myself, but I'm not trying to prove anything to anybody. That's not why I'm doing this. This is for myself. I'm not putting the guys on test here, or men against women. I just want to play against the best and see what happens" (cited in Mariotti, 2003a, p. 110). She stated, "I'm just doing it for personal reasons. I'm curious to see how I do, and if I raise the level of women's golf, that's a bonus. It's really just for me" (cited in Mariotti, 2003b, p. 142). Sorenstam added, "I like to compare myself maybe with a mountain climber. This will be Mt. Everest for me, and I believe I have practiced for this for years. I feel like I have nothing to lose. Nobody expects anything from me" (cited in Mariotti, 2003b, p. 142).

Through Sorenstam's own interpretation, the story of her playing in the Colonial was not that different from what other athletes consistently do, which is challenge themselves. Boxers move up in weight class, baseball players leave Asia or Latin America to play in the major leagues, and basketball players leave Europe to play in the National Basketball Association all with the thought of challenging themselves against the best competition. Some columnists agreed with Sorenstam's perspective of an athlete testing her own ability. MacMullan (2003) did not place the larger gender significance on Sorenstam playing in the Colonial, stating, "Sorenstam isn't taking on the PGA and the Colonial with a mantra of proving women superior to men. She is simply trying to stretch her own limits—not the limits of the entire female population" (p. 1). MacMullan added, "It's hard to imagine how anything that bad can come of this opportunity to reach a little higher, and a little further. One weekend, regardless of what happens, should not erase a career studded with accomplishments, nor should one weekend revolutionize the place of women in the world of golf" (p. 1). She concluded, "I have no idea where Sorenstam will finish, but it doesn't much matter to me. I've already enjoyed her leap out of the box as much as anything she'll do on a golf course" (MacMullan, 2003, p. 1). Brennan (2003a) would agree with MacMullan's assessment, pointing out that "Sorenstam says playing in the Colonial is all about challenging herself, about seeing how good she is, about trying something new. Admirable pursuits all, and undeniably true, considering Sorenstam's character" (p. 10c).

Anderson (2003a) offered a completely different perspective on the challenge of gender competition and more closely aligned his writing with the perspective of Sorenstam challenging herself, pointing out that it was the golf course, and not the other male players, that Sorenstam was competing against. Anderson (2003a) claimed that "only she can be on, or off, her game. She's not playing against the 113 men in the Colonial, she's playing against the Colonial course. No matter how far some of the men hit their drives, they can't prevent her from hitting her drives, which average about 270 yards, into the fairway. They can't prevent her from holing birdie putts" (p. D2). PGA veteran Greg Norman even stated, "It's not Annika versus 70 men, it's Annika versus the course" (cited in MacMullan, 2003, p. 1). Sorenstam even commented, "My golf ball doesn't know where it is" (cited in Anderson, 2003a, p. D2). The athlete challenging herself frame would be more interested in her score and how she finished in relation to par, rather than if she made or missed the cut, which directly relates to her performance in comparison to the male players.

One final perspective that was presented in regards to the Sorenstam's motivation for playing frame was that she was playing to simply promote herself. Lupica (2003) commented, "It is also fair to wonder how much of this is Sorenstam herself, and how much of it is her handlers, trying to push product here with a woman golfer who has become more famous now for entering a big men's tournament than she has for winning all her women's tournaments combined" (p. 56). This position was not widely expressed by other columnists. Anderson (2003a) commented, "Considering Sorenstam's shy nature, she's not here for the publicity. And she's not here to learn how many of the men she can beat. She's here, as she has often said, to test herself, to see how well she plays from the men's tees on a prestigious course in a prestigious tournament" (p. D2).

The Magnitude of the Event Frame

Sorenstam's announcement that she was playing in the Colonial transformed the tournament into a sports event spectacle. There are many sports games, but some become elevated because of their storyline. In the Colonial, it was more than the golf course and more than the male golfers that Sorenstam was playing against. The event aspect of her playing in the tournament, where there were going to be many reporters and a large invested audience watching her perform, elevated the pressure. Over 600 media credentials were handed out for the Colonial.

The Colonial became a major television event with Sorenstam playing, as the USA Network expanded its coverage to show all of her rounds on Thursday and Friday. The USA Network also began its coverage on Thursday at 10 a.m., to show Sorenstam play her entire opening round. CBS began its Saturday coverage an hour earlier to focus on Sorenstam's performance. It was not that she was playing the golf course on a Tuesday afternoon with no spectators; it was about her ability to perform on this stage. The pressure of the media scrutiny would be the difference between these rounds of golf and every other round of golf that Sorenstam had ever played, including her playing in an LPGA major. In terms of the magnitude of the event, Sorenstam commented, "I'm not worried about my golf game, but I'm worried about whether I can keep my mind straight. This is something that I've never experienced. It's a total test for me" (cited in

Mariotti, 2003a, p. 110). She stated, "I don't think I'd be a professional today if I was afraid of embarrassing myself" (cited in Mariotti, 2003a, p. 110).

In terms of the magnitude of the event, Mariotti (2003b) commented, "On a course longer and tougher than any she has seen on the LPGA Tour, she basically must play the greatest golf of her life, as dozens of suspicious male competitors, a lively gallery, 600 media members, and a beady-eyed world watch her every swing, step, and expression" (p. 142). Cowlishaw (2003a) wrote that "Sorenstam has to be prepared not only to face the daunting challenge of playing Colonial from the men's tees but to hear criticism of her unique invitation that will bring a massive sideshow" (p. 1c). He added, "But during a Tiger-less lull in the men's tour, some excitement will be generated. So applaud her for accepting the challenge" (Cowlishaw, 2003a, p. 1c). Lupica (2003) added, "There is no question that Sorenstam is showing us all something, men and women, by putting herself on the line this way, and ought to be cheered for that" (p. 56).

The scrutiny and pressure not only came from the media and the fact that the audience would be paying close attention, but other PGA players. Lopresti (2003a) wrote, "Their (PGA) tour has simply been borrowed for a weekend, to scratch Annika Sorenstam's itch. The suspicion is that a good many PGA golfers are not entirely comfortable with what is happening at the Colonial. Only a few chose to blab and incur the public relations collateral damage for their words" ("Male golfers opposed"). The reaction of other players on the men's tour to Sorenstam's playing in the Colonial became a critical element of the story. Tiger Woods commented, "It's great that she's playing, but it will only be great for women's golf if she plays well. I think if she goes out there and posts two high scores, then it's going to be more detrimental than it's going to be good" (cited in Mariotti, 2003a, p. 110). Woods also stated, "I think it will be more fair to her if she could play four or five tournaments—then you could judge on those results." He then added, "I'm sure if she did play four or five, she'd get on a roll . . . in one tournament a lot could go wrong" ("Tiger encourages Annika," 2003).

The most striking criticism of Sorenstam's participation came from Vijay Singh, who stated, "If I miss the cut, I hope she misses the cut because I don't want to get beat by a lady" (cited in Cowlishaw, 2003a, p. 1c). Singh added, "This is the men's tour. There are guys out here trying to make a living. It's not the ladies tour. If she wants to play or if any lady for that matter wants to play on the men's tour, they should have to qualify" (cited in Cowlishaw, 2003a, p. 1c). Nick Price, defending champion at the Colonial, also thought Sorenstam should have had to qualify to play and claimed her entry into a men's event, "reeks of publicity" ("Tiger encourages Annika," 2003). Scott Hoch, added that by Sorenstam playing in the Colonial people will realize "how much separation there is between us and the ladies tour" ("Tiger encourages Annika," 2003). These perspectives clearly see her playing as a gender competition rather than an athlete testing herself.

The reaction of some of the men's players created another frame that emerged— reporters defending Sorenstam's right to play. Boswell (2003) pointed out that "Sorenstam didn't get into the Colonial on a court order or through a loophole. It's standard PGA Tour procedure—eight sponsor exemptions. Some events invite famous old coots who aren't competitive but can draw a few extra fans. Well, Sorenstam will draw thousands. And far better TV ratings than the men—without her—could have hoped to pull" (p. 1). The PGA players who expressed displeasure with Sorenstam's appearance were consistently criticized. Mariotti (2003a) argued, "If she's fearless enough to become the first female in 58 years to compete on men's turf—brave enough to risk the reputation of women's golf, the advancements of women's sports and, let's not sugar-coat this, the pride of women everywhere—the least the boys in the clubhouse can do is stop heckling her" (p. 110). Brennan (2003a) commented, "Women who play golf for a living know what some, and perhaps many, male pros think of them. The word that comes to mind is inferior" (p. 10c). She added, "Any woman who dares to be different, who launches herself into a man's world in a unique or groundbreaking way . . . knows there most likely will be a serious backlash from the men in that world against her and her very presence in their midst. In fact, if she's long on perspective, she might even be a little disappointed if she didn't trigger such a reaction" (Brennan, 2003a, p. 10c).

Expectations and Predictions of Sorenstam's Performance Frame

The framing of the story evolved throughout the tournament based on Sorenstam's performance. The columnists' articles prior to the event focused on expectations, predictions, and what Sorenstam needed to accomplish for her participation to be deemed a success. The articles after each round focused on her performance, if it was successful, and what it meant as an accomplishment to Sorenstam individually, men's and women's golf, and men's and women's sports in general. Sorenstam helped define her own expectations by stating, "If I shoot the best golf I know how, I can shoot par. I'm being realistic in saying level par will be a good score for me on this course. If I do that, I will feel like I'm a winner inside" (cited in Mariotti, 2003b, p. 142).

Prior to playing, making the cut was one hurdle Sorenstam had to clear in order to be deemed a success. One betting line in Las Vegas had a two-day score total of 153 and a 4-1 underdog to make the cut. Tiger Woods provided a sense of what an accomplishment making the cut would be, stating, "I would think it was a fantastic performance—no doubt about it" ("Tiger encourages Annika," 2003). Regarding her making the cut, Sorenstam commented, "I'm very optimistic I'll be here Sunday. I've got to think positive. If I waited another three months or three years, I wouldn't be more ready" (cited in Mariotti, 2003b, p. 142). Mariotti (2003b) defined the expectations and success clearly on her making the cut, claiming that "the difference between making history and making us yawn is simple. Sorenstam needs to survive the cut at Colonial. That doesn't mean she has to shoot an even-par 140 over the first two rounds, but she'd better be fairly close" (p. 142). He predicted, "Much as I'd love to see her send tremors through sports, much as it would prove an elite female athlete can compete with men, I'm afraid Annika won't last beyond Friday. Not that I don't admire her brave experiment, but she would have to be at her precise, ball-striking best to approach the low 70s either day. She'll be hitting long irons and fairway metals when the PGA players are hitting short irons" (Mariotti, 2003b, p. 142).

Brennan (2003b) predicted that Sorenstam would shoot a 74-73 for a total of seven-over-par and would not make the cut, stating, "She won't be awful, not at all, but she will make just a few too many mistakes to qualify to play on the weekend" (p. 7c). She added, "I hope Sorenstam makes me look ridiculous. I hope she shoots even par . . . and makes the cut by a stroke or two. That's my heart talking. But my head says something else" (Brennan, 2003b, p. 7c). Anderson (2003a) was one of the few who predicted that Sorenstam would make the cut, writing, "Maybe it's wishful thinking, but I believe she will make the cut" (p. D2). He added, "If Sorenstam is on her game, she's certainly capable of shooting, say, 72-70" (Anderson, 2003a, p. D2). Cowlishaw (2003a) offered a more long-term prediction, stating, "Sorenstam doesn't pose a threat to anyone. She will play and she probably will miss the cut and she will return to the LPGA Tour and that will be the end of it" (p. 1c).

Analysis of Sorenstam's Performance Frame

Annika Sorenstam's overall results at the Colonial were shooting 71 on Thursday, 74 on Friday, finishing five-over-par, and failing to make the cut. The sentiment of many columnists prior to the tournament was that her achieving that measure was critical in her playing being evaluated as a success. The columnist predictions were largely correct in that Sorenstam did not make the cut, but their articles after the tournament no longer viewed making the cut as the critical measure that would determine success. In the evaluation by newspaper columnists, both her performance and her attitude were consistently applauded, and therefore her participation, despite missing the cut by four strokes, was described as a success.

There were actually two very different rounds and reactions, after the first day of play and for the event as a whole. After her one-over-par, 71 in the first round, Anderson (2003b) stated, "It's the most memorable round of golf ever played by a woman. It's also the most memorable 71 by anyone. Send her scorecard to the World Golf Hall of Fame. Even better, put it in a time capsule. Not for the score. For the situation. And for the adulation" (p. D1). Anderson (2003b) also offered a comparison of her round to some of the most historic rounds ever played in golf, recognizing Johnny Miller's 63 to win the 1973 United States Open, Jack Nicklaus' 65 to win the 1986 Masters at age 46, and Ben Hogan's 67 to win the 1951 United States Open, stating, "Sorenstam's 71 was equally special" (p. D1).

After her first round, Brennan (2003c) commented, "If she wanted to, Sorenstam could withdraw from the Colonial on Friday morning, pack up and fly home, because she already has done what she came here to do. She wondered if she could compete at the top level of the game of golf. She now has her answer. She most definitely can" (p. 11c). Brennan (2003c) also quickly placed Sorenstam's first round in historical perspective, stating, "No matter what she does on Friday, make the cut or miss it, Sorenstam's Thursday round should be packaged by itself and remembered as one of the magnificent moments in women's sports history. This isn't hyperbole. It's already right up there with the King-Bobby Riggs match, the 1999 Women's World Cup soccer tournament, the signing of Title IX and the performances of Babe Didrikson Zaharias. That's how wonderful it was" (p. 11c).

After not playing as well on Friday and missing the cut, some comments were tempered. Mariotti (2003c) analyzed Sorenstam's Friday performance, writing, "Brave as she was, charming as she was, cool and triumphant as she was Thursday, Dreamboat Annika was slightly out of her element" (p. 134). All of the writers still characterized Sorenstam's playing in the Colonial as a resounding success and essentially changed from their initial definition of having to make the cut as determining success. Mariotti (2003c) stated, "In the biggest picture, her gender-crossing experiment was worthwhile, bringing attention to her considerable talents and women's golf and attracting the interest of millions, including little girls who today are asking their parents how to swing the club. And she handled herself with poise, grace, and dignity, hardly embarrassing herself" (p. 134). He added, "Perhaps she doesn't have the game to compete consistently against the men, but Sorenstam still took home a victory more significant than any score. She won over the majority of her critics, in the process narrowing a perception gap older than Adam and Eve. By proving she could play respectably in spurts, she might have turned to the traditionally excruciating concept of a man losing to a woman—a boy losing to a girl—into a less painful experience" (Mariotti, 2003c, p. 134). He concluded, "We won't remember her deficiencies as much as her contributions" (Mariotti, 2003c, p. 134).

Brennan (2003d) stated, "She turned the Colonial, a sleepy little tour stop, into one of the most memorable sports events of the year" (p. 13c). She also commented, "To judge Sorenstam on one week's effort, perhaps as few as 36 holes, is not entirely fair, yet it's the undeniable consequence of the decision she made to play here. To burden her with the fate of all womankind in sports, as many pundits have, also is a bit much, but it's part of that same reality" (Brennan, 2003b, p. 7c). Jenkins (2003b) argued, "We should do this every year. The best female player from the LPGA Tour should receive an annual invitation to play in the Colonial. Annika Sorenstam's presence here transformed an ordinary golf tournament into a historic event, and a not-insignificant experiment. It's one worth repeating. Colonial now has a unique status" (p. 7c).

Cowlishaw (2003c) concluded, "The 2003 Colonial will belong forever to Annika Sorenstam. And there is absolutely nothing wrong with that" (p. 1c). He added, "Two rounds of golf don't confirm or deny anything. This was a story of a champion athlete doing what few champions or people at the top of their field, period, ever consider. That's risking total embarrassment" (Cowlishaw, 2003c, p. 1c). Cowlishaw (2003c) also indicated there were no losers by having Sorenstam compete in the Colonial, stating, "So if it was good for Annika and the men and women who cheered her and for both tours (PGA and LPGA) and for the TV ratings, just how bad could this have been for anyone?" (p. 1c). Recognizing her performance was a remarkable achievement considering the enormous pressures, Cowlishaw (2003d) noted, "This one-shot experiment will heighten awareness of her presence on the LPGA Tour. At the same time it did nothing to soil the reputation of either the Bank of America Colonial or the PGA Tour. That might not have been the case had Sorenstam shot a pair of 80s" (p. 1c).

Many of the columnists tried to examine what impact Sorenstam's performance would have on the larger sports scene and an even larger societal scene. Anderson (2003b) commented, "Just as Tiger Woods' success has inspired more blacks to play golf, what Sorenstam did yesterday (Thursday) will surely inspire more girls as well as more women, young and old, to play golf" (p. D1). He added, "All those young and old men and women, and all those boys and girls were there to cheer Sorenstam because, whether they played golf or not, they could identify with what she was doing: testing her game and her psyche against the men from the men's tees. And she more than passed the test. Give her an A" (Anderson, 2003d, p. 11).

In evaluating her own performance, Sorenstam commented, "I wish I could have played better. The crowds were so fantastic and giving me so much support, I didn't want to let them down" (cited in Mariotti, 2003c, p. 134). She also spoke to the magnitude of the event, commenting, "This was much more than I expected. The course being longer, being under the microscope, I didn't perform as well as I can. I'm emotionally drained because I gave it all I had. I was nervous, and when that happens, I lose the feeling in my hands. That's something I have to work on" (cited in Mariotti, 2003c, p. 134).

Although trying to downplay the gender angle prior to the tournament, Sorenstam did recognize and address the potential gender significance. She stated, "It's great to see the little girls. I hope that they feel like when they grow up that they can play golf, but also follow their dream and to follow their heart. That's what I'm doing. So it's wonderful to see every little one here" (cited in Anderson, 2003b, p. D1). Sorenstam added, "I hope my dream lets little girls live their dreams. Hopefully, all of this takes women's golf way higher" (cited in Mariotti, 2003c, p. 134).

Conclusion

As soon as Annika Sorenstam accepted an invitation to play in the Colonial, an interesting sports, and human interest, story was created. The interest in how Sorenstam would perform is evident as the two-day audience for Thursday and Friday set a record for the USA Network's 22 years of televising the PGA tour. The PGA Tour also had its highest number of hits in one day on its website, www.pga.com. Sorenstam immediately was the dominant storyline and the winner of the Colonial golf tournament became secondary, as Cowlishaw (2003d) wrote, "Sometimes tournaments are about more than who stood in the winner's circle" (p. 1c). Even Colonial tournament winner Kenny Perry acknowledged Sorenstam's presence, commenting, "I'll probably be remembered as the guy who won Annika's event, that's OK with me" (cited in Cowlishaw, 2003d, p. 1c).

For major sports events, even though they are viewed live on television by many, people still look for analysis to place the event in some sort of meaningful context. Even with the growth of sports talk radio and television commentary, it is the newspaper columnists that still have the responsibility of providing such analysis. How newspaper columnists frame the coverage of the event they are witnessing is a factor in how people perceive the story. The presented frames gain a status of importance in comparison to the frames that are ignored. The initial intrigue of Sorenstam participating in the Colonial was obviously centered on the gender competition frame that was created. The question of can the best female golfer compete with the men in a men's event created a compelling storyline. Once the storyline was presented, it did not matter if Sorenstam succeeded or failed—the reporters had an interesting story.

In analyzing the framing of Sorenstam's playing in the Colonial, a few different frames other than the gender angle emerged. One notable frame is that of an athlete challenging herself against better competition. Through the interplay between those two frames, another critical frame emerged—the expectations and predictions of what would be deemed a success for Sorenstam and the analysis of her performance after the tournament. The most interesting aspect of the columnists' analysis relating to the gender and athlete challenging themselves frames is that the expectation that had been placed on Sorenstam as to what would mean a successful performance was not achieved.

At the outset it was the gender competition that was the relevant frame, as evidenced by all of the columnists making predictions about whether or not she would make the cut, a measure determined by her performance relative to other male players. The relevant frame, however, evolved and the examination of the columnists' writings demonstrates that, in the end, it can be argued that the relevant frame was that of an athlete challenging herself against the best competition, under intense scrutiny. The reasoning for this conclusion is that after the Colonial, the columnists focused on and praised Sorenstam for her own individual score, despite not making the cut. All of these reporters already knew that Sorenstam was a tremendously talented golfer based on her LPGA credentials. All athletes, however, have the task of being able to perform on the grandest of stages. The performance of Sorenstam can be deemed a success by the sports columnists because she demonstrated her ability under the difficult circumstances of intense scrutiny and pressure.

The analysis of the columnists represented a sort of reversal that eventually wound up embracing Sorenstam's comments, as prior to the tournament, while many columnists focused on the gender angle, she downplayed it and focused on an athlete challenging herself. Yet, after the tournament there was an acknowledgement by Sorenstam of the potential gender implications, while the columnists focused on her athletic accomplishment.

Overall, the societal impact that two rounds of golf can have are difficult to evaluate. Sports reporters will be off to the next event and begin covering and framing the next major sports competition. Some of the impact on Sorenstam can be provided. Sorenstam maintained that after the Colonial, she would not play in another event on the PGA Tour, stating, "It's a tour for the best players in the world. It's something I don't want to push" (cited in Mariotti, 2003c, p. 134). The week following the Colonial, Sorenstam returned to the LPGA, where her appearance and her new national notoriety helped double ticket sales at the Kellog-Keebler Classic. As for her golf game, in the two weeks following the Colonial, Sorenstam won both tournaments with a 17-under-par to win the 54-hole, Kellog-Keebler Classic and the LPGA major championship. After winning the major, Sorenstam stated, "Winning is what it's all about. At Colonial, it was the journey to winning. Maybe with all that pressure I experienced then, that's what helped me pull through today" (Associated Press, 2003).

References

Anderson, D. (2003a, May 22). Lady in red will make the cut at the Colonial. *New York Times*, p. D2.

Anderson, D. (2003b, May 23). "I'll never forget this day in my life." *New York Times*, p. D1.

Anderson, D. (2003c, May 24). "I love what I do," and the crowd knows it. *New York Times*, p. D1.

Anderson, D. (2003d, May 25). Can Sorenstam, at center stage, inspire a mixed U.S. Open? *New York Times*, p. 11.

Associated Press (2003, June 9). Sorenstam uses clutch to top Park. *Newark Star-Ledger*, p. 50.

Associated Press (2003, May 15). Tiger encourages Annika to play more than one. Retrieved May 15, 2003, from http://sports.espn.go.com/golf/story?id=1553446.

Boswell, T. (2003, May 13). Larry, Moe and Curly. *Washington Post*, p. 1.

Brennan, C. (2003a, May 15). In Sorenstam's venture, Singh plays role of whiner to a tee. *USA Today*, p. 10c.

Brennan, C. (2003b, May 22). Here's hoping Sorenstam doesn't play by my numbers. *USA Today*, p. 7c.

Brennan, C. (2003c, May 23). Sorenstam proves herself against the best. *USA Today*, p. 11c.

Brennan, C. (2003d, May 27). Annika accomplished more with her achievement than she realizes. *USA Today*, p. 13c.

Cowlishaw, T. (2003a, May 14). Singh's wrong, but at least he speaks mind. *Dallas Morning News*, p. 1c.

Cowlishaw, T. (2003b, May 19). Singh doesn't need the circus to tame a Tiger. *Dallas Morning News*, p. 1c.

Cowlishaw, T. (2003c, May 24). Annika ties for 96th, but everyone's a winner here. *Dallas Morning News*, p. 1c.

Cowlishaw, T. (2003d, May 26). Lasting memories: Annika and a pair of 61s. *Dallas Morning News*, p. 1c.

Crosset, T. W. (1995). *Outsiders in the clubhouse*. Albany, NY: State University of New York Press.

Duncan, M. C., Jensen, K., & Messner, M. A. (1993). Separating the men from the girls: The gendered language of televised sport. *Gender and Society, 7*, 121-137.

Entman, R. (1993). Framing: Toward clarification of a fractured paradigm. *Journal of Communication, 43*(4), 51-58.

Fishman, M. (1997). News and nonevents: Making the visible invisible. In D. Berkowitz (Ed.), *Social meaning of news: A text-reader* (pp. 210-229). Thousand Oaks, CA: Sage.

Fortunato, J. A. (2001). *The ultimate assist: The relationship and broadcast strategies of the NBA and television networks*. Cresskill, NJ: Hampton Press.

Gamson, W. A. (2001). Foreword. In S. D. Reese, O. H. Gandy, & A. E. Grant (Eds.), *Framing public life: Perspectives on media and our understanding of the social world* (pp. ix-xi). Mahwah, NJ: Lawrence Erlbaum Associates.

Gamson, W. A., & Modigliani, A. (1989). Media discourse and public opinion on nuclear power: A constructionist approach. *American Journal of Sociology, 95*(1), 1-37.

Gandy, O. H. (2001). Epilogue—Framing at the horizon: A retrospective assessment. In S. D. Reese, O. H. Gandy, & A. E. Grant (Eds.), *Framing public life: Perspectives on media and our understanding of the social world* (pp. 355-378). Mahwah, NJ: Lawrence Erlbaum Associates.

Garcia, M., & Stark, P. (1991). *Eyes on the news.* St. Petersburg, FL: The Poynter Institute.

Jamieson, K. H., & Waldman, P. (2003). *The press effect: Politicians, journalists, and the stories that shape the political world.* New York: Oxford University Press.

Jenkins, S. (2003a, May 22). This has some guys really teed off. *Washington Post*, p. D1.

Jenkins, S. (2003b, May 24). An invitation worth repeating. *Washington Post*, p. D1.

Kane, M. J., & Greendorfer, S. L. (1994). The media's role in accommodating and resisting stereotyped images of women in sport, pp. 28-44. In P. Creedon (Ed.), *Women, media, and sport.* Thousand Oaks, CA: Sage.

Kaneva, N., & Lenert, E. (2003). Who wants to be a millionaire? How the press framed the role of the public in the dispute between Time Warner Cable and Disney's ABC Network in May 2000. *The New Jersey Journal of Communication, 11*(2), 149-163.

Lippmann, W. (1922). *Public opinion.* New York: Macmillan.

Lopresti, M. (2003a, May 14). Male golfers opposed to playing against Sorenstam have a point. Retrieved May 15, 2003, from http://www.usatoday.com/sports/columnist/lopresti/2003-05-13-lopresti_x.htm.

Lupica, M. (2003, May 18). Swinging for the fences. *New York Daily News*, p. 56.

MacMullan (2003, February 13). Start is what matters, where Sorenstam finishes at the Colonial is irrelevant. *Boston Globe*, p. 1.

Mariotti, J. (2003a, May 20). Sorenstam already ahead of the game. *Chicago Sun-Times*, p. 110.

Mariotti, J. (2003b, May 22). Sadly, Sorenstam stands little chance. *Chicago Sun-Times*, p. 142.

Mariotti, J. (2003c, May 25). Sorenstam loses battle, wins war. *Chicago Sun-Times*, p. 134.

Mariotti, J. (2003d, May 30). Sorenstam gets real—and is better for it. *Chicago Sun-Times*, p. 167.

McCombs, M. E., & Reynolds, A. (2002). News influence on our pictures of the world. In J. Bryant & D. Zillmann (Eds.), *Media effects: Advances in theory and research* (2nd ed., pp. 1-18). Mahwah, NJ: Lawrence Erlbaum Associates.

Nelson, T. E., Clawson, R. A., & Oxley, Z. M. (1997). Media framing of a civil liberties conflict and its effect on tolerance. *American Political Science Review, 91*, 567-583.

Reese, S. D. (2001). Prologue—Framing public life: A bridging model for media research. In S. D. Reese, O. H. Gandy, & A. E. Grant (Eds.), *Framing public life: Perspectives on media and our understanding of the social world* (pp. 7-31). Mahwah, NJ: Lawrence Erlbaum Associates.

Rintala, J., & Birrell, S. (1984). Fair treatment for the active female: A content analysis of *Young Athlete* magazine. *Sociology of Sport Journal, 1*, 231-250.

Scheufele, D. A. (2000). Agenda-setting, priming, and framing revisited: Another look at cognitive effects of political communication. *Mass Communication & Society, 3*(2&3), 297-316.

Tuggle, C. A. (1997). Television sport reporting of female athletics: Quantitative and qualitative content analysis of ESPN Sportscenter and CNN Sports Tonight. *Journal of Broadcasting & Electronic Media, 41*, 14-24.

Yioutas, J., & Segvic, I. (2003). Revisiting the Clinton/Lewinsky scandal: The convergence of agenda setting and framing. *Journalism & Mass Communication Quarterly, 80*(3), 567-582.

Assessing the Impact of Sport Editorials and Cognitive Complexity on Social Behavior

DANIEL C. FUNK
MARK PRITCHARD

Abstract

Consumer socialization has been defined as the process by which individuals develop skills, knowledge, and attitudes relevant to their functioning in the marketplace. Despite widespread acceptance of the media's influence on society, research has provided limited understanding on how a person's prior knowledge and direct experience (i.e., cognitive complexity) related to a sport object moderates the influence of media on behavior. The present study extends this line of inquiry by empirically examining the role sport editorials have on shaping social behavior towards a professional sport team among consumers with high and low levels of cognitive complexity. A repeated measure mixed experimental design was used to examine the interaction between cognitive complexity and editorial type on social behavior toward a professional baseball team (N = 154). These data revealed that complexity stabilized the sport editorial's influence and individuals with limited prior knowledge and direct experience were more susceptible to the editorial's bias. The results highlight the importance of developing and maintaining beneficial and symbiotic relationships with local and regional print media to shape general consumer behavior towards a sport organization and players.

Assessing the Impact of Sport Editorials and Prior Experience on Attitude and Social Behavior

Consumer socialization has been defined as the process by which individuals develop skills, knowledge, and attitudes relevant to their functioning in the marketplace (Hoff & Ellis, 1992; Ward, 1974). Research has examined the role of socializing agents in the psychological and behavioral development of children and adults (Frankenberger & Sukhdial, 1994; Moore, Raymond, Mittelstaedt, & Tanner, 2002; Moschis & Moore, 1979) and specifically within the context of leisure and sport (James, 2001; Kelly, 1972). Among the socializing agents examined, mass media continues to receive considerable attention (Cobb-Wallgreen, Ruble, & Donthu, 1995; Krugman & King, 2000; Rose, Busch, & Kahle, 1998). The present study empirically examines a specific form of mass media—sport editorials and their role in shaping social behavior towards a professional sport team.

The pervasiveness of mass media consumption in the form of electronic and print media in North American society has been widely recognized by sport sociologists (Eitzen & Sage, 2003; Smith 1988). A symbiotic relationship continues to exist between sport and mass media (Nichols, Moynahan, Hall, & Taylor, 2002; Sage, 1990). Sport organizations receive free publicity in the form of event coverage, while the media receives programming and content to augment their "product." This in turn drives viewer ratings, circulation (consumption), and advertising revenue.

A predominate position within the social science literature is that individuals form impressions and opinions from information provided by a variety of sources, but that intermediaries such as media, most notably television and newspapers, are increasingly playing a dominant role (Dalton, Beck, & Huckfeldt, 1998; Domke, 2001; Emmers-Sommer & Allen, 1999; Sprio, 2001). As suggested by Entman (1989), "The media do not control what people prefer . . . they influence public opinion by providing much of the information people think about and shape how they think about it" (p. 361). The media's influence on shaping attitudes and behaviors has primarily been studied from two perspectives: 1) the cognitive effects of how information is framed and processed (e.g., how events and candidates are perceived) (Drew & Weaver, 1990; Schmidt, 1993), and 2) the potential persuasiveness of media content (e.g., news coverage, editorials, cues) (Dalton et al., 1998; Erikson, 1976). Despite the widespread acceptance of the media's influence on society, media research on the interaction between information processing and content has provided little understanding of the dynamic process in which new information directs social behavior. Within sport, there are compelling reasons to expect that content and information processing will differentially influence beliefs and feelings based upon individual characteristics (e.g., Funk & James, 2001; Mahony, Madrigal, & Howard, 2000; Petrick, Backman, Bixler, & Norman, 2001; Pritchard, Havitz, & Howard, 1999).

Theoretical Foundation

Consumer socialization theory provides a useful framework to gain new insight into how individual characteristics and newspaper editorials shape adult sport behavior. Consumer socialization is the process by which people acquire skills, knowledge, and attitudes related to their functioning as consumers in the marketplace (John, 1999; Moschis & Churchill, 1978; Ward, 1974). This perspective suggests that social learning (e.g., modeling, reinforcement) is an outcome of environmental factors that influence the development of preferences for products and services from early childhood through maturity (Bandura, 1977; Crawford, Godbey, & Crouter, 1986). Specific agents (parents, peers, and mass media) represent environmental factors that interact with the learner through which information, social mores, and values are conveyed and exchanged (John, 1999). Social learning theory has been used to understand the development of beliefs and attitudes toward leisure in general (Iso-Ahola, 1980), recreation activities (Burch, 1969), sport participation (McPherson, 1976) and competitive sport teams (James, 2001). The present research utilizes socialization theory as a framework to examine three specific elements of socialization theory: socializing agents, structural variables, and outcomes among adult sport consumers (see Figure 1).

SOCIALIZING AGENTS

Social Stimuli

(e.g., exposure to sport media)

SOCIAL STRUCTURES

Consumer Characteristics

(e.g., cognitive complexity)

SOCIAL OUTCOMES

Consumer Response

(e.g., social behavior)

Figure 1: Conceptual Model of Sport Consumer Responses to Media Effects

Socializing Agent

Socializing agents represent persons, institutions, or organizations that communicate norms, attitudes, and behavior through social interaction (Bush, Smith, & Martin, 1999). Environmental forces that shape adult behavior toward various objects such as sport are linked to prior social learning as a child. As the person matures, the impact of various socializing agents is expected to change (Moore et al., 2002). In a meta-analysis, Emmers-Sommer and Allen (1999) concluded that mass media become increasingly important in shaping the behavior of children as they mature. A great deal of research has been devoted to understanding the direct and indirect impact of mass media in shaping attitudes (Domke, 2001; Moy, Pfau, & Kahlor, 1999), cognitive learning and knowledge (Drew & Weaver, 1990), opinions (Gamson & Modigliani, 1989; Schmidt, 1993), information processing (Entman, 1989) and, more recently, behavior (Moore et al., 2002). Mass media has also received considerable attention as an important institution for shaping adult consumption activities (Bandura, 1986; Ward, 1974; Bush et al., 1999; Rose, Bush, & Kahle, 1998; Trevino, Webster, & Stein, 2000).

Socializing Agents in Sport

The bulk of sport socialization research has been devoted to understanding the impact that environmental forces have on children from birth to adolescence from two different perspectives: socialization into sport and socialization through sport (Eitzen & Sage, 2003; James, 2001). Research has demonstrated that people are drawn to sport due to the influence of formal channels (parents, peers, coaches, mass media, teachers) and informal channels (school, church, and community-based programs) (Kenyon & McPherson, 1973; McPherson, 1976; Spreitzer & Snyder, 1976). These socializing agents have been found to be instrumental in shaping the social learning process among young people (Hoff & Ellis, 1992; McPherson, 1976). For adults, mass media, friends, the influence of one's spouse/partner, coworkers, and the emphasis a community places on sport or supporting a team are suggested to become more important (Funk & James, 2001).

Research in sport management has primarily focused on one specific socializing agent for adults: mass media. The majority of research has concentrated on television's impact by examining visual pleasure (Duncan & Brummett, 1989), behavior during viewing (Gants, 1981), style of commentary (Comiskey, Bryant, & Zillman, 1977), and exploitation of violence (Bryant & Zillman, 1989). Other researchers have examined differences in media consumption among participants and spectators (Burnett, Minion, & Smart, 1993), coverage of sporting events (Hansen & Gauthier, 1989; McDaniel, 2002), the interactions between website provider and consumer for professional sport teams (Beech, Chadwick, & Tapp, 2000), and the persuasiveness of recreational brochures (Manfredo & Bright, 1991). Although this line of inquiry illustrates the link between mass media and adults, the descriptive nature of this research provides limited information for understanding how the mass media influences outcomes such as attitudes, values, knowledge, and behaviors in sport.

Sociologists suggest that mass media can construct information in such a way that it promotes dominant group interests as normal (Sage, 1990; Eitzen & Sage, 2003) and influences what we think and feel about our social and political environment. Media coverage can influence public opinion by controlling what individuals know about an event in the absence of actual observation or firsthand knowledge (Bartels, 1993; Entman, 1989). Although television is widely recognized as a key source for developing information and spectating/viewing sport events (Eitzen & Sage, 2003; Lobmeyer & Weidinger, 1992), newspapers continue to be an important source in the distribution and consumption of sport information (Nichols et al., 2002). Previous efforts devoted to understanding the relationship between the individual and sport television have diverted attention from studying an equally important media agent: the effect of print editorials in newspaper sport sections. One compelling reason for focusing on sport editorials is the credibility and popularity readers place on newspapers in general, and editorials in particular.

Newspaper as Socializing Agent

Newspapers continue to play a vital role in public affairs, informing readers and providing in-depth information about activities, particularly at the local level (Gamson & Modigliani, 1989; Nichols et al., 2002). For example, St. George and Robinson-Weber (1983) observed that the amount of exposure to newspapers is predictive of political participation. Drew and Weaver (1990) reported that newspapers stimulate cognitive learning. Schmidt (1993) found that public attitudes related to labor unions were influenced by the amount of media coverage of union activities from 1947-1985. Moy et al. (1999) observed that newspaper reading was related to favorable attitudes toward schools and criminal courts.

Recent research has also found that newspapers are perceived as one of the more credible sources for news. Schweiger (2000) reported that newspapers were rated as more credible than television and web media forms on 9 of 11 categories (e.g., more thoroughly researched, more detailed and critical, better balanced, more competent, more professional). Spiro (2001) observed that newspapers were given more credibility than online news and television. In addition to the credibility, the popularity of newspapers and particularly the sport section suggest the need for study.

The Newspaper Association of America (NAA) reported that printed newspapers represent a $57 billion industry, with more than 2,000 newspapers in the United States and Canada. The association's most recent study (n = 26,005, 18 years & older) found that over half of all adults (55.5 percent) in the 50 largest U.S. markets read a daily newspaper, and that nearly two-thirds (63.9 percent) read one on Sunday (NAA.org, 2002). Particularly germane here is the finding that the sport section is the second most widely read section after the general news.

Today, regardless of newspaper size or day of the week, 25-50 percent of story space is devoted to covering sport and represents the best link to a given demographic such as young males (Eitzen & Sage, 2003). The present sport section in newspapers has become increasingly diverse, including editorials about women's sports, coverage on recreational sports, listing the names of local residents participating in amateur athletics, and providing daily accounts of local pro, college, and high school team activities. The structure of newspapers also remains fundamentally different from other forms of sport media. Sport programming decisions for electronic media are driven by audience ratings and ad revenue, while newspapers have historically remained immune to these considerations (Eisten & Sage, 2003, Nichols et al., 2002).

Unfortunately, the production and delivery of sport media has not been immune from criticism levied at the broader media culture about its transmission and construction of social reality. Newspaper publishers continue to emphasize the right to freedom of the press but socio-political and economic pressures often flavor reports given about local sport teams and events (Sage, 1990; Schweiger, 2002). Such pressure can lead beat reporters, columnists, and feature writers to manipulate editorials that introduce their own biases or follow a specific agenda (Hackett, 1984). Eitzen and Sage (2003) suggest that in many instances,

"Stories are withheld or distorted, and sports news is edited to ensure a favorable public image of the home team" (p. 253). The challenge then for publishers is to produce a quality sport section that does not compromise the newspapers' integrity with inaccuracies and self-serving agendas.

Adding further weight to the matter, editorial units have been found to be quite persuasive due to the credibility recipients attach to the source (Petty & Cacioppo, 1986; Dalton et al., 1998). Dalton et al. (1998) reported that editorials that favored a specific candidate directly influenced reader preferences for that candidate. In this context, source credibility operates as a peripheral cue related to the message argument, and has an important role in the message's processing and in determining the outcome of a persuasive effort (Chaiken & Maheswaran, 1994). Source credibility becomes more influential in situations where low processing of the information occurs (Petty & Cacioppo, 1986). Sport editorials are more likely to be perceived as formal or neutral sources (e.g., Not-for Profit, Consumer Report, Public Service Announcements) rather than a paid advertisement with profit-oriented motives, giving the reader more confidence in the message (Schiffman & Kanuk, 2000). Hence, the pressure from management coupled with the popularity of newspapers and the persuasive source characteristics attributed to editorials make efforts to understand the ways in which sport editorials influence social behavior toward sport teams compelling.

Structural Variable: Cognitive Complexity

In most views of socialization, social structural variables are those factors that influence outcomes directly or indirectly via an interaction with other socializing agents. Social structural variables have included individual characteristics related to age, gender, ethnicity, income, education, and family structure (Bush et al., 1999). However, the relationship between social structural variables and both attitude and behaviors remain largely ambiguous. The present study utilized two individual difference characteristics: prior knowledge and direct experience related to a sport team as a social structural variable to provide some clarity (Funk & James, 2001; Petrick et al., 2001).

Prior knowledge refers to the functional knowledge or the amount of relevant knowledge that accompanies an individual's attitude related to a sport team (Funk & Pastore, 2000). Individuals who possess greater levels of knowledge about an object are more likely to evaluate an object consistently with previous beliefs due to greater cognitive resources available and the extensive linkages between the attitudes and other cognitive components (Eagly & Chaiken, 1993). Attitudes based upon higher levels of prior knowledge are more likely to moderate the attitude-behavior relationship (Kallgren & Wood, 1986), less likely to change (Wood, 1982), and more likely to predict behavior (Davidson, Yantis, Norwood, & Montano, 1985) than attitudes based upon limited functional knowledge. The amount of attitude-relevant knowledge has generally been measured by asking participants to list everything they know and can remember about an object or self-reports on how knowledgeable they feel about an object.

Direct experience refers to the degree of prior experience, participation, or the amount of direct contact one has had with team-related activities (Funk & Pastore, 2000). Attitudes based upon direct experience are reported to have greater clarity, held with more confidence, and are more consistent with behavior than attitudes not based upon direct experience (Doll & Ajzen, 1992). Attitudes formed via direct experience have been found to be more resistant by linking the attitude object to beliefs and prior experience, persistent and predictive of behavior (Fazio, Chen, McDonald, & Sherman, 1982). Direct experience has been assessed with self-report measures asking individuals how involved they were in activities related to an object or if they have committed any actions in regards to an object.

Taken together, prior functional knowledge and direct experience can be referred to as "cognitive complexity" because jointly they provide an individual with the ability to resist the popularity of newspapers and the persuasive source characteristics attributed to editorials (Pritchard, Havitz, & Howard, 1999). Cognitive complexity can reduce discrepancy between one's initial position and conflicting information to stabilize attitude formation and subsequent behavior. In recent research that examined patron commitment to specific travel services, Pritchard, Havitz, and Howard (1999) provided initial evidence that information complexity contributed to a person's resistance to change (i.e., commitment's root tendency). Cognitive complexity could well contribute to the strength of resistance and allow the individual to refute or block persuasive communication that conveys negative information about a preferred object or attractive information about competing alternatives (Petty, Hauvgedt, & Smith, 1995). Resistance to change one's assessment of an object or issue is often thought to denote an evaluative response that's characterized by a high degree of prior experience and knowledge (Ajzen & Madden, 1986). In sport and leisure research, efforts have drawn upon prior knowledge and direct experience to examine attitudinal loyalty toward sport teams (Funk & Pastore, 2000), prior golf participation to understand repeat behavior (Petrick et al., 2001).

In summary, the literature reviewed suggests that a person's cognitive complexity may directly influence attitude stability and indirectly influence social behavior. The level of complexity should moderate attitudinal reaction to persuasive editorials and stabilize subsequent behavior. Further study on the interaction between cognitive complexity and persuasive information, albeit in newspaper sport editorials, would extend understanding of the role that newspapers play in shaping behaviors toward sport organizations. We suspect that a reader's level of cognitive complexity will determine the degree of influence a sport editorial will have in any subsequent behavioral change (Petty, Cacioppo, & Schumann, 1983). A reader's initial position will determine the extent of self-generated cognitive and affective thoughts produced in response to the sport editorial that will in turn influence behavior (Burkrant & Unnava, 1995).

Outcomes: Social Behavior

The outcome measure chosen for the present study was social behaviors toward a sport team. The type of information processed can determine an individual's positive or negative feelings toward an object based upon normative and subjective beliefs (Fishbein & Ajzen, 1975). In line with this perspective, sport editorials would serve as the socializing agent to influence an individual's normative and subjective beliefs about a team based upon the type of cognitive processing that occurs. However, the level of cognitive complexity should intercede and operate as a structural variable that moderates the influence of sport editorials on subsequent behavior.

Social identity theory offers a framework to understand the influence that editorials have on reader behavior (Tajfel & Turner, 1979). Individuals strive for a positive social identity that has cognitive, emotional, and evaluative implications for subsequent social behavior. The literature on sport spectator and sport fans has identified a number of behaviors that generally focus on self-presentational concerns or image-maintenance (Cialdini, Borden, Thorne, Walker, Freeman, & Sloan, 1976; Hirt, Zillmann, Erickson, & Kennedy, 1992). Individuals realize that favorable evaluations of a positive source by others may be transferred to them (Heider, 1958) as well as unfavorable evaluations of a negative source (Synder, Lassegard, & Ford, 1986). A successful sport franchise provides individuals with self-presentational strategies to create or maintain positive self-image through public behavior demonstrating team association (Gladden & Funk, 2001). Individuals can also derive enhanced self-esteem by privately drawing a connection between themselves and a positive source unrelated to the assessment by others (Cialdini et al., 1976; Boen, Vanbeselaere, & Feys, 2002). Hence, behavioral outcomes should be positively related to the valence of the editorial for individuals with minimal cognitive complexity. However, individuals with more prior knowledge and direct experience are less likely to be influenced by the position advocated by the columnist and less change in behavior will occur.

Methods

A repeated measure mixed experimental design was used to examine the interaction between cognitive complexity and editorial type on social behavior toward a professional baseball team. A convenience sample of undergraduates (N = 154) located in close proximity to a professional team was utilized for the pre test. Participants included 88 males and 66 females with an average age of 24. A survey was administered that contained 17 items to measure direct experience (3 items), prior knowledge (5 items), personal relevance

(5 items), and intent to engage in social behavior (4 items) related to a Major League Baseball franchise (see Appendix A). Prior knowledge, direct experience, and personal relevance were measured using Krosnick et al.'s 1993 scale that has been validated in a sport context (Funk & Pastore, 2000). The personal relevance scale was included to measure an individual's level of involvement with a team in order to provide an internal test of validity for the social structural variable cognitive complexity. Objects or issues generally considered to be personally relevant have significant consequences for individual life as well as the elaboration and processing of persuasive material (Petty, Cacioppo, & Schumann, 1983). The social behaviors were designed to capture behavioral intent based upon image-management concerns by individuals privately drawing a connection between themselves and a sport team. The four 7-point Likert-type scales were incorporated from previous work in sport and leisure (Beard & Ragheb, 1983; Funk & Pastore, 2000).

Seven weeks later, the students participated in a post-test for extra course credit. Participants were recruited via a sign-up procedure for a project described as a "Sports Media Evaluation" study that would take place in a 30-minute session. Eleven experimental sessions with groups of 10-20 were utilized. All conditions were represented in each session. Upon arrival, each participant was given a packet of material containing four pages. Participants were randomly assigned to either a positive or negative editorial condition through distribution of experimental packets upon arrival (Campbell & Stanley, 1963).

The first page of the packet informed respondents that "newspapers and magazines are often given readability index scores," and the study was interested in assessing the "validity" and "favorability" of these scores among college student populations. Participants were instructed to read the articles from various newspapers' sport editorials in the packet of material as they would if they encountered them in a magazine or newspaper and that their impressions of the articles would be solicited. A pro and counter version of the three fictitious sport editorials were designed to elicit favorable and unfavorable thoughts and responses based upon a set of statements and arguments embedded in each version (Petty & Cacioppo, 1986; Petty, Haugtvedt, & Smith, 1995). Consumer research often employs a single-message methodology, where participants read or listen to a single persuasive message supporting one product or side of an issue (Haugtvedt & Petty, 1992).

On page two of the experimental packet, three sport editorials appeared with fictitious newspaper logos and authors. After reading the editorials, participants were instructed to turn the page and respond to five statements related to author characteristics and favorability of the articles. Participants were asked to not turn back to the previous page and examine the articles. After the article-rating task was completed on page 3, participants were instructed to turn the page and respond to a series of questions. The questions on page 4 were identical to the 12 items to measure direct experience, prior knowledge, and intent to engage in social behavior completed in the pretest. At the conclusion of the study, participants were debriefed and excused.

Statistical Analysis and Results

Scale analysis revealed that each subscale had inter-reliability measures above the .70 threshold: Direct Experience (a = .87), Prior Knowledge (a = .92), Personal Relevance (a = .82), and Social Behavior (a = .89) from the pretest. A cognitive complexity measure was created using a factor score from direct experience items and knowledge items using principle components factor analysis with varimax rotation (M = 3.00, SD = 1.98, a = .95). A median split on cognitive complexity was used to place respondents into a low (n = 80) and high (n = 74) cognitive complexity group (Haugtvedt, Petty, & Cacioppo, 1992). The distinctiveness of the two groups was assessed by examining the level of team involvement (i.e., 5-item personal relevance scale). An ANOVA provided evidence of distinctive group membership, with involvement levels in the low complexity group (M = 3.32, SD = 1.94) and high complexity group (M = 13.83, SD = 6.62) on a scale of 1.40 to 15.87 $F(1,154) = 213.37$, $p < .01$.

The validity of the editorial bias was confirmed as respondents who received the positive editorials rated the editorial as very favorable toward the team (M = 6.33, SD = .73) while respondents who received the negative articles rated the editorial as more negative toward the team (M = 1.50, SD = 1.01) on a

7-point scale. Respondent's cognitive complexity scores were used to conduct a 2 x 2 x 3 (Pre Test vs. Post Test x Complexity Level x Editorial Type) mixed-design analysis of variance (ANOVA) on behavior. The means and standard deviations are reported in Table 1. Repeated measures test revealed a main effect of time for intention to engage in social behavior $F(1, 150) = 149.91$, $p < .01$. However, the main effect was qualified by a Time x Cognitive Complexity interaction $F(2, 150) = 3.53$, $p < .03$. Post-tests revealed that high complexity individuals did not change their intentions to engage in social behavior regardless of editorial position. However, the intentions of individuals with minimal cognitive complexity were shaped by the bias of the editorial.

Table 1: Social Structural and Outcome Variables: Means, Standard Deviations, and Internal Consistency Measures (N = 154)			
Social Structural Variables	**M**	**SD**	a
Direct Experience	2.93	1.71 .	87
Knowledge	3.07	1.72	.92
Personal Relevance	2.62	1.47	.82
Outcome Variables			
Social Behavior Pre Test	2.19	1.32	.89
Social Behavior Post Test	2.63	1.20	.83

Table 2: Editorial Type x Time x Cognitive Complexity for Behavior (N = 154)				
	Pre Test		Post Test	
Cognitive Complexity	Pro Editorial	Counter Editorial	Pro Editorial	Counter Editorial
Low	1.24 (.38)	1.49 (.36)	1.54 (.57)	1.18 (.42)
High	3.40 (1.75)	3.79 (1.45)	3.54 (1.83)	3.67 (1.59)

Discussion

These data illustrate the relative influence sport editorials have on shaping the direction of public behavior toward a professional sport franchise. The level of cognitive complexity was observed to moderate the sport editorial influence on intentions to engage in social behaviors. The complexity level appeared to stabilize the evaluations of the editorial among individuals with more direct experience and prior knowledge while individuals with less complexity were more susceptible to the editorial's bias. These data revealed that individuals with minimal complexity were more likely to defend the franchise publicly, be seen as a fan of the team, and place a high priority on watching, reading, and listening activities related to the team after reading the positive editorials. In contrast, individuals who read the negative editorials became less willing to engage in behavior.

The fluctuations in social behavior for these individuals appear to stem from the potential self-presentational concerns produced by the valence of the editorial (Heider, 1958). The favorable team editorials served as a persuasive source cue that induced positive evaluative responses toward engaging in a self-esteem enhancement strategy through public affiliation with the team (Cialdini et al., 1976; Petty & Cacioppo, 1986). Likewise, the unfavorable editorials cued negative evaluative responses that lead to a self-esteem protection strategy by disassociating or distancing oneself from the team (Hirt et al., 1992; Synder, Lassegard, & Ford, 1986). The motivation for engaging in impression management appears to extend from both the public level as well as being unrelated to the assessment by others (Boen, Vanbeselaere, & Feys, 2002: Wann & Branscombe, 1993).

These data illustrate how cognitive complexity moderates the influence of sport editorials and stabilizes social behavior. Sport editorials operate as a socializing agent that induces processing and subsequent self-presentation behavioral strategies for individuals with less functional knowledge and prior direct experience. These data support prior research that illustrates the persuasive characteristics of editorials and their influence on shaping public opinion (Dalton et al., 1998; Hackett, 1984; Moy et al., 1999). The results highlight the important socializing role that print media (i.e., via newspaper columnists) plays in shaping the evaluations of consumers toward a sport team amongst adults within a community.

Implications for Sport Marketing

Public relations is a multidisciplinary approach within marketing designed to utilize media and community relations to help shape public attitudes and behaviors towards brands, services, issues, and people (Baskin, Aronoff, & Lattimore, 1997). As a management function, public relations can help achieve organizational objectives by communicating with relevant internal and external publics within a non-sponsored framework. As stated by Heltzer (2000), "The real talent is not the writing of publicity but the creation of publicity" (p. 205). The present study provides support for this notion by reinforcing to sport marketers the efficacy of editorials for influencing social behavior in a sport context. These data emphasize the need for developing and maintaining beneficial and symbiotic relationships with local and regional print media to shape editorial content in regards to sport organizations and players.

The generation of publicity related to a sport organization via print media remains advantageous over traditional advertising and promotions due to the enhanced credibility of the message (Chaiken & Maheswaran, 1994; Nichols et al., 2002). For athletic teams within larger geographic markets, individuals with greater cognitive complexity (i.e., direct experience and prior knowledge with the sport team or product) are less likely to be found. Subsequently, these individuals will be less influenced by media coverage and the position advocated by columnists than individuals who have limited prior experience with the team. Since the majority of a team's consumer base will have limited cognitive complexity, media relations can be advantageous over traditional advertising and promotions for shaping social behavior. Such behavior may not necessarily translate into increased ticket sales but may induce positive support for public funding efforts.

Limited sport research has evaluated the impact that non-traditional advertisement-based communication has on influencing public attitudes through the media. For example, the unprecedented growth in venue construction within the 1990s ($16.1 billion) highlights the important role the media may have in shaping public attitudes and behavior toward building new or renovating existing facilities (Howard & Crompton, 2003). In this context, influencing public opinion to support local and state tax referendums for construction projects is most likely to be successful through strategic building of relationships with local and regional newspaper columnists to leverage the impact that print media has on public sentiment. The credibility of the print source, author, and the use of repetition within this non-sponsored framework become a strong component of the persuasive communications success (Eagly & Chaiken, 1993). These strategies are likely to work equally well for managing media-based communication for new and emerging sport and leagues.

Limitations

The current study has several limitations that suggest the need for further research. First, the current study did not examine a random sample of a community's general population, and thus respondent characteristic and socio-demographic factors may limit the findings related to extent and type of change from the media-based communication (Wells, 1993). Second, acquiescence and social desirability on the part of individuals responding to attitude statements poses potential response set concerns. Third, cognitive recall of facts embedded in the editorials and attitudinal measures were not used in the present study. Their inclusion in future research would provide more in-depth understanding of information processing and latent forces that shape and direct behavior. Finally, dichotomizing cognitive complexity using season ticket holders versus single game attendees may provide a clearer picture of attitude change.

Conclusion

In conclusion, these findings demonstrate cognitive complexity's role in stabilizing the influence of sport editorial bias on intention to engage in social behavior related to a professional sport team. The cognitive complexity level a person possesses in relation to a sport team provides a mechanism to make informed judgments and evaluations about informational content in a highly persuasive form of media. Hopefully these findings may generate additional interest into the nature and role that processing media-based information has on shaping public attitudes.

References

Ajzen, I., & Madden, T. J. (1986). Prediction of goal-directed behavior: Attitudes, intentions, and perceived behavioral control. *Journal of Experimental Social Psychology, 22*, 453-474.

Bandura, A. (1977). Self-Efficacy: Towards a unifying theory of behavior change. *Psychological Review, 84*, 191-215.

Bandura, A. (1986). *Social foundations of thoughts and action.* Englewood Cliffs, NJ: Prentice-Hall.

Bartels, L. (1993). Messages received: The political impact of media exposure. *American Political Science Review, 87*, 267-285.

Baskin, O., Aronoff, C., & Lattimore, D. (1997). *Public relations: The profession and the practice (4th Ed).* Boston, MA: McGraw-Hill.

Beard, J. G., & Ragheb, M. G. (1983). Measuring leisure motivation. *Journal of Leisure Research, 15*(3), 219-228.

Beech, J., Chadwick, S., & Tapp, L. (2000). Surfing in the Premier League: Key issues for football club marketers using the Internet. *Managing Leisure, 5*(2), 51-64.

Boen, F., Vanbeselaere, N., & Feys, J. (2002). Behavioral consequences of fluctuating group success: An internet study of soccer-team fans. *Journal of Social Psychology, 142*(6), 769-781.

Burch, W. R. (1969). The social circles of leisure: Competing explanations. *Journal of Leisure Research, 1*, 125-147.

Bryant, J., & Zillman, D. (1983). Sports violence and the media. In J. H. Goldstein (Ed.), *Sports violence* (pp.195-210). New York: Springer-Verlag, Inc.

Burnett, J., Menon, A., & Smart, D. T. (1993). Sports marketing: A new ball game with new rules. *Journal of Advertising Research, September/October*, 21-35.

Bush, A. J., Smith, R., & Martin, C. (1999). The influence of consumer socialization variables on attitude toward advertising: A comparison of African-American and Caucasians. *Journal of Advertising, 28*, 13-24.

Campbell, D. T., & Stanley, J. C. (1963). *Experimental and quasi-experimental designs for research.* Boston, MA: Houghton Mifflin.

Cialdini, R. B., Thorne, A., Walker, M. R., Freeman, S., & Sloan, L. R. (1976). Basking in reflected glory: Three (football) field studies. *Journal of Personality and Social Psychology, 34*(3), 366-375.

Chaiken, S., & Maheswaran, D. (1994). Heuristic processing can bias systematic processing: Effects of source credibility, argument ambiguity, and tasks performance on attitude judgment. *Journal of Personality and Social Psychology 66*, 460-473.

Cobb-Wallgreen, C. J., Ruble, C. A., & Donthu, N. (1995). Brand equity, brand preference, and purchase intent. *Journal of Advertising, 24*(3), 25-40.

Comisky, P., Bryant, J., & Zillman, D. (1977). Commentary as a substitute for action. *Journal of Communication, 27*, 150-153.

Crawford, D. W., Godbey,G., & Crouter, A. C. (1986). The stability of leisure preferences. *Journal of Leisure Research, 18,* 96-115.

Dalton, R. J., Beck, P. A., & Huckfeldt, R. (1998). Partisan cues and the media: Information flows in the 1992 presidential election. *American Political Science Review, 92,* 111-126.

Davidson, A. R., Yanits, S., Norwood, M., & Montano, D. E. (1985). Amount of information about the attitude object and attitude-behavior consistency. *Journal of Personality and Social Psychology, 49,* 1184-1198.

Doll, J., & Ajzen, I. (1992). Accessibility and stability of predictors in the theory of planned behavior. *Journal of Personality and Social Psychology, 63,* 754-765.

Domke, D. (2001). The press, race relations, and social change. *Journal of Communication, 51,* 317-344.

Drew, D., & Weaver, D. (1990). Media attention, media exposure, and media effects. *Journalism and Mass Communication Quarterly, 67,* 740-748.

Duncan, M. C., & Brummett, B. (1989). Types and sources of spectating pleasures in televised sports. *Sociology of Sport Journal, 6,* 195-211.

Eagly, A. H., & Chaiken, S. (1993). *The psychology of attitudes.* Forth Worth, TX: Harcourt Brace Jovanovich, Inc.

Eitzen, D. S., & Sage, G. H. (2003). *Sociology of North American sport* (7th ed.). New York: McGraw-Hill.

Emmers-Sommer, T. M., & Allen, M. (1999). Surveying the effect of media effects: A meta-analytic summary of the media effects research in human communication research. *Human Communication Research, 4,* 478-497.

Entman, R. M. (1989). How the media affect what people think: An information processing approach. *Journal of Politics, 51,* 347-370.

Erickson, R. (1976). The influence of newspaper endorsements in presidential elections. *American Journal of Political Science, 20,* 207-234.

Fazio, R. H., Chen, J., McDonald, E. C., & Sherman, S. J. (1982). Attitude accessibility, attitude-behavior consistency, and the strength of the object-evaluation association. *Journal of Experimental Social Psychology, 18,* 339-357.

Fishbein, M., & Ajzen, I. (1975). *Beliefs, attitudes, intentions, and behavior: An introduction to theoretical research.* Reading, MA: Addison-Wesley.

Frankenberer, K. D., & Sukhdial, A. S. (1994). Segmenting teens for AIDS preventive behaviors with implications for marketing communications. *Journal of Public Policy & Marketing, 13,* 133-150.

Funk, D. C., & James, J. D. (2001). The Psychological Continuum Model (PCM): A conceptual framework for understanding an individual's psychological connection to sport. *Sport Management Review, 4,* 119-150.

Funk, D. C., & Pastore, D. L. (2000). Equating attitudes to allegiance: The usefulness of selected attitudinal information in segmenting loyalty to professional sports teams. *Sport Marketing Quarterly, 9*(4), 175-184.

Gladden, J. M., & Funk, D. C. (2001). Understanding brand loyalty in professional sport: Examining the link between brand association and brand loyalty. *International Journal of Sports Marketing & Sponsorship, 3,* 67-94.

Gamson, W. A., & Modigliani, A. (1989). Media discourse and public opinion on nuclear power: A constructionist approach. *American Journal of Sociology, 1,* 1-37.

Gantz, W. (1981). An exploration of view motives and behaviors associated with television sports. *Journal of Broadcasting, 25,* 263-275.

Hackett, R. A. (1984). Decline of a paradigm? Bias and objectivity in news and media studies. *Critical Studies in Mass Communication, 1,* 229-259.

Hansen, H., & Guthier, R. (1989). Factors affecting attendance at professional sport events. *Journal of Sport Management, 3,* 15-32.

Haugtvedt C., & Petty, R. E. (1992). Personality and persuasion: Need for cognition moderates the persistence and resistance of attitude changes. *Journal of Personality and Social Psychology, 63,* 308-319.

Heider, F. (1958). *The psychology of interpersonal relations.* New York: Wiley, 1958.

Helitzer, M. (2000). *The dream job: Sports, publicity, promotion and marketing* (3rd ed.). Athens, OH: University Sports Press.

Hirt, E. R., Zillmann, D., Erickson, G. A., & Kennedy, C. (1992). Costs and benefits of allegiance: Changes in fan's self-ascribed competencies after team victory versus defeat. *Journal of Personality and Social Psychology, 63*, 724-738.

Hoff, A. E., & Ellis, G. D. (1992). Influence of agents of leisure socialization on leisure self-efficacy of university students. *Journal of Leisure Research, 24*, 114-126.

Howard, D. R., & Crompton, J. L. (2003). *Financing sport* (2nd ed.). Morgantown, WV: Fitness Information Technology.

Iso-Ahola, S. E. (1980). *The social psychology of leisure and recreation.* Dubuque, IA: Wm. C. Brown.

James, J. D. (2001). The role of cognitive development and socialization in the initial development of team loyalty. *Leisure Sciences, 22*, 233-261.

John, D. R. (1999). Consumer socialization of children: A retrospective look at twenty-five years of research. *Journal of Consumer Research, 26*, 183-213.

Kallgren, C. A., & Wood, W. (1986). Access to attitude relevant information in memory as a determinant of attitude-behavior consistency. *Journal of Experimental Social Psychology, 22*, 328-338.

Kelly, J. R. (1972). Work and leisure: A simplified paradigm. *Journal of Leisure Research, 4*, 50-62.

Kenyon, G. S., & McPerson, B. D. (1973). Becoming involved in physical activity and sport: A process of socialization. In G. L. Rarick (Ed.), *Physical activity: Human growth and development* (pp. 303-332). New York: Academic Press.

Krosnick, J. A., Boninger, D. S., Chuang, Y. C., Berent, M. K., & Carnot, C. G. (1993). Attitude strength: One construct of many related constructs? *Journal of Personality and Social Psychology, 65*, 1132-1151.

Krugman, D. M., & King, K.W. (2000). Teenage exposure to cigarette advertising in popular consumer magazines. *Journal of Public Policy & Marketing, 19*, 183-188.

Lobmeyer, H., & Weidinger, L. (1992). Commercialism as a dominant factor in the American sport scene: Sources, developments, perspectives. *International Review for the Sociology of Sport, 27*, 309-327.

Mahony, D. F., Madrigal, R., & Howard, D. (2000). Using psychological commitment to team (PCT) scale to segment sport consumers based on loyalty. *Sport Marketing Quarterly, 9*, 15-25.

Manfredo, M. J., & Bright, A. D. (1991). A model for assessing the effects of communication on recreationist. *Journal of Leisure Research, 23*, 1-20.

McDaniel, S. R. (2002). An exploration of audience demographics, personal values, and lifestyles: Influence on viewing network coverage of the 1996 Summer Olympic Games. *Journal of Sport Management 2*, 117-131.

McPherson, B. D. (1976). Socialization in toe the role of sport consumer: A theory and causal model. *Canadian Review of Sociology and Anthropology, 13*, 165-177.

Moschis, G. P., & Churchill, G.A. (1978). Consumer socialization: A theoretical and empirical analysis. *Journal of Marketing Research, 15*, 599-609.

Moschis, G. P., & Moore, R. L. (1979). Decision making among the young: A socialization perspective. *Journal of Consumer Research, 9*, 101-112.

Moore, J. N., Raymond, M. A., Mittelstaedt, J. D., & Tanner Jr., F. J. (2002). Age and consumer socialization agent of influences on adolescents' sexual knowledge, attitudes and behavior: Implications for social marketing initiatives and public policy. *Journal of Public Policy & Marketing, 21*, 37-52.

Moy, P., Pfau, M., & Kahlor, L. (1999). Media use and public confidence in democratic institutions. *Journal of Broadcasting & Electronic Media, 43*, 137-158.

Newspaper Association of America. (2002). Retrieved February 18, 2004, from http://www.naa.org.

Nichols, W., Moynahan, P., Hall, A., & Taylor, J. (2002). *Media relations in sport.* Morgantown, WV: Fitness Information Technology.

Petty, R. E., & Cacioppo, J. T. (1986). The elaboration likelihood model of persuasion. In L. Berkowitz (Ed.), *Advances in Experimental Social Psychology* (Vol. 19, pp. 123-205). San Diego, CA: Academic Press.

Petty, R. E., Cacioppo, J. T., & Schumann, D. (1983). Central and peripheral routes to advertising effectiveness: The moderating role of involvement. *Journal of Consumer Research, 10*, 135-146.

Petty, R. E., Haugtvedt, C., & Smith, S. M. (1995). Elaboration as a determinant of attitude strength: Creating attitudes that are persistent, resistant, and predictive of behavior. In R. E. Petty & J. A.

Krosnick (Ed.), *Attitude strength: Antecedents and consequences* (pp. 93-130). Mahwah, NJ: Lawrence Erlbaum Associates, Inc.

Petrick, J. F., Backman, S. J., Bixler, R., & Norman, W. C. (2001). Analysis of golfer motivations and constraints by experience use history. *Journal of Leisure Research, 33,* 56-70.

Pritchard, M. P., Havitz, D. R., & Howard, D. R. (1999). Analyzing the commitment-loyalty link in service contexts. *Academy of Marketing Science, 27,* 333-348.

Rose, G. M., Bush, V. D., & Kahle, L. (1998). The influence of family communication patterns on parental reactions toward advertising: A cross-national examination. *Journal of Advertising, 27,* 71-85.

Sage, G. H. (1990). *Power and ideology of American sport: A critical perspective.* Champaign, IL: Human Kinetics.

Schiffman, L. G., & Kanuk, L. L. (2001). *Consumer behavior* (7th ed). Englewood Cliffs, NJ: Prentice Hall.

Schmidt, D. E. (1993). Public opinion and media coverage of labor unions. *Journal of Labor Research, 14,* 151-164.

Schweiger, W. (2000). Media credibility—experience or image? A survey on the credibility of the World Wide Web in Germany in comparison to other media. *European Journal of Communication, 15,* 37-59.

Smith, G. J. (1988). The noble sports fan. *Journal of Sport and Social Issues, 12,* 54-65.

Spiro, K. (2001). Public trust or mistrust? Perceptions of media credibility in the information age. *Mass Communication & Society, 4,* 381-403.

Spreitzer, E. A., & Snyder, E. E. (1976). Socialization into sport: Parent and child reverse and reciprocal effects. *Quarterly for Exercise and Sport, 53,* 263-266.

St. George, A., & Robinson-Weber, S. (1983). The mass media, political attitudes and behavior. *Communication Research, 10,* 487-508.

Swinyard, W. R., & Coney, K. A. (1978). Promotion effects on a high-versus-low involvement electorate. *Journal of Consumer Research, 5,* 41-48.

Snyder, C. R., Lassegard, M. A., & Ford, C. E. (1986). Distancing after group success and failure: Basking in reflected glory and cutting off reflected failure. *Journal of Personality and Social Psychology, 51,* 382-388.

Tajfel, H., & Turner, J. C. (1979). An integrative theory of intergroup conflict. In W. G. Austin and S. Worchel (Eds.), *The social psychology of intergroup relations.* Montery, CA: Brooks/Cole.

Trevino, L. K., Webster, J., & Stein, E. W. (2000). Making connections: Complementary influences of communication media choices, attitudes and use. *Organization Science, 111,* 163-182.

Ward, S. (1974). Consumer socialization. *Journal of Consumer Research, 1,* 1-14.

Wann, D. L., & Branscombe, N. R. (1993). Die hard and fair weather fans: Effects of identification on BIRGing and CORFing tendencies. *Journal of Sport and Social Issues, 14*(2), 103-117.

Wells, W. D. (1993). Discovery-oriented consumer research. *Journal of Consumer Research, 19,* 489-501.

Wood, W. (1982). Retrieval of attitude-relevant information from memory: Effects on susceptibility to persuasion and on intrinsic motivation. *Journal of Personality and Social Psychology, 42,* 798-810.

Appendix A: Measurement Details

Direct Experience

Three variables were used to represent the amount of direct experience participants had with the Cleveland Indians. They were:

How often have you participated in pre-game activities related to Cleveland Indians games? (7-point scale)

Participants indicated whether they had participated in the following activities: attended, watched or listened to an Indians game, read or talked about the Indians, obtained information about the Indians on TV, or listened to talk radio. The possible range of this variable was 1 to 8.

How often have you participated in post-game activities related to the Cleveland Indians games? (7-point scale)

Knowledge

Five variables were used to represent the degree of knowledge. They were:

How much information would you say that you have about the Cleveland Indians? (7-point scale)

How much knowledge do you have about the Cleveland Indians? (thermometer scale)

If you were to list everything that you know about the Cleveland Indians, how long would the list be? (4-point scale)

"Compared to other teams, I consider myself to be an expert about the Cleveland Indians." (4-point scale)

Some students tell us that they consider themselves to be very knowledgeable about some teams. About other teams, they say they have little or no knowledge. How knowledgeable do you consider yourself about the Cleveland Indians? (7-point scale)

Personal Relevance

Five variables were used to represent participants' attention to relevant information about the Cleveland Indians. They were:

Some students tell us that with some sports teams, they pay close attention to relevant information in magazines, newspapers, and on television about the team. With other teams, however, they say they devote little attention to relevant information. How closely do you pay attention to information about the Cleveland Indians? (7-point scale)

How interested are you in obtaining information about the Cleveland Indians? (7-point scale)

When you keep up with the news by reading magazines, newspapers, or by watching television, how closely do you pay attention to stories about the Cleveland Indians? (3-point scale)

How important is information about the Cleveland Indians to you? (thermometer scale)

"I am very interested in information about the Cleveland Indians." (4-point scale)

Social Behavior

Four variables were used to reflect participants' behavior related to the Cleveland Indians. All items were assessed using 7-point Likert-type scales. They were:

How willing are you to defend the Cleveland Indians publicly, even if it causes controversy?
Following the Cleveland Indians is not a high priority among my leisure activities.
It would be difficult for me to be a fan of the Cleveland Indians baseball team.
I support the idea of increasing my free time to engage in activities (i.e., watching, reading, listening, etc.) to follow the Cleveland Indians.

Sports Public Relations: The Strategic Application of Public Relations to the Business of Sport

MARIA HOPWOOD

Abstract

In today's competitive business environment, it is increasingly the case that in order to attract and keep customers and others interested and loyal to the organisation, high quality products and services are no longer enough. Contemporary organisations have come to understand that they can differentiate themselves and their offerings and also gain a competitive advantage by developing the public relations function as part of their communications and relationship building strategies. This same understanding is also true for sports organisations and the promotion of the sport product. The transactions and relationships that exist in all modern sports are frequently of a commercial nature, and it is now the case that "market pressure imposes an instrumental rationality on sporting institutions, just as it tends to do so on the institutions that comprise civil society as a whole."[1] A direct result of the complex nature of contemporary sport and the way in which it has developed into a consumer commodity has resulted in a much greater interest in how sports are managed and organised.

Public relations practice in sport is rarely evident, yet to the contemporary sport business it has much to offer. Research was conducted in order to find out if and how professional sports organisations use public relations. Cricket was particularly chosen because, though not enjoying the same popularity as soccer in the UK, it does have an extremely loyal following and widespread support at a grass roots level. A critical finding from this research is that the communications strategies recommended for use in cricket are equally applicable and can undoubtedly offer the same potential benefits to all sports.

1. Hargreaves, J. (1998) *Sport, power and culture: A social and historical analysis of popular sports in Britain.* Cambridge: Polity Press.

Applying the Public Relations Function to the Business of Sport

"Sport personifies much of what humanity is about: community, the pursuit of physical excellence and the full range of emotions" (Smith and Westerbeek, 2004).

Cricket is one of the oldest team sports which is played and enjoyed with passion the world over. Preston, Ross, and Szymanski (2001) point out that most contemporary team sports were not formally organised until the 19th century, but the rules of cricket were first documented in 1744. Before being displaced by soccer, cricket was the original national sport of England and, in the view of many, it still holds that place. Millions of fans throughout the world follow this sport which, whilst steeped in heritage and tradition, is showing the world that it is at the cutting edge of progressive sport with the diversification into Twenty20 cricket, which is now attracting significant attention in the Southern Hemisphere. It is cricket's innovative philosophy and its proactive approach to sports marketing which was the original impetus for this study.

There can be no doubt that for huge numbers of consumers, sport is of vital importance. Whether they consume their sport as participants or observers, people are spending increasing amounts of time and money in the process of sports consumption. Some sports have far greater numbers of consumers than others, and the compelling attractions of the shopping mall and other leisure pursuits are becoming recognised as powerful competition. Also, it is very obvious that in order for sporting organisations to compete and survive in the marketplace, they have to, whether they like it or not, become much more business oriented.

This paper is a qualitative critical evaluation and analysis of the current level of public relations activity in English domestic First Class County cricket. The paper is the outcome of research which began in September 2002 and which was concluded in April 2003. The basis for this paper is a completed case study of Durham and Yorkshire County Cricket Clubs. These two clubs were chosen as the focus of the research because Durham CCC is the youngest First Class County Club and Yorkshire is one of the oldest—two very different organisations, then, operating in the same industry sector and market place. Both clubs currently reside in the second division of the English County Championship, are culturally and ideologically very different, and, because they are both located in the North of England, are great rivals.

Compared with soccer, and despite being, as far as some are concerned, the original national sport, cricket has not attracted anywhere near the same amount of support and financial backing. As a spectator sport, cricket is facing the fact that the traditional structure of the game does not have wide appeal. The governing body for UK cricket, the England and Wales Cricket Board (ECB), is funding and promoting initiatives to widen the appeal of cricket, from providing cricket equipment to inner-city schools to encouraging greater female participation in the sport. At the professional level, although the National team attracts sponsorship and significant ECB backing, the County teams are finding that in order to remain viable business and sporting propositions, they have to increasingly adopt a strategic vision. A fundamental component of this strategic vision is the creation of successful marketing and communications strategies that will contribute to the bottom line and ultimate long-term survival of the Club.

In today's increasingly competitive business environment, some clubs are realizing that in order to attract and keep customers and others interested and loyal to the organisation, high quality products and services are no longer enough. Contemporary organisations have come to understand that they can differentiate themselves and their offerings and also gain competitive advantage by developing the public relations function as part of their communications and relationship building strategies. This same understanding is also true for sports organisations. The transactions and relationships that exist in all modern sports are frequently of a commercial nature, and it is now the case that, according to Hargreaves (1998) and others, market pressure imposes an instrumental rationality on sporting institutions, just as it tends to do so on the institutions that comprise civil society as a whole.

A direct result of the complex nature of contemporary sport and the way in which it has developed into something of a consumer commodity has resulted in a much greater interest in how sports are managed and organised. The modern perspective of sport is that it has evolved dramatically from its position as an important social phenomenon during the 1960s into its current status as a significant economic and political phenomenon. Now, in the early years of the 21st century, sport is widely regarded as a cultural subsystem of modern society. As a result of the vast numbers of individuals who regularly participate in, watch, or otherwise engage in sporting activities, it has also become big business.

This study was conducted in order to find out if and how professional cricket clubs use public relations. Cricket, though not enjoying the same popularity as soccer, does have an extremely loyal following and widespread support at a grass roots level. The sport does, however, suffer from a serious and long-held image problem, which is proving difficult to reverse and which is undoubtedly affecting cricket's potential to attract essential media and financial support. The England and Wales Cricket Board does have a marketing orientation and disseminates good practice throughout the 18 First Class County Clubs. Each club, however, is responsible for promoting the game at a local level, but it is evident that no unified or consistent promotional strategy currently exists.

Public relations is still considered to be a young profession and, by some, a disreputable activity. However, public relations is proving to be a valuable tool in the organisational armoury, and it is felt that it is of just as much value to the sporting organisation as to the business organisation. Primary research was conducted with marketing and public relations professionals, playing and coaching staff, and sponsorship and media managers. The consensus is that public relations is essential to the future success of the sport, but the reality is that it is not formally implemented to the extent that it should be or, in the opinion of many within the game, needs to be.

It is an accepted fact that professional sport is one of the major profit and loss industries in our contemporary society. At the beginning of the 21st century, the most popular leisure pursuits in the Western world are sports related, involving countless numbers of individuals as participants or observers, and many more in the highly profitable business of satisfying innumerable sports-related needs and wants. Although modern sport's contribution to the global economy is indisputable, it is surprising to learn that, as Horne, Tomlinshon, and Whannel (1999) observe, one striking feature of much sport is precisely the way that it is not organised as a business. The main reason that most sports are seemingly uncomfortable with the associations of capitalism and entrepreneurship is that they remain heavily influenced by their historical developmental traditions.

Modern cricket, perhaps more than most contemporary popular sports, struggles not only with the legacy of its privileged past but also with the fact that it is, in Birley's (1999) words, freighted with extraneous moral overtones. The widespread practice of describing unacceptable behaviour as "not cricket" helps to perpetuate the myth that cricket is the gold standard for the sportsmanlike behaviour that belongs to the age of imperialism and gentility. As a direct result of this legacy, professional cricket has, as Birley goes on to say, struggled to keep pace with the tempo of the age, and has sometimes seemed to be lost in a dream-world of past glories and outworn social attitudes. An outcome of this is that cricket has found regarding itself as a business particularly problematic and, accordingly, provided the main impetus for this study.

Most modern spectator sports, of necessity, operate as businesses and are having to adopt and adapt to the core business functions of marketing, finance, and human resource management. Soccer has long enjoyed success as a business venture, a fact that is borne out by the huge financial sums that have become commonplace in the game. Cricket, on the other hand, has shown a reluctance to express itself in business terms, but has come to accept that if it is to survive and compete for media and supporter attention, it has to modernise and behave as a commercial enterprise. In order to maintain its licence to operate, cricket must regard itself as part of the entertainment industry and compete for its share of the global market. A key objective of this strategy is building and maintaining mutually beneficial relationships with a range of publics, an objective that can only be achieved through the systematic and structured implementation of excellent public relations.

Contemporary professional cricket faces considerable challenges, the most pressing of which is to generate interest in what is seen by many as a game which belongs to a bygone age being played at stuffy and unwelcoming county clubs. If cricket is to have a viable future, it must address its image problems and must become more appealing to a demographically different audience than has traditionally been the case. Public relations, more than the other elements of the contemporary promotional mix, offers a potential solution. UK sport generally and cricket especially have yet to reap the potential rewards offered by adopting a strategic public relations philosophy, yet, as is evident from the findings of this research, where a public relations focus exists, there is much to be gained.

It is encouraging to note that cricket in the UK has undergone some significant developments since this research began and that public relations has played a significant part in these innovations. In June 2003, the Twenty20 Cup was launched, surrounded by some traditional English doubts and complaints from the cricket establishment that such a game was just "not cricket." However, Twenty20 cricket in 2004 is proving to be exactly the kind of product that appeals to a range of different publics, and cricket grounds throughout the country have been reporting sell-out attendances for these games. It is evident that this shorter form of cricket is pumping new lifeblood into the game. The year 2004 saw the first international version of Twenty20, a match played between the England and New Zealand women's cricket teams. In July 2005, Australia played England in the first full Twenty20 international match at Lords, the home of cricket. In order to demonstrate the ever-growing appeal of shorter form cricket in the global sports arena, July 2004 saw the inaugural ProCricket matches being played in the US, and a similar version is being played in South Africa. As well as offering an alternative to the traditional cricket format, Twenty20 is proving to be exactly the type of product extension that the game needs. As Booth (2004) said, "Call it hit-and-giggle if you like. Call it fast food. Call it blasphemy. Just don't call it irrelevant."

Methods

The research interest was to analyse public relations practice in English County Cricket and to offer a strategy for effective, proactive public relations. By using a case study approach, the primary research conducted for this study revealed the extent to which key stakeholder publics in contemporary First Class County cricket understand and utilise public relations. Case studies were written on Durham and Yorkshire County Cricket Clubs, focusing on, amongst other things, issues of regional identity and the differing operational practices of both a young modern club and one that has a long and successful cricket history. Communication and relationship building strategies were analysed, and, by applying key theoretical principles of public relations, insight and understanding were gained regarding a sport that is frequently both misunderstood and overlooked. A key finding from the research is that the communications strategies recommended for use in cricket are equally applicable and can offer the same potential benefits to all sports.

The English are frequently characterised and even stereotyped as being passionate about sport. As well as actively participating in a whole range of sports for leisure and fitness reasons, as a nation, we spend huge amounts of our free time as sport spectators either in front of our televisions and radios, or live at the ground or stadium. According to Cashmore, the contemporary fascination with sport has much to do with the fact that by consuming sport in various ways, we view and do it for nothing more functional than avoiding what we do during the rest of our working week. It is therefore not surprising that sport has, over recent years, become the focus of extensive academic research. A large part of such research has been conducted in the area of sports science, but as the amounts of money to be made in and by sports increase, they and their participants have become lucrative business prospects. As a result, sports marketing and promotions have become and continue to be fruitful and dynamic areas of study.

In the UK, the sport that captures most attention in terms of spectators, finance, the media, and academics is "the national game"—soccer. As a nation, the English are fanatical soccer supporters and, even if individuals are not supporters of particular clubs, the whole country will grind to a halt in order to be able to watch England beat Argentina. The patriotic fervour widely reported in the media during May and June 2002, and the attendant "feel-good factor" that was enjoyed by both business and society during the time that the national soccer team was keeping the country's World Cup glory hopes alive, are both significant illustrators of the power that sport can exert over a vast range of publics.

Although cricket is played and watched all over the world by huge numbers of people, it is only those who are interested in the game who will have been aware of the 2003 Cricket World Cup. It undoubtedly attracted media coverage and offered a whole range of sponsorship and commercial opportunities, but these will all have been to a much lesser extent than is the case with soccer. Cricket generally has been rather slow to capitalise on the enormous potential benefits of customer relationship building, perhaps having a tendency to be somewhat complacent about supporter loyalty. Why is this? What is it about cricket that has given it the perceived status of soccer's "poor relation?" What can be done to get cricket off the back pages and into the lifestyle sections of the newspapers? Why do cricket clubs not attract the same kind of support that soccer clubs do? What role could public relations play in changing attitudes and behaviour towards cricket generally? Such questions and others led to this particular research interest.

Cricket at all levels of the game has received a great deal of criticism in recent years for an apparent inability, even reluctance, to take the requisite steps towards adapting to changing market demands. The sport has also suffered from a serious image problem. One of the aims of this study was to attempt to discover the reasons for such negative associations through both primary and secondary research. It was clear that the only way to get a realistic snapshot of actual prevailing attitudes and practices in cricket was through making personal contact with people involved in the sport. Arrangements were made to interview a wide range of personnel who were associated with cricket in differing capacities, as this would give a broad but representative range of perspectives and views of the game. Respondents comprised public relations and marketing personnel, club CEOs, sponsorship and media managers, players, and coaches.

In selecting individuals to be interviewed, a purposive sample was identified and agreed upon. Visits were made to Durham and Yorkshire CCC headquarters at the Riverside in Chester-le-Street and Headingley in order to conduct personal, face-to-face interviews. Other interviews were conducted over the telephone, as this was more convenient for all the participants. The personal, face-to-face interviews were designed to be semi-structured and open-ended, as it was felt that this approach would generate a more detailed response and would put interviewees more at ease. Interviewees were sent the questions via email in advance of the interviews and were given the opportunity to decline answering specific questions if required. This did not happen and no question had to be changed or deleted. Each of the personal interviews was tape-recorded with the permission of all interviewees, and notes were made during the telephone interviews. All interviews were transcribed and analysed in detail in order to develop and produce a "thick description," which has been useful in establishing the quality of the research. The main advantages of such interviews were that the researcher was able to control the line of questioning and tailor it specifically to the study whilst gathering important information from the interviewee.

Secondary research took the form of consulting a variety of literature sources, namely key texts and journals and other print material. A range of significant key scholarly texts were identified, the majority of which deal with sports from a social science perspective. An extensive preliminary literature search suggested that texts dealing specifically with cricket were few. Most general sports texts tend to have short, though significant, pieces on cricket. The greater majority of cricket-related writing tended to focus on the history and development of the sport or were specifically about cricket clubs or players. A particularly interesting issue is that of cultural identity and its impact and influence on cricket and its supporters. This is an issue which has created much academic interest but with specific focus on soccer. One aim of this study was to take and apply some of these key theories usefully to cricket.

An extensive range of print media, particularly newspapers and special interest magazines, were also used. New media such as online information sources also provided relevant material. Both Durham and Yorkshire have websites, as do the ECB and ICC. CricInfo, a website dedicated to the sport, has an extensive article archive and useful links to a range of alternative information sources which have proved helpful.

In addition, public relations literature and theoretical material was also consulted and applied to the research. Specific elements of public relations theory were appropriate to this study. For example, in determining the extent and application of public relations activity conducted by the two clubs, reference is made to the public relations planning process, communication models and theories, stakeholder and publics theories, and image and identity theories. At no time did it become necessary to adapt or alter the research methodology as the research progressed. As the basic methodology was sound, reliable, and achievable, the quality of the research and its outcomes were in no way or at any stage compromised or threatened.

Results

A key factor to emerge from the research is that public relations is extremely important at Durham County Cricket Club. Vicky Laverick, the club's Public Relations and Marketing Executive, is the personification of the club's commitment to this element of their marketing and promotion strategy, as prior to Vicky's engagement the post did not exist. Durham CCC's approach to public relations is the exception rather than the rule among the 18 First Class Counties. Vicky is one of only a very few dedicated public relations personnel, which is indicative of the widespread disregard for public relations in domestic cricket. Marketing is very much a feature of all the County Clubs and each club has a marketing manager or the equivalent, but public relations tends to be incorporated into the marketing activities rather than being used as a communications tool in its own right. From the research conducted at Durham, it is evident that even here, where there is a keenly proactive approach to public relations, such activity is not always considered to be a priority, and there is a constant struggle for budgets and resources. This apparent neglect of public relations is a risky strategy that must be addressed, particularly as it contradicts the ECB's much more proactive approach to public relations.

The greatest barrier to implementing public relations strategies in cricket is lack of finance. Although the ECB is financially secure, the Counties are reliant on the ECB for funding. However, in order to survive, the clubs have to generate their own income, and largely depending on location and relationships with key publics and stakeholders, some Counties are more financially secure than others. There appears to be a case to answer here that the ECB needs to redress the balance somewhat and allocate specific resources for public relations activity. It is suggested that if cricket were treated more like a business, the ECB could adopt the role of "head office" in overseeing the activities and performances of the "branch offices." More of a corporate approach to public relations would assist greatly in ensuring a better corporate image and identity for the game. This would allow the Counties to continue promoting their regional identity but under the England and Wales Cricket Board corporate umbrella.

It is evident that there is currently a distance between the ECB and the Counties. Any marketing and public relations activity has to be cleared with the ECB before implementation, but visits to the Counties by their governing body are rare. It is also evident that the ECB seems to focus much more on the England national team than on the Counties. This skewed balance was particularly noticeable during the early part of 2003, as very little information had been made available about the new Twenty20 tournament, which was widely regarded among players and officials alike as a resuscitation strategy for the sport. The tournament, which had its inaugural games in June, had, during the writing up of the research, yet to be fully marketed. According to Paul Grayson, this was a tactical mistake. In his opinion, public relations is vital to the long-term survival of the game of cricket, and he cited this particular issue as an example of a typical but disappointing failure to act proactively. This view was further repeated by both James Bailey and Andrew Pratt from Durham, who both held the view that the time to be disseminating the message to the publics was already at hand, but that it was unable to happen because the ECB was still engaged in research and development and a sponsor had not been secured. However, the political wrangles in which cricket had reluctantly become involved at the World Cup rather overshadowed the development of the domestic game—another factor, perhaps, in the argument that ECB focus tends to be directed towards the national team. It is, however, encouraging for public relations practice to discover that much greater use of public relations at County level features as a significant element of the ECB's long-term strategy for the game.

Durham CCC allocates part of the marketing budget for public relations activities because of a perceived need and because the Chairman, Bill Midgley, and the Chief Executive, David Harker, are active, high-profile spokespeople for the Club with personal involvement with a range of key publics and stakeholders. This proactive approach, which is actively encouraged throughout the Club, is being observed with great interest by many involved with the sports promotion. The reality is that much more in terms of practical public relations needs to be done, but certain limitations are imposed which have long-term implications for the survival of both the club and the game. The Club's policy of nurturing local young cricketers by developing them through the Durham academy before they graduate into the First and Second teams is a key element of the club's public relations strategy and one that is well-regarded by the club's supporters and members. Of the 20 2003 playing staff, 14 are from the North East and have been playing together, according to Andrew Pratt, since the age of 13. Durham CCC's attitude to player development is a key strength in that it extends throughout the Club from its programme of coaching youth cricket in the region's schools, through the Durham Schools Cricket Association, which has county representative teams in all age groups from Under 11 to Under 16 as well as women's teams, into the Academy and First teams. The County youth teams receive coaching from the academy coaches and players and specialist coaching is offered to young elite players. Players of all ages are valued and made to feel part of the Club, which is a key element in developing player loyalty.

The resource issue in regard to public relations at Durham CCC needs to be monitored to ensure that financial backing is put into place to optimise the communications efforts. This is clearly something that does not seem to be widely recognised in the modern game. The following comment by James Bailey illustrates this very clearly: "Cricket is such a break even business. One of the main reasons that First Class Counties don't have any PR or even marketing is that it doesn't add to your bottom line immediately. They'll concentrate on selling sponsorship or corporate hospitality, which has a big impact. Durham is a break even business but we're very much focussed on the long-term." The same theme is identified by Vicky Laverick: "There's so much we could do here really, it's just having the resources to do it. We don't have resources to measure the effectiveness of articles printed in particular magazines. If we can't evaluate it, it makes you wonder whether it's worth it. We don't have resources to pay media clippings agencies to scan every publication." The role that public relations has to play in the overall promotion of cricket and, specifically, Durham CCC cannot be overemphasised. Since its inception as a First Class County, Durham CCC has relied heavily on the support of the local spectators and businesses and readily admits that without such stakeholder support, the club will be unable to survive as a going concern.

Of all the First Class County cricket clubs in the United Kingdom, Yorkshire CCC is the club that many would agree, supporters and non-supporters alike, is the most traditional and well-known. Yorkshire CCC is one of the very few sporting institutions which is recognisable to a wide audience, many of whom are not the slightest bit interested in cricket. In fact, Yorkshire CCC, until very recently, was synonymous with cricket, meaning that both "cricket" the word and cricket the sport were inextricably linked with the Club, and the word "Yorkshire" could even be extended as a connotation for the sport. The whole Yorkshire approach to cricket has become legendary. Much of what has been written on that subject together with stories that have grown around some of the famous players through the years has created a mythology about the Club. A key feature of Yorkshire CCC is the fact that it has successfully positioned itself as a corporate brand, something that many of its competitors have still to achieve. An issue worth analysing, however, is how relevant is Yorkshire CCC's mirror image to contemporary cricket and how does this image match the existing actual image?

Yorkshire CCC, unlike Durham CCC, does not have a dedicated public relations professional on the marketing team. In her role as Marketing and Sponsorship Manager, Liz Sutcliffe describes public relations activity as being important, but it is not given specific financial resources. The approach to marketing communications at Yorkshire CCC appears to be very successfully integrated and, like Durham CCC, the income generating focus is not exclusively on cricket. Though there is clearly a place for public relations, other techniques, which are clearly not aimed at the grass roots supporter, seem to be more important at Yorkshire. This is a clear example, which seems to be very common in domestic cricket, of public relations being subsumed or even overlooked in favour of other organisational functions and activities which are perceived as being more lucrative and cost effective. For example, as a method of generating club loyalty and as a lucrative income stream, 2003 has seen a concerted push of hospitality packages which are being promoted using carefully targeted personal appeals. Although hospitality packages are thoughtfully targeted at corporate client publics, which have the potential to be very lucrative, there is a tangible sense that, for the long-term survival of both the Club and the game, it is the younger publics that need better targeting. This is something that is relatively new at Yorkshire CCC, the acceptance that if a younger public is targeted, they can potentially be tied into the Club for a long time. As with the many other First Class Counties, Yorkshire CCC is having to compete for support with local premier league soccer clubs and the recognition that young supporters are much more likely to be attracted to a shorter and more dynamic game is something that the Clubs are having to face up to and accept. With the advent of the Twenty20 Cup, Yorkshire CCC is, like Durham CCC, hoping that this will be product that will fill the gap in the market.

One particularly noticeable characteristic of Yorkshire CCC is that there seems to be a tendency to internalise problems and issues which, in terms of reputation management, is ill-advised. As Hutton et al. (2001) state, reputation management, if it is to emerge as a significant business function, clearly rests on a foundation of what is traditionally termed "public relations." The fact that the Club does not have a dedicated public relations function yet and seems apparently content to rely on history, tradition, and perhaps mythology to assuage potentially damaging image and reputation issues suggests a possible lack of understanding concerning reputation management. It became apparent during the interview with Liz Sutcliffe that current efforts at Yorkshire CCC are more concerned with trying to encourage greater numbers of spectators through the gates for the forthcoming season.

The overwhelming justification for developing a proactive approach to public relations and reputation management is found in Hutton et al.'s findings that a good reputation is fundamental to any organisation's success. It is evident from the research at both Durham and Yorkshire that cricket clubs, which depend upon continual replenishment of supporters for their long-term viability, need to be especially mindful of the implications of ignoring the basic principles of public relations.

Discussion/Conclusion

Recent research into the operation of professional English cricket is unanimous on one particularly incontrovertible issue, which is that the modern game is strategically vulnerable. In 1997, Shibli and Wilkinson-Riddle (1998), among others, detailed a number of observations about the financial strength of the First Class counties which was based upon the 1995 year-end accounts. Despite a number of radical changes being made at every level of the game since the late 1990s—such as the introduction of the 10-match triangular NatWest Series between the national and visiting teams, the central contracting of England players, the introduction of a two-division promotion and relegation competition for the County Championship, as well as one-day National Cricket League and day/night matches—at the game's highest levels, the focus must continue to be on making cricket accessible to a wider audience.

In order to consider how the game can move forward, it is necessary to review a number of observations concerning the financial strength of the 18 First Class County clubs. From research conducted by Shibli and Wilkinson-Riddle, it is apparent that a significant amount of gross income is generated by commercial activities, but this falls far below the amount needed to pay for the core activity, leading to an unsatisfactory situation for all the clubs where the commercial income shows static profitability, a high degree of volatility, and therefore inherent unreliability. With only 34% of gross revenue coming from the England and Wales Cricket Board, lucrative additional income streams are therefore essential to the survival of the county clubs. Shibli and Wilkinson-Riddle's research suggests that cricket's current financial difficulties are a direct consequence of a number of microenvironmental factors. Most significant among these are that county cricket continues to rely upon grant income from the ECB, County Championship matches have not generated enough support from the public, member subscriptions are falling year after year, and commercial income is unlikely to grow sufficiently to present clubs with the necessary financial support. Findings such as these point to the anachronistic nature of cricket management and illustrate the persistent problematic financial situation peculiar to a sport in which most clubs operate at a loss and are, in fact, subsidised by cricket followers. Unlike soccer club directors who embrace such initiatives as share flotations as a way of attempting to raise revenue, cricket clubs have historically relied upon membership fees, gate-receipts, and "general fund-raising rituals," such as bazaars, to keep their club functioning.

The apparent reluctance by those at the sport's highest levels to regard cricket as a business has its roots in the very origins of the modern game. The fact that it took more than 130 years to change the County Championship to a two-division, more competitive tournament is yet a further illustration of the resistance to change that continues to permeate the sport. It is, however, undoubtedly the case that these powerful influences persist and that they regularly provide the ammunition with which to launch, albeit sometimes ill-informed, attacks. It is this persistent and unfortunate image of the game that presents it with perhaps the most pressing public relations challenge of all, that is to create an image that is appealing and relevant to today's more demanding and sophisticated audiences. An emergent fact from the primary research is that although the modern game is proving to be more attractive to audiences with a different demographic to the traditional cricket audience, much more needs to be done. All the players and coaches interviewed were unanimous in supporting the notion of getting close to the people who really matter and giving them more of what they really want to see—a view which was further endorsed by Nicky Peng of Durham CCC, who said, "Crowds want to see big shots and action, we need to encourage people to come and watch. You can see by the Norwich Union League how much the people love it; with coloured clothing and floodlights, it brings a different dimension to cricket." The ECB's recent own market research found that "some groups of consumers felt that there was a lack of buzz and excitement associated with cricket compared to other sports, particularly with the county game. Younger and potentially new cricket audiences made clear that they wanted forms of entertainment with enough excitement to justify the leisure time and money they would invest in purchasing a match ticket." There is clearly a recognition that cricket must continue in its attempts to become much more consumer focussed and that a systematic public relations orientation can help in achieving that objective.

A dominant phrase in the lexicon of contemporary public relations and marketing communications is "relationship building." Public relations practice historically has been directed towards managing communications. However, within the last five years, academics have begun to conceptualise the practice of public relations as relationship management, and research has become centred on critically examining the range of variables that impinge upon organisation-public relationships. The findings of such research continually show that effectively managed organisation-public relationships affect key public member attitudes, evaluations, and behaviours. Actual recent research conducted by Bruning (2001) and also Hutton et al. (2001), though not applied to cricket club publics, is nonetheless relevant. The fundamental tenet of such research is that publics will display long-term loyalty and repeat purchase behaviour to a company, brand, or service if a relationally-based grounding is applied to organisational public relations practice. This theory of relationship building is completely consistent with Grunig's Two-way Symmetric Model of Public Relations, which is characterised as follows:

Purpose	Mutual understanding
Nature of Communication	Two-way; balanced effects
Communication Model	Group ⇌ Group
Nature of Research	Formative; evaluative of understanding
Leading Historical Figures	Bernays, educators, professional leaders
Where Practiced Today	Regulated business, agencies
Estimated Percentage of Organisations Practicing Today	15% (including Durham County Cricket Club)

Characteristics of the Two-Way Symmetric Public Relations Model

The research findings for this dissertation indicate that this model is evident in the communication strategies of both Durham and Yorkshire CCCs but that Durham is more proactive in creating two-way symmetric communication strategies than Yorkshire. The obvious implication of such findings is that there is need for trained public relations practitioners at all First Class County Clubs.

Hutton et al. (2001) state that relationships are of significant importance and relevance to people who are direct stakeholders of the organisation, such as employees, customers, stockholders, and others who usually are the organisation's most important publics. They also make the interesting observation that a reputation is generally something an organisation has with strangers, but a relationship is generally something an organisation has with its friends and associates. The relevance of these findings to cricket clubs and the sport in general is clear. Creating the correct image for both the sport and clubs is necessary and essential, as this will develop the reputation that in turn forms the alchemy which turns strangers into long-term friends and associates. The primary research conducted for this dissertation underpins this theory and is encapsulated in Vicky Laverick of Durham CCC's view that "your company reputation and image is what it's all about, and if you don't have that, it doesn't matter how good your product is. If people think it's rubbish but it's not, there isn't much you can do about it, so you really have to manage your reputation." Proactive relationship building strategies present an achievable critical success factor for cricket. According to Richard Nowell, "Relationship building with all key publics is critical but it is vitally essential to forge relationships with children. The role of the sponsor is to get things for the kids to do, it (cricket) needs to take itself to the public a lot more."

This section began with the notion that for publics to become more widely engaged with cricket, it is necessary for those involved in the game, whether administrators, players, or the media, to communicate all that is desirable about the sport and its teams frequently and consistently. This goes to the very heart of the human communication theories which form the foundations of modern public relations. It is argued here that an acknowledgement and awareness, at least, of the influence of particular communication theories can only assist in the construction of highly effective public relations strategies for cricket clubs. Two specific and accessible communication theories worth discussing in this context are the theories of social penetration and social exchange. Social penetration theory, as originally developed by Altman and Taylor (1973) and analysed by Heath and Bryant (1992), is completely relevant to public relations in cricket quite simply because social penetration refers to the process whereby people come to know one another in varying degrees of detail and intimacy. This theory views the quality of communication—what is exchanged between relational partners—as vital to the development and maintenance of relationships; positive communication produces positive relationships, whereas negative communication results in negative ones. One of the keys to relationship development is what the participants remember about previous encounters with one another. Memorable and positive experiences are critical to all relationship building founded on social penetration theory. Here, the metaphor of "penetration" helps in explaining the idea that cricket club-publics relationships can be developed on the basis of "getting into" and, by association, getting to know each other in order to achieve the mutual understanding of two-way symmetric public relations.

In order for cricket clubs to further nurture lucrative relationships of the kind that have the potential to "draw in" future generations of supporters, an understanding of social exchange theory is necessary: According to social exchange theory, individuals (publics), who are involved in interactions that they want to be positive, define and negotiate what they consider to be required for positive and negative communication, and "agree" on the rules and behaviours required to foster the relationship. Heath and Bryant (1992) state that interpersonal communication is a symbolic process by which two people are bound together in a relationship, provide each other with resources, or negotiate the exchange of resources. This theory, then, sits at the very heart of public relations practice.

A conclusion to be drawn from the aforementioned theories is that many of the relationship-building strategies, which are fundamental to human interpersonal communication, can be perfectly adapted to cricket club-publics relationships. It is undoubtedly the case that both key public members and the cricket club will benefit when public relations activities are managed utilising relational perspectives. It is also extremely likely that when publics are able to feel as though they have a relationship with their club, the halo effect will occur whereby the overall image of cricket as a sport will be greatly improved.

By applying Grunig's situational theory of publics to the concept of relationship management, it is evident that cricket clubs, through a better understanding of how their publics operate, will be able to devise much more effective communications strategies. Organisations need to establish relationships with their publics, and publics seek to establish relationships with their chosen organisation for reasons of mutual benefit. Most publics, which include stakeholder publics such as, in the context of both Yorkshire and Durham CCCs, members, players, spectators, and the local community, are passive. Mutual interest and acknowledgement exists, but for the greater part of the relationship, publics and organisation are content to function without significant formal communication. However, it is imperative that in order to maintain positive relationships, the organisation does not take these publics for granted or overlook them when communication becomes a necessity. Both Yorkshire and Durham CCCs have commented upon falling membership numbers and low gate numbers at matches, particularly the County Championship games. A key finding of the primary research for this study is that there is clear evidence that certain key stakeholder publics in cricket have been allowed to become active—they are actively demonstrating their dissatisfaction with the clubs or the sport in general by not buying into the game. This has clear implications for cricket's future and is an issue that needs to be addressed at the sport's highest levels.

> "As for the future of the game, some very tough decisions need to be made. Cricket is in the entertainment business and has to take its customers very seriously. . . . What does cricket need to do to change people's perception that it is merely a game rooted in the past and no longer relevant to today's helter-skelter society?"

The above statement, which appeared in the February/March 2003 edition of the Cricket Society Bulletin, is an excellent summation of the current state of English cricket. The extensive media coverage of the Cricket World Cup has undoubtedly raised awareness and created interest in and discussion about the game that should be welcomed by all its constituent parties. One of James Bailey's key stated objectives for the game has been met—cricket has been moved from the back pages to not only the lifestyle pages of many publications, but also the front page. It would seem that now is the time to capitalise on people's awareness and to take the opportunity to keep cricket in the public eye.

This heightened awareness of cricket has resulted in some recent important announcements surrounding the game. On March 12, 2003, npower announced its sponsorship of the new Twenty20 Cup. The Durham County Cricket Club website welcomed this announcement with the comment that "we are excited by what the ECB is doing to broaden the appeal of cricket." This is an example of a significant third party endorsement for cricket—the product as npower is already extensively involved with the sport. It is especially significant because in 2002, it became the first Test sponsor to actively market matches to families and children, with designated npower "Lion's Den" areas at the games. This project introduced over 6,500 children to Test cricket.

It is apparent from the research findings that the Twenty20 Cup is regarded as cricket's potential saviour. Everyone consulted during the course of this research was unanimous in their opinion that cricket has to change and that by creating a shortened, fast-paced version of the traditional one-day game, that will last just two hours and 45 minutes and be played under floodlights and in coloured clothing, new publics will be reached and drawn into the game. The Twenty20 Cup is the result of the ECB's own market research, which has proved to be invaluable in helping to develop a more consumer-focused approach to cricket. The ECB anticipates that this venture will yield long-term benefits that will help the game within England and Wales to become stronger at all levels, both professional and amateur. Changing the structure of a game which to many is outdated and irrelevant is an important first step, but it is clear that much more can be done at the club level in developing and maintaining satisfying long-term relationships with a range of existing and intensely loyal publics and the new publics which will be created by the new tournament. A systematic commitment to proactive public relations is undoubtedly the key. A management commitment to ensuring that the function is professionally applied and resourced will be rewarded by the extensive long-term benefits that are the result of establishing and implementing the symmetric public relations model.

It is evident from the research that those involved in the game recognise the need for and actively encourage what Peters and Waterman (1982) refer to as "Staying close to the customer." This is an example of the active symmetrical communication which is practised extensively in what Peters and Waterman termed "Excellent Organisations." Grunig (1992) says that it is only a small leap in logic to conclude that excellent organisations should have an excellent public relations function to manage this symmetrical communication. Durham CCC with its existing commitment to public relations is well on the way to achieving excellence. If public relations is allowed a greater strategic role at the Club, there is real potential here for Durham to enjoy a competitive advantage that will affirm its position as an innovative market leader in the sport. As Richard Nowell from Karen Earl Sponsorship Limited observes, "Durham CC brings innovation to the game in terms of what they are doing as far as PR and marketing are concerned. Many other cricket clubs (including First Class Counties) don't do PR and I feel that this is a big mistake."

Players should be used much more strategically for public relations purposes. Youngsters are attracted to the sport because they want to emulate and get close to the players that they admire. Cricket has the advantage of being much more accessible than other sports like soccer, and identifying and training playing staff to coach young players, as well as making players available on match days to sign autographs and play in the nets, is a cost effective approach to relationship management. In Nowell's opinion, "Players need to understand their role as ambassadors—they need to be consumer friendly. Cricketers have short contracts and are only tied to the county for a few months—building goodwill is important to ensure that players will engage with PR effort. On a local level, you need to get involved with local people. The counties don't have any money so players need to be worked harder in terms of PR. Get players to talk to the media as a way of generating loads of free advertising. Players need media training. Take players to the publics, make them human, get people to relate to them—cricket needs a David Beckham."

Essex CCC's Paul Grayson endorses this view. He feels that it is incumbent on all senior cricket players to engage in "active public relations" and thinks it should be a compulsory part of an international player's training, at all ages and levels. Andrew Pratt refers to situations where players have felt disadvantaged because they did not have the requisite communications skills training and, though "you have to learn from experience," he feels that players are underutilised in public relations terms because they do not have the relevant training and expertise. It is clear, therefore, that the Clubs have the potential to derive significant benefits if they develop their players as public relations tools, which means that they also need to invest players with the skills to become confident media spokespeople. "Cricket has to work a lot harder to get column inches," Pratt says. "Counties are very wary of the media but it's important to give local journalists access to the players. Get to know the media a lot more, build relationships. Durham uses their players for PR—the more interviews players do, the better the club's relationship with the media. Relationship building with media is critical. ECB need to train more players to become media savvy."

Both the cricket clubs and cricket in general must be thoroughly aware of who their publics are and be able to categorise them in accordance with Grunig's (1992) typology of publics. Reference has been made to the fact that, perhaps as a result of lack of awareness or understanding of publics behaviour, key stakeholder publics in cricket have changed from being passive to active, a situation which needs to be addressed and reversed. Acknowledging the existence of active publics in cricket has to be a priority for both the policymakers at the highest levels of the domestic game and the senior CEOs at the cricket clubs. It is imperative, for the future well-being of both the clubs and cricket, that strategies are set in place which allow for both the continual monitoring of publics and the organic adaptation of the organisation. This can be achieved by installing public relations personnel who, by virtue of their profession, perform what organisational theorists call a "boundary" role.

Marketing and promotions are evidently the functions with which the clubs and the sport are most comfortable. The perhaps rather reluctant acceptance that cricket is a business and thus needs to operate as one is manifest in the promotional strategies in place at both Durham and Yorkshire CCCs. However, in response to Nowell's view that "cricket needs to take itself to the public a lot more," a final observation needs close attention. In their research into public relations and marketing practices, Ehling, White, and Grunig (1992) found that both marketing and public relations are important functions for any organisation. However, when public relations was subsumed into marketing, as tends to be the case in the cricket clubs, organisations were deprived of one of those two critical functions. It is therefore recognised that if the public relations function is to derive its optimum capabilities and benefits, public relations departments must exist separately from marketing departments, or if that is not viable, then the two functions must be conceptually and operationally distinct within the same department.

The case for public relations in cricket has been made. The 2003 season saw the most significant structural changes to the domestic game for many years. It seems appropriate, therefore, that the extensive innovations which are beginning to be seen on the field of play are underpinned and optimised by similar innovations in the boardroom. Maximising the obvious potential and benefits of public relations has to be done now in order to secure the future of the modern game.

References

Altman, I., & Taylor, D. (1973). *Social penetration: The development of interpersonal relationships*. New York: Holt, Rinehart and Winston.

Birley, D. (1999). *A social history of English cricket*. London: Aurum Press.

Booth, L. (2004). The spin. *Guardian Unlimited*. Retrieved May 15, 2004, from http://sport.guardian.co.uk/thespin/.

Boyle, R., & Haynes, R. (2000). *Power play: Sport, the media & popular culture*. Harlow, UK: Pearson Education Limited.

Bruning, S. D. (2001). Axioms of relationship management: Applying interpersonal communication principles to the public relations context. *Journal of Promotion Management, 7*, 3-15.

Cashmore, E., (1990). *Making sense of sports* (2ⁿᵈ ed.). London: Routledge.

Cutlip, S. M., Centre, A. H., & Broom, G. M. (2000). *Effective public relations* (8ᵗʰ ed.). Upper Saddle River, NJ: Prentice Hall Inc.

Dunning, E. (1999*). Sport matters: Sociological studies of sport, violence and civilisation*. London: Routledge.

Ehling, W. P., White, J., & Grunig, J.E. (1992). Public relations and marketing practices. In J. E. Grunig (Ed.), *Excellence in Public Relations and Communication Management*. Hillsdale, NJ: Lawrence Erlbaum Associates, pp. 357-393.

Grunig, J. E. (Ed.). (1992). *Excellence in public relations and communication management*. Hillsdale, NJ: Lawrence Erlbaum Associates Inc.

Hargreaves, J. (1998). *Sport, power and culture: A social and historical analysis of popular sports in Britain*. Cambridge, UK: Polity Press.

Heath, R. L., & Bryant, J. (1992). *Human communication theory and research: Concepts, contexts, and challenges*. Hillsdale, NJ: Lawrence Erlbaum Associates, Inc.

Helitzer, M. (2001). *The dream job: $port$ publicity, promotion and marketing* (3ʳᵈ ed.). Athens, OH: USP Sports Press.

Hill, J., & Williams, J. (Ed.) (1996). *Sport and identity in the north of England*. Keele, UK: Keele University Press.

Hill, J. (2002). Sport, leisure & culture in twentieth-century Britain. Basingstoke, UK: Palgrave Macmillan.

Holt, R. (1989). Sport and the British: A modern history. Oxford, UK: Oxford University Press.

Horne, J., Tomlinshon, A., & Whannel, G. (1999). *Understanding sport: An introduction to the sociological and cultural analysis of sport*. London: E & FN Spon.

Houlihan, B. (2003). *Sport and society: A student introduction*. London: Sage.

Hutton, J. G., Goodman, M. B., Alexander, J. B., & Genest, C. M. (2001). Reputation management: The new face of corporate public relations? *Public Relations Review, 27*, 247-261.

Jarvie, G., & Maguire, J. (1994). *Sport and leisure in social thought*. London: Routledge.

Peters, T., & Waterman Jr., R. H. (1982). *In search of excellence: Lessons from America's best-run companies*. London: HarperCollins Business.

Preston, I., Ross, S. F., & Szymanski, S. (2001). Seizing the moment: A blueprint for reform of world cricket. Unpublished manuscript, available at http://www.ms.ic.ac.uk/stefan/.

Shank, M. D. (2002). *Sports marketing: A strategic perspective* (2ⁿᵈ ed.). Upper Saddle River, NJ: Pearson Education Inc.

Shibli, S., & Wilkinson-Riddle, G. J. (1998). An examination of the first class county cricket Championship as an effective structure for producing equivalently proficient Test match teams, *Managing Leisure, 3*, 85-97.

Smith, A., & Westerbeek, H. (2004). *The sport business future*. Basingstoke, UK: Palgrave Macmillan.

Rugby League: A Game in Crisis

JANE SUMMERS
MELISSA JOHNSON MORGAN
MICHAEL VOLKOV

Abstract

This study examines the issue of crisis and reputation management strategies in Australian sporting clubs and finds that not only are individual clubs unaware of the potential impact of such crises on their organizations, but that they also have no training, contingency plans, or strategies to handle crises of any sort either at this or at the national league level. It uses the Australian Rugby League organization as a case study for examining these issues and concludes with several recommendations for improving crisis management and communications policies in Australian sporting organizations and for their stakeholders.

Many public and private organizations prefer to ignore the reality that "bad things" can happen, either through denial of their vulnerabilities or through myopia about their successes and strengths (Elliott, 2002). A crisis can be defined as any problem or disruption that triggers negative stakeholder reaction and extensive public scrutiny (Newman, 2003). Effective crisis management lies in continuous learning processes designed to equip managers with the capabilities, flexibility, and confidence to deal with sudden and unexpected problems or events (Robert & Lajtha, 2002). Good crisis leaders are those who can make fast decisions under pressure and who can keep the big picture consequences of actions and words in mind when making these decisions (Boin & Lagadec, 2000). In 2004, the Rugby league in Australia was both ill-prepared and ill-advised to effectively deal with a sex scandal involving a number of their players on an official club tour. In classic crisis escalation, what should have been a serious but easily dealt with problem became a major reputational and institutional crisis for the league, its sponsors, its players, and its fans.

Introduction

Many public and private organizations prefer to ignore the reality that "bad things" can happen, either through denial of their vulnerabilities or through myopia about their successes and strengths (Elliott, 2002).

Crises by their very nature are unpredictable and varied, and when considering preparing a crisis management plan, firms should anticipate the worst thing that could happen and then make a plan to deal with it effectively (Newsom, Scott, & Vanslyke Turk, 1993). Linked to a good crisis management plan should be a crisis communication plan which spells out the people, the actions, and the processes that will be used to communicate with the press, employees, and other stakeholders in the event of a crisis. Failure to communicate is one of the biggest mistakes made in a crisis situation.

In 2004, the Rugby league in Australia was both ill-prepared and ill-advised to effectively deal with a sex scandal involving a number of their players on an official club tour. In classic crisis escalation, what should have been a serious but easily dealt with problem became a major reputational and institutional crisis for the league, its sponsors, its players, and its fans.

This paper seeks to explore the issues inherent in crisis management and crisis communication as they apply to sporting organizations through a review of the relevant literature in this area. The extent of crisis management preparedness in Australian sporting organizations and the level of knowledge of the role and function of communications in crises management will be reviewed through an extensive examination and review of media commentary relating to this particular crisis. Over 160 different media releases from the popular press, sport commentaries, and news sites both in Australia and from overseas were reviewed in dating from February 22 (the date of the first alleged incident) to July 22, 2004. These commentaries were reviewed in relation to the literature and, from this, several recommendations for improving crisis management and communication's policies in Australian sporting organizations have been proposed.

Literature

A crisis can be defined as any problem or disruption that triggers negative stakeholder reaction and extensive public scrutiny (Newman, 2003). Effective crisis management lies in continuous learning processes designed to equip managers with the capabilities, flexibility, and confidence to deal with sudden and unexpected problems or events (Robert & Lajtha, 2002). Good crisis leaders are those who can make fast decisions under pressure, keep the big picture consequences of actions and words in mind when making these decisions (Boin & Lagadec, 2000), and understand and effectively use communication strategies to manage the crisis. Managers who do not do these things run the risk of escalating the crisis, coming under the scrutiny of the media, having the crisis seriously interfere with the normal operations of the organization, and jeopardizing the reputation of the organization (Fink, 1986).

The key role in any crisis management and crisis communication plan is to be prepared and to have the plan well rehearsed and well known to all key management staff (Shearlean & Lynne, 2002). Essentially the plan should have four main features: (1) to have clearly defined response strategies; (2) to have appropriate resources available and responsibilities assigned; (3) to maintain ongoing corrective action and reactions during the course of the crisis; and (4) to have an evaluation and follow-up stage (Sharon, 1999). We will examine each of these areas in brief.

Clearly Defined Response Strategies

It is generally noted that the quality of initial response by an organization to a crisis will largely determine how much damage a crisis eventually does to the reputation of the organization. A crisis needs to go public within the first three to six hours of the event (Newsome, Scott, &Vanslyke Turk, 1993) and the message that is sent needs to be well considered and prepared. In dealing with the media in a crisis, the way it is handled will largely determine not only how the organization is made to appear but it will also have an impact on that organization's rapport with the media for years to come (Adams, 2000). Organizations have an inertia period of approximately two days where their response to the crisis and their reaction to the media interest in the crisis will largely determine the degree of long-term damage to the organization (see Figure 1).

Organizations with a well prepared plan generally have in place a "telephone tree" which details who calls whom during a crisis and who is the designated corporate spokesperson. Internal communications are also important during a crisis, with senior management needing to clearly communicate the facts of the crisis to staff, as well as the plan for addressing the crisis (Browne, 2003). It is important to have a single voice for the organization with a concise message, and that everyone in the organization knows what that message is and who will deliver it.

Appropriate Resources and Responsibilities

It is important during crises to realize that all staff involved in the organization will need additional support, information, and timely decisions. It is critical to a successful crisis management plan that the appropriate staff are given the time and information needed to adequately deal with the media, to make the necessary administrative decisions that might be required, and to possibly even counsel or support employees. Organisations that do not allocate sufficient resources to this task simply add more stress to the system (Browne, 2003).

Similarly it is also important to have considered the personalities, training, and skills of staff in the preparation of a crisis management and communication plan. One of the key aspects of successfully dealing with a crisis involves successful dealings with media—and there are many people in senior positions in organizations that may not be well equipped to complete this task. Many senior staff have a strong urge to stay out of the news, fearing the criticism and possibly tough questions that are likely to be asked of them, particularly in a crisis (Hadaway & Seidel, 2003). Therefore, allocation of media responsibilities in crisis plans should take account of the training and ability of staff and where appropriate additional training and practice prior to a crisis is advisable.

Maintain Ongoing Corrective Action and Reactions During the Course of the Crisis

When communicating in a crisis situation, the spokesperson needs to have all the relevant information, and he or she also needs to be able to verify the accuracy of that information. It is important that this individual not speculate, make up information, nor discuss potentially sensitive legal or personal details of the situation (Shearlean & Lynne, 2003). Being open and responsive to the media is also important, as this will help to minimize comments that suggest the organization is trying to hide something or that they are evasive in some way. Keeping the media updated with new information, constantly reinforcing what the organization is doing to address the crisis, understanding that no matter what that there will be criticism of the actions and decisions being made, and understanding the audience for your message will all help (Browne, 2003). Organizations in crisis need to adopt a positive "high ground" in attitude to their responses to criticism. There will be many situations where the media and others will try and bait you into being defensive or apologetic. Staying calm, explaining the situation, and what action the organization is taking is the hallmark of a successful crisis leader (Browne, 2003).

Evaluate and Follow-up

Once the crisis has passed it is then necessary to review the performance of the organization and to assess the damage (if any) to the corporate reputation. In the aftermath, you must ensure that any communications reflect the concern and action being taken. It is important to emphasize that the organization has attempted to be fair and transparent in its actions and reactions to the crisis, and to also communicate the steps being taken to ensure that the possibility of a similar crisis occurring is minimized. This might include such things as training, changes to policies and procedures, changes to structures or physical facilities, and so on (Shearlean & Lynne, 2003). Monitoring all media that refers to the crisis to verify accuracy of new information and to correct misinformation as it occurs is also an important part of the evaluation phase.

Finally, the post-crisis stage can also bring with it recurring problems associated with the amnesia syndrome—that is, the belief that as soon as the event is over, everything returns to the way it was before (Boin & Lagadec, 2000). When any crisis hits, there should be a number of fundamental questions asked about how and why the crisis occurred and what needs to be done in the future to prevent its reoccurrence.

A crisis then follows a reasonably predictable path as illustrated in Figure 1, where following a period of inertia in which the organization is given a period of grace and the media and public wait to see what will happen, the organization can react in one of two ways: positively, where they follow the theoretical advice and recommendations mentioned above; or negatively, where the organization does not deal with the media appropriately, nor do they have a well managed plan of response. The negative response will ultimately lead to an antagonistic media coverage, long-term brand damage, and possibly fatal public response and opinion.

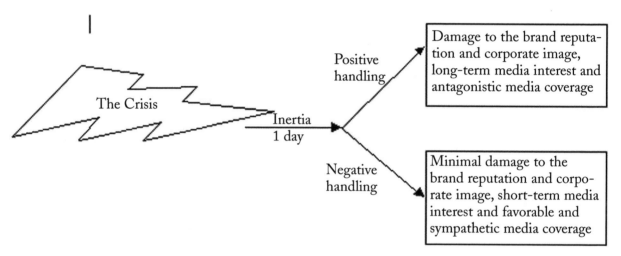

Figure 1. The crisis pathway

In summary then, crises by their very nature are unpredictable and difficult to define. One person's critical incident could be another's crisis. Crisis that involve reputation are the most difficult to contain and require careful and well planned communications strategies. The key to the successful management of any crisis appears to be common throughout the literature: be prepared, be rehearsed, invest in media training, tell the truth, have one central and focused voice and message for the organization, make information widely available and be responsive to media, and, finally, learn the lessons from past crises to help avoid similar problems in the future.

The Crisis Cycle

When we examine crises in organizations, it becomes very evident that there is predictability to the cycle or progression of the crises process. Figure 2 shows this cycle. The solid line in Figure 2 represents the organization's progress and public opinion while the dotted line represents media interest in the crisis and in the organization. It can be seen that when a crisis hits an organization, there will be almost instantaneous negative public opinion and alarm (depending on the nature of the crisis). There will be immediate media attention and a desire to know what has happened and what the organization intends to do about the situation. Following the immediate crisis, the organization then enters an inertia period, as previously mentioned (Figure 1), where both the media and public wait to see what will happen. This is the critical point that will determine whether the organization's progress then follows path A or path B. In path A, the organization cooperates with the media, outlines an appropriate and responsible course of action, and is seen to be taking the "right" action in response to the crisis. In this case, public opinion will gradually return to a more normal level and media attention also begins to quickly wane.

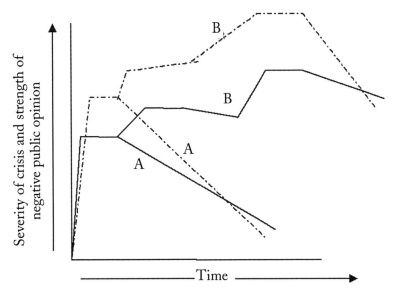

Figure 2. The crisis cycle

When an organization does not handle the crisis well and fails to implement appropriate crisis communications, being both responsive to and receptive to the media, then path B is likely to eventuate. In this path, the negative public opinion will once again begin to escalate and associated media interest will grow. What generally happens in this scenario is that the media will begin to suspect there is more to the story than is being released, and they will be tempted to investigate on their own. This generally results in new information about either the organization, its employees, or the victims of the crisis (if applicable) coming to the public, thus causing new crises for the offending organization, and also causing further damage to public opinion. If this path continues, then the public image fall-out and damage to the brand can leak into the industry in general and other brands within the same product category can be affected.

Thus an organization planning for crises needs to be aware that, if left unchecked, a crisis can escalate dramatically and can drawn in issues, people, and organizations that were not implicated by the original problem. When this happens it is far more difficult for an organization to regain public opinion and brand equity. The tail end of the path line B in Figure 2 reflects this loss of ground in terms of public opinion and also the increased length of time before media interest wanes.

Sporting organizations, like many other organizations that deal with celebrities, have the potential to be exposed to many different types of crises, just by virtue of the celebrity status of their athletes (Chilton, 2002). The adulation and high profile status of many sports people can result in some of them acting "above" the law and failing to appreciate the rules of the "real" world that still apply in their fantasy existence. High profile athletes are often paid large sums of money, given access to other famous people and places, treated like royalty in relation to their wants and desires, and this can all create a situation where their behavior can lead to conflicts with the law and with their sponsors or their organizations.

In this case, we examine the sex scandal that preoccupied the Australian Rugby League code in early 2004, and how both the club and the league handled the crisis. In the analysis, information relating to other sex scandals in sport will be considered, and, in particular, the crisis management and communication plans of the league and the club will be critiqued with suggestions for future "best practice" offered.

Method

This paper follows a particular crisis involving a National Rugby League team, the Canterbury Bulldogs, in Australia, during the 2004 season. The National Rugby League (NRL) has 15 teams in the competition, with the Bulldogs being one of the oldest. The club was established in 1935, and during that time has won 7 premiership titles. In the 2003 season, the club was leading the competition when it became known that they had violated salary cap regulations, and, as a consequence, they were stripped of competition points, causing them to miss out on the finals series and possibly the premiership itself.

The case follows events from 21 February 2004, when news broke that players from the club were accused of gang raping a woman following a preseason game. Through an analysis of media reports and news stories, we trace the club's crisis management procedures and compare them to the theoretical models proposed in the literature. A number of interviews were then conducted with CEOs of various football clubs (the CEO of the Bulldogs declined an interview) about the general management practice in the league in relation to crisis management before concluding with recommendations for this club and other sporting clubs on how to best handle crises.

Results

A timeline of news stories is provided chronicling the escalation of public sentiment in relation to this crisis, and the crisis cycle is used to assist the analysis. Extracts and comments from these news reports show how poor handling and poor communications processes exacerbated the crises and caused it to spread to the league in general and then to other football codes.

Day 1. The Crisis Occurs 21 February

The story breaks in major national newspapers and on other electronic media that an alleged rape has occurred after a preseason game with six players from a national rugby league team—The Bulldogs. In addition, press reports suggest that a number of players had been on a drinking binge at three venues and had also been fighting with locals.

Days 6 – 11. Inertia Stage

During this stage, nine new news stories appear in major daily, weekend, and national papers. The first reaches the public announcing an inquiry into the matter by the NRL league. The league chairman is quoted as saying, "We are conducting our own investigation into what happened at **** last weekend. We in no way intend to interfere with what the police are doing. It is clear that there are some matters outside the central allegation and outside the police investigation that are of concern to the NRL." He is also noted as being concerned with the image of the game on the eve of the season kickoff and the need to obtain an independent view of the events.

The woman who made the rape allegations will have her evidence videotaped as she re-enacts the events on the night of the alleged attack. She alleges that players forced her into group sex and threw her into the swimming pool at the resort where the club was staying. The club's players have given their version of events, which are noted to have done more damage than good, as they admitted to group sex and drinking during the weekend. Bulldogs spokespeople are angered that comments have been made to the media by players when they had been specifically told not to talk to "outsiders."

Other news stories provide comments by reporters that the Bulldogs involved had "been on the defensive," with all stating that any sex that was had was consensual. Players had been advised not to talk to the media, but many ignored that demand, admitting to wild parties and group sex during this preseason weekend. Even more damaging were comments from players that this was just a typical night for the players—one quote in particular went, "Some players just love a bun (woman who engages in group sex). Gang banging is nothing new for our club or most other clubs in the league." Further players were noted to have described the woman as a "scrag."

The NRL chairman was quick to voice disgust at the "gang banging" comment. The chairman of the Bulldogs was also quoted as not condoning those actions. Further on in this article, it also noted that a similar incident occurred with this club in the same preseason situation 12 months earlier and no charges were brought. There were also comments from other players in the league that it was the fault of the sport and the fans that this sort of thing happened. Players are paid large sums of money, they are idolized and live a fantastic lifestyle and could sometimes make behavior decisions that were outside the bounds of "normal" behavior. They couldn't help themselves.

The NRL spokesperson suggested that the league has been attempting to control and minimize the likelihood of these incidents by holding seminars lecturing players on avoiding dangerous situations (which includes young women eager to flirt with players) and by employing security guards to accompany teams. The chief of the league expressed a desire to see the gossip and media discussion about the incident stopped and "hoped that sufficient measures were in place to put an end to the sex scandals." An education and welfare committee would be looking to investigate the protocols for clubs for away games, and he called on clubs and players to focus on their responsibilities as role models in football and the community.

In spite of this discussion regarding whether the players in question did or did not rape the woman, there were also comments appearing in the press from sport commentators calling for some concrete reaction from the league and the club in relation to these players more so from the perspective that they had clearly breached the club's code of conduct, with up to 11 clauses and sub clauses noted that these players had potentially breached. Why hadn't the club disciplined these players in light of these conduct breaches, regardless of the actions of individuals in relation to the alleged rape? Players were noted to have clearly broken the rules and should face heavy fines and suspensions.

Other news commentators began to voice the concern that a couple of the club's sponsors may be getting "itchy" feet at this stage. It was particularly noted that charities were reconsidering their association with the Bulldogs club after allegations that group sex was a common practice. One charity source was quoted as saying, "They were paralyzed by the scandal and felt that this was just the tip of the iceberg in sport generally." The incident overshadowed the season launch of the league and the marketing department for the NRL seriously considered pulling a commercial, specifically targeted at women, due to the current climate, however logistically impossible this was at such a late stage of the campaign. Most of the new season ads were aimed at 18- to 25-year-olds, families, and women, because it is known that women comprise 40 percent of their market. There are now questions about the long-term impact of this case on that sector of the market.

Days 12 – 15. Negative opinion and media antagonism begins to surface

Twenty more stories appear in this period from major national and international papers. A number of online news services and sport information services have also picked up the story and are making comments. Talks of crisis meetings at the Bulldogs club and police interviews with the players at the centre of the scandal begin to circulate. The club chairman makes the suggestion that this type of behavior is not to be tolerated and, if found guilty, players will face heavy fines, suspensions, or possibly dismissal, but no action will be taken at this stage. In carefully addressing the club's lack of action, he quotes legal advice and reinforces that the club does not condone violence, threats, victimization, intimidation, or the humiliation of women. Further investigations are also opened into allegations that a woman making the same complaints 12 months earlier had been discouraged from taking her case further. There are comments about the possible loss of sponsors and fans and possible loss of government funding for the NRL depending on the outcome of the investigations. To make matters worse, on the same day, players who are to be interviewed by the police are photographed attending the meeting in thongs, t-shirts, caps, and sun visors—no club uniform was worn by any player. Comments about the club's checkered 2003 season with salary cap breaches and large fines are raised again in most media commentaries.

The NRL considers removing all images of the club in question from the $3.5 million advertising campaign, but is unable to do this completely. Wherever possible, club representation is removed—particularly in the ads targeted at families. Experts agree that these ads will not address the fundamental image problem now facing the league. It is only the behavior of players that can now go some of the way to undoing the damage done. In the short term, the club and the league prepare for loss of sponsorship. Comments are also noted by the NRL chief about the lack of action taken by the league against these players and his call for calm and understanding until the end of the police investigations.

In the short time thereafter, more comments are made concerning the police interviews and the new information that the Bulldogs club held "truth" meetings before meeting with the police, where players aired their version of events in front of each other to give them all the opportunity to hear what everyone else had to say. Questions are raised about the quality of the personal player interviews following this meeting. The "group" story clearly paints the woman in question as the lustful initiator of multiple sexual encounters—all consensual. Criticism is also leveled at the police, who failed to interview the players individually immediately after the assault was reported. Players have been instructed not to talk to outsiders about the case. The report from the NRL investigator into general player misconduct finds no evidence that players misbehaved against female patrons on the evening of the alleged rape.

Calls begin to appear that it is the responsibility of the clubs to educate young players that ignoring community standards degrades them and the sport that they play. Team bonding sessions are not good forums and these rites of initiation are not acceptable in modern society. Why were the players out drinking anyway, and where were the club's managers? The media comments further that perhaps the coach's arrogance and the club's tolerance of this behavior have somehow contributed to the problems and culture of the club. On the club's website, for example, under the headings of Born, Height, Weight, Test Matches, and Personal notes, all the coach could summon was "unknown."

New allegations come to light at this stage with a woman claiming sexual assault in early February by two players from another NRL club. Police investigate this one as well. It is also found that the chief executive of that club knew of the allegations and decided not to inform the national league. More media comments appear concerning a heated exchange between this person and the chairman of the NRL.

The chief of the NRL is noted as looking "drained, even hollowed out." However, articles appear in which he seems to be trying to calm down talks of a crisis in the league, and in which he begins to talk of the future and of making the game even better after these events have subsided. However, other commentators note the reviews being made by a number of sponsors of the club in question and the league in general with millions of dollars at stake. Professional sponsorship companies also worry, with some citing this scandal as a negative for everyone involved in sports sponsorships because these allegations highlight the uncontrollable nature of sport—and this is a factor that sponsors will now consider carefully. Reports of similar sex allegations from sports around the world are also now being reviewed, with comparisons to Kobe Bryant and members of a number of Premier League Soccer clubs. Some also suggest that the female market segment may also shrink with these types of allegations becoming more common.

One report also notes that the NRL has employed a female university journalism lecturer to counter the perceived culture of misogamy in the game. One player refuses to give DNA samples, citing it a violation of his civil liberties and against his religion. As this player does not drink and insists he was in bed at the time of the alleged assault, the club supports his stance.

Comments appear in general media from NRL players and other clubs that the players are the real victims in this scandal. The story being pushed is that the players are mostly good, God-fearing blokes who unfortunately sometimes fall prey to women out to make trouble for them. Most commentators of course have scathing sarcasm in response to this view. However, we now also see news stories about the families of the other players in the club that were not implicated in the alleged rape and how they were tucked up in bed at the time. The stories discuss the discomfort and anger they feel at their men being smeared with this scandal. Other players in the league also comment on how this is affecting them, and how people are making nasty comments to them because they are NRL players.

Another player—the captain of the national rugby league team—at a media lunch to launch the new season, makes a distasteful joke (in front of TV cameras and the press) about the sex scandal. He apologizes to all through the national media, citing a lack of judgment and expressing genuine remorse, and is spared further punishment.

The prime minister is quoted as expressing his sorrow for the fans of the rugby league after their sport has been "gutted" by the recent sex scandal. He stresses that if a crime has been committed then people should pay the full penalty, but people should be presumed innocent until proven guilty. The bulk of people who support this sport are decent people who care about their sport, their families, and their country, and this is a positive that we should focus on.

Other articles comment on the difficult times for the club, the edginess of sponsors, and the return of the board of directors of the Bulldogs club at the AGM.

Days 16 – 20. New crisis point reached and continued negative public opinion and media interest and attention

Media attention continues to be high, with 16 new stories appearing in major daily and national papers. The media has started to dig for more information about the club's history and player transgressions. The Bulldogs club loses two of its major sponsors, resulting in a loss of revenue of about $650,000. Both organizations cite overwhelming pressure from their customers and fear of an impact on their brand image through continued association with the club. The club expresses their sadness at the decision but offers no other comments.

From the media come comments that most people thought that the issues raised by the sex scandal in February would subside after a week (the usual span of sports scandal) and yet after two weeks there appears to still be plenty of interest and plenty of news. Apart from the inept handling by the club of the incident and inappropriate comments made to the media by players, it appears that new allegations of sexual assault by two players from another club have kept up the media's interest. Added to this is the national television news story on "60 Minutes" in which the woman who alleged sexual assault from the same club 12 months ago is interviewed and her story aired. Commentary is also quick to include the fact that Australian sports people are not alone in the world when it comes to sex scandals; however, it seems that the media is always interested in them and all the sordid details.

The club then releases a copy of a letter of support from the manager of the hotel where the alleged rape took place. In his letter the manager commends the behavior of the players and also notes that players were not drunk and disorderly, that there were no fights, and that he was unaware of any other incidents in relation to player behavior.

A third sponsor leaves the club stating, "With the adverse publicity we don't want anything to do with the club." This sponsorship was worth $100,000 to the club. Police are still calling for information to assist in their investigation, stating that a seventh player was seen walking away from the area where the attack took place and that they would like to talk to this player.

The chairman of the club doubts that this player exists; however, if this is the case, then that player should come forward and give evidence. He also insists that he is "laying down the law," vowing that any player who is found guilty of the assault will not have a future in the club. He cautions that the players should be considered innocent unless proven guilty. The club's website has been flooded with comments from both fans calling in their support and from others calling for more action by the club.

Others in the league call for the NRL to get tough on players' off-field behavior to limit the number of possible incidents like this one. There is a call for the club to punish the players, even if cleared of the assault charges, for breaching the club's code of conduct and for bringing the game into disrepute.

A school in the heart of the Bulldogs' club territory requests that another competitor club conduct a junior development coaching clinic planned for the school after concerns about the sex scandal intensify among parents and school authorities, who ultimately deem the club's culture inappropriate for children. The principal of the school cites overwhelming parent support for distancing the children from these players while the investigation is underway. In the same report, another minor sponsor has also left the club while another sponsor requests more control in the contract to allow them to exit if the police investigations result in criminal charges against players.

Another article cites the cancellation of a rugby league linked schools extravaganza which is to be held in Sydney in April. Up to 1,000 school children were to be involved, but Department of Education officials have abandoned the idea following the sex scandals in the NRL. External sports commentators are now suggesting that poor player conduct has been a time-bomb waiting to explode for years and that this is all too common in many sports. For too long players have been getting away with blue murder, and clubs have turned a blind eye because of the players' ability on the field. In many cases, the behavior tolerated in the clubs would be revolting to normal people. The NRL announces a program of education courses relating to community standards, racial vilification, sexual discrimination, and harassment for officials, coaches, and players. While this is seen as a good idea, many question why it is necessary at all. Why don't these players know what decent behavior is?

Days 21 – 26. Continued negative media attention and general public support begins to wane

Twenty-four new stories appear during this period, with media interest still high. More allegations of sexual assault appear in relation to other clubs and the scandal begins to spread to other codes and other teams in the league. The NRL chief comments that the sex scandal has damaged the game and has focused the media spotlight on the off-field behavior of players. One of the lessons learned is that the media cannot be blamed for the problem and that clubs need to work more proactively with the media when problems occur. At this time, there are still no results from the police investigation.

The second NRL club to face sexual assault allegations is also confident that the club will recover; however, their chief executive officer announces his decision to stand down. He insists that this is a decision he has been contemplating for some time and has nothing to do with the sex scandal.

More sexual assault claims are laid against footballers from a different code (Australian Rules Football – AFL). Two women claim assault of a serious nature which are denied by the players. A review of the NRL sex scandal case (which is still under police investigation three weeks after the event) is also given. Talk begins to circulate about a national television broadcast in which a woman will be interviewed about an alleged pack rape by AFL players a few years ago. The woman did not go to the police at the time. The producer of the program says that the purpose of the show is to determine whether there is an endemic problem within the football codes regarding attitudes toward women.

The mother of an 18-year-old intellectually disabled girl claims her daughter was gang raped by four rugby league players the previous month. This information is aired on another national television show and police investigate the claim. Meanwhile the state crisis centre manager states that a number of women claiming they had been sexually assaulted by footballers had called the centre following recent allegations involving NRL players.

Stories appear in relation to the claims about AFL players. The police are investigating and the club has condemned the action if proven to be true. The club in question has a history of off-field misbehavior by players, and this is a culture that the current president and coach are trying to change. The AFL says it is approaching SBS to get more information about claims aired last night on their national broadcast. The Chief of the AFL expresses his disappointment with the allegations and a strong desire to work with the police to resolve the issue. He also criticizes SBS for its reluctance to hand over information in relation to claims made on their program. He urges other women who feel they may have experienced abuse at the hands of the AFL to come forward to the AFL as their first port of call.

Two of the club's main sponsors review their involvement with the club and ask for a detailed briefing about the club's position and the players' involvement.

The coordinator of the Melbourne rape crisis unit comments that it is not unusual for women to complain they had been raped by professional footballers and other sportsmen. There is a culture within sport that allows sexual violence against women, and the sports are complicit in letting that culture continue. AFL has now fallen into the cesspit occupied for the past month by rugby league, and, even if it emerges, the mud will remain caked over it. From an external commentator's perspective, most worry that the club did not express any concern for the women involved. Their statements stick clearly to the letter of the law and show concern only for the image of the club and the reputations of the players. They do not seem to have any compassion for the alleged victims and obviously see this as an admission of guilt.

The woman who claimed she was sexually assaulted by a group of NRL players has identified the players from club photos. A taxi driver who took the woman and an unnamed player to the hotel on the night in question is also re-interviewed by police. It is also announced that the woman was argumentative outside a nightclub before leaving to go to the player's hotel. Players waiting for taxis are seen to reject her advances and it is stated that the woman had had consensual sex with a player in the nightclub earlier in the evening.

The club's football manager is sacked today by the board because he allowed players to publicly present themselves at police interviews wearing thongs and T-shirts. He is also stated to have failed to ensure that the club's code of conduct was observed at all times during the team's ill-fated trip in the preseason. On two occasions, players presented themselves at the police station dressed casually despite a management directive to wear more appropriate attire. They were also two hours late for their appointments. The players involved would also be fined by the club. Police announce they are still investigating claims of a gang rape against an 18-year-old intellectually disabled girl by rugby league players. These players are not affiliated with any national club. The mother complains that these men "competed" as they raped her daughter, and this takes the actions of football players to a new low.

More speculation circulates about the NRL gang rape scandal, with rumor and comment about what happened still under discussion. One article announces that this is the football sex scandal that won't go away. Clubs in all codes are attempting to reinforce to players their expectations for behavior and treatment of women; however, one club president has announced that the problems facing the league are caused by predatory women who target footballers. Further, these footballers are often young and inexperienced without the emotional maturity to make decisions, and, when you add alcohol into the mix, then you are just asking for trouble.

A multi-million dollar sponsor of the AFL will quit the sport if the sex scandals continue. The club is currently playing a wait-and-see game, and sponsors are waiting for the results of the police investigations. The majority of the players are outstanding people and leaders in the community—we shouldn't let the behavior of a small number tarnish the good work of all the others.

Days 26 – 30. Action taken but the impact of the crisis spreads to other clubs and other football codes

Media interest remains high, with 39 new stories appearing in this period. The AFL states that women are important to the league, with almost 50 percent of club memberships and attendances being made up of women. In May, there will be a summit about the role of women in the AFL, and there is mounting pressure for the league to appoint a female commissioner. While the AFL has generally had a relatively clean reputation and has done little to offend its family target audience, they still have skeletons in the closet. The AFL appears to have done a better job of educating players and the culture of group sex is not as common; however, under-the-counter payments and bribes are issues that can also impact the league's reputation. Also of concern is the lack of interest or compassion for the women at the centre of all these allegations. A back-page story in one newspaper the day after the police announced their investigations pondered whether the two players would be available for the first game of the season on that weekend. Is this really all the fans care about?

The NRL is noted as having its greatest public relations disaster, and allegations from the club in question have only served to entrench the feelings and prejudices of many about the behavior of rugby league players in general. Another article comments on the culture of the NRL as repulsive, with players swaggering into police stations in beach gear, the Australian captain so insensitive that he makes a tasteless joke, players make foul-mouthed statements wearing T-shirts designed to provoke and trivialize the incident. Supporters defend the code with unsophisticated and crude arguments that ignore facts and common decency. Players note that group sex is common; there are reports of clubs making payments to ensure that unseemly matters do not make the headlines. One club manager says he gets 50 phone calls a week complaining about footballer's behavior. Players, their management, officials, and the media are all at fault because victory has always been put before virtue—hush everything up to keep the star on the field. These clubs think that they are above the law, and it is no wonder then that the players think the same thing. But perhaps this is the dawn of a new sporting culture—maybe the new generation will stop the drinking, gambling, and groupie mentality, and both players and clubs will not need special training in how to behave?

A former NRL club manager sacked for not enforcing club code of conduct will bring legal proceedings against his club this week. The players in question have all had suspended fines for their lack of dress standards.

The chief executives of both the AFL and the NRL meet this week for crisis talks about the sex scandals. They discuss strategies to assist in these situations. While the chiefs of each league have been praised for their open and accountable approach to the claims, some players in the NRL have been less than helpful both with the police and the media. There is some discussion about various AFL clubs paying large sums of money to women accusing players of rape so that they wouldn't take their cases to the police or the media. Both leagues state that they are doing everything possible to educate players to their responsibilities; however, at the same time, most people know what is right and wrong and have their own values, and there is not much the football club can do about that. Some footballers are idolized, and hero worship has its own drawbacks for players.

The chief executive of the NRL club at the centre of the sex scandals resigns. The police investigation continues. The club and the league reluctantly accept the resignation, calling him an honorable man. The club needs a new era of accountability and nepotism, and reluctance to answer to community standards will not be tolerated. It appears that this is the price for attempting to discipline players and for sacking the club manager for their roles in the sex scandal that has been plaguing the club for six weeks. As the club's CEO, he absolutely defended the players in relation to the scandal, but 10 days into the affair he became shocked by reports about his players' behavior, including the consensual group sex that was supposedly a common part of their off-field behaviour. He breaks ranks and notes that this attitude is appalling to his family values and his faith and he couldn't condone it.

One commentator notes the responsibility for the media to report sport as it is and to call on-field violence and off-field gang rapes crimes, rather than treating them as some form of macho sporting activity. This then may go some of the way to improving the image of modern professional sport and give our young people a more balanced view of right and wrong.

Rape scandals show no sign of abating with another eight cases of alleged gang rape reportedly set to become public within weeks. Two more AFL clubs are set to be put in the media spotlight and nine players from these clubs are accused of gang raping two women at a nightclub.

More news about the resignation of the NRL club's CEO and his acceptance of responsibility for the incident which has cost his club over $600,000 in sponsorship as well as fines from the league. Other reports surface that the players are running this club and that they are responsible for the CEO's resignation, as they were unhappy with his decisions regarding the sacking of the manager and penalties applied to players. Officials of the club are concerned by the financial impact of the disaster with lower attendances and less sponsor support.

A large number relate fresh claims of gang rape against AFL players. Comments are made that the first NRL incident has sent shock waves through all football clubs, with all scrambling to minimize the damage to their reputations.

One insider comments on the difficulty juggling egos and economics where the demands of old-guards football boards and new-style business are often in conflict. The resignation of three top football administrators in 10 days raises many questions. The NRL club at the centre of the storm adopts the old-guard approach, which is to kill the messenger and blame the media for the firestorm. The circle the wagons approach takes no account of modern business practices or of modern crisis management theory. While many question the club's decision not to name players involved nor discipline them for breaches of conduct, the result is that many executives are unable to satisfy the multitude of demands of pampered stars. The NRL club in question is now saying that its players engaged in immoral acts which were not illegal and that this may cost some of these players their careers.

If the sex scandal was not enough, the NRL club now faces allegations of recreational drug use claiming that prominent players from the club tested positive for cocaine use last year and the club simply imposed a fine. The club is under no obligation to name the player involved and all clubs have different policies on how to handle this issue. The second NRL club to be named in the sex scandal has continued their investigation and have been said to have cooperated fully with police

Days 31 – 34. New crisis shocks the club and the league and public discontent and dissatisfaction spreads

New crises hit the Bulldogs club and 10 new stories appear. Media interest begins to wane, with public opinion reaching a low point. Players from the NRL club alleged to have gang raped a woman in March now stand accused of testing positive to cocaine use.

More general comments are made about the ongoing police case and the allegations of drug abuse by certain players, plus a call from club officials and supporters for players and the club to get their act together. More comments about the disastrous publicity for both the NRL and the club in question, and about how the new drug abuse scandal is threatening the future of both the club and the league.

The news reports a violent brawl in the crowd supporting the NRL club at their game over the weekend. The NRL is threatening to ban all Bulldogs supporters and to fine the club for the violent behavior of their fans. Extra security will now be provided at all Bulldogs games and, if this happens again, the club will be taken from the league.

A few independent sports writers claim that as each day passes, more victims come forward and more poor off-field behavior is reported. Even if only half of these allegations are true, there is a serious problem in the code, and the question is asked, "Will this stop women supporting the code and allowing their daughters to support it as well?" The way we treat our young professional footballers has contributed to this attitude toward women and to the acceptance of this behavior. They are paid large sums of money, told they are elite athletes, and we treat them like national heros. Over time they begin to believe that they exist in a world beyond the law and beyond normal social behavior. Players are also arrogant, believing that they will not get caught when they do engage in inappropriate behavior. The only way to address this is for the clubs themselves to get serious. Clubs need to take a good look at the culture which has created this monster and, if not addressed, then football will never be the same again.

More comments are made about the Bulldogs club and their fans disappointing behavior—comments that fans and others are getting sick of the NRL not taking any action against players in the sex scandal from earlier in the season. The Bulldogs have been penalized four competition points for their fans behavior.

Days 35 – 51. Some positive action taken but more public discontent and comment about lack of general action and lack of interest in the larger issues

Media interest continues to wane even though the Bulldogs appear to be taking some positive action at last. Only 12 stories appear during this phase. A new chief executive officer is appointed for the Bulldogs club, and he is committed to changing the club's current culture, including one of secrecy with the media.

The families and wives of the Bulldogs players implicated in the sex scandal are interviewed. The shameful culture of the change room, where women are mere playthings and the sports star is both greedy and lacking in moral responsibility, is discussed. The club, in addition to problems with its culture, has also failed the public relations test with contempt for community standards. The culture where players expect and usually get everything for free is well known and promoted. Group sex and sharing and keeping score of sexual conquests are considered to be a normal part of football activity—but do the sponsors and the fans really support this notion and how do parents feel about these men being role models for their children?

The national footy show, which highlights issues relating to NRL in a humorous way, finally addresses the Bulldogs issue and the larger issue of sex and violence in the code and the fact that this club has had a particularly bad history with crowd and fan violence. However, the issues of too much money, too much alcohol, and too much time are not tackled.

It is discovered that another NRL club used players to judge a bikini pageant at a local night club, and women's rights groups comment that this sends exactly the wrong message to the community and the club just isn't taking these issues seriously. The club insists that their involvement with the pageant was at the request of one of their sponsors, and that it was all strictly above board. The new CEO of the Bulldogs takes on the old culture and vows to clean up the club's image and players' off-field performance. There is more general discussion about the issues of the last month and the lack of a decision by police about the outcome of the investigation hanging over the heads of the Bulldogs club.

The NRL withdraws sexy merchandise after feminists warned that it was tacky and could further alienate female fans. Images on the website show women exposing their breasts, and they could be downloaded onto mobile phones. There are general negative comments about the NRL and the Bulldogs club and the decision by the NRL to withdraw the sexy merchandise. Some say the NRL and the club have failed to learn the lessons of the last couple of weeks.

The Bulldogs announce that any players charged over the sexual assault issue earlier in the season will be stood down immediately. There is also general discussion about the club's woes and problems with the board in terms of their inability to control player behavior. The Bulldogs sign a new sponsor to replace the two major sponsors who left following the sex scandal earlier in the season.

Days 65 – 66. Police findings released, club again in trouble with the media, and fresh negative issues emerge

Even though this represents the official end to the crisis, media interest is low with only nine stories appearing in major newspapers. No international papers break the news. The police findings are announced with no players charged over alleged gang rape earlier in the season. While the police investigation suggests that a sexual assault had taken place, there was not enough evidence to charge players. The Bulldogs club has responded to the announcement with a "us-against-the-world" tone suggesting that this was full vindication and players were even demanding front-page apologies. None of this shows that the club had recognized the larger problem with the league and their behavior. The NRL immediately fines the six players involved with breaches of conduct and for bringing the game into disrepute totaling $500,000. The NRL chief apologizes for upsetting the public with comments in relation to the police findings in the sex scandal. Writers state that the NRL doesn't "get it" and that their behavior is a classic example of the problems facing the league and football in general.

Discussion

Theoretical models suggest that when a crisis hits, there is a window of opportunity when the organization can, and should, react decisively and positively with the media—the inertia stage. This stage can last up to a couple of days, depending on the particular crisis and the availability of information. Following inertia, public opinion can either become supportive and positive, or it can turn negative and antagonistic. Organizations who are defensive and uncommunicative with the media often find this is the result. Being open and responsive to the media helps to minimize comments that the organization is trying to hide something or that they are evasive in some way (Browne, 2003).

As we can see by the press comments in the first few days of the Bulldogs crisis, their reaction to the problem, their lack of sensitivity to the alleged victim, and their aggressive stance with the media resulted in the negative path (path B in Figure 2) being taken, the consequence of which has been antagonistic press coverage, loss of brand image, and negative sponsor and public support. In addition, their response has also resulted in the league itself being drawn into the crisis and, in turn, suffering associated brand damage. Worse still in this case, the sport of football in general has also been implicated by the negative impact of the crisis and has also been tarnished with the negative brand image.

The literature also suggests that in order for a crisis management strategy to be successful, a clearly defined response strategy is required where everyone in the organization knows who is responsible for what and what actions need to be taken. In the case of the Bulldogs, there was no clearly defined strategy and, further, players and management did not appear to have a clear notion of who was to speak with the media and who wasn't. This resulted in different stories being released to the media, an aggressive stance being taken in relation to media, and a perception that the club lacked sensitivity as to the seriousness of the issue.

The next most important element in a crisis plan is to have adequate resources available to manage the crisis and to allow the spokespeople for the organization to investigate the issue and report appropriately. In the case of the Bulldogs, it appears that limited resources were allocated as the club gave the media the impression that the crisis was really not a significant one and, further, that there was no additional information to be gained from continuing any investigation. Once again, the lack of sensitivity to the victims and the lack of appreciation of public opinion in relation to the crisis caused the club's actions to be perceived in a very negative light.

As highlighted in the literature, organizations need to maintain ongoing corrective action and reactions during the course of the crisis. In the case of the Bulldogs, the public and the media became increasingly frustrated with the apparent lack of action taken by the club toward the players involved, regardless of their legal situation. People wanted to see some form of justice done; to see the players implicated suspended because of their contravention of the club's code of conduct would have appeased many. The lack of action by the club and their constant reiteration that they could not prejudice the police investigation did little to sway public opinion. This approach also resulted in increased media interest, which in turn resulted in additional aggrieved women being found and brought into the media spotlight, as well as bringing other unrelated club issues, such as drug use, illegal salary payments, and management in-fighting, into the reporting. The end result was a picture of a club that was arrogant, unacceptable in their attitudes toward women, and lacking in moral and professional behavior. Further, the media investigations also resulted in the sex scandal issue being identified in other clubs and in other football codes, thus spreading the crisis and causing irreversible damage to the game.

Interviews with two CEOs of other NRL clubs at this time revealed that in the same circumstances they would have immediately suspended players pending the outcome of the investigation based on those players breaking club rules (being out past a curfew hour and drinking) and also to soothe public opinion and to be seen taking decisive action. One can only assume that if the Bulldogs club had been more open and helpful with both the police and the media that path A (Figure 2) would have been followed and the damage to the code and to other football clubs may have been averted.

Finally, crisis management plans all suggest a period of review and reflection with the aim of improving plans and tactics being the final step in a well coordinated plan. In the case of the Bulldogs, it appeared that even when the police verdict dropping charges against players was released, the club was still antagonistic and lacking in any form of apology or regret about the actions of the players involved.

Conclusions and Implications

This case is an example of a national sporting organization that has failed to adequately plan for the possibility of a crisis involving the off-field behavior of their players. Further, the history of the club in question indicates that over the last two seasons they have had a number of crises that have not been well handled in terms of their media relations or in terms of an appropriate crisis management strategy. In 2003, the club was hit with a salary cap crisis and, in 2004, the sex sandal hit. The club in question did not appear to reflect and review its management operations or strategies to deal with crises as a result of either incident. Worse still for this club was the fact that their actions and poor handling of the incident caused the negative media coverage to spread to the league in general and to the code on a larger basis.

It would seem from this analysis that the off-filed behavior of footballers has long been the subject of public concern and condemnation, and yet football clubs have largely chosen to ignore the problem in deference to the star billing of many of their players. Discussions with two CEOs from other clubs in the league suggested that the corporate culture within the Bulldogs was also largely to blame for the aggressive and unrelenting media interest in the story and for the unceasing questions in relation to the management and control of this particular club. In addition, the lack of appreciation of the long-term impact of this sort of crisis on the club and its fans and sponsors resulted in major brand image damage and deterioration of the brand image of the league in general.

This case highlights the need for sporting clubs of any level to recognize and plan for player-related crises. The increasing adoration and hero worship afforded national sports people and the culture of sex, drinking, and debauchery that prevails in many contact sports should highlight to clubs at all levels the need to be prepared and to have in place appropriate strategies to handle such crises. It would appear from this case study that media training and education for key management is also a significant factor in achieving a positive and successful outcome. In this case, the Bulldogs were suspicious, antagonistic, and unresponsive to media involvement, which only served to fuel their interest in the case and force a negative and unsympathetic viewpoint from the relevant media commentators.

Interviews with two other CEOs from NRL clubs also highlighted that crisis management plans were not common both within individual clubs and within the league in general and that perhaps it was time to take a more professional approach and to recognize the potential problems when dealing with elite athletes and to plan and rehearse appropriate strategies to cope with crises when they arise.

It is recommended that future researchers in this area investigate why clubs are resistant to putting in place appropriate crisis management plans and whether this is a problem more endemic in one sporting code over any other. It is highly likely that a sporting culture that has accepted immoral or anti-social player behavior in the past will be less able to see the benefits of adopting and practicing a crisis management plan. Future researchers should also consider the implications and demands of all relevant sport publics and stakeholders in their analysis, as it is likely that the conflicting demands of these groups may have a significant impact on the development of a crisis plan and the implementation of same.

This paper has limitations in that it is largely exploratory in nature and lacks empirical support for the propositions made. However, anecdotal evidence from media reviews and discussions with management involved in the football industry in Australia suggest that these findings are not isolated, but rather, more disturbingly, they are endemic of a sporting industry that has not fully accepted the transition to professional sports and the responsibilities to fans and sponsors that come with that move.

References

Adams, W. (2000). Responding to the media during a crisis: It's what you say and when you say it. *Public Relations Quarterly, 45*(1), 26–29.

Boin, A., & Lagadec, P. (2000). Preparing for the future: Critical challenges in crisis management. *Journal of Contingencies and Crisis Management, 8*(4), 185–191.

Booth, S. A. (2000, December). How can organizations prepare for reputational crises? *Journal of Contingencies and Crisis Management, 8*(4), 197–207.

Browne, T. (2003). Powerful crisis communications lessons. *Public Relations Quarterly, 48*(4), 31–35.

Chilton, D. (2002). The pitfalls of star power. *Marketing Magazine, 5*(13), 23–25.

Elliot, C. (2002, October). Crisis management. *PG Gas Magazine,* 18–24.

Hadaway, R. T., & Seidel, E. M. (2003). Turn fear, loathing of media into aplomb. *Plastics News, 15*(40), 8–10.

Shearlean, D., & Lynne, M. (2002). Crisis communication by the book. *Public Relations Quarterly, 47*(3), 30–36.

Newsom, D., Scott, A., & Vanslyke Turk, J. (1993). *This is PR: The realities of public relations.* Belmont, CA: Wadsworth.

Newman, M. (2003). Don't be caught by surprise. *Commercial Property News, 17*(10), 33–35.

Fink, S. (1986). *Crisis management: Planning for the inevitable.* New York: AMACOM.

Robert, B., & Lajtha, C. (2002, December). A new approach to crisis management. *Journal of Contingencies and Crisis Management, 10*(4), 181–191.

SECTION III

FINANCIAL MATTERS AND SPORT MARKETING

Zero-Based Sport Marketing Management: A Management and Budgeting Tool for Sport Managers

DENNIS L. BECHTOL

Abstract

The decision to use the zero-based budgeting process for a sport organization may be derived from three critical factors affecting the organizational management philosophy. First, the organization may have decided to restructure as a means of making a new commitment to the sport product, sport program, or the sport marketing effort. Secondly, as a result of this new commitment, new marketing plans may have been added to the sport organization in the form of strategic marketing planning. These may include new promotional ideas, addition of marketing strategy, or an entire new approach to a specific sport marketing campaign. Thirdly, with this new restructuring attitude, new managerial personnel may have been hired to further develop the organization and its management team.

As a result of this new commitment and new philosophy towards the promotion of this sport operation, an ideal or more accurate budgeting system is being required. With this change of attitude, the organization wants a budgeting procedure that would force the program to identify and analyze what they are going to do, set goals and objectives, make the necessary operating decisions, and evaluate changing responsibilities and workloads—not after the budgeting process, but during it.

The sport organization may especially want to focus on the zero-based budgeting plan. They may feel this plan, with its "decision package" for each activity or category, included an analysis of cost, purpose, alternative course of action, measures of performance, consequences of not performing the activity, and its benefits. There are pluses and minuses in every proposed budget for developing a new paradigm of the sport marketing operation. It is important for the organization to conduct a budget analysis, rather than accepting the previous year's data without examining need from zero base. With this in mind, starting from a zero-based analysis would benefit the organization whether there was increased or decreased funding for marketing operations. Zero-based management allows the manager to know what people in the organization *value* as per their individual budget allocations. This is a management tool, not a form of budgeting.

Sport and facility organizations can benefit and add value by utilizing zero-based management in the following manner:

- Improve plans and budgets
- Follow-up on the benefits of the zero-based analysis during the operation year
- Develop a managerial communication process where a new manager can become quickly informed and provide quality managerial decision-making and accountability

Research Background

This paper on zero-based sport management is a result of descriptive theory developed from a qualitative study on intercollegiate athletic directors (see Bechtol, 2002). The main purpose of this study was to describe the managerial roles and activities of selective NCAA Division I athletic directors. To accomplish this main purpose, data were collected through the process of passive observation, interviewing, physical and environmental documentation, archival record collection, cultural and physical artifact collection, and proxemic contact documentation.

An initial review of literature revealed that researchers have used varying ways to describe and analyze managerial roles and work activities. Mintzberg (1968) designed a new categorical classification of managerial work by developing 10 managerial roles divided into interpersonal, information, and decisional role categories.

A review of literature conducted after data collection and analysis indicated several studies describing the athletic directors' work roles as multi-functional and similar in importance and function to those of business managers. Although athletic directors' duties and responsibilities were stated, there was no evidence of actual field study documentation.

To achieve the stated purpose of the study, a research study was designed utilizing qualitative research techniques to examine selective athletic directors in their naturalistic environment. It was based on data collected from five Division I athletic directors over a period of one work week of passive observation, interviewing, documentation, and artifact data collection. Upon completion of data collection, similar patterns of data were observed consistently at all five research sites. If this had not been observed, further research subjects and sites would have been sought to carry the study to theoretical saturation.

Results gained through data analysis resulted in a description of the athletic directors' managerial roles and activities as multi-functional in nature. The chronological record showed athletic directors who spend a great deal of time in their office environment conducting desk work and telephone communications in an administrative role. The largest proportion of verbal contacts also took place in the athletic directors' offices. Out of office time was spent traveling, and conducting and participating in meetings. The athletic directors spent very little time touring their organization and conducting unscheduled meetings. Based on observation, after-business hours and weekend-hours work activities accounted for almost 25% of the athletic directors' working time. The athletic directors appeared not to be conscious of the full utilization of their executive assistants as a function of time management. They appeared to lack delegation skills that may have saved them personal time to conduct other work-related activities.

This study represents a small step in the direction towards gaining deeper understanding of the professional lives and experience of the managerial elite of NCAA Division I intercollegiate athletics. Additional work is needed to further investigate issues that could not be investigated within the limitations of this study.

Work Activities Related to Athletic Departmental Budget

One of the most dominant findings that emerged from this study concerned the activities of the athletic directors in relation to the athletic department budget. In other words, "Did the athletic directors' activities change with size of departmental budget?" Based on the chronological record of working activities, the work activities of all five athletic directors appeared to be categorically the *same* despite the level of athletic budget. At the time of data collection, the five research site university athletic budgets ranged from just under $5 million to slightly over $28 million. This was a significant range of revenues for the athletic directors to manage. Most of this revenue was generated by football and basketball gate receipts. Funds that were raised specifically to support the athletic program ranged from $2-6 million. Two of the five athletic departments were essentially self-sufficient, (i.e., no state or university funds were utilized). A third site was self-sufficient to the extent that it utilized state monies for capital building projects only. This university had excess funds of over $4 million which was donated to the capital project fund. Another site supported its budget with no state or university funding except a voluntary student fee which brought in just over $1 million per year. One athletic department had an athletic reserve fund of close to $10 million. This particular athletic program gave the university $5 million from this fund for capital project land acquisition.

Descriptive Theory

Specifically, this study was concerned with generation of descriptive theory, *not* the testing of hypothesis or theory. After data are initially analyzed and described, areas of particular significance emerged and a higher level of analysis may be undertaken (e.g., Strauss & Corbin, 1990; see also Erlandson & Harris, 1993). In this study, *two* areas of significance emerged; these data were selectively coded and connected with other coded data to develop substantive or speculative theory (i.e., also known as inductive or descriptive theory).

The first area was revealed through the analysis of interview and observational data in which the athletic directors expressed a desire to have more contact and increased exposure to the main campus. They stated a belief that this desire could be realized if they projected a more positive image of the athletic department. The obstacle to fulfilling this desire for campus contact and image building was the difficulty for the athletic director to find the time to conduct these work activities. An analysis of the data revealed the athletic directors spent very little time conducting on-campus communications. Thus, the *consequences* were a lack of exposure for the athletic department to the general campus community. An *alternative* action would be to develop personal time management skills allowing additional time to conduct these new communication activities.

The second area of data selectively coded for the purpose of developing substantive theory were current program or institutional control and *budget management* issues facing intercollegiate athletics today. These issues may include coach and player behavior, gender equity, recruitment and eligibility, and specific budgetary issues regarding program funding and operation.

The athletic directors in this study spent the largest amount of time in an administrative role (58%), and the largest amount of work time conducting desk and telephone activities (54%). The greatest number of all verbal contact (80%) and of all time spent in verbal contact (67%) was conducted in the athletic director's office. The athletic directors spent the least amount of time walking around their organization on tours. A substantive theory was built on the premise that if the athletic directors spent a great deal of time in an administrative role, in their office, at their desks, they had inadequate time to conduct organizational tours. Based upon a causal-solution analysis process, these activities produce the consequence of possibly less programmatic and organizational control. An alternative action could be developed that would allow the athletic directors to have more time to spend outside of their offices monitoring organizational work activities, which could produce a consequence of increased organizational control.

One technique to allow the athletic directors the additional time needed to conduct these new work activities would involve developing a higher level of personal time management skills. Work activities relating to correspondence and telephone calls seemed to consume the largest amount of desk work time. It was found that only one athletic director used micro-cassette dictation for executive assistant transcription as a means of conserving desk work time and expediting the turnaround of correspondence. This same individual was also the only one to consistently utilize the executive assistant in conducting outgoing telephone calls. The executive assistant would place the outgoing telephone calls, which conserved desk time spent waiting for the party to take the call, or time involved in leaving messages. Interestingly, this same athletic director spent a higher proportion of time conducting organizational tours than did any of the other athletic directors.

For the athletic director—or, for the purpose of this paper, the athletic manager—to obtain new time management skills, a plan-of-action (POA) should be developed and would include learning (1) dictation skills; (2) how to better utilize the executive assistant; (3) how to utilize zero-based budgeting (especially for the new athletic manager); and (4) how to develop specific strategic programs to increase on-campus contact between athletics and academics.

The theory described is purely substantive (i.e., based on phenomenon specific to this study) in nature. However, if one were to extrapolate these data to the entire group represented in this study (i.e., NCAA Division I athletic directors), perhaps some light would be shed on the lack of program control which is recognized in the field. For example, if one were to assume that these previously outlined data were reflective of all NCAA athletic directors, and a composite picture of the average athletic director was constructed, it would reveal an athletic director or manager in an administrative position who spends a great deal of time conducting his or her own correspondence and telephone communications; one who spends little time outside the office touring and showing visibility throughout the athletic organization; and one who desires to enhance organizational control, image, and communication between the athletic department and the main university campus, but ambiguously makes little time available to conduct and develop these activities.

Zero-based Budgeting

Pyhrr (1973) is credited with developing and pioneering the process of zero-base budgeting. Essentially, zero-based budgeting is a process of information accountability leading to the preparation of an operating budget. During the "call to budget" process, the individuals involved are instructed to develop their budgets from a zero sum, starting from zero and building their budget requests based upon documentation of decision packages according to budget category. The entire budget request must be documented from developing goals and objectives to explaining consequences and developing alternatives for organizational operations.

Zero-based Process

According to Pyhrr (1973), there are two basic steps of zero-base budgeting:

1. Developing "decision packages." This step involves analyzing and describing each discrete activity—current as well as new, in one of more decision packages.
2. Ranking "decision packages." This step involves evaluating and ranking these packages in order of importance through cost/benefit analysis or subjective evaluation. (p. 5)

These two steps are further divided into a specific four-step process consisting of identifying the decision-making teams, preparing the team category components budget requests, evaluating and ranking these budget requests, and finally preparing the annual budget (see Leith, 1990; Kramer, 1979).

Identifying decision-making teams

Decision-making teams are those groups within the organization having authority or having been assigned the task of developing an annual budget. This team may be allocated operational funds within the operational structure. This process could involve all levels of management and the inclusion of the followers within each of these managerial levels (e.g., facility management might include operations, sales and marketing, and events, depending upon organizational structure).

Preparing the team category components requests

Within each decision-making team there are specific budget areas or categories related to their operational responsibilities. This section identifies and prepares these categories as part of the budget request. This is not only an identification of category, but an in-depth analysis of need and a justification for that needed budget item and financial allocation. After identifying each category, and specifying a budget request for each of these categories, a detailed documentation justifying each category must be made. Leith (1990) describes the following specific types of information needed for sport organization zero-base documentation:

> A description of what you need; a statement of why you need these requested items; a list of what objectives the requested items will serve or benefit; the proposed costs and benefits of your budget requests; and the alternatives (i.e., different ways of performing the same function) for accomplishing your objective if the request is denied (Leith, p. 62).

Phyrr (1973) also suggests adding an area to discuss "the proposed consequences should you not receive the budget amount requested" (p. 6). Accurate forecasting in each category is critical to the success of the entire budget process. Examples of a basic team category analysis and documentation are shown in Figures 1 and 2.

Evaluating and ranking the budget request

After budget analysis and forecast justification of each team category budget request, you are ready for the final operational step in the process. This last step consists of evaluating and ranking each team category followed by an overall ranking of specific team components. An example might be the specific breakdown of team categories for a sport and entertainment facility where specific category teams were developed for operations, sales and marketing, and event operations. Following the completion of each of these team category budget requests (i.e., including documentation and justification of expense), the ranking process can begin based upon fiducial priority. This ranking takes place within each team category, and within each team category decision package. Upon completion of the individual team rankings, an overall ranking of the most prioritized decision packages would take place. The idea is to prioritize and rank each team category decision package as per the goals and objectives of the organization. This is the critical success factor for accurate zero-based budgeting. Does your documentation and justification equate to an accurate ranking in aligning the budget request with the goals and objectives of the organization? Again, this is the process of learning how to get "more for less" within the structure of the organization. An example of a basic zero-based budget ranking system is shown in Figure 3.

Preparing the annual budget

The preparation of the zero-based budget takes away the bias of speculation when preparing the overall budget. The final organizational decision maker has hard data to consider when preparing the final budget. The organization can still utilize a line-item incremental budgeting process. However, accurate well-thought out zero-based data are present to assist in the decision making process.

DECISION PACKAGE (1 of 4) (1 & 2 shown)   PACKAGE   A

Package Name: 000 Salary/Wages   Ranking: 1

Statement of Program (Needs, Goals, & Objectives)

A-1   To provide maximum adequate salaries for all staff coaches according to university guidelines. To maintain a high ratio to retain quality assistant staff coaches.

A-2   To provide an adequate salary base to attract and retain a quality secretarial/clerical staff. The emphasis being on quality, not quantity.

A-3   To increase the number of graduate assistants. The goal is to increase numbers to adequately support each specialty (i.e., position) coaching assistant.

A-4   To ensure grant-in-aid will operate efficiently and effectively as per NCAA guidelines. The creation of positive attitudes and culture related to the continued development of an ethical recruiting process is the major goal of this program.

Benefits
An overall salary/wage plan is required to focus on new commitment to excellence at WXYZ University.

Consequences and Alternatives
• Elimination or reduction of position or positions would result in defeating the university focus on commitment to excellence in developing a quality football program.
• Combining assistant coaching positions to consolidate salaried positions.
• Utilize more graduate assistants instead of full-time assistant coaches.
• Decrease the number of full-time secretarial/clerical staff.
• Seek part-time secretarial staff.
• Give partial grant-in-aid scholarships to certain student athletes.

Proposed Dollar Cost of Package "A" Budget: $2,434,833*

* See operating budget summary

Note: Figure design was adopted from Leith (1990) and Pyhrr (1973).

Figure 1:   Example of WXYZ NCAA football program zero-base budget, including decision package 1 of 3 (i.e., package 1 and 2 only shown).

Zero-based Management

The majority of the previous text has been documentation leading to this section on zero-based management for the sport and entertainment manager. The foundational qualitative research helped develop theory as to the sport manager's roles and activities. One of the concerns that emerged from this study was the consciousness of having "to do more with less" when it comes to financing and promoting a sport event or sport organization. This particular study revealed a genuine need for time and information in the working lives of intercollegiate elite athletic managers. This appears to remain true for not only the sport industry, but for all organizations operating in current economic conditions. The applied suggestion to maintaining institutional or organizational control was to develop a type of zero-based management—not necessarily zero-based budgeting in the strictest sense, but a form of zero-based management where operational teams take a closer look at what they do from an organizational financial perspective. This concept utilizes zero-based concepts as a management tool, not as a strict budgetary process. This would be especially helpful for the new sport and entertainment marketing manager (i.e., facility or arena manager, etc.) as the zero-based concepts increase the communication process within the organization. As a new manager, it is difficult to initially understand what departmental directors and staff value when it comes to

Package Name: 010 Travel   Ranking: 2

Statement of Program   (Needs, Goals, & Objectives)

B-1   Travel for administration and the team fluctuate with the number of home games. It also fluctuates with the distance to be traveled to each away game. The goal is to schedule away games that are within a reasonable travel distance, while maintaining a quality competitive schedule.

B-2   Travel for recruiting needs to be on a developmental increase to keep pace with the program's strides for excellence. Our goal is to also maintain recruiting policy within NCAA regulations, but also to increase our budget within these guidelines. Travel for recruit visits to campus and travel for scouting should remain constant as per NCAA regulations. Our goal is to increase this expense on a strategic developmental basis.

B-3   Meals for travel and student athletic training table expenditures must be increased to upgrade the program quality. A consistent monitoring of diet and training techniques is critical for a successful program. New training facilities as a result of capital budgeting invokes an increase and upgrade to this budget.

Benefits
Travel activities for the football program required to maximize the quality development of the program.

Consequences and Alternatives
• Cut back and/or eliminate the travel package, which could force a step backwards in the development of the football program.
• Utilize university vehicles for travel as much as possible, and accrue travel expense only when recruits visit the campus.
• Travel less for recruiting (i.e., use more telephone contact).
• Make training table available only in key situations to alleviate or control expenses. Sacrifice continuity of diet and training table.
• Rethink team hotel expenses for home games (i.e., stay in own local residences prior to home games)

Proposed Dollar Cost of Package "B" Budget: $536,000*

* See operating budget summary

Note: Figure design was adopted from Leith (1990) and Pyhrr (1973).

Figure 2: Example of WXYZ NCAA football program zero-base budget, including decision package 2 of 3 (i.e., package 1 and 2 only shown).

finances and financial allotments. The new manager can become much more quickly informed leading to higher quality decision making when utilizing zero-based management.

So, how do you make it zero-based management and not zero-based budgeting? The answer to this question is to simplify the process. Zero-based budgeting has never been easy; thus, it is rarely utilized as the sole process of budgeting. There appears to be very little current usage of the zero-based process for budgeting. Specific organizations have modified the process to accommodate their organizational needs. Literature reveals examples of the zero-based budgeting process do exist, such as the state of New Jersey adopting what they call "target-based budgeting." The most revealing difference in this approach is that there are no decision packages required for the target budget. Actually, in this process there are two zero-based processes operating at the same time. One is the target budget consideration as a part of target package rankings both by the unit submitting them and by the budget office. This appears to work as a checks and balance system (Goertz, 1993).

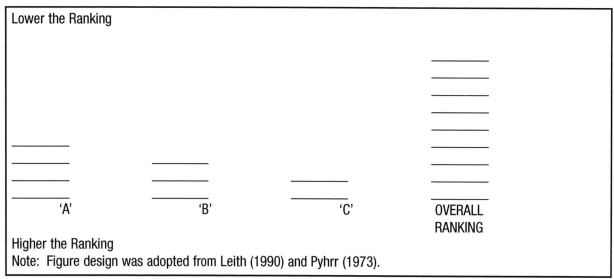

Figure 3: Ranking of decision packages for a formal zero-based budget, team category and component budget requests.

Much of the literature referring to the usage of the zero-based process is directed to public organizations. Posner (1999) reports another variation of the zero-based budgeting process in describing the "performance budgeting" process within the public sector. This is a process where expected program outcomes are linked to budget levels. The determination of budget levels is dependent upon zero-based justification of allocations in relation to specific outcomes. Public school based management appears to have taken to the zero-based process as well. Weller (1995) discusses an alternative to downsizing utilizing the TQM (i.e., total quality management) process as a means to cost effectiveness. This concept addresses the TQM process along with the application of zero-based budgeting.

In relation to the sport industry and specific to Major League Baseball, the Chicago White Sox utilize a modified zero-based budgeting process. The purpose is to "ensure that the organization's plans are in sync with its current financial position" (Dennis, 1998, p. 1). Generally, sport organizations appear to use a zero-based process as a means to justify and track future expenditures (Fried, Shapiro, & DeSchriver, 2003).

The management of operational expenses with any organization, and especially with sport marketing management organizations, is a significant component of the marketing management control and evaluating process (Kotler, 2003; Shank, 2002). So, why not use zero-based management as a tool for communication and justification of expenditures? Why not have open communication and get a handle on what your staff values as important to operations? In the past, it has just been too hard to do this type of process.

Zero-based budgeting is not easy, but zero-based management is very easy to implement and control in relation to organizational outcomes. There are two critical success factor components to designing and implementing a zero-based management program. *First*, make the process *easy*! This means to, *secondly*, *adapt* the zero-based process to the specifics of your organization. Simplify the decision categories by developing an easy to use zero-based form that can be attached and delivered to staff members and back to management via e-mail. If a new manager is implementing this process, get out of the office and discuss the process on an individual basis. Get to know the staff, their values, and the ability to improvise and create new avenues of production. The critical success factor is knowing your staff's organizational behavior related to operational budgeting, and receiving the dissemination of information from the organizational "doers." It is a two-way street. The staff gets a feeling that their input is valued, and the sport manager receives valuable information allowing for more accurate organizational forecasting and decision making. Figures 4 and 5 illustrate simplified versions of the zero-based process leading to zero-based management.

Marketing Expenditure Classification	Previous Fiscal Year Actual	Current Fiscal Year Budgeted	Next Fiscal Year Requested
Personal Selling (Promotional Campaigns)	$	$	$
Advertising	$	$	$
Sponsorship	$	$	$
Public Relations (Community Relations)	$	$	$
Market Research	$	$	$

Figure 4: General simplified zero-based management forms (adapted from the zero-based budgeting process). Figure shows an overview of budget operation categories as per previous, current, and projected allotments.

Program Costs	Continuation of Current Level of Funding	Assuming a 10% Reduction in Funding	Assuming a 25% Reduction in Funding
Personal Selling (Promotional Campaigns)	$	$	$
Advertising	$	$	$
Sponsorship	$	$	$
Public Relations (Community Relations)	$	$	$
Market Research	$	$	$
TOTALS	$	$	$

Note: Base upon this basic form, an organization can adapt a team category request form, leading to the input of data into the above overview budgeting form. This category request form should have specific areas for budget justification. These would include sections for exploring the consequences of budget reduction, and an alternative POA (i.e., plan of action) should there be a reduction in budgetary allotments.

Figure 5: General simplified zero-based management forms (adapted from the zero-based budgeting process). Figure shows an overview of budget operation categories as per current funding level, and forecasted projected reductions of funding allotments.

References

Bechtol, D. (2002). Structured observation description of the managerial roles and activities of selected NCAA division I athletic directors. *International Journal of Sport Management, 3*(1), 11-33. (Permission granted for reprint)

Dennis, A. (1998). Budgeting for curve balls. *Journal of Accountancy, 186*(3), 89-92.

Erlandson, D. A., Harris, E. L., Skipper, B. L., & Allen, S. D. (1993). *Doing naturalistic inquiry: A guide to methods.* Newbury Park, CA: Sage.

Fried, G., Shapiro, S. J., & DeSchriver, T. D. (2003). *Sport finance.* Champaign, IL: Human Kinetics.

Goertz, R. K. (1993). Target-based budgeting and adaptations to fiscal uncertainty. *Public Productivity & Management Review, 16*(4), 425-427.

Kotler, P. (2003). *Marketing management* (11th ed.). Upper Saddle River, NJ: Prentice-Hall.

Kramer, F. A. (1979). *Contemporary approaches to public budgeting.* Cambridge, MA: Winthrop.

Leith, L. M. (1990). *Coaches guide to sport administration.* Champaign, IL: Leisure Press.

Mintzberg, H. (1968). *The manager at work—determining his activities, roles, and programs by structured observation.* Unpublished doctoral dissertation, M.I.T. Sloan School of Management, Cambridge.

Posner, P. L. (1999). Performance budgeting: A critical process, *Public Manager, 28*(3), 8.

Pyhrr, P. A. (1973). *Zero-based budgeting: A practical management tool for evaluating expenses.* New York: John Wiley & Sons.

Shank, M. D. (2002). *Sports marketing: A strategic perspective* (2nd ed.). Upper Saddle River, NJ: Prentice Hall.

Strauss, A., & Corbin, J. (1990). *Basics of qualitative research: Grounded theory procedures and techniques.* Newbury Park, CA: Sage.

Weller, D. L. (1995). School restructuring and downsizing: Using TQM to promote cost effectiveness. *The TQM Magazine, 7*(6), 11-24.

SECTION IV

SPONSORSHIP AND SPORT MARKETING

Fulfilling Sponsorship Goals: Evaluation of Major League Soccer Team Websites

COREY BRAUN
VASSILIS DALAKAS
JOE FERNANDEZ
ANDREA LANSFORD

Abstract

Using the official websites of the Major League Soccer teams, this study found no one individual team website meets all the goals sponsors seek to achieve by sponsoring a property. However, the study revealed the MLS teams could improve the sites to better benefit the sponsor by creating a website presence for the sponsor that provides appreciation, enhances awareness, and positively positions the sponsor and its ability to increase sales.

Introduction

In a 2003 survey of sponsorship decision-makers, the International Events Group (IEG) found that 38% of the respondents mentioned "presence on property website" as an extremely valuable benefit for sponsors (IEG Sponsorship Report, 2003). This benefit was listed along with other well-established benefits like "category exclusivity" and "on-site signage." In a similar survey in 2002, 30% of the respondents mentioned this benefit as extremely valuable; given the increasing use of the internet, one can expect the significance of such a benefit to continue to rise.

In addition to the desired benefits sponsors expect from potential sponsorship opportunities, they also have goals they expect the sponsorships to help them accomplish. The results of another IEG survey (IEG Sponsorship Report, 2001) showed the following top six goals of sponsorships:

- 68% – to increase brand loyalty
- 65% – to create awareness/visibility
- 59% – to change or reinforce their image
- 45% – to drive retail/dealer traffic
- 43% – to showcase community/social responsibility
- 35% – to stimulate sales/trial/usage

Given the importance sponsors place on having a presence on the property website, we examined how prevalent and useful such presence is. We specifically focused on the websites of all 10 teams of Major League Soccer (MLS). Through the study, we intended to evaluate which teams did the best and worst job in benefiting their sponsors through their websites. Moreover, we expected to identify how properties may help their sponsors accomplish their goals through the presence on the website.

Methodology

During the 2003 MLS season, we assessed each MLS team on an individual basis. We visited each team's site. We analyzed the sites using 11 different criteria that are connected to the desired goals of sponsors. We looked for each sponsor and evaluated how easy it was to find the sponsor, the nature of the sponsor's web presence, the number of clicks it took to get from the team's homepage to the sponsor's name or logo, how identifiable the logo was, and was there a link to the sponsor's own website. We also looked at how the sponsors were represented overall on the site by asking the following four questions:

1. Did the team website indicate any appreciation for the sponsors?
2. Did the team website include encouragement to support the sponsors?
3. Did the team website suggest that the sponsors are integral to the success of the team?
4. Did the team website have a separate page for all the sponsors?

Some of these criteria overlap in defining multiple goals. The following is a list of the goals with the corresponding criteria that pertain to each.

To increase brand loyalty: To what extent the website expresses gratitude, appreciation, and encouragement, crediting the team's success to the sponsors.

- Does the website indicate any appreciation for the sponsors? (Yes or No answer)
- Does the website include any encouragement to support the sponsors? (Yes or No answer)
- Does the website suggest that sponsors are integral to the success of the team? (Yes or No answer)
- Does the website have the sponsors listed on a separate sponsor page? (Yes or No answer)

To create awareness and visibility: To what extent the sponsors have a presence on the website.

- Is the sponsor mentioned on the homepage of the team? (Yes or No answer)
- Is the sponsor's name/logo easily identified? (Yes or No answer)
- How many clicks does it take to actually see a sponsor's name/logo? (relative number answer)
- Is the sponsor's name listed? (Yes or No answer)
- Is the sponsor's logo present? (Yes or No answer)
- Does the website have the sponsors listed on a separate sponsor page? (Yes or No answer)

To change or reinforce their image: To what extent the presence of the sponsor on the website affects the way people view the sponsor.

- Does the website indicate any appreciation for the sponsors? (Yes or No answer)
- Does the website include any encouragement to support the sponsors? (Yes or No answer)
- Does the website suggest that sponsors are integral to the success of the team? (Yes or No answer)

To drive retail/dealer traffic: To what extent the presence of the sponsor on the website allows for easy access to the sponsor's business.

- Is there a link to the sponsor's page? (Yes or No answer)
- What is the destination of the link? (open-ended answer)

To showcase community/social responsibility: To what extent the presence of the sponsor on the website affiliates the sponsor with social involvement in relation to the team.

- Does the website indicate any appreciation for the sponsors? (Yes or No answer)
- Does the website include any encouragement to support the sponsors? (Yes or No answer)
- Does the website suggest that sponsors are integral to the success of the team? (Yes or No answer)

To stimulate sales/trial/usage: To what extent the presence of the sponsor on the website promotes the increase of sales or usage of the sponsor's products or services.

- Is there a link to the sponsor's page? (Yes or No answer)
- What is the destination of the link? (open-ended answer)

Findings/Results

Is the sponsor mentioned on the homepage of the team?

Only 8.3% of the 406 sponsors found on all the MLS sites had presence on the team's homepage. The New England Revolution had all 12 of its sponsors on the homepage, proving to be the best in this category, and the Metro Stars and San Jose Earthquakes did the worst because neither team mentioned any of their sponsors on the team's homepage.

Table 1	
Team	Sponsor on Homepage
Chicago Fire	1
Colorado Rapids	3 of 26
Columbus Crew	5 of 60
D.C. United	6 of 28
Dallas Burn	2 of 99
Kansas City Wizards	3 rotating
L.A. Galaxy	1 rotating
Metro Stars	None
New England Revolution	all 12
San Jose Earthquakes	None
sponsors on homepage	33/406

Is the sponsor's name/logo easily identifiable?

With the exception of the Columbus Crew site, where only half of the sponsors names or logos are identifiable, all the logos or names on the other sites were easily identifiable.

How many clicks does one need to actually see a sponsor's name/logo?

The average number of clicks to actually see sponsors who were not listed on the homepage of each team was 1.5 clicks. Six sites (Chicago Fire, Columbus Crew, D.C. United, Dallas Burn, Kansas City Wizards, and Metro Stars) took two clicks, three sites (Colorado Rapids, L.A. Galaxy, and San Jose Earthquakes) took only one click, and the New England Revolution site took zero clicks (given that the sponsors are listed on the team's homepage).

In analyzing the results of this question, it is also necessary to consider the ease of finding the sponsors from the homepage of the team. Every site called their sponsors something different and had them listed under various links on the homepage. Some actually had a sponsor link directly listed on the homepage. Others had them in small print at the very bottom of the homepage. Several labeled their sponsors as corporate sponsors, local sponsors, small business partners, or in the case of L.A. Galaxy, they were labeled on the homepage as Hotlink. Some links were very easy to find. They were clearly labeled on the homepage as partners or sponsors. Others took over 30 minutes to find. For example, to find the Metro Stars sponsors, one had to first go to tickets, then to small business partners. It was very difficult to find. Overall, though it may have taken two clicks to get the sponsor page, it could have been very easily identified on the homepage. Furthermore, though some sites only took one click, finding that link on the homepage may have been very difficult.

Is the sponsor's name simply listed, just a logo, or both name and logo?

Of the 406 sponsors from all 10 MLS team websites, 21.9% were simply listed, 65.8% showed only the sponsor's logo, and 12.3% showed both the name and the logo. On an individual basis, Metro Stars only listed (using names and not logos) over 80% of their sponsors. Three teams had only logos: the L.A. Galaxy, the New England Revolution, and the San Jose Earthquakes. Only three website gave some of their sponsors the benefit of having both their name and their logo listed. D.C. United did this for 100% of its sponsors.

Table 2			
Team	simply listed	just logos	both
Chicago Fire	21	21	0
Colorado Rapids	14	12	0
Columbus Crew	0	41	19
D.C. United	0	0	28
Dallas Burn	19	80	0
Kansas City Wizards	21	16	0
L.A. Galaxy	0	59	0
Metro Stars	14	0	3
New England Revolution	0	12	0
San Jose Earthquakes	0	26	0
	89	267	50

Is there a link to the sponsor's page and what was the nature of that link?

Sixty percent of the sponsors were given hyperlink capabilities. More than 95% of those were linked directly to the sponsor's homepage. Eight went to homepages that mentioned soccer or the MLS team, one went to a form for a sweepstakes being performed by the sponsor, two went to schedules of the season, and a few were not able to be located.

Table 3		
Team	sponsor link	
Chicago Fire	4	home
Colorado Rapids	24	18 home, 1 TV schedule, 4 home w/ soccer mentioned, 1 can't be found
Columbus Crew	5	4 home, 1 sweepstakes entry
D.C. United	28	28 homepages
Dallas Burn	95	2 can't be found, 1 e-mail contacts, 4 home w/soccer mentioned, 88 homepages
Kansas City Wizards	7	7 homepages
L.A. Galaxy	49	49 homepages
Metro Stars	3	3 homepages
New England Revolution	12	11 homepages, 1 MLS schedule
San Jose Earthquakes	14	14 homepages
	241/406	

Does the website indicate any appreciation for the sponsors?

Half of the sites (Chicago Fire, Columbus Crew, D.C. United, Dallas Burn, and Metro Stars) indicated some appreciation, thanks, or gratitude towards their sponsor. Most basically said, "We would like to thank our sponsors." Some went so far as to say "We proudly salute our sponsors."

Does the website indicate any encouragement to support the sponsors?

Only two of the sites (D.C. United and Metro Stars) encouraged those who visited the site to support the sponsors. For example, the D.C. United site said, "Please click on these links to visit their sites and support the sponsors that support our sport."

Does the website suggest that sponsors are integral to the success of the team?

Two teams directly stated that the support from the sponsors was integral to the success of the team. The Chicago Fire said, "One reason for the great success of the Chicago Fire is its impressive roster of marketing partners in Chicagoland"; and the Columbus Crew site referred to its sponsors as "The Cornerstone to Success."

The following chart summarizes the findings for the previous three questions.

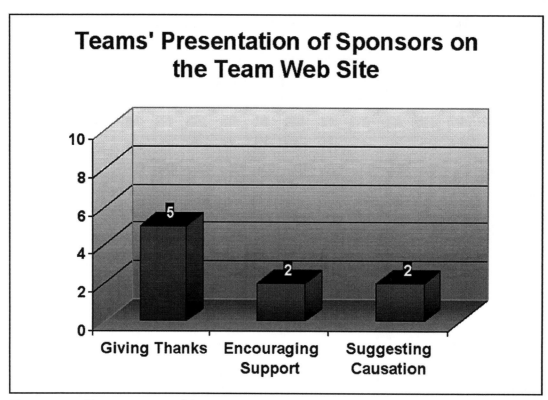

Figure 1: Presentation of Sponsors.

Discussion

There was no individual team that was able to fulfill the goals that a sponsor looks for in sponsoring a team. Each team had pieces of what the sponsors are looking for, and some did an excellent job with those different features. However, it would be very simple to provide sponsors with features that accomplish the goals they seek. The following is an example webpage that achieves each goal of the sponsors.

To increase brand loyalty, the sponsor is mentioned as an integral part of the success of the team and shown much gratitude. The sponsor's logo and name are displayed directly on the homepage to increase awareness and visibility. They are once again recognized as integral to success, showing that the fans' favorite team could not go on, in order to reinforce their image and showcase the sponsor's community and social responsibility. Each name and logo links directly to some part of the sponsor's own website, in order to drive retail/dealer traffic and stimulate sales or trial usage. The sponsor is easy to find, its name and logo are identifiable, and they are provided with the means to reach their goals.

Overall, our findings indicated that the MLS team websites did little to help the sponsors achieve the goals that the sponsors seek to obtain through sponsoring a property.

Though some of the teams did a better job than others, not one of the sites provided a complete package deal that fully benefited the sponsors. Some sites did not express their gratitude to the sponsors that have given significant amounts of money to these teams. Less than half displayed the sponsor's logo on the homepage. This feature would be a huge benefit for sponsors since most fans do not go to the website to search for the sponsor page. If the sponsor's name or logo was on the homepage, it is more likely to give the sponsor visibility and a greater public awareness. Another finding that supports our hypothesis deals with not identifying a team-sponsor relationship. Most of the teams in the MLS league could not play without the investments from outside sources. This past season, the L.A. Galaxy brought in the first ever profits for any team in the league, and the amount was very low. The teams need the support of sponsors in order to survive. If fans know that the sponsor gives money to their favorite team and that is the reason that their favorite team can still play, then they are more likely to support that sponsor by purchasing its products because that sponsor supports their favorite team.

References

Chicago Fire (2003). Chicago Fire homepage. Retrieved November 1, 2003, from http://www.chicago-fire.com.

Colorado Rapids (2003). Colorado Rapids homepage. Retrieved November 1, 2003, from http://www.col-oradorapids.com.

Columbus Crew (2003). Columbus Crew homepage. Retrieved November 1, 2003, from http://www.the-crew.com.

Dallas Burn (2003). Dallas Burn homepage. Retrieved November 1, 2003, from http://www.dallasburn.com.

DC United (2003). DC United homepage. Retrieved November 1, 2003, from http://www.dcunited.com.

Kansas City Wizards (2003). Kansas City Wizards homepage. Retrieved November 1, 2003, from http://www.kcwizards.com.

Los Angeles Galaxy (2003). Los Angeles Galaxy homepage. Retrieved November 1, 2003, from http://www.lagalaxy.com.

Major League Soccer (2003). MLS homepage. Retrieved November 1, 2003, from http://www.mlsnet.com.

Metro Stars (2003). Metro Stars homepage. Retrieved November 1, 2003, from http://www.metrostars.com.

New England Revolution (2003). New England Revolution homepage. Retrieved November 1, 2003, from http://www.revolutionsoccer.net/home.

Performance research/IEG study highlights what sponsors want. (2001, 16 April). *IEG Sponsorship Report, 20*(7), 1, 4-5.

San Jose Earthquakes (2003). San Jose Earthquakes homepage. Retrieved November 1, 2003, from http://www.sjearthquakes.com.

Sponsorship grabs larger share of marketing budgets: Findings from IEG/performance research sponsor study. (2003, 10 March). *IEG Sponsorship Report, 22*(5), 1, 4-5.

Utilizing Youth Sport Sponsorships to Break Through the Media Clutter

ERIC J. NEWMAN

Abstract

As the cost of media continues to rise and entertainment opportunities continue to grow, minor league teams are looking for ways to better utilize their shrinking media budgets. This study looks at reallocating traditional media budgets and utilizing current sponsors to gain positive brand exposure through strategically aligned community youth sport sponsorships. The youth sport consumers are distributed across the family life cycle (youth participants, parents, siblings, grandparents, and relatives), providing exposure to a wide range of sports-interested consumers. A number of variables are utilized in strategically choosing the youth sport sponsorships, including family sports involvement, sports knowledge, purchase ability, and the willingness to purchase game tickets and licensed merchandise. The consumer's attitude toward the minor league team was positively affected by the youth sports sponsorships with increased team goodwill, brand name awareness, and an involvement in family activities.

The youth sport sponsorship relationships also provide a positive attitude change toward the minor league team by the community, current fans, and current sponsors of the minor league team.

Introduction

Minor league baseball is constantly challenged by all the entertainment opportunities available to its consumers and the increased costs of media. One challenge a minor league baseball team president faced was a lack of measurement for the success of his radio buys. He explained how there were no significant differences in attendance when there were no radio advertisements for a two-week period. Due to the lack of any measurable return on his radio buys, the team president contemplated reducing or eliminating his radio advertisements. It was suggested that the minor league baseball fans be surveyed to determine the effectiveness of the radio buys and where to reallocate that budget if they proved to be not effective. Over a three-game home stand 1,043 fans were surveyed.

The survey revealed that the number of radio stations currently used could be decreased to the three most popular with the target market. The three radio stations were chosen by a 2 to 1 margin with 28% of the fans feeling it was very important to advertise on each of those specific stations.

The money saved from the elimination of radio stations was then reallocated to strategically build relations with regional youth sport teams and leagues. Specific youth athletic leagues would be sponsored that fit the demographics and psychographics of the fans. This money would not be reallocated to charity; instead, it would be strategically placed in leagues of current and future fans. The households targeted would already be interested in sports because of their current involvement with youth sports. They would have the purchasing power for game tickets, concessions, and team merchandise.

Media Costs

Minor league teams are looking for ways to better utilize their media budgets. Their market is generally geographically defined and local (Stilson, 2004). Being a minor league team at a small stadium in a local market limits the revenue, requiring some measurable return on all media purchased.

Radio has faced more competition over the past 40 years (Raymond, 2000) and is currently hoping for better times (Bachman, 2003). The television, vinyl records, eight tracks, cassettes, CDs, digital computer, DVDs, and now digital satellite have all provided alternatives to radio. Drivers like to hear music in their vehicles while they drive, but now they have many choices to choose from. Radio listeners are very fragmented with all the stations and options to choose from. Even drivers who do listen to the radio tend to have all their favorite stations preprogrammed so that they can change the station quickly during commercial breaks. They may also like their music commercial free by playing CDs or subscribing to satellite digital commercial free radio.

Depending on where the consumers are driving, they are generally expected to be more focused on the road than the music. One of the limitations of radio is that it is used regularly as background noise at home and in the office. Advertisers are paying for all consumers to have the opportunity to hear the advertisement, not taking into effect the majority who are not paying attention or channel switching.

When surveyed, only 6.8% of the fans had heard a team advertisement on the radio. With the cost of media continuing to rise, a single 60-second radio spot can cost $200 during peak driving hours. When adding the required frequency for effective radio advertising, the costs multiply quickly. Three radio spots can equal the cost of sponsoring a youth athletic team for the whole season. The costs of sponsoring a youth team can also be shared with current minor league sponsors. Most youth Little League teams average 12 players. If the team goes to four minor league games in a season, the concessions alone will come close to paying for the team sponsorship. That is not factoring in the ticket costs and if more than one person joins the youth at the game.

Another justification for reallocating some of the radio budget is that only 6.8% of the fans heard a radio advertisement. Also, 48.5% of the fans said they would look in a newspaper for game time information. Thirty-three percent of the minor league fans said they would visit the team website for game information.

Sponsorships

In the current study, we looked at Little League baseball as the youth sport because it is a natural fit with minor league baseball. Youth sports were selected since 60% of the minor league baseball fans are accompanied by a child 17 years of age or younger. Little League baseball was also chosen because the leagues are very selective in giving access to its coaches and team parents. Being within the same sport provided opportunity to interact with the league in a way other marketers could not. It also provided the opportunity to be like a big brother to the league and work on building a longstanding relationship. The Little League relationship also provides access to the team coaches and team parents. Our survey showed that youth baseball parents receive their information from either the coach or team parent.

It was very challenging trying to build the original relationship with the Little League. The leagues are run by volunteers who are very skeptical and cautious of advertisers trying to take advantage of the league. Trust is a major issue in relationships (Morgan & Hunt, 1994), and the Little League didn't trust that we would follow through with our promises, just like many of their other so-called sponsors. It has been an issue with many leagues that are trying to keep what they say is true to the sport. They are trying to keep the commercialization away from local ball fields and feel that many of the advertisements are not appropriate for the fields and youths (Weiss, 1999). There have been problems—specifically, parents getting upset—when team sponsors are associated with alcohol (White, 1998). We had to prove to the league that we were there in the best interest of the youth athletes and willing to commit to a long-term relationship. A number of our current sponsors expressed difficulty in getting access to the youth athletic market. This is the perfect opportunity to promote baseball in general and to get our team name associated with the players and fans of Little League baseball. This also provides opportunity for our sponsors to expand their exposure and association with baseball at all levels.

Current Sponsors

The cost of team and league sponsorships can be offset by utilizing current minor league sponsors. Many of our sponsors, such as food and beverage companies, are very interested in building relationships with the current youth sports market. Utilizing our current sponsors helped in gaining positive brand exposure through the strategically aligned community youth sport sponsorships. For example, during one visit to the Little League fields, our sponsors provided Corn Nuts and a sponsor's bottled water. We as a sponsor had permission to give away items associated with our minor league team. The exposure did not stop at the youth participants—family members also became involved. The youth sport consumers are distributed across the whole family life cycle (youth participants, parents, siblings, grandparents, and relatives), providing exposure to a wide range of sports-interested consumers.

The youth sport sponsorship also provides a positive community attitude toward the minor league baseball team by the community. It shows the minor league team giving back to the community by pleasing the recipients, current fans, as well as city and county officials.

Choosing Leagues

Rather than participate equally in all the Little Leagues in the area, the teams and leagues are strategically selected. This strategic selection does not affect any general donations committed to the league as a whole. The goal is to choose the teams and leagues that most closely match the target market of our minor league baseball team. When our fans were asked what activities they participated in, 40% of the fans missed our games due to activities involving youth. That shows that many of our fans are involved with youth activities that coincide with our baseball season. It was also shown that 23% of the fans missed games due to organized youth sports. That is high considering most youth sports such as football, basketball, soccer, and volleyball participate during our off-season. The majority of our fans were also highly interested in game day promotions that involved youth. Fifty-seven percent of our fans felt that events that involve youth at the games, such as kids in uniforms and on-field promotions, increased their overall enjoyment of the games.

As stated earlier, the reallocation of a portion of the radio budget to the Little League sponsorships is not a donation but an investment. The teams and leagues then have to match similarly to the fan base of the minor league team. The following variables are looked at in differentiating the teams.

Education – The current county has an educational level of 15% with a college degree, while 36% of the minor league baseball fans have a college degree. Educational attainment has been shown to be very important in a competitive youth sports market. This competitiveness shows a need for camps, gear, and club team sports. The education level has been shown to increase involvement in youth activities, with a better understanding of the need for continued training. Youth athletics have been shown to be most competitive in the higher educated, higher household income regions. The higher the educational level, the higher the income (Census, 2004), which provides the financial ability to continue in youth sport involvement. Leagues were chosen by looking at the school districts and comparing API (Academic Performance Index) scores. Those scores provided a baseline to study the demographic information of the specific areas. Those scores did coincide with a higher educated geographic area to look for league and team sponsorships.

Household income – County median household income is $31,140, whereas over 57% of the fans have a household income over $50,000. Only 17% of the fan base was below the median income, which could account for the "single and currently in college" group. Household income is very important, as it provides the ability to purchase tickets and concessions at the stadium. The additional income also provides more discretionary income for the licensed merchandise.

The consumer's attitude toward the minor league team was positively affected by the youth sports sponsorships with increased team goodwill, increased minor league team awareness, and increased involvement in family activities. Parents and fans both expressed excitement and appreciation for the increased involvement in youth activities. By providing representatives to many of the Little League games, parents and coaches were provided the opportunity to discuss events that would be of interest to them. One of the recommendations coming from those discussions was a clinic where the youth athletes would be provided the opportunity to learn baseball skills from the minor league team players and coaches.

The Clinic

Being a sponsor and contributor to Little League baseball provided the opportunity to bring the youth players to the stadium for a baseball clinic. At the clinic, 62 parents were surveyed and interviewed to judge the success of the clinic and determine the direction of future clinics. Current sponsors of the minor league team were given the opportunity to help sponsor the clinic. There was no problem gathering sponsors or player volunteers. The clinic was advertised by using flyers, stadium announcements, and by contacting coaches and team parents. Of the participants, 57% heard about the clinic through their coach or team parent. Twenty-one percent came because of the flyers handed out at the Little League games, 16% heard through other sources, and 6.5% heard the stadium announcement.

Youth athletes from 33 different schools participated in the clinic. The participants represented nine different geographical leagues, with 79.2% of the youth coming from just three leagues. The cost of the clinic was not an issue since it was completely sponsored and free to the youth participants. The three leagues that were highly represented were also identified as teams/leagues to sponsor due to their demographic match of the minor league baseball team demographics. In contrast, 89% of the parents whose youth attended the clinic planned on attending the minor league game later that day, with 80% planning on staying for the entire game. The survey also indicated that 92% of the parents whose child participated in the clinic were interested in and willing to pay to participate in a three-day summer clinic. It was also recommended that a small token be charged for the one-day clinic by the parents to provide additional value and commitment.

Conclusion

In prior years, the relationship with Little League baseball was one-directional with the minor league team providing game tickets and a charity donation to the league with little return. The minor league team would provide free game tickets for the Little League with very disappointing redemption rates. The new strategic relationships with specific Little League teams has increased ticket redemption from less than 10% to over 80% for some games.

The reallocation of the radio budget has provided a measurable return and goodwill with the Little League teams. The clinics, for example, give youth the opportunity to experience the stadium with the minor league coaches and players. The experience can then be shared in 33 different schools as the youth athletes go back to their school.

The decrease in radio advertising has not shown any negative effects on attendance. The three key radio stations have increased there visibility at the minor league games with new on- and off-air promotions. Attendance was compared to the previous year's attendance levels, with the current year providing slightly higher attendance rates. There has also been a noticeable difference in the amount of children wearing Little League uniforms at the games. The minor league baseball team is already making plans for additional clinics next year and increasing its sponsorships within youth activities.

References

Bachman, K. (2003). Waiting game. *Brandweek, 44*(35), SR15.

Morgan, R. M., & Hunt, S. D. (1994, July). The commitment trust theory of relationship marketing. *Journal of Marketing, 58*, 20-38.

Raymond, J. (2000). Radio-active. *American Demographics, 22*(10), 28-31.

Stilson, J. (2004). Radio scraps for its future. *Advertising Age, 75*(5), 22.

United States Census Bureau (2000). Census report. Retrieved March 4, 2004, from http://www .census.gov.

Weiss, J. (1999, October 28). Sign of the times\Newton ballfield plan pits advertising vs. ambience. *Boston Globe*, B1-3.

White, C. (1998, July 17). Girl opposed to alcohol banned after protest. *USA Today*, C14.

SECTION V

ENDORSEMENT, BUILDING BRAND, AND PROMOTIONAL STRATEGIES

Sports Celebrities as Endorsers: An Analysis of Tiger Woods

DAN DRANE
DENNIS PHILLIPS
ALVIN WILLIAMS
BRIAN CROW

Introduction

Each year, companies pay millions and millions of dollars to athletes for endorsement of their products. This phenomenon is not limited to just large companies. Smaller companies with limited marketing budgets are also beginning to utilize athletes to promote their products. In return for this large investment in endorsements, athletes are supposed to achieve a number of marketing objectives, such as capturing the interest of consumers, fortify the image of the product, enhance recollection of the brand name, augment product attractiveness, enhance credibility of the marketing message, and boost the probability of consumer purchase (Thwaites, 1995).

The most popular athlete endorsers with both fans and sponsoring companies are top names in highly visible sports such as Tiger Woods, Jeff Gordon, and Michael Jordan (Till, 2001). While some argue that companies are reaching a point of diminishing returns with the utilization of expensive athletes, some still find a very lucrative market for their endorsements (Shevack, 1998). Tiger Woods has a $100 million deal with Nike and recently signed on with General Motors to endorse their Buick brand for 10 years. Michael Jordan once signed a 25-year contract with Nike and still makes $35 million per year in endorsements (Sirak, 2004). Retired boxer George Foreman even signed a lifetime deal with Salton for $137.5 million. Stars in little known sports have also begun to take advantage of endorsement opportunities. For example, skateboarder Tony Hawk earns $1.5 million per year in endorsements alone (Moukheiber, 1999).

The research for this paper focuses on Tiger Woods' effectiveness as an endorser and whether or not he is really worth the big bucks he demands. The research investigates consumers' awareness of Woods' endorsements and purchase intentions based on his endorsement in 2000 and again in 2004. Particular interest is also given to Woods' endorsement contract with Nike.

Historical Development

Although it is common practice today, the use of celebrities as endorsers is not a recent phenomenon. Celebrities have been used as product endorsers since the late nineteenth century (Erdogan, 1999). The use of Queen Victoria in connection with Cadbury's Cocoa is an example of early utilization of celebrities (Sherman, 1985). The use of professional athletes as product endorsers have propagated since the 1920s, when Babe Ruth endorsed Pinch Hit Chewing Tobacco and Baby Ruth candy bars (Stotlar, Veltri, & Viswanathan, 1998). From the 1930s to the 1970s, the use of sports celebrities as endorsers grew significantly. Much of this is due to the emergence of cinema and later the popularity of commercial radio in the 1930s and commercial television in the 1950s (McDonough, 1995).

The use of celebrities in general as product endorsers has risen dramatically. Howard (1979) estimated that one in every six advertisements utilized celebrity endorsers in 1979. By 1988, Motavalli (1988) estimated that figure had grown to one in five. In 1997, about 25% of commercials utilized celebrity endorsers (Shimp, 1997). The use of sports celebrities as endorsers increased notably in the late 1980s and 1990s as companies progressively spent more money for athletic product endorsements (Lane, 1994; Lane & McHugh, 1995; Lane & Midgett, 1993). In terms of actual monetary value, it is estimated that companies in the United States paid more than $1 billion to sport celebrity endorsers alone in 1996 for endorsement contracts and licensing rights (Lane, 1996). It is safe to argue that the use of celebrities, including sports celebrities, has reached the level that it can be accepted as common practice in marketing strategy.

Celebrity Versus Non-Celebrity Endorsers

Companies have a vast ability to control created spokespersons since they develop these characters. They can develop characters that are harmonious with their brands and target audiences, and guarantee that these characters are endorsing only their particular product (Tom et al., 1992). Conversely, in the case of celebrity endorsers, companies have very limited influence over the celebrity's public persona. Tom et al.'s results indicated that created endorsers were more successful in creating a link to the product than celebrity endorsers. They attributed these findings to the single utilization of created endorsers with the brand and their unambiguous persona representing the brand's distinctiveness.

Mehta (1994) also found no significant differences in attitudes towards brand, advertising, and intentions to purchase the endorsed brand between celebrity and non-celebrity endorsed products; however, differences were found in cognitive responses produced by receivers. Receivers gave more attention to the brand and its features in non-celebrity conditions whereas in the celebrity condition receivers focused more on the celebrity in advertising. In contrast, Atkin and Block (1983) found that celebrity endorsers fashioned more positive attitudes towards advertising and greater intentions to purchase than non-celebrity endorsers.

Agrawal and Kamakura (1995) and Mathur, Mathur, and Rangan (1997) conducted two noteworthy studies designed to assess the economic worth of celebrity endorsers. The authors utilized Event Study Methodology, which is used to identify the valuation effects of marketing decisions to assess the impact of celebrity endorsement contracts on the expected profitability of a firm. Both studies found that the use of celebrity endorsers was desirable and effective.

Based on academic findings and company reports, it is safe to contend that celebrity endorsers are more effective than non-celebrity endorsers in creating desirable marketing outcomes such as positive attitudes towards advertising, brand awareness, intentions to purchase, and, in fact, actual sales. This is especially true when companies utilize celebrities whose public persona corresponds with the products and target audiences and who have not previously endorsed products.

Models of Celebrity Endorsement Strategy

Selecting celebrity endorsers is an inexact science; however, many scholars have attempted to construct models to aid in their selection. Carl Hovland and his associates presented one of the earliest models, the Source Credibility Model, in 1953 (Erdogan, 1999). Three additional models have been developed since that first model: the Source Attractiveness Model (McGuire, 1985), the Product Match-Up Hypothesis (Kamins, 1990), and the Meaning Transfer Model (McCracken, 1989).

Source Credibility Model

Although a number of dimensions have been proposed to the Source Credibility Model since its inception, it is normally thought to consist of the two major aspects of trustworthiness and expertise (Pornpitakpan, 2003). Information from a credible source can have an effect on opinions, beliefs, attitudes, and behavior through a process called internalization. Internalization takes place when receivers acknowledge a source influence in terms of their personal attitude and value structures (Erdogan, 1999).

Trustworthiness refers to the audience's degree of acceptance and confidence in the speaker and the message (Hovland, Janis, & Kelley, 1953). Companies can benefit from the value of trustworthiness by opting for endorsers who are commonly regarded as honest, believable, and dependable (Shimp, 1997).

Expertise refers to the degree to which an endorser is perceived to be a source of valid assertions. This dimension of source credibility has also been referred to as "competence" (Whitehead, 1968) and "authoritativeness" (McCroskey, 1966), and includes the perceived knowledge, experience, or skills possessed by the endorser. Whether the endorser is really an expert or not is not important, only how the target audience perceives the endorser (Ohanian, 1991).

Source Attractiveness Model

The Source Attractiveness Model contends that the effectiveness of a message depends upon the endorser's likeability, familiarity, and similarity. Likeability is defined as affection for the endorser based on the endorser's physical appearance and behavior, familiarity as knowledge of the endorser through exposure, and similarity as resemblance between the endorser and the intended audience. It is important to understand that attractiveness does not simply mean physical attractiveness, but can include a number of variables such as athletic prowess, intellectual skills, personality, and lifestyle (Erdogan, 1999).

Based on the belief that physically attractive people are more liked and in turn more effective in producing favorable responses, advertisers tend to prefer to use physically attractive endorsers rather than unattractive ones. Research on physical attractiveness of endorsers supports this strategy (Pornpitakpan, 2003).

Product Match-up Hypothesis

The Product Match-up Hypothesis proposes that messages communicated by the endorser and the product message should be harmonious for the advertising to be effective. For example, an endorser who is perceived to possess athletic prowess will be more effective when matched with a sport-related product. Conversely, there will be a minimal influence on consumer attitudes toward the product if it is not related to the user's athletic endeavors. Mirsa and Beatty (1990) supported the match-up hypothesis with their findings that recall and affect toward the brand were enhanced when the celebrity and the brand were perceived to be a good fit or matched. Kotler (1997) also found that utilizing an endorser with congruence to the product leads to greater believability in the advertisement. In further support of the match-up hypothesis, Evans (1988) found that the absence of connection between the endorser and product can cause the audience to focus on the endorser rather than the product and also lead consumers to believe that the endorser is only promoting the product for their financial benefit.

Meaning Transfer Model

In the Meaning Transfer Model, it is proposed that celebrity endorsers embody symbolic meanings that transcend the person and are passed on to the products (McCracken, 1989; Brierley, 1995). There is a conventional path for the movement of cultural meaning in this process. First, the meaning resides in the celebrity. The meaning is then conveyed to the product when the celebrity endorses the product. In the last stage, the meaning is transferred from the product to the consumer (McCracken). In support of this model, Fowles (1996) contends that advertisers' motivation for utilizing celebrities to endorse products lie in the fact that people identify with images of celebrities, and so the advertisers' hope is that people will consume products associated with celebrities.

Pros & Cons of Sport Celebrity Endorsers

Pros

Due to increased competition for consumer consciousness and the proliferation of new product development, companies have utilized attention-creating sports stars to assist with marketing efforts. Sports celebrities can help products stand out from surrounding clutter in the advertising arena, therefore enhancing effective marketing communications by cutting through excess noise in the marketing process (Sherman, 1985). The fundamental nature of an endorsement marketing strategy utilizing sports celebrities consists of forming an emotional tie between the consumer and the athlete, thus improving both brand and product awareness and enriching the image of the company (Stone, Joseph, & Jones, 2003). Using famous and recognized athletes as a strategy to "transfer meaning" implies that consumer perceptions of sports celebrities such as success, power, attractiveness, and athletic prowess can be passed on to the product basically by connecting the product with the athlete.

Another advantage of using sport celebrities as endorsers is that they can supply both free publicity and testimony for a product or service, especially when the product has contributed to their level of performance. Source credibility is also enhanced with the use of sports celebrities in endorsements. This tends to generate a more positive attitude toward the endorsed product, as well as increased intention to purchase (Kamins, 1990). Foe example, Nike's golf ball sales soared after Tiger Woods won the U.S. Open at Pebble Beach using a new Nike golf ball.

In addition to creating favorable consciousness of the endorsed product, Agrawal and Kamakura (1995) have confirmed that sports celebrities serving as product endorsers often positively impact the stock prices of the companies they represent. The stock prices of five companies that Michael Jordan endorsed while playing for the Chicago Bulls increased by $2.9 billion two weeks before the beginning of the 1995 NBA season. The rise in stock price was attributed to the rumor that Jordan would be rejoining the Bulls following his brief retirement the previous season (Crawford & Niendorf, 1999).

Cons

Professional athletes possess a level of athleticism and skill in their chosen sports that cannot be refuted. Therefore, they are not lacking in source credibility. However, skill level alone does not automatically make an athlete a good candidate to become a successful endorser of products (Stone, Joseph, & Jones, 2003). A number of studies have explored the use of celebrity endorsers in general and discovered that the utilization of celebrities as endorsers of products is not always beneficial. Till and Shimp (2000) suggest that negative publicity regarding a celebrity endorser has a tendency to have a harmful impact on the perceptions of a company, particularly when negative events surrounding the celebrity has been exposed prior to the relationship with the company. Consumers also tend to pay more attention to the negative information associated with a celebrity endorser in an ad campaign than positive publicity generated by the endorser

(Ahluwalia, Burnkrant, & Unnava, 2000). Langameyer and Shank (1993) found that consumer perceptions of non-profit organizations decreased when associated with celebrities perceived as having a negative image. Numerous endorsements by the same celebrity amplifies the individual's liability and reduces their credibility (Tripp, Jensen, & Carlson, 1994). Calcott and Lee (1994); Scott (1994); and Pollay and Lavack (1993) have all noted that the increased level of risk associated with using celebrity endorsers has resulted in advertisers using more images of deceased celebrities and animated characters because they are more immune to bad publicity.

As mentioned previously, researchers universally agree that for endorser ads to be successful, the endorser must be both trustworthy and credible. Athletes matched with sport-related products would seem to be a natural and reasonable fit in terms of their perceived source credibility, but not always an appropriate fit in terms of personal character. The negative publicity generated by socially unaccepted behavior and illegal actions of popular sports figures in recent years is of particular concern to advertisers. The media has reported incidents of professional athletes being involved in murder charges, illegal drug distribution, fathering children out of wedlock, illegal gambling activities, and use of anabolic steroids and other banned substances. Advertisers are weary of the negative publicity that is now commonly associated with some of today's premier sports figures. In turn, this bad publicity has resulted in a smaller number of long-term endorsement contracts for athletes (Shevak, 1998). Sport celebrity endorsers exert a considerable influence on the way consumers view endorsed products, and this influence can deeply affect the company's image, both positively and negatively (Till, 2001).

Methodology

A simple seven-question survey was developed for this study. Three questions gained information regarding the demographic characteristics of age, gender, and race. Two questions ascertained the respondents' frequencies of playing and watching golf. The last two questions garnered information about the number of companies respondents knew that Tiger Woods endorsed and their intention to purchase products based on his endorsement.

The survey was administered in 2000 (n = 996) and again in 2004 (n = 806) to determine differences in Woods' effectiveness as an endorser during the time frame. In 2000, students in an undergraduate marketing class were asked to have friends and family fill out the surveys. In 2004, students in an undergraduate club management class were asked to do the same. The authors utilized analysis of variance (ANOVA) to determine relationships between the demographic variables, frequency of playing golf, and frequency of watching golf with knowledge of which products Woods endorsed, knowledge of Woods' endorsement of Nike products specifically, and intention to purchase based on Woods' endorsement. In addition, frequency distributions were used to provide descriptive results for the variables.

Results

Table 1 presents frequency distributions for the demographic variables measured in the two different years.

The sample from 2000 knew an average 1.64 products that Tiger Woods endorsed. In 2004, the sample knew an average 1.73 products that he endorsed. The group from 2004 also had more intentions to purchase products based on his endorsement. In 2000, 9.6% of the respondents indicated they purchased products based on Woods' endorsement. By 2004, this figure had risen to 17.0%. The sample from 2004 also had more knowledge of Woods' endorsement of Nike products. In 2000, 77.0% of respondents knew of his Nike endorsement and 81.9% knew of it in 2004.

In 2000, 18-25 and 26-35 year-olds were able to name more products that Woods endorsed than 35-50 year-olds ($p<.05$). However, in 2004 there was no statistically significant difference among the age groups in knowledge of the companies Woods endorsed. In both years, men were more knowledgeable of the companies he endorsed ($p<.05$). For products endorsed, there was no statistically significant difference

Table 1		
	2000	2004
Age		
Under 18	3.7%	7.2%
18-25	53.2%	46.7%
26-35	13.5 %	18.6%
35-50	20.9%	13.8%
51 and up	8.7%	13.8%
Gender		
Female	43.0%	41.8%
Male	57.0%	58.2%
Racial/Ethnic Group		
American Indian	.5%	2.0%
Asian/Pacific Islander	.2%	3.3%
Black, not Hispanic	18.5 %	28.5 %
Hispanic	1.5%	4.0%
White, not Hispanic	79.3%	62.2%
Play Golf		
Never (0 time per year)	57.7%	45.4%
Seldom (1-5 times per year)	20.7%	19.1%
Moderately (6-10 times per year)	15.4 %	9.9%
Actively (11-30 times per year)	6.0%	11.0%
Often (more than 30 times per year)	8.0%	14.5%
Watch Golf		
Never	36.7%	29.4%
Seldom	36.8%	32.1%
Moderately	15.4%	19.9%
Actively	4.4%	10.5%
Often	6.6%	8.1%

among race for either year. In 2000, respondents that never play golf knew fewer companies endorsed by Woods than all other categories ($p<.05$). Those that played seldom knew fewer than the other three groups ($p<.05$), and those that played moderately knew fewer companies he endorsed than those who played actively ($p<.05$). These results were identical for 2000 when the variable of watching golf was measured. In 2004, respondents that never play golf also knew fewer endorsements of Woods ($p<.05$). Respondents that play golf seldom also knew fewer companies endorsed in 2004 than the other three groups of moderately, actively, and often ($p<.05$). The results for respondents watching golf in 2004 were the same as playing golf with the exception of moderate watchers knew fewer companies Woods endorsed than those who watched actively and often ($p<.05$).

In 2000, respondents in the under 18 age group purchased products based on Woods' endorsement more than any other age group, but only significantly more (statistically) than the 35-50 year old age group ($p<.05$). There was no statistical significance in purchase intentions among the age groups in 2004. There was no gender difference in purchasing products based on Woods' endorsement in 2000; however, men purchased products more based on his endorsement in 2004 ($p<.05$). In 2000, blacks purchased more products based on Woods' endorsement than whites ($p<.05$). There was no difference among race in 2004. Those that played golf often were influenced to purchase products based on Woods' endorsement more than all other groups ($p<.05$). In 2004, respondents that played golf actively and often purchased more than those who played never and seldom ($p<.05$). In 2000, those who watched golf often purchased more based on Woods' endorsement than those who watched never, seldom, and moderately ($p<.05$). Respondents that never watched golf also purchased fewer products based on his endorsement than those who watched golf actively in 2000 ($p<.05$). In 2004, respondents that watched golf often purchased more based on Woods' endorsement than those who watched golf never, seldom, and moderately ($p<.05$). Those who watched golf never and seldom also purchased fewer products than those who watched actively in 2004 ($p<.05$).

In 2000, respondents in the 18-25 and 26-35 year-old age groups had significantly more knowledge (statistically) that Woods endorsed Nike products than those in the 35-50 and over 51-year-old age groups ($p<.05$). However, there was no difference in knowledge of his Nike endorsement among age groups in 2004. Men knew more of his Nike endorsement in both years ($p<.05$). There was difference among race in either year for knowledge of Woods' endorsement of Nike products. In both 2000 and 2004, those who never played golf knew less of Woods' Nike endorsement than all other groups ($p<.05$). These results are identical for both years for the variable of watching golf ($p<.05$).

Conclusions

The results of this study show that Tiger Woods has become more effective as an endorser from 2000 to 2004. Not only did the 2004 group recall more products that Woods endorsed, they also had a greater intention to purchase products based on his endorsement. More people were also aware of Woods' relationship with Nike in 2004. Although not definitive, these results would indicate that Nike is getting a good return on their investment in Woods. The other companies Woods represents might not be as lucky. If 82% of respondents knew of his endorsement of Nike but could only recall 1.7 of the companies he endorsed, then awareness of the other companies was not that high.

Of particular note is the change in results among older adults. The 51-and-older age group was only able to recall 1.14 companies that Woods endorsed in 2000. By 2004, this number had grown to 1.72. The 35-50-year-old age group knew 1.28 companies he endorsed in 2000 and 1.73 in 2004. Although all age groups had a higher intention to purchase based on Woods' endorsement in 2004, the largest jumps were in the two older age groups. These two age groups also had the most increase in knowledge of Woods' endorsement of Nike products.

Woods' effectiveness as an endorser also seems to have had an impact on the white population. In 2000, white respondents knew 1.64 products he endorsed. By 2004, white respondents knew 1.81 products Woods endorsed. This was more than any other racial group. While black respondent actually had a slightly lower intention to purchase based on Woods' endorsement in 2004, the intention to purchase among white respondents increased dramatically. In 2000, white respondents had the least amount of knowledge regarding Woods' relation with Nike. By 2004, whites had more knowledge of Woods' Nike endorsement than any other racial group except for American Indians.

As would be expected, respondents that play and watch more golf had higher awareness of Woods' endorsements and intention to purchase based on his endorsement in both years. However, there was an increase in purchase intention based on Woods' endorsement for those who play and watch golf never, seldom, and moderately in 2004. These same three groups also had a greater knowledge of his Nike endorsement in 2004.

More and more athletes are venturing into the endorsement business and this limited study should shed some light on their effectiveness, especially in the case of Tiger Woods. Studies have shown that the utilization of sports celebrities as endorsers is an effective marketing strategy. The key to effective athlete endorsements seems to be finding a congruent fit between the sports celebrity and product endorsed.

References

Agrawal, J., & Kamakura, W. A. (1995). The economic worth of celebrity endorsers: An event study analysis. *Journal of Marketing, 59*, 56-62.

Ahluwalia, R., Burnkrant, R. E., & Unnava, H. R. (2000). Consumer response to negative publicity: The moderating role of commitment. *Journal of Marketing Research, 37*, 203-214.

Atkin, C., & Block, M. (1983). Effectiveness of celebrity endorsers. *Journal of Advertising Research, 23*, 57-61.

Belch, G. E., & Belch, M. A. (1995). *Introduction to advertising and promotion: An integrated marketing communication perspective.* Chicago: Richard D. Irwin, Inc.

Brierley, S. (1995). *The advertising handbook.* London: Routledge.

Calcott, M., & Lee, W. (1994). A content analysis of animated spokes characters in television commercials. *Journal of Advertising, 23*(4), 1-12.

Crawford, A. J., & Niendorf, B. (1999). The Michael Jordan effect. *American Business Review, 17*(2), 5-10.

Dickenson, N. (1996, May 3). Can celebrities ruin a launch? *Campaign,* p. 24.

Erdogan, B. Z. (1999). Celebrity endorsement: A literature review. *Journal of Marketing Management, 15*, 291-314.

Evans, R. B. (1988). *Production and creativity in advertising.* London: Pitman Publishing.

Fowles, J. (1996). *Advertising and popular culture.* London: Sage Publication Ltd.

Hovland, C. I., Janis, I. K., & Kelley, H. H. (1953). *Communication and persuasion.* New Haven, CT: Yale University Press.

Howard, A. (1979). More than just a passing fancy. *Advertising Age, 50*, S-2.

Kamins, M. (1990). An investigation into the match-up hypothesis in celebrity advertising: When beauty is only skin deep. *Journal of Advertising, 19*(1), 4-13.

Kotler, P. (1997). *Marketing management: Analysis, planning, implementation, and control.* Englewood Cliffs, NJ: Prentice-Hall.

Langmeyer, L., & Shank, M. (1993). Celebrity endorsers and public service agencies: A balancing act. *Proceedings of the 1993 American Academy of Advertising,* 197-207.

Lane, R. (1996). Nice guys finish first. *Forbes, 158*(14), 236-242.

Lane, R. (1994, December 19). The golden bull and the golden bear. *Forbes, 155*(14), 234-242.

Lane, R., & McHugh, J. (1995, December 18). A very green year. *Forbes, 156*(14), 212.

Lane, R., & Midgett, W. (1993, December 20). The super 40. *Forbes, 154*(14), 94-96.

Mathur, L. K., Mathur, I., & Rangan, N. (1997). The wealth effects associated with a celebrity endorser: The Michael Jordan phenomenon. *Journal of Advertising Research, 37*(3), 67-73.

McCracken, G. (1989). Who is the celebrity endorser? Cultural foundation of the endorsement process. *Journal of Consumer Research, 16*, 310-321.

McCroskey, J. C. (1966). Scales for the measurement of ethos. *Speech Monographs, 33*, 65-72.

McDonough, J (1995, Spring). Bringing brands to life. *Advertising Age,* 34-35.

McGuire, W. J. (1985). Attitudes and attitude change. In G. Lindzey & E. Aronson (eds.), *Handbook of social psychology* (pp. 233-346). New York: Random House.

Mehta, A. (1994). How advertising response modeling (ARM) can increase ad effectiveness. *Journal of Advertising Research, 34*(3), 62-74.

Mirsa, S., & Beatty, S. E. (1990). Celebrity spokesperson and brand congruence: An assessment of recall and affect. *Journal of Business Research, 21*, 159-173.

Mooij, M. (1994). *Advertising worldwide: Concepts, theories and practice of international, multinational and global advertising.* London: Prentice-Hall International.

Motavalli, J. (1988, January 11). Advertising blunder of the rich and famous. *Adweek,* p. 18-19.

Moukheiber, Z. (1999, November 29). Later, skater. *Forbes, 164*(13), 108-110.

Ohanian, R. (1991). The impact of celebrity spokesperson's perceived image on consumers' intention to purchase. *Journal of Advertising Research, 31*(1), 46-52.

Pollay, R. W., & Lavack, A. M. (1993). The targeting of youths by advertising marketers: Archival evidence on trial. *Advances in Consumer Research, 20*, 266-271.

Pornpitakpan, C. (2003). Validation of the celebrity endorsers' credibility scale: Evidence from Asians. *Journal of Marketing Management, 19*, 179-195.

Scott, L. M. (1993). Images in advertising: The need for a theory of visual rhetoric. *Journal of Consumer Research, 21*, 252-253.

Sherman, S. P. (1985, August 19). When you wish upon a star. *Fortune, 112*(4), 66-71.

Shevak, B. (1998, October 5). The brand should be the star, not the athlete. *Brandweek, 39*(37), 5.

Shimp (1997). *Advertising, promotion and supplemental aspects of integrated marketing communication.* Fort Worth, TX: The Dryden Press.

Sirak, R. (2004). The golf digest 50. *Golf Digest, 55*(2), 106-110.

Stone, G., Joseph, M., & Jones, M. (2003). An exploratory study on the use of sports celebrities in advertising: A content analysis. *Sport Marketing Quarterly, 12*(2), 94-102.

Stotlar, D. K., Veltri, F. R., & Viswanathan, R. (1998). Recognition of athlete-endorsed sports products. *Sport Marketing Quarterly, 7*(1), 48-56.

Thwaites, D. (1995). Professional football sponsorship: Profitable or profligate? *International Journal of Advertising, 14*(2), 149-164.

Till, B. D. (2001). Managing athlete endorser image: The effect of endorsement product. *Sport Marketing Quarterly, 10*(1), 35-42.

Till, B. D., & Shimp T. A. (2000). Endorsers in advertising: The case of negative celebrity information. *Journal of Advertising, 27*(1), 67-82.

Tom, G., Clark, R., Elmer, L., Grech, E., Masetti, J., & Sandhar, H. (1992). The use of created versus celebrity spokesperson in advertisements. *The Journal of Consumer Marketing, 9*(4), 45-51.

Tripp, C., Jensen, T., & Carlson, L. (1994). Effects of multiple product endorsements by celebrities on consumer attitudes and intentions. *Journal of Consumer Research, 20*, 535-547.

Whitehead, J. L. (1968). Factors of source credibility. *Quarterly Journal of Speech, 54*(1), 59-63.

Branding Athletes: If the Athlete is the Brand, Does the Product Matter?

RON GARLAND
JAN CHARBONNEAU

Abstract

The benefits that brands accrue from celebrity and celebrity athlete endorsement, the characteristics of effective celebrity endorsement, and the risks involved for brands are all topics that have been well researched. The focus of academic literature has primarily been on the transfer of the celebrity image to the endorsed brand or product through the endorsement process. Apart from Till (2001), few studies have investigated the influence of the product endorsed upon the image of the celebrity athlete endorser—in essence, reverse image transfer.

This paper reports the results of an exploratory study investigating reverse image transfer. Selected attributes from Ohanian's (1990) 15 item source-credibility scale were used to first establish celebrity athlete image and then post-test this image after respondents had been exposed to a series of print advertisements featuring the celebrity athlete endorsing either a positively or negatively perceived product. The results were unequivocal: Endorsing negatively perceived products, such as cigarettes, damages celebrity athlete images in terms of both attractiveness and trustworthiness. Conversely, positively perceived products, such as orange juice, appear to have no statistically significant effect on celebrity athlete image. These results have implications for athletes, their agents, and their corporate partners when considering endorsement proposals. Choice of product for endorsement does matter! As internationally recognised celebrity athletes such as David Beckham and Anna Kournikova increasingly draw substantial amounts of their income from brand endorsement, or even reinvent themselves as brands in their own right, there is a need to understand this reverse image transfer.

Literature Review

Introduction

Having celebrity athletes endorse brands is a prominent part of many companies' promotional strategies. The benefits that accrue to brands from such celebrity endorsement are well documented (see, for example, Kamins, 1990; Erdogan, 1999; James & Ryan, 2001; Pornpitakpan, 2003) and the academic literature is quite voluminous. Focus has been on the transfer of celebrity image onto endorsed product or brand, but few studies, apart from that of Till (2001) in the USA, have investigated the influence of the brand or product upon the image of the celebrity athlete endorser—in essence, reverse image transfer. This paper investigates reverse image transfer and closely replicates the work of Till (2001), albeit in a New Zealand setting, but using international celebrity athletes.

Celebrity Athlete Endorsement

Brooks and Harris (1998) noted that celebrity athlete endorsement has excited the interest of practitioners, students, and researchers alike, while Erdogan, Baker, and Tagg (2001) commented that a recent literature review by their first author unearthed 45 recent academic articles on that topic in mainstream marketing and communication academic journals. In the context of this paper, a celebrity athlete endorser is a publicly recognised sports star who uses that public recognition to help another party (usually a corporate client) sell or bolster the image of specific goods or services.

In an earlier article, Erdogan and Kitchen (1998) provide a cogent summary of the reasons for the growth of celebrity endorsers in marketing communications. These include

- qualities such as physical attraction, sex appeal, and likeability, which can be transferred to the products being endorsed;
- "cutting through the advertising clutter"—celebrities can attract and maintain attention by their mere presence; and
- helping brand makeovers, brand re-launches, and brand re-positioning, especially when a new or enhanced athletic image is required.

Obviously there are negative aspects to celebrity endorsement, especially when celebrities are involved in scandals, disappear from public attention through injury or loss of form, become overexposed by too much product involvement, or even overshadow the brand they are endorsing. Nonetheless, "even though research findings are equivocal about the ability of celebrities to stimulate actual purchase behaviour, the positive impact of celebrity endorsers is well documented" (Erdogan & Kitchen, 1998, p. 17).

Development of Multiple-Item Scales to Measure Celebrity Endorsement

Atkin and Black (1983) traced some of the earlier use of celebrity athletes (post-World War II up to the 1970s) in advertising, noting the influence that various celebrities provided to a range of goods and services. Attitude changes in a positive direction were accredited to the celebrity's presence. Kahle and Homer (1985) extended this research perspective and were among the first to formally acknowledge, using social adaptation theory, how attractive-looking endorsers can produce an attitudinal change. Meanwhile, Kamins (1990) was opining on the "match-up hypothesis," the perceived level of "fit" between celebrities' images and the products or services they are endorsing. Then Ohanian (1990) introduced a scale (the source-credibility scale) measuring a potential celebrity's suitability for endorsing specific products. She went to some trouble to define source credibility, commenting that its usage in advertising had been handicapped by many different executions, finally settling on source credibility being "a communicator's positive characteristics that affect the receiver's acceptance of a message" (p. 41). Her review of the literature highlighted how celebrity endorsement really rested upon two themes: source credibility and source attractiveness. The former is, in turn, comprised of two main factors—expertise and trustworthiness—while the latter (attractiveness) "depends on the source's 'familiarity,' 'likability' [*sic*], 'similarity' and 'attractiveness' to the respondent" (Ohanian 1990, p. 41). She concluded that "credible sources are more persuasive than are sources of low credibility" (p. 42), then introduced her three component celebrity endorser's credibility scale on the premise that "with the increased use of celebrities in advertising, a valid instrument measuring a celebrity endorser's credibility is essential for understanding the impact of using such individuals in advertising" (p. 42). After the scale performed well on a series of reliability and validity tests, Ohanian (1990) suggested that it could replace single-item scales for assessing celebrity endorsers. Subsequently, Garland and Ferkins (2003) in New Zealand, and Pornpitakpan (2003) in East Asia, have confirmed the Ohanian scale's validity and reliability for international settings.

Relevant Celebrity Endorsement Research

Recently, Stone, Joseph, and Jones (2003), Burton and Kahle (2001), and James and Ryan (2001) have explored issues related to sport heroes' gender in celebrity athlete endorsement. The latter authors investigated tertiary students' attitudes to female sports stars as endorsers, using three different product categories scored against six popular female athletes. Their results supported Kamins' (1990) "match-up hypothesis" with the celebrity athletes' images "fitting" with various product images. Expertise (one of Ohanian's source-credibility scale's three key dimensions—see Figure 1) was deemed crucial in athlete-product fit although trustworthiness and attractiveness (the other two key dimensions of the Ohanian scale) were sometimes associated too. Notwithstanding the research discussed above, and citing work by Miciak and Shanklin (1994), James and Ryan (2001) stated that the former had "concluded after interviewing a large number of advertising agencies and corporations that most did not undertake adequate research with regard to celebrity endorsers" (p.1), while Brooks and Harris (1998) suggested that "researchers and practitioners clearly have much work to do to bring a sense of order to the understanding of celebrity athlete endorsement" (p. 43).

Erdogan and Kitchen (1998) discuss how "academic research findings are equivocal about what are the important dimensions of celebrity endorsers" (p. 18). Their main criticism is that source credibility—attractiveness, trustworthiness, expertise—"effectively disregards the meaning of interaction between celebrity and brand." They went to say that "[t]hese interactions could cause endorsers to be inappropriate for some products, regardless of their credibility or attractiveness" (p.18). They also suggest that the celebrity's previous endorsements ought to be considered. In a later paper, Erdogan, Baker, and Tagg (2001) investigated British advertising agency managers' celebrity choice factors. Their findings confirm that choice factors for celebrity selection are influenced by the type of product being endorsed. Thus, matching celebrity to product is crucial, followed by the celebrity's overall image, then his/her cost, trustworthiness, controversy risk, familiarity, prior endorsements, and likeability.

Undoubtedly, celebrity endorsers break through media clutter and hold viewers' attention (Dyson & Turco, 1998; Erdogan & Baker, 1999). They contribute to brand name recognition, create positive associations with the brand, and assist in developing distinct and credible brand personalities (Kamins, 1990; Ohanian, 1990). Athletes provide particularly compelling testimonials for products that have contributed to their sporting performance and success (Dyson & Turco, 1998). If this concept of meaning transfer can be reversed, then it is possible for endorsed brands to attach some of their underlying images to the endorser. Hence it can be suggested, as Till (2001) did, that in this age of celebrity athletes pursuing their own branding opportunities, reverse image transfer (from product or brand back to endorser) ought to be a consideration. Till (2001) demonstrated how celebrity athlete endorsers' own images can be adversely affected by association with negatively perceived products, especially products, such as tobacco, with well documented health risks. He saw the possibility of reverse image transfer—the impact of the brand on the endorser—as worthy of investigation and of value to celebrities in matching their own brands (themselves) with potential endorsement opportunities.

Methodology

Our study is a close replication of Till's (2001) study with adjustments for the New Zealand sport environment. The hypothesis to be tested (derived from Till's 2001 work) was "that while a positively perceived product will have little or no effect on respondents' perceptions of celebrity athlete endorsement, a negatively perceived product will have a substantial effect."

Till's pre-testing work, which called for two products on either end of the "positive-negative" product continuum, resulted in the choice of orange juice and chewing tobacco. New Zealanders do not have a tradition of chewing tobacco. Thus, cigarettes were substituted instead and pre-testing revealed a substantial level of negative connotations with that product.

To remove any specific confounding branding influences in the experiment, the two products, orange juice and cigarettes, were presented to respondents as "brand X orange juice" and "brand X cigarettes." And, just as Till (2001) did, we removed any chance of an effect from choice of endorser by creating two fictitious endorsers, one male (whom we christened "Marty") and one female (whom we christened "Franny"), for our study. The next decision was to choose a sport. Rugby football is New Zealand's national winter game, played by both men and women, and it became our selection. For the purposes of our study we now needed to choose two top athletes from the world of sport to represent "athletes as their own brands." Who better to choose than David Beckham (this research was conducted prior to his recent notoriety regarding the Rebecca Loos affair) and Anna Kournikova? Both these sporting stars have recognition and earnings from their endorsement activities that far exceed their incomes from sport prize money.

These decision outcomes discussed above resulted in two experiments:

- Comparison of two fictitious celebrity rugby players (one male, one female) endorsing two "generic" products (brand X orange juice and brand X cigarettes).
- Comparison of two named celebrity athletes (David Beckham and Anna Kournikova representing athletes as their own brands) endorsing the same two "generic" products.

Eight versions of our questionnaire were constructed as follows:

- Version 1: Generic rugby player Marty endorsing orange juice
- Version 2: Generic rugby player Marty endorsing cigarettes
- Version 3: Generic rugby player Franny endorsing cigarettes
- Version 4: Generic rugby player Franny endorsing orange juice
- Version 5: Branded athlete David Beckham endorsing orange juice
- Version 6: Branded athlete David Beckham endorsing cigarettes
- Version 7: Branded athlete Anna Kournikova endorsing orange juice
- Version 8: Branded athlete Anna Kournikova endorsing cigarettes.

Background information provided in the questionnaires for the generic rugby players Marty and Franny was restricted to the following: "Marty was a professional rugby player who represented his country at the 2003 World Cup. He was acclaimed by his teammates as one of the best players in his position."; and "Franny was a rugby player who represented her country at the 2002 World Cup. She was acclaimed by her teammates as one of the best players in her position." The only background information provided in versions 5-8 of the questionnaire for David Beckham and Anna Kournikova was "David Beckham is England's former football captain and played for Manchester United before moving to Real Madrid" and "Anna Kournikova, the Russian tennis star is the winner of many doubles tournaments."

Apart from the questionnaire versions as outlined above, our research instruments for each product (orange juice and cigarettes) and each subject (celebrity both fictitious and "branded") were three black and white print advertisements mocked up with the subjects in casual clothing, a photograph of the product, and the following by-lines and body copy:

- (subject) ONLY drinks BRAND "X" orange juice
- (subject) ONLY drinks BRAND "X," the juice with more orange
- (subject) and BRAND "X" orange juice . . . a winning combination!

- (subject) ONLY smokes BRAND "X" cigarettes
- (subject) ONLY smokes BRAND "X" . . . the cigarette with more PUFF
- (subject) and BRAND "X" cigarettes . . . a winning combination!

Ohanian's (1990) source-credibility scale became the instrument for evaluating our sample's perceptions of each celebrity's attractiveness and trustworthiness both before and after the product match-up experiment. Apart from her own validity and reliability testing in 1990 and 1991, Ohanian's scale has been tested in a number of non-U.S. settings (see, for example, James & Ryan, 2001; Garland & Ferkins, 2003; Pornpitakpan, 2003). We chose to use only the first 10 attributes of Ohanian's 15-point semantic differential source-credibility scale because the final five points are "expertise" attributes and our selected athletes were all either independently judged or created by us as experts in their chosen sport (see Figure 1 for the attributes of Ohanian's 1990 source-credibility scale).

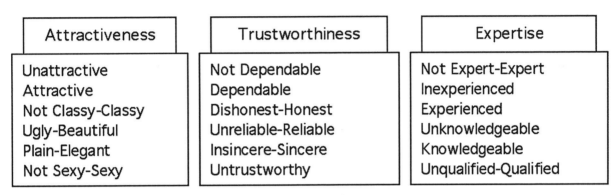

Figure 1. Ohanian's 15 point source-credibility scale

Respondents were all undergraduate business students from one campus of Massey University, New Zealand. The research was carried out at the beginning of several marketing lectures without any prior publicity, and, once completed and collected, the survey instrument was incorporated into lecture content. Students can be appropriate samples for experiments such as in this study as they are often market innovators (Nikas, 1999). In total, 240 respondents (n = 128 males and n = 112 females) completed our survey, split equally into eight groups with n = 30 respondents receiving one of the eight versions (see above).

Firstly, respondents completed several demographic questions, then a "level of interest in sport" question, and then a screening question on the level of appropriateness (using a 9-point semantic differential scale: anchors—not appropriate; appropriate) for an athlete to endorse orange juice or to endorse cigarettes. Then the celebrity athlete (either generic or named) was presented to respondents by way of a PowerPoint slide (picture), along with the brief biography specified above. Respondents now scored their subject on 10 attributes (attractiveness and trustworthiness) of the Ohanian (1990) 15-point source-credibility scale (see Figure 1). Next came three print advertisements (for each celebrity athlete paired with his/her particular product) with the pace for viewing each advertisement controlled by the authors as they administered the questionnaire. Once this viewing phase was completed, respondents completed the same evaluation (again using 10 of the 15 attributes of Ohanian's source-credibility scale) for their celebrity athlete as before, thereby completing the "before exposure, after exposure" experiment.

Results and Discussion

At the beginning of the questionnaire, respondents had been requested to score athletes in general (using a nine-point semantic differential scale) on "appropriateness" to endorse orange juice and cigarettes. This initial question provided context in the form of a benchmark result for the experimentation to follow.

Results of these benchmarks are presented in Table 1 and are unequivocal: Orange juice is entirely appropriate for celebrity athletes to endorse, cigarettes are not! Hence orange juice is perceived as a positive product while cigarettes are very definitely negatively perceived.

Table 1: Celebrity athlete appropriateness to endorse orange juice, cigarettes

Product	Mean	Std deviation	Sample size
Orange juice	7.09	1.57	237
Cigarettes	1.86	1.73	234

Our hypothesis was that the endorsement of a positive product (orange juice) would have little or no effect upon a celebrity athlete's perceived credibility, but endorsement of a negatively perceived product (cigarettes) would result in a negative impact on perceived credibility. Table 2 displays the grand means for each treatment (version) and demonstrates clearly that the endorsement of orange juice by either a generic celebrity athlete or a named celebrity athlete has little or no effect as hypothesized. Equally as clear is the denigration of celebrity athlete credibility through endorsement of cigarettes. The change in respondents' evaluations brought about by pairing generic and named celebrity athletes with cigarettes in mock-up print advertisements is always in the negative direction (see treatments 2,3,6,8 in Table 2). In each of these cases, mean evaluations fell by statistically significant (at the .05 level) amounts. Perhaps of even more interest is the harsher evaluations meted out to female athletes (compared to males) when endorsing cigarettes. Remember, our sample was almost evenly split between male and female respondents.

Table 2: Evaluation of celebrity athletes by product category

Treatment (n=30 each)	Product	Pre-test Mean	Post-test Mean	T	p
1. Generic male athlete	Orange juice	4.45	4.49	-.24	.82
2. Generic male athlete	Cigarettes	4.58	4.20	2.19	.04*
3. Generic female athlete	Cigarettes	5.21	4.69	3.83	.01*
4. Generic female athlete	Orange juice	5.13	5.23	-1.39	.18
5. David Beckham	Orange juice	5.05	4.84	1.49	.15
6. David Beckham	Cigarettes	4.67	4.32	2.41	.03*
7. Anna Kournikova	Orange juice	5.21	5.33	-.88	.39
8. Anna Kournikova	Cigarettes	5.32	4.67	3.74	.01*

* Statistically significant at .05 level on simple ANOVA.

Further investigation within particular attributes of source-credibility (see Table 3) reveals that respondents are especially harsh in their scoring of the athletes on the trustworthiness dimension's attributes (dependability, honesty, reliability, and sincerity) when they were paired with the negative product, cigarettes. Nevertheless, interesting side issues emerge on closer inspection of the scores for the two named celebrity athletes. It would appear that Anna Kournikova is dealt particularly severe evaluations when associated with cigarettes, stemming from decreasing values for both dimensions (attractiveness and trustworthiness) and on all but two of the attributes, whereas David Beckham is perceived less severely although he too loses some appeal on the trustworthiness dimension. The generic female athlete (Franny) scores very similarly to Anna Kournikova on these attributes leading us to speculate that associating with a negatively perceived product poses greater risks for female athletes than male athletes (in keeping with our previous finding).

Table 3: Celebrity athletes & cigarettes: attributes of attractiveness & trustworthiness

Ohanian's (1990) attributes	Generic male athlete		Generic female athlete		Beckham		Kournikova	
	Pre-test mean	Post-test mean	Pre-test mean	Post-test mean	Pre-test mean	Post-test mean	Pre-test mean	Post-test mean
Attractiveness	5.07	4.70	5.57	5.30	4.77	4.60	6.17	5.40*
Classiness	4.87	4.30*	4.87	4.63	5.00	4.30*	5.31	4.38*
Beauty	4.90	4.50*	5.70	5.40	4.63	4.40	5.97	5.60*
Elegance	4.73	4.30*	5.07	4.60*	4.80	4.63	5.76	4.97*
Sexiness	4.43	4.21	5.23	5.10	4.73	4.47	6.43	6.03
Dependability	4.37	4.23	5.20	4.53*	4.50	4.27	4.77	4.30
Honesty	4.23	4.03	5.13	4.40*	4.47	4.23	4.83	4.27*
Reliability	4.57	3.97*	5.10	4.41*	4.57	4.03*	4.76	3.86*
Sincerity	4.37	3.83*	5.10	4.31*	4.73	4.17*	4.90	4.03*
Trustworthiness	4.27	3.90	5.17	4.20*	4.50	4.07*	4.87	3.90*

* Statistically significant at the .05 level on simple ANOVA.

These results have implications for athletes, their agents, and their corporate partners when endorsement opportunities are under consideration. Choice of product for endorsement does matter in that reverse transfer can occur, suggesting the need to pre-test celebrity-product match-up opportunities. As celebrity athletes such as David Beckham and Anna Kournikova increasingly derive substantial amounts of their income from brand endorsement or even try to reinvent themselves as brands in their own right, the potential for reverse image transfer needs to be part of their endorsement decision making.

References

Atkin, C., & Block, M. (1983). Effectiveness of celebrity endorsers. *Journal of Advertising Research, 23*(1), 57-61.

Brooks, C. M., & Harris, K. (1998). Celebrity athlete endorsement: An overview of the key theoretical issues. *Sport Marketing Quarterly, 7*(2), 34-44.

Dyson, A., & Turco, D. (1998). The state of celebrity endorsement in sport. *Cyber-Journal of Sport Marketing, 2*(1). Retrieved October 20, 2003, from http://www.ausport.gov.au/fulltext/1998/cjsm.

Erdogan, B. (1999). Celebrity endorsement: A literature review. *Journal of Marketing Management, 15*(4), 291-314.

Erdogan, B., & Baker, M. (1999). Celebrity endorsement: Advertising agency managers' perspective. *Cyber-Journal of Sport Marketing, 3*(3). Retrieved October 20, 2003, from http://www.ausport .gov.au/fulltext/1999/cjsm.

Erdogan, B. Z., Baker, M. J., & Tagg, S. (2001). Selecting celebrity endorsers: The practitioner's perspective. *Journal of Advertising Research, 41*(3), 39-48.

Erdogan, B., & Kitchen, P. (1998, April). Getting the best out of celebrity endorsers. *Admap*, 17-20.

Garland, R., & Ferkins, L. (2003, December). Evaluating New Zealand sports stars as celebrity endorsers: Intriguing results. *Proceedings of ANZMAC Conference*, University of South Australia, Adelaide, AU.

James, K. & Ryan, M. (2001). Attitudes toward female sports stars as endorsers. *Proceedings of ANZMAC Conference*, Massey University, Auckland, NZ, 1-8.

Kahle, L., & Homer, P. (1985). Physical attractiveness of the celebrity endorser: A social adaptation perspective. *Journal of Consumer Research, 11*(3), 954-961.

Kamins, M. (1990). An investigation into the "match-up hypothesis" in celebrity marketing: When beauty may be only skin deep. *Journal of Advertising, 19*(1), 4-13.

McCracken, G. (1989). Who is the celebrity endorser? Cultural foundations of the endorsement process. *Journal of Consumer Research, 16*(3), 310-321.

Miciak, A., & Shanklin, W. (1994). Choosing celebrity endorsers. *Marketing Management, 3*(3), 50-59.

Nikas, C. (1999, 5-18 May). Just ad celebrity. *Ragtrader*, 22-23.

Ohanian, R. (1990). Construction and validation of a scale to measure celebrity endorsers' perceived expertise, trustworthiness, and attractiveness. *Journal of Advertising, 19*(3), 39-52.

Ohanian, R. (1991). The impact of celebrity spokespersons' perceived image on consumers' intention to purchase. *Journal of Advertising Research, 13*(1), 46-55.

Pornpitakpan, C. (2003). Validation of the celebrity endorsers' credibility scale: Evidence from Asians. *Journal of Marketing Management, 19*(1/2), 179-195.

Stone, G., Joseph, M., & Jones, M. (2003). An exploratory study on the use of sports celebrities in advertising: A content analysis. *Sport Marketing Quarterly, 10*(1), 35-42.

Till, B. (2001). Managing athlete endorser image: The effect of endorsed product. *Sport Marketing Quarterly, 10*(1), 35-42.

Understanding and Adapting to Cultural Diversity in International Sport Marketing

JAIME OREJAN

Introduction

Communication is a growth business, and the world has been shrinking for quite some time. In 1603, it took three days to get vital messages from London to Edinburgh. By the mid 1800s, the invention of the telegraph cut this time to three hours. Forty years later, the telephone reduced this time yet again to three minutes or less. Nowadays, communication can be done in less than three seconds by e-mail.

Satellites have merged the world's media. Teleconferencing systems now link executives across oceans without even the buffer-time of a plane journey. Screen trading enables the banker to deal at the touch of a button, shifting currencies and shares at the speed of light.

Does all this mean the end of the personal touch? Or the end of understanding the world's cultural diversities?

Yes, the world has become more global, and communication has become easier and faster. Unfortunately, we know less about our cultural differences than at any other time in our history. It is this lack of understanding and appreciation of other cultures that causes many blunders in international business.

Consistent with the overall reduction of trade barriers worldwide, international sport marketers are looking for ways to capitalize on opportunities to sell their products overseas. Given the prevalence of sports and sport products in the international marketplace, it is imperative that sport marketers understand the cultural issues associated with selling and advertising in foreign markets. Pitts and Stotlar (2002) noted that sport business personnel have a common bond with their counterparts in other countries through their athletic experience, but that culture variations on appropriate business and etiquette can sabotage chances for success.

According to Root (1994), blunders in international business are commonly traceable to ethnocentric assumptions unconsciously held by managers, especially the belief that foreigners think and behave much like people at home even though they may speak another language. Because they are usually wrong in one respect or another, ethnocentric assumptions lead to poor strategies in both design and execution.

Cultural differences can affect any and all entry strategy decisions, and all decisions depend on cross-cultural communication, which in reality is the lifeblood of international business transactions. Any time a message or product crosses cultural boundaries, there is a potential for misunderstanding arising from largely unconscious cultural differences.

International managers are communicators across cultures; they are transmitters of their own culture, and agents of change in foreign cultures (Sumatra, 1989). This means that they need to deal with foreign nationals in face-to-face encounters. They also need to design and execute marketing communications, such as advertising, addressed to foreign nationals.

Rick (1993) noted that the expatriate manager is most directly involved in managing cultural differences, followed by headquarters managers who make frequent business trips abroad. But even in an international company or organization, home country managers should learn to appreciate and understand cultural differences, because at the very least they are members of a communications system that includes foreign nationals. A frequent complaint of country managers is their inability to communicate with ethnocentric managers at the corporate level, due to a lack of understanding of cultural differences, and language in particular (Root, 1994).

The pervasive influence of cultural differences on communication in international business dealings merits a more thorough treatment. In this article we attempt to describe the nature of culture and those of its elements that influence international marketing operations, as well as a guide to think in international and global terms.

What is Culture?

Culture is a widely recognized word, and defining the concept of culture is so challenging and complex that it is difficult to define it in short, simple terms. It seems that each anthropologist has a definition. In fact, Kroeber and Kluckhon (1952) identified over 160 different definitions of the term *culture*. Hoebel (1960) described culture as "the sum total of learned behavior traits which are manifest and shared by members of a society" (p. 168).

Culture, according to Kahler and Kramer (1977), provides the members of a society with a means to comfortably interact with their environment and each other. People think and act according to the norms of the culture in which they have been reared. Values and beliefs adopted from the family, reference, and social groups provide individuals with a sense of security and help them function in the society.

Terpstra (1997) noted that culture is not biologically transmitted; any given culture or way of life is learned behavior which depends on the environment and not heredity. Hodgetts and Luthans (1991) believe that culture is learned through both education and experience, and that cultures constantly undergo change as people adapt to new environments. In fact, in most countries, the culture of the early 21st century is not the same as that of the 1960s or 70s.

Anthropologists, as described by Hall (1977), do agree on three features of every human culture. First, he noted, culture is not inherited, but rather learned by a process called *enculturation*. Second, the knowledge values, beliefs, customs, and mores that make up the culture are interrelated to form a more or less *integrated whole*. Third, culture consists of learned behavior traits which are shared by members of a societal group and distinguish that group from other groups with different cultures.

To be successful in international business, we must understand the cultures of other countries and learn how to adapt to them. To an extent, all individuals are home country oriented; the challenge in international business is learning how to broaden our perspective to avoid making decisions based on misconceptions (Cassidy, 1992).

One cause of these misconceptions, according to Knotts (1989), is ethnocentrism, the belief that one's way of doing things is superior to others. Knotts noted that there are a number of forms of ethnocentric behaviors. Some of the most common include patronization, disrespect, an aura of superiority, and inflexible behavior.

Ethnocentric behavior can be avoided by learning about the culture where one will be doing business. Perhaps the easiest way to grasp the complexity of culture is to examine its varied aspects, and this can be done by learning or studying the elements of culture.

Elements of Culture

Culture, as stated earlier, is a complex, multidimensional subject, and the same applies to the varying definitions of the elements of culture. Terpstra (1997) and Rugman and Hodgetts (1995), in trying to understand the nature of culture, examined eight major elements of culture: language, religion, material culture, values and attitudes, aesthetics, education, manners and customs, and social institutions.

Language

Language is the most obvious difference between cultures. It is inextricably linked with all other aspects of a culture, and reflects the nature and values of that culture. Language is critical to culture because it is the primary means used to transmit information and ideas. Knowledge of the local language can help in four ways (Rugman & Hodgetts, 1995). First, it permits a clearer understanding of the situation. With direct knowledge of a language, a businessperson does not have to rely on someone else to interpret or explain. Second, language provides direct access to local people who are frequently more open in their communication when dealing with someone who speaks their language. Third, an understanding of the language allows the person to pick up nuances, implied meanings, and other information that is not being stated outright. Finally, language helps the person to better understand the culture.

One of the best examples of the value of language is to know the meaning of everyday idioms and clichés. A former fellow classmate from Latin America, with limited knowledge of the English language, was baffled when other students saluted her with the words "What's up?" Confused by the unfamiliar idiom, she constantly looked upwards, not knowing or understanding what the words meant in the American English context. In other cases, the meaning of idioms and clichés differ from one country to another, although the same language is spoken. For instance, in Britain a "torch" means a flashlight, whereas in the United States the word means fire or flame.

Knowledge of another language is also important, because direct translation may be inadequate or misleading (Rugman & Hodgetts, 1995). In fact, in many languages around the world, certain words do not exist. Thus, to convey the meaning for a word that does not exists in another language requires an extensive and detailed translation. In many cases, literal translations are not accurate. This is more evident in advertising. For example, General Motors introduced its Chevrolet Nova into Latin America without realizing that the words *no va* in Spanish mean "no go." Not a very stimulating name for an automobile (Axtell, 1994).

In another example, Gibson and Hodgetts (1991) pointed to a laundry detergent company that wished it had contacted a few locals before it initiated its promotional campaign in the Middle East. All of the company's advertisements pictured soiled clothes on the left, its box of soap in the middle, and clean clothes on the right. But, because in that area of the world people tend to read from right to left, many potential customers interpreted the message to indicate the soap actually soiled the clothes.

The English language has a rich vocabulary for commercial and industrial activities, reflecting the nature of the English and American societies. However, many less industralized societies have only limited vocabularies for industrial and commercial activities, but have richer vocabularies for matters important to their culture (Terpstra, 1997). Eskimos, for example, have many words to describe snow, whereas English has one general term. At the same time, in America, the subculture of skiers has a richer vocabulary for snow than the non-skiers.

Because language is such an obvious difference, everyone recognizes that it must be dealt with. Anyone planning a career—or, at the very least, anyone dealing in international business—should learn a foreign language, and while it is not detrimental to anyone's career, it is extremely advantageous. If a career is going to be exclusively involved in a particular country, learning the language will be very useful; however, learning German or Japanese for someone not involved with those countries is no great help. Most of us do not know where a career will lead; therefore, it is best to study a language with large international coverage. Americans are fortunate in having English as their native tongue, for English comes as close to being a world language for international dealings. French and Spanish follow English as the languages most frequently used in conducting international business.

Religion

Religion reflects beliefs and behaviors of a nation which cannot be verified by empirical tests (Terpstra & David, 1985). In other words, the religion of a culture provides the best insights into that culture's behavior. Therefore, although the international company is primarily interested in knowing how people behave as consumers or workers, management's task will be aided by an understanding of why people behave as they do (Terpstra, 1997).

The extent to which religion influences the cultural profile of a society depends on whether a particular religion is dominant or state sanctioned, the importance that society places on religion, the degree of religious homogeneity in the society, and the degree of tolerance for religious diversity that exist in the society (Mendenhall et al., 1995). Some evidence suggests that devoutly religious individuals are more likely to endorse the dominant cultural profile of a society (Burris, Branscombe, & Jackson, 2000).

There are a number of major religions in the world, including Catholicism, Protestantism, Judaism, Islam, Hinduism, Buddhism, and Confucianism. Religions influence lifestyles, beliefs, values, and attitudes and can have a dramatic effect on the way people in a society act toward each other and toward those in other societies (Rugman & Hodgetts, 1995). Religion can also affect the work habits of people, and this can have some economic implications. In the United States, it is common to hear people talk about the Protestant work ethic, which holds that people should work hard, be industrious, and save their money. This work ethic, according to Rugman and Hodgetts (1995), helped develope capitalism in the United States because of the importance it assigned to saving and capital reinvestment.

Religious holidays vary greatly among countries, not only from Christian to Muslim, but even from one Christian country to another. Italy, for example, has 13 religious holidays, depending on how Sundays fall. Religion also affects work and social customs from the days of the week on which people work to their dietary habits. Even major holidays are often tied to religion. On December 25th, Christmas Day, many Americans exchange gifts. However, the Dutch exchange gifts on St. Nicholas Day (December 6), the Russians do it on Frost Man's Day (January 1), and, in many Latin countries, as well as in Latin-oriented communities in the United States such as Miami, this activity is often carried out on Wise Men's Day (January 6).

Although Christianity is currently the dominant religion worldwide, its percentage of followers is projected to be relatively stable in the near future, with Islamic religions and Hindus representing an increasing percentage of the world population (Barrett, 1982). Of course, religions are not evenly distributed across the planet, with some religions concentrated in specific geographic regions (Thomas, 2002). For example, Islam is largely concentrated in Asia and Africa, and Shinto almost exclusively in Japan. Obviously, therefore, religion has a greater influence in some cultures than others.

Material Culture

The tools, artifacts, and technology that people of a society make are considered material culture. Material culture involves techniques and physical things, but only those made by man, as opposed to those found in nature (Tersptra, 1997). For example, a tree per se is not part of a culture, but the Christmas tree is, and so is an orchard. Material culture is directly related to the way a society organizes its economic activities.

When studying material culture, we consider how people make things, who makes them, and why—technology and economics, respectively. Technology includes the techniques used in the creation of material goods; it is the technical know-how possessed by the people of a society. Economics is the manner in which people employ their capabilities and the resulting benefits (Cateora, 1983).

A society's technology is important because it influences the national standard of living and helps to account for the country's values and beliefs. If a country is technologically advanced, the people are less likely to believe that fate plays a major role in their lives and are more likely to believe that they can control what happens to them (Rugman & Hodgetts, 1995). Thus, their values are more likely to be materialistic because they have a higher standard of living.

In the subject of economics are the production of goods and services, their distribution, consumption, means of exchange, and the income derived from the creation of utilities. Material culture affects the level of demand, the quality and types of products demanded, and their functional features, as well as the means of production of these goods and their distribution (Cateora, 1983).

In the big and diverse economy of the United States, almost any good can find a market. In less developed nations, however, marketers will find increasingly limited markets, where they can sell only part of their product line, or perhaps none of it (Tresptra, 1997). The better we see and understand the picture of the material culture in world markets, the better able the firm or organization will be able to identify the best prospects. The prospects in countries where the principal agricultural implement is the machete will differ from those in which it is the tractor. Similarly, the prospects in countries where the principal sport is football (soccer) will differ from the United States in which it is American football.

The marketing implications of the material culture of a country are obviously many. Electrical appliances will sell in Western Europe (England, France, Denmark), but will have few buyers in countries where less than 1 percent of homes have electricity. Even where electricity is available, the distribution of income may limit the desirability of certain products. An electric carving knife is acceptable in the United States, but in less developed or affluent nations, not only are they unattainable and unwanted, they are likely considered a waste, since disposable income could be spent more meaningfully on housing, clothing, or food (Cateora, 1983).

Perhaps the most subtle role of international marketing is that of agent of cultural change (Terpstra 1997). When a company or organization introduces its new product(s) into a new market, it is, in effect, seeking to change the country's material culture. The change may be fairly modest—a new food item—or it can be more dramatic—a machine that changes agricultural or industrial technology in the host country. An international organization must be sure that changes it introduces are in accordance with the interests of the host country, as the people may resent the company's market penetration, viewing it as a form of "Americanization" or "imperialism."

Values and Attitudes

Much of human behavior depends on attitudes and values. These values often have a religious foundation and usually imply approbation or a moral judgment. Our values and attitudes help determine what we think is right or appropriate, what is important, and what is desirable (Hodgetts & Luthans, 1991). An attitude is a persistent tendency to feel and behave in a particular way toward some object (Luthans, 1989). A number of attitudes relate to economic activities, such as attitudes toward work, achievement, and private property.

Values influence culture. In the United States, for example, we assign equality in the workplace, which has resulted in legislation and action against sexual discrimination. This change in value is reflected in new attitudes toward dealing with those guilty of such discriminations (Rugman & Hodgetts, 1995).

The attitudes that emanate from values directly influence international business. For example, Russians believe that McDonald's food is superior to their own (value) and are willing to stand in long lines in order to eat there (attitude). Similarly, Swiss chocolate manufactures know that U.S. customers believe Swiss chocolate products are of high quality (value), so companies emphasize their Swiss origins and thus generate high sales (attitude), as noted by Hogetts and Luthans (1991). In other cases, there are negative attitudes toward foreign-made products, causing firms to deemphasize their origin—such as Firestone tires, which is owned by Bridgestone, a Japanese company.

International managers must have an understanding of attitudes and values to be able to develop effective marketing programs. Because of the impossibility of achieving intimate knowledge of a great number of markets, they must rely on help from others in addition to research.

Aesthetics

Aesthetics refers to the artistic tastes of a culture, such as the arts, folklore, music, drama, dance, color, and form (Tersptra, 1997). Aesthetics are of particular interest to the international marketer because of their role in interpreting the symbolic meanings of a variety of methods of artistic expression, color, and standards of beauty of a particular country (Cateora, 1983). Without the culturally correct interpretation of a society's aesthetic values, product styling is seldom successful. Insensitivity to aesthetic values not only leads to ineffective advertising and package design, but it can also lead to offending the proposed customer or creating a negative impression.

There are many aspects of aesthetics that make cultures different. For example, in the United States we use colors to identify emotional reactions; we "see red," we are "green with envy," or we "feel blue" (Tersptra, 1997). Black is for mourning in Western countries, whereas white is often the color of mourning in Eastern nations. Certain colors have particular meanings because of religious, patriotic, or aesthetic reasons (Rugman & Hodgetts, 1995). Thus, the international marketer needs to know these patterns in planning products, packages, branding, and advertising. Advertising must be culturally sensitive, as the right choice of colors, illustrations, and appeals will be related to the aesthetic sense of the buyer's culture, rather than the marketer's culture. Aesthetic values influence behavior, and we need to understand aesthetic values if we are to appreciate another culture.

Education

Education influences many aspects of culture. Literate people read widely and have a much better understanding of what is happening in the world. Additionally, higher rates of literacy usually result in greater economic productivity and technological advance. Education also helps to provide the infrastructure that is needed to develop managerial talent (Rugman & Hodgetts 1995). Education is a critical factor in understanding culture.

To most Americans, education usually means formal training in school. In this sense, the natives or primitives of Africa are not educated—that is, they have never been to school. This definition, however, is too restrictive. Education, as explained by Tersptra (1997), includes the process of transmitting skills, ideas, and attitudes, as well as training in particular disciplines. Thus, even primitive people have been educated in this broader sense, meaning that they are educated according to the culture in which they live.

The international marketer must learn to be an educator, since the products and techniques the international firm or organization brings into another culture are generally new to that market. Thus, the international firm must educate consumers about their new product, its uses, and its benefits. While this will not be accomplished using the traditional or formal educational system normally used to accomplish its educational goals, its success will be constrained by that very system (Cateora, 1983).

The international marketer should also be concerned about the educational situation in foreign markets because it is a key determinant of the nature of the consumer market and the kinds of marketing personnel available. This lack of education can have some implications—for example, advertising programs and packaging labels will need to be adapted if consumers are largely illiterate. If girls and women are excluded from formal education, marketing programs will be different than those aimed at the American housewife. In less developed nations, education affects literacy, which in turn affects marketing promotion. The quality of marketing practices will depend on how well the educational system prepares the people of the host nation.

Manners and Customs

Customs are common or established practices. Manners are behaviors that are regarded as appropriate in a particular society (Rugman & Hodgetts, 1995). In many countries around the world, social customs and manners are quite different from those in the United States. For example, a sturdy handshake is part of the American cultural repertory. Yet in the Middle East the visitor gets a flaccid, "dead" handshake that a male may associate with femininity or unfriendliness. To the Arab, the hearty grasp is a sign that the American has more brawn than brains (Root, 1994). Similarly, in Arab countries it is considered bad manners to shake hands with an individual of higher authority unless this individual makes the first gesture to do so.

In Latin countries it is acceptable to show up late for a party, whereas in England and France, promptness is valued. When an American has a 9:00 a.m. appointment in Latin America, he/she may be kept waiting a half-hour or longer (Root, 1994). The American may find this behavior insulting, particularly since he or she has come a long way to meet this individual. To the Latin American individual, this is not an insult, and the meeting is still very important.

Customs also dictate the way companies advertise and market their products (Pollack, 1994). An American airline in Brazil advertised "rendezvous lounges" on its jets. In Portuguese, "rendezvous" means a room hired for lovemaking. According to Root (1994), when Pepsi-Cola ran an ad in the Taiwan issue of Reader's Digest, it used the slogan "Come alive with Pepsi!" Unfortunately, the Taiwanese translation told its readers, "Pepsi brings your ancestors back from the dead!" In Germany, the same slogan was translated, "Come out of the grave with Pepsi!"

Unless business firms understand the customs and manners of the country in which they are doing business, they are likely to have trouble marketing and selling their products effectively.

Social Institutions

Social institutions or social organizations refer to the way people relate to other people, and they differ somewhat from society to society. Thomas (2002) noted that identifying ourselves with a particular social group places boundaries around our group (in-group) and defines nonmembers as an out-group.

The primary kind of social organization is based on kinship, and in the United States the key unit is the family, which includes the father and mother and the unmarried children in the household. The family unit elsewhere is often larger, including more relatives, such as the large joint family found in Hinduism. In many other less developed nations there is also a large extended family (Terpstra, 1997). Those who call themselves brothers in Zaire include those whom we call cousins and uncles in the U.S.

The extended family in developing nations fulfills several important social and economic roles. The extended family provides mutual protection, psychological support, and a kind of economic insurance for its members, and although the importance of the extended family is decreasing, it is still quite significant in many parts of the world.

To the international marketer, the extended family means that consumption decision making takes place in a larger unit and in different ways. The extended family, by having pooled their resources, may allow for larger purchases.

Another kind of grouping is based on age, especially in the United States and some of the more affluent industrialized nations. We have recognized both the "senior citizen" and the "teenage" subcultures. Senior citizens usually live as separate economic units with their own needs and motivations. Although teenagers do not live apart from their families, they are a separate economic force to be reckoned with in marketing (Terspstra, 1997).

Another aspect of social organization concerns the role of women in the economy. Women seldom enjoy parity with men as participants in the economy, and their participation often declines more in less developed countries, and more so in nations where their role is diminished by religious beliefs. The extent to which women participate affects their role as consumers, consumption influencers, and workers in the money economy, as well as their attainment of formal education.

According to Cook (1975), even developed countries exhibit significant differences in attitude toward female employment, such as the Germans, who are more critical of wives' employment than are the people of any other large Western country.

In spite of this constraint, the economic role of women is undergoing notable change in many countries, and many have been hired as managers in such unlikely places as Brazil and particularly Saudi Arabia, where Arab women have been among the most restricted.

Conclusion

A complete and thorough appreciation and understanding of the many elements of culture may very well be the single most important gain to a foreign marketer when preparing international marketing plans and strategies. A marketer may have control of the product offered to a particular market overseas—its promotion, price, and distribution methods—but they will always have limited control over the cultural environment within which these plans must be implemented.

Planning marketing strategy in terms of the uncontrollable elements of a market is necessary in a domestic market, but when a company is operating internationally, the task is complicated by a new environment influenced by elements unfamiliar and sometime unrecognizable to the marketer. For these reasons, it is important to study and make the effort to absorb enough understanding of the foreign culture in order to be able to cope with the uncontrollable features. It is probably safe to generalize that of all the tools a foreign or international marketer must have, those that help generate empathy for another culture are definitely the most valuable.

References

Axtell, R. (1994). *The do's and taboos of international trade: A small business primer.* New York: John Wiley & Sons, Inc.

Barrett, D. B. (Ed). (1982). *World Christian encyclopedia: A comparative study of churches and religions in the modern world.* New York: Oxford University Press.

Burris, C. T., Branscombe, N. R., & Jackson, L. M. (2000). For god and country: Religion and the endorsement of national self-stereotypes. *Journal of Cross-Cultural Psychology, 31*(4), 517-527.

Cassidy, S. (1992, 12 October). Defining the cosmo girl: Check out the passport. *New York Times*, p.C8.

Cateora, P. (1983). *International marketing* (5th ed.). Homewood, IL: Richard Irwin, Inc.

Cook, A. (1975). *The working mother.* Ithaca, NY: Cornell University Press.

Gibson, J., & Hodgetts, R. M. (1991). *Organizational communication: A managerial perspective* (2nd ed.). New York: Harper Collins.

Hall, E. (1977). *Beyond culture.* Garden City, NY: Doubleday.

Hodgetts, R., & Luthans, F. (1991). *International management.* New York: McGraw-Hill, Inc.

Hoebel, A. (1960). *Man, culture and society.* New York: Oxford University Press.

Kahler, R., & Kramer, R. (1977). *International Marketing* (4th ed.). Cincinnati, OH: South-Western Publishing Co.

Knotts, R. (1989, January-February). Cross-cultural Management. *Business Horizons*, p.32.

Kroeber, A. L., & Kluckhohn, F. (1952). Culture: A critical review of concepts and definitions. *Peabody museum papers, 47*(1). Cambridge, MA: Harvard University Press.

Luthans, F. (1989). *Organizational Behavior* (6th ed.). New York: McGraw-Hill, Inc.

Mattock, J. (2003). *Cross-cultural communication: The essential guide to international business.* London, UK: Kogan Page.

Mendenhall, M. E., Punnett, B. J., & Ricks, D. (1995). *Global management.* Cambridge, MA: Blackwell.

Pitts, B. G., & Stotlar, D. K., (2002). *Fundamentals of sport marketing* (2nd ed.). Morgantown, WV: Fitness Information Technology.

Pollack, A. (1994, February 20). Myths aside, Japanese do look for bargains. *New York Times*, p. E5.

Ricks, D. A. (1993). *Blunders in international business*. San Francisco, CA: Berrett-Koeler.

Root, F. (1994). *Entry strategies for international markets*. New York: Lexington Books.

Rugman, A., & Hodgetts, R. (1995). *International business: A strategic management approach*. New York: McGraw-Hill, Inc.

Sumatra, G. (1989). *Managing across borders*. Cambridge, MA: Harvard University Press.

Terpstra, V. (1987). *International marketing* (4th ed.). New York: The Dryden Press

Terpstra, V., & David, K. (1985). *The cultural environment of international business*. Dallas, TX: South-Western Publishing.

Thomas, D. C. (2002). *Essential of international management: A cross-cultural perspective*. London, UK: Sage Publishing, Inc.

The Challenge of Building Brand Equity: A Look at Cases in North America and Europe

ANDRÉ RICHELIEU
VINCENT COUVELAERE

Abstract

Sports teams generate an emotional response from their fans that is stronger than in any other industry. In an effort to capitalize on the emotional relationship they share with their fans, professional sports teams try to position themselves as brands. As part of a comparative research program between North American and European sports teams, this paper examines the strategies and actions French soccer* and Canadian hockey teams implement in order to build and exploit their brand.

Since not every team can grow into an international brand, the League should at least create favourable conditions so that all teams can build and leverage their brand equity to the best of their potential. The League can only gain by doing so, since beyond the coherence and continuity it must ensure across markets, the League's brand as a whole is as strong as the weakest individual team brand.

Introduction

A professional sports team has the potential to build what is known as brand equity, by capitalizing on the emotional relationship it shares with its fans (Underwood, Bond, & Baer, 2001). Brand equity is defined in terms of the marketing effects uniquely attributable to the brand: "when certain outcomes result from

---

* For a more extensive discussion of French soccer clubs, see Couvelaere, V., & Richelieu, A. (2005). Branding strategy in professional sports: The case of French soccer teams. *European Sport Management Quarterly, 5*(1), 23-46.

the marketing of a product or service because of its brand name that would not occur if the same product or service did not have that name" (Keller, 1993, p. 1). The brand equity of a company becomes the promise it makes to its customers to meet their expectations and deliver value on a continuous basis (Aaker, 1994; Kapferer, 1998).

A brand has both an accounting and commercial value (Keller, 1993). First, an accounting value in terms of assets valuation for balance sheet, merger, acquisition, or divestiture purposes. Different methods of brand evaluation have been suggested in this regard (Barwise et al., 1989). Second, a strong brand translates into additional sales of products and services because of the brand awareness and recognition, as well as the promise of quality customers associate with the brand (Kapferer, 1998). With higher costs, greater competition, and flattening demand, companies try to increase the efficiency of their marketing expenses. Consequently, managers need a better understanding of consumer behaviour in order to make better marketing strategy decisions (Keller, 1993).

With this in mind, some teams have gone beyond their status as mere sports teams and have established themselves as brands in their own right (Bobby, 2002; Burton & Howard, 1999; Shannon, 1999). Examples include the Manchester United, Real Madrid, the New York Yankees, and the Dallas Cowboys. These clubs epitomize the success of an aggressive brand strategy by well-endowed big market teams. However, some smaller market teams in North America and Europe are following suit (Bobby, 2002; Shannon, 1999).

Sports teams generate an emotional response from their fans that is stronger than in any other industry (with the exception of actors and singers) (Underwood, Bond, & Baer, 2001). With a strong brand, a team can potentially develop and nurture the loyalty of fans, which helps generate additional revenues through the sale of a variety of goods and services (Burton & Howard, 1999; Gustafson, 2001; Mullin, Hardy, & Sutton, 2000). For example, today, the Glasgow Celtic soccer club generates more money from merchandise sale than from TV rights and sponsorship combined (Glasgow Celtic, 2004; Worsley, 2001). Indeed, strong brands have a financial value that is inherent to their ability to generate additional revenues for the company (Bousch & Loken, 1991; Kapferer, 1998).

However, still relatively few teams seem proactive in building and leveraging their brand, and a lot of academic work remains to be done on brand equity in professional sports (Burton & Howard, 1999; Desbordes, Ohl, & Tribou, 2001; Mullin, Hardy, & Sutton, 2000). The purpose of our research is to examine what strategies and actions French and Canadian teams use to build and exploit their brand.

Like in other European championships, the French Professional Soccer League (LFP, first division) has a relegation/promotion format that challenges the stability and continuity of soccer teams: Saint-Étienne just came back in first division in 2004, Marseille has spent several years in second division, and the legendary Reims has disappeared in anonymity. Furthermore, it is only recently that soccer teams in France changed from non-profit to profit organizations, which means that French soccer teams can now be managed as companies (Bolotny, 2002). Even though the championship is not as unbalanced as in some European countries (Netherlands, Portugal, Scotland), huge disparities remain between top tier clubs and the rest of the pack.

Six Canadian hockey teams compete with 24 American teams in the National Hockey League (NHL), the top professional hockey league in North America. In recent years, with skyrocketing salaries (representing 75% of their gross revenues), the challenge Canadian teams face is putting a toll on their survival: Canadian teams are "importing" players in U.S. dollars, their revenues are in Canadian dollars (which has lost value toward the U.S. dollar in the last 10 years), they face a heavy tax burden, and their markets are much smaller than those of the majority of U.S. teams (Li, Hofacre, & Mahony, 2001). Hence, what strategies and actions could these French and Canadian teams use in order to survive and eventually prosper?

We will start our investigation with the review of the literature. Second, we will underline the methodology used. Third, we will present the results of the research. A discussion will follow, and we will end the paper with a conclusion and some recommendations.

Literature Review

A brand is "a name, a word, a sign, a symbol, a drawing, or a combination of these, which aims at identifying the goods and services of a company and differentiates them from the competitors" (Kotler, Filiatrault, & Turner, 2000, p. 478).

A brand is a differentiating asset for a company (Kapferer, 2001; Keller, 1993). Through its brand, a firm creates and manages customers' expectations (Aaker, 1994). Successful brands are able to quickly establish a strong emotional and personal relationship with the customer. As a result, this relationship can potentially trigger trust and loyalty toward the brand (Bedbury & Fenichell, 2002; De Chernatony, 2001). For this reason, companies that own strong brands try to turn the customer's attention to their brand image (Aaker, 1994; Rijkenberg, 2002).

A brand is a promise a company makes to its customers, and this promise is built on the coherence and continuity of the brand's products (Aaker, 1994; Kapferer, 1998; Kapferer, 2001). High levels of brand awareness and a positive brand image should increase the probability of brand choice, as well as generate higher consumer loyalty and reduce vulnerability to competitive marketing actions (Keller, 1993).

A sporting event is intangible, short-lived, unpredictable, and subjective in nature (Holbrook & Hirschman, 1982; Levitt, 1981; Mullin, Hardy, & Sutton, 2000; Gladden, Milne, & Sutton, 1998). It is produced and consumed at the same time and it comes with a strong emotional commitment from the fans (Mullin, Hardy, & Sutton, 2000). In this regard, a strong brand can and should help a professional sports team capitalize on the emotional attachment with the fans, in order to instil trust and trigger fan loyalty (Holt, 1995). In return, this trust and loyalty can help the sports team leverage its brand equity and generate additional revenues through the sale of goods and services, within and outside the sports arena, through brand extension (Bottomley & Doyle, 1996; Dawar & Anderson, 1994; Gustafson, 2001; Sunde & Brodie, 1993). For example, merchandise sales in Canada and the United States accounted for USD $3 billion in 2001. They represent 18% of the global sales for sports licensed products (*Sport Business Group*, 2002).

Strong sports brands are able to make the customers live the brand at different moments of their daily lives. Because the brand is relevant, it is able to transcend the sports arena (Richelieu, 2004). This being said, the team must have a minimum level of success on the field. Otherwise, it becomes difficult to ask the fans to associate themselves with a losing team, success being a fundamental dimension in sporting events (*Future Brand*, 2002), but also because the symbolic benefits (needs for social approval or personal expression and outer-directed self-esteem; Keller, 1993) attached to the sports teams are limited or inexistent.

Furthermore, being a brand can enable a sports team to position itself against other teams and entertainment offerings in the market: sports teams must be innovative and competitive in how they seduce their fans and ensure both affordability and accessibility (Mullin, Hardy, & Sutton, 2000). All the more so since sports teams are battling for the entertainment money of customers against other leisure alternatives, such as festivals, movies, restaurants, traveling, etc. (Burton & Howard, 1999). Why should the customers spend their emotions, time, and money on a sports team? Mullin, Hardy, and Sutton (2000) suggest that teams should build "a positive attitude with reciprocity." This means that sports team marketers should try to create a relationship based on reciprocity between the fans and the team, which shows the fans that they are appreciated and valued. In return, this can help increase the fans' sense of belonging toward their team. For instance, some sports teams put photos of their fans taken at the stadium on their website, which are regularly updated.

Based on a review of the literature (Aaker, 1994; Gladden, Milne, & Sutton, 1998; Kashani, 1995; Keller, 1993; Richelieu, 2004; Underwood, Bond, & Baer, 2001) and the case analyses we have completed, there are three steps that lead to the development of brand equity in professional sports: i) Defining the identity of the sports team; ii) Positioning the sports team in the market; and iii) Developing a brand strategy (Figure 1). The identity and positioning represent what Kashani (1995) refers to as the strategic construction of the brand; or, in other words, the foundations of the brand strategy (Gladden, Milne, & Sutton, 1998). It is only with a clear identity and strong positioning that marketing actions become relevant and can

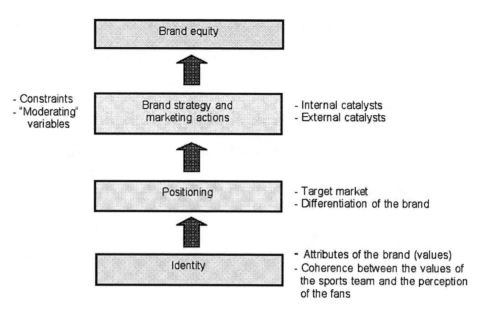

Source: Richelieu (2004)

Figure 1: A framework for building sports teams' brand equity

then serve the purpose of leveraging the brand equity of a sports team. As Keller (1993, p. 2) underlines it, "Brand equity exists when the consumer is familiar with the brand and holds some favourable, strong, and unique brand associations in memory."

We followed this conceptual model when analysing the strategies and actions used by French soccer and Canadian hockey teams in building and exploiting their brand equity. So, how do French soccer and Canadian hockey clubs try to develop their brand equity? And what can we draw from their initiatives in order to establish some guidelines for professional sports teams?

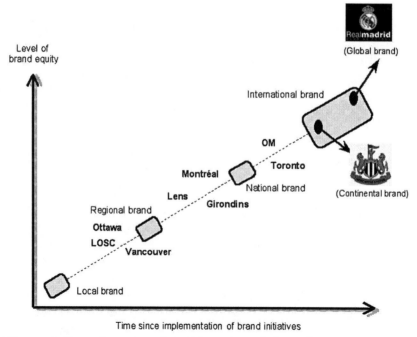

Figure 2: Brand equity of the French and Canadian teams

Research Methods

The methodology is qualitative in nature. We proceeded with in-depth case analyses of four French soccer teams and four Canadian hockey teams. The research is exploratory.

Case Selection

There are 20 soccer teams evolving in the French Professional League (LFP), and six Canadian teams among the 30 that make up the National Hockey League (NHL). In each league, we chose four teams.

Case analysis limits the number of companies that can be studied within a reasonable timeframe, at a reasonable cost. Eisenhardt (1989) recommends using between four and 10 cases in order to allow, on the one hand, an in-depth analysis of each case, and on the other, a relative diversity to increase the validity of the results. Cases should be selected according to their ability to provide information: the major determinants for the number of cases are the quality of the information the cases provide and the observational capabilities of the researcher rather than the sample size (Patton, 1980).

As such, we chose our teams by convenience. First, we looked for teams that were initiating brand and/or marketing actions. Second, we wanted to have a sample of teams that were at different levels of brand equity in both leagues. Indeed, we believe that a sports team could reach four levels of brand equity along the "brand equity pipeline" (local, regional, national, or international; see Figure 2): "Given the limited number of cases which can usually be studied, it makes sense to choose cases such as extreme situations . . . in which the process of interest is 'transparently observable'" (Eisenhardt, 1989, p. 537).

Sample

In France, we chose Lille Olympique Sporting Club (LOSC), Racing Club de Lens (RC Lens), Girondins de Bordeaux, and Olympique de Marseille (OM); in Canada, the Montréal Canadiens, the Ottawa Senators, the Toronto Maple Leafs, and the Vancouver Canucks.

French soccer and Canadian hockey teams have interesting similarities that allow us to study them together: their resources are generally very limited; they live in the shadow of strong rivals (either European or American teams); and it is only recently that they realized their potential to leverage their brand equity, which they now try to develop.

Data Collection and Data Coding

For the purpose of this study, we collected primary and secondary data.

We conducted in-depth interviews with vice presidents, marketing directors, and general managers of the eight teams studied between December 2002 and June 2003. Data was collected during one-on-one interviews, using a semi-structured questionnaire that had open-ended questions. Four areas were covered during the interviews: i) general information on the sports team; ii) marketing and brand strategy of the sports club; iii) catalyst factors used by the team to build and leverage their brand; iv) constraints and hurdles faced by the team in building and leveraging their brand.

Reliability of the instrument was reinforced by using a questionnaire which remained the same in its structure and the sequence of questions for every interview. However, some minor adjustments had to be made in order to take into account the specificities of all the teams studied and the fact that the teams were evolving in two different sports, two different leagues, and two different countries.

Each one-on-one interview was held on the site of the respective team and lasted approximately an hour and a half. One or two persons were interviewed for each team, depending on the expertise and availability of the respondents (Matear, Gray, & Irving, 2000). Interviews were held in the offices of the teams studied. The main criteria for selecting a suitable subject in a case study is the quality of information:

therefore, the managers who were interviewed had a direct involvement in their team brand and marketing endeavors. Moreover, the interviewees should understand the purpose of the study and the measures solicited by the interviewer (Cavusgil & Zou, 1994; Matear, Gray & Irving, 2000; Pellemans, 1999). This is why we always interviewed the best managers available.

The summary of each interview was written out 24 hours following the interview, as recommended by Lofland and Lofland (1995). Also, to assure the accuracy of the interview data, the managers were contacted again after the interview by e-mail or by phone in case of doubt about the information, or to obtain additional information.

Moreover, in order to increase the validity of our data, scientific papers, sports articles, team documents, and media articles (print and electronic) were consulted. In some cases, we were able to consult secondary data prior to the interviews, which helped us collect more specific information regarding the teams and their brand endeavours during the interviews.

As far as data analysis is concerned, content analysis was used. For every team, we formerly analysed the brand strategy, marketing actions, and constraints teams face, thus extracting the essence of the primary and secondary data (Pellemans, 1999).

The validity was ensured through the use of several sources of information, the number of cases studied, and the comparisons we made between the cases (Perrien, Chéron, & Zins, 1986).

Results

Presentation of the French Soccer and Canadian Hockey Teams

The French soccer teams. The four French teams we studied have a long history and tradition (Table 1).

Table 1: An overview of the French soccer teams				
	Lille Olympique Sporting Club (LOSC)	Racing Club de Lens (RC Lens)	Girondins de Bordeaux (Girondins)	Olympique de Marseille (OM)
Web site address	www.losc.fr	www.rclens.fr	www.girondins.com	www.olympique demarseille.com
Established	1944	1906	1881	1899
Record	French Champions (2) Cup Champions (5)	French Champions (1) League Cup (1)	French Champions (5) French Cup (3) League Cup (1)	French Champions (9) French Cup (10) European Champions
Key attributes (values) of the brand	Fighting spirit Solidarity Conviviality Modernity.	Unconditional passion for soccer Desire to win Search for perfection Respect of others Confidence Humility.	Up-market brand Tradition Finesse Prestige.	Warm Emotional Sympathetic
Formal brand strategy	Yes Started in 2000-2001 Capitalizing on relational marketing to develop the consumption for the LOSC brand.	Yes Started around 1998 Brand extension as a down- or mid-market brand.	Yes Started around 1999-2000 Brand extension as an up-market brand.	Yes Started around 2002 Externalizing the brand strategy through partners (Adidas).

Lille Olympique Sporting Club (LOSC; 2004) was founded in 1944. It quickly established itself as the best French soccer team after the Second World War, winning two championships and five cups between 1946 and 1955. But between 1955 and 2000, the club relegated six times in second division; at best, it was a "middle of the pack" team. Back in first division in 2000, the team, newly privatized, had great ambitions: becoming a modern sports and entertainment company with a new stadium the managers intended to start building at the end of 2003.

Racing Club de Lens (RC Lens; 2004), founded in 1906, became a professional team in 1934. In 1969, with the economic recession in the region, the team switched back to amateur status. For more than 20 years, RC Lens hit some snags, finally reclaiming its place in first division in 1991. After winning the championship in 1998, RC Lens rediscovered its ambitions: the team became competitive at the national and continental levels and the budget increased to 50 million euros for the 2002-2003 season. The focus was geared toward developing new talent from within the organization, in order for the club to remain competitive and financially viable.

Girondins de Bordeaux (2004), founded in 1881, became a professional team in 1937. They won their first championship in 1950. It was in the 1980s that the team had its best years, winning three titles (1984, 1985, and 1987), two cups (1986 and 1987), and taking part in two Champions Cup semi finales (1985 and 1987). However, excessive spending sent the club into bankruptcy and second division in 1991. In the mid-1990s, the team got back on track. In 1999, the television group M6 bought the club and, in the same year, the Girondins won their fifth championship in history. Today, M6 injects money into the team for its operating budget, but also into a new training facility that enables the team to develop new talent and remain competitive.

Olympique de Marseille (OM; 2004), founded in 1899, is one of the most prestigious teams in France, if not the most. It has won nine championships, 10 cups, and one Champions League cup. Olympique de Marseille lived its glory days between 1986 and 1993, with Bernard Tapie as president. But one week after its Champions League win against Milan A.C. in 1993, a corruption scandal, combined with a huge deficit, sent the club into second division. Since the 2002-2003 season, a new OM is being built. With new management in place, the club wants to ensure financial viability and autonomy by June 2004 by controlling expenses and increasing revenues.

The Canadian hockey teams. Of the four teams we studied, two have a long lasting tradition (Montréal and Toronto), and two are more recent teams (Ottawa and Vancouver) (Table 2).

The Montréal Canadiens (2004) were established in 1908 and have won the Stanley Cup (championship trophy) an NHL record 24 times. The Montréal Canadiens are one of the six original teams which were part of the NHL when the League started its operations in the early 1900s. More than just a hockey team, it is an institution in Montréal and in Canada. The team has long been seen as the team of French Canadians, which explains its nickname, the "Habs" (for "Habitants," the French Canadians settlers). In the last five years, the team has had its share of problems and is undergoing a restructuring process. The glory days are a distant memory.

The Toronto Maple Leafs (2004) were established in 1927, and the team has had glorious times up until the late 1960s, when it won the Stanley Cup for the last time. Toronto is also one of the original six teams of the NHL, as well as an institution in Toronto and in Canada. Top sports brands have been located in their respective cities for an extended period of time, which helps establish the brand over time (Future Brand, 2002). Toronto's jersey is highly recognizable and displays the Canadian maple leaf. While the Montréal Canadiens were seen as the francophones' team in Canada, the Toronto Maple Leafs were identified as the anglophones'. Since the 1990s, the team is a Stanley Cup contender again. Toronto has won 11 Stanley Cups.

Ottawa (2004) first had a hockey team between 1901 and 1934, before the franchise was moved to St. Louis and disappeared.[1] The Senators have been back in Ottawa since 1992. The Senators operate in a historically fragmented market. Indeed, "because of the vacuum created by the departure of the original

---

1 In North America, professional sports teams are franchises. Business people acquire the right to exploit a team and its brand from the league, but the team remains the property of the league. Franchises can be contracted or moved to another city for financial purposes, which can alienate fans.

	Montréal Canadiens (Habs)	Ottawa Senators (Sens)	Toronto Maple leafs (TML)	Vancouver Canucks (VC)
Table 2: An overview of the Canadian hockey teams				
Web site address	www.canadiens.com	www.ottawa senators.com	www.torontomaple leafs.com	www.canucks.com
Established	1908	1992 (modern era)	1901-1934 (the early years)	1927 1970
Record	24 Stanley Cups	11 Stanley Cups	(7 as Ottawa Senators; 4 as Ottawa Silver Seven)	11 Stanley Cups Stanley Cup finalist (2)
Key attributes (values) of the brand	History and tradition of success Authentic Professional Dynamic.	Part of the community Good product on the ice (Stanley Cup contenders) Good entertainment.	Traditional but contemporary True grit and inspired play. Canadian Transcending generations (mass appeal). Delivering value to customers and shareholders.	Close knit team Authentic Integrated in the community Canadian
Formal brand strategy	No Trying to position the team to younger customers.	No Being a brand, more a result of marketing actions Trying to build the fan base and move the fans along the emotional continuum.	Yes Started in 1999 Leverage trough merchandising and broadcasting.	No Being a brand, more a result of the message sent to the community (Canucks = underdogs) Capitalizing on a clearer team identity.

Senators, some Ottawa residents have associated themselves with the Canadiens, others with the Maple Leafs, and others with the remaining four original NHL teams" (Boston, Chicago, Detroit, or New York) (Ottawa Senators vice president, Marketing). This situation is a challenge for the Senators brand (Moore, Wilkie, & Lutz, 2002). Since 2000, the team is a Stanley Cup contender.

The Vancouver Canucks (2004) were established in 1970 and have never won the Stanley Cup, even though they played in the finals in 1982 and 1994. The Canucks are competitive again, after some difficult years in the 1990s. The Canucks have long lived in the shadow of the Edmonton Oilers, the dominant team in the western part of Canada for much of the '80s and beginning of the '90s. The Canucks are a relatively young franchise that went through some soul searching as will be shown in the next section. However, their brand awareness is on the rise and the team is now a force to be reckoned with on the ice.

Identity and Positioning

Identity and positioning of French soccer teams. All four teams studied seem to know where they stand in terms of identity. Some, however, appear to be more advanced than others in their reflection. One of them is Lille Olympique Sporting Club.

Following a market research, Lille Olympique Sporting Club identified four key values the fans wanted the club to promote—namely, fighting spirit, solidarity, conviviality, and modernity, which is displayed on the LOSC website (LOSC, 2004): "LOSC intends to rely on these four values in order to create a universe around the brand and develop the purchase of LOSC products and services" (LOSC Marketing Director). For instance, conviviality refers to the interaction between the team and its fans, and the involvement of the players in their community. In this regard, LOSC sponsors youth soccer teams in the Lille region, which play with a LOSC badge on their jersey. This can potentially trigger the sense of belonging to the team among young customers who can become LOSC fans, if they are not already, and remain fans for years to come (Bobby, 2002; Burton & Howard, 1999; Holt, 2002; Mullin, Hardy, & Sutton, 2000).

The identity of the RC Lens is strongly linked to its values, which it defined in 1997. These fundamental values are i) the unconditional passion for soccer (the RC Lens fans live and die with the team), ii) the desire to win, iii) the search for perfection, iv) respect for others, v) confidence, and vi) humility. "The objective is to position the club as a convivial sport entity that tries to win, makes people, young or old, proud to be fans of the RC Lens, during but also before and after the games" (RC Lens General Manager). In other words, provide fans with the experiential and symbolic values defined by Keller (1993). Even though it has entered the modern era of soccer, RC Lens wants to remain close to its fans. RC Lens aims at nurturing an identity that is coherent with its history, fans, and core values. Thus, the team is able to trigger emotional value and psychological proximity with its fans (Kapferer, 2001) by transcending the sports arena, gender, age, and social differences (Burton & Howard, 1999).

The managers of Girondins de Bordeaux are aware of the importance of their brand. They want to preserve its identity, which was built over time and based on certain values: essentially an up-market brand, with tradition, finesse, and prestige. This brand identity is strongly linked to the region and its history. Indeed, Bordeaux is a "bourgeois" city with old traditions. Furthermore, in order to reinforce the identity of the Girondins brand and nurture its up-market positioning, the style of the logo has been modified to provide a more British look. The scapular and the traditional colors (white and navy blue) have been kept. The founding date has been added to the logo in order to reinforce the traditional dimension of the brand (Girondins, 2004).

The identity of the Olympique de Marseille brand is consistent with the values of the city, as underlined by the marketing director of the team during the interview: "warmth, emotional and sympathetic." The managers of the team believe they have a strong brand that stands for itself. What they need to do is monitor the evolution of the image of the brand, without it being affected by on-field performance. Indeed, a brand evolves in time and managers need to make sure this evolution is in line with the attributes of the brand they want to promote (Aaker, 1994; Kapferer, 1998). The OM brand changes with the city: since 2002, the club has evolved toward a better image thanks to an improved efficiency, professionalism, rigor, and transparency.

Identity and positioning of Canadian hockey teams. All four Canadian teams seem to know where they stand in terms of their identity and the attributes of the brand. In this regard, being Canadian, authentic, and part of the community appear to be essential values to the four Canadian teams: phrases like "we are part of our community," "we have grassroots programs to get closer to people," and "we want to give back to the community" came up very often during the interviews. Being in relatively small markets,[2] with the exception of Toronto and, to a lesser extent, Montréal, these teams need to develop closer links with fans and compete for the entertainment money of consumers (Burton & Howard, 1999).

The Montréal Canadiens want to leverage their brand based on four key attributes: history and tradition, authenticity, professionalism, and dynamism. History and tradition are linked to the longevity of the franchise (100 years in 2006), the renowned players who have put on a Canadiens uniform, and the impressive record of the team (24 Stanley Cups). However, an obsession with history does not mix well with the recent performances on the ice. Second, the team has long been seen as authentic and French Canadian; the team could now take advantage of its appeal across Canada and position itself more as Canadian.

2 Montréal: 2.5 million people; Ottawa: 1 million; Toronto: 5 million; Vancouver: 1.5 million.

Third, the hiring of a new and competent general manager who has won five Stanley Cups with the Canadiens (Bob Gainey) and better communication with the younger audience the team wants to attract should help improve professionalism. Fourth, dynamism is an attribute the new management team brings, as the image of the club has long been conservative.

The Ottawa Senators have three key values they want to build on: i) being part of the community, ii) having a good product on the ice, and iii) offering good entertainment. Being part of the community is very important for a young franchise. Indeed, community involvement increases the sympathy fans have for the players, which can reinforce the identification of the fans to the players, but also their sense of belonging to the team, and, by extension, this can help the team become a brand with a social conscience (Mullin, Hardy, & Sutton, 2000; Keller, 2003). And finally, the Senators aim at offering an entertainment experience to the fans that come to the arena (Corel Centre) through the game itself, but also through the "bells and whistles" that surround the game: music, mascot (Spartacat), contests, ambience in the stands, etc. As a result, the brand awareness of the team is increasing.

The Toronto Maple Leafs emphasize five essential values: i) traditional but contemporary, ii) true grit and inspired play, iii) Canadian, iv) transcending generations, and v) delivering value to customers and shareholders. Great players have worn the blue and white jersey with the maple leaf crest, and today the team has its superstar, Mats Sundin. The Maple Leafs are proud of their history, but at the same time, they look toward the future (traditional but contemporary). An example is the new logo on the shoulders of the jersey: a stylized "TML," which stands for Toronto Maple Leafs. Furthermore, the brand is considered by the managers to transcend generations: younger and older fans associate themselves with the Toronto Maple Leafs. Also, the management realizes that the product at the arena is too expensive to build a value proposition for the fans, "which leads to a class stratification of the product offered" (Toronto Maple Leafs vice president, Marketing).

The Vancouver Canucks have four values: i) being a close-knit team, ii) authentic, iii) integrated in the community, and iv) Canadian. As a matter of fact, the Canucks are looking for genuine players who work hard and will blend in well with the team and the community, not superstars. Each player has a nickname and is involved in the Vancouver area. Truly, the Canucks are more competitive than ever before. Furthermore, the team emphasizes its Canadian roots, the maple leaf being displayed on all promotional material. The name and the logo themselves encompass the Canadian identity of the team and triggers emotion from fans: "Canucks" means French Canadian and the logo is now a stylized Aboriginal whale. A genuine, community-oriented brand that appeals to families has won the heart of Vancouver citizens who now see the Canucks as "the team of the city of Vancouver" (Vancouver Canucks, Marketing Director).

Marketing and Brand Strategy

Marketing strategy and brand strategy of French soccer teams. All four French soccer teams studied appear to have not only a marketing strategy, but also a brand strategy. These brand strategies have been implemented in the late nineties and beginning of 2000.

In the case of LOSC, the brand strategy is based on the vision of the managers and the four values that have been identified through market research: fighting spirit, solidarity, conviviality, and modernity. Since the identity and positioning which make up the strategic construction of the brand (Gladden, Milne, & Sutton, 1998; Kashani, 1995) are clear, it becomes easier to capitalise on and leverage the brand equity through catalyst factors we will underline in the next section.

RC Lens has transformed its marketing activities with the idea of leveraging its values, while shaking up its image of a friendly club that is not always taken seriously. This is a challenge in terms of brand strategy: if the team does not want to alienate its original core fan base and because it remains a regional brand, the RC Lens brand is, in a way, limited to remaining a down- or middle-market brand. This has an impact on, among other things, its merchandising initiatives across France (Chaudhuri & Holbrook, 2001; Mullin, Hardy, & Sutton, 2000).

The brand strategy of Girondins de Bordeaux is in line with the identity of the city of Bordeaux and its region. Anchoring the brand in the local environment can help leverage it in order to increase the association of the fans to the brand. The actions undertaken by the team lie on the development of different brands that target soccer fans, but also a regional clientele looking for an up-market brand. This brand extension is congruent with the identity and positioning of the Girondins (Bottomley & Doyle, 1996), which will be presented in the next section.

As far as OM is concerned, their brand strategy has been implemented in the late 1990s. The club first decided to internalize its activities (merchandising, shops, etc.), then chose to externalize. In this regard, a limited marketing team collaborates with partners in relation to sponsoring and merchandising. This strategy aims at increasing profitability and reducing the uncertainty associated with the team's performance on the field. A key partner is adidas for both the design and distribution of team merchandise.

Marketing strategy and brand strategy of Canadian hockey teams. Interestingly, if all the Canadian teams studied are aware of the importance of branding, only one team (Toronto Maple Leafs) has a formal brand strategy and is proactive in this regard. The managers of the three other teams have underlined that "being a brand is a result of our marketing actions." In fact, it should be the other way around: marketing actions should reflect and enhance both the identity and positioning of the team (Aaker, 1994; Keller, 1993). The attributes of the brand that managers have identified and presented to us do not translate into a brand strategy.

There might be three reasons for this paradox. First, it is only recently that Canadian hockey teams have understood the importance of branding, and branding initiatives are still under construction. Second, Canadian teams are facing major economical constraints: for instance, 75% of the teams' revenues go to players' salaries, which does not free up a lot of resources to build a brand. Third, the NHL controls the marketing and branding of the teams beyond a 150 km radius. This means that NHL teams cannot seal agreements with licensors for national coverage. On one hand, this policy imposed on the teams discourages their commercial initiatives. Indeed, with the exception of Toronto, it is often not profitable enough for a Canadian team to launch local marketing actions because of the relatively small size of their market. On the other hand, being confined to their territory, small market teams do not have the ability to put their brand out and make it visible on a larger scale, in order to become part of the consideration set of customers across North America. This means that the sales of their products are generally marginal outside of their local market. And a brand should have the opportunity to transcend its original market (Richelieu, 2004).

As far as the Toronto Maple Leafs are concerned, they implemented their brand strategy around 1999. The managers believe the team needs to exploit its brand equity in order to ensure its growth, by being true to the values of the team. Two avenues are considered in order to leverage the TML brand: merchandising and broadcasting. In this regard, the Maple Leafs have launched different lines of products and a TV channel called Leafs TV.

Catalyst Factors Used by Sports Teams

We define catalyst factors as variables that can help a professional sports team leverage its brand. Catalyst factors represent a set of tools a team might use in order to establish itself as a brand and reinforce its brand image. Internal factors usually belong to the sports team or are controlled by it. External factors are environmental elements or factors that are out of the immediate control of the sports team (Richelieu, 2004; see Table 3).

Catalyst factors for French soccer teams. When analysing the catalyst factors used by the four French soccer teams, one element stands out: merchandising. Beginning in 2000, French soccer teams have improved their merchandising initiatives to the point that in some instances, they have no reason to envy their British or North American counterparts. These initiatives strengthened and were congruent with the identity and positioning of the respective French clubs (Chaudhuri & Holbrook, 2001; Mullin, Hardy, & Sutton, 2000). Merchandising is not an end in itself and an overextension could dilute the brand (Aaker, 1994; Keller, 1993). However, merchandising helps teams take advantage of an established brand and generate

Table 3: Catalyst factors, constraints and "moderating" variables in building and leveraging a sports team brand

Catalyst factors	Constraints and "moderating" variables
Internal catalyst factors	**Constraints**
"Fans bonding with the team"	Fashion
Entertainment experience for the fans	Trend phenomenon
Team's involvement in its community	Decrease in loyalty
Competent managers	Decrease in customer loyalty toward brands
Physical facilities	Less and less loyalty from the players toward their team
Marketing actions	Life cycle of sports leagues
On-field jerseys	Maturity or decline phase of professional sports leagues
Sale of team's merchandise	General entertainment offering
Players' management	Competition from other entertainment alternatives
Promotional campaigns	
Commercial partnerships	
Customer Relationship Management programs (CRM)	
External catalyst factors	**"Moderating" variables**
Market size	Legal framework
Access to a large fan base and lucrative TV deals	Centralization in managing the league's brands
Industry changes	Legal status of the team
Merger of sports with the entertainment and communications industries	Finances
	Resources of the team
Technological advances	On-field performance
Development of new means of communications	Winning

much-needed additional revenues (Burton & Howard, 1999; Mullin, Hardy, & Sutton, 2000; *Sport Business Group*, 2002; Worsley, 2001).

Specifically, Lille Olympique Sporting Club has an exclusive agreement with Décathlon stores, which design and distribute the team jersey. It enables LOSC to have a unique jersey compared to the teams sponsored by adidas, Nike, Puma, or Umbro. This unique jersey enhances the value of the LOSC brand. From a distribution perspective, this agreement is also part of a marketing strategy used to leverage the LOSC brand and position it as a reference in France, and maybe even in Europe (*La Voix du Nord*, 2001).

RC Lens develops its own line of complementary products, even food products, like milk (*L'Équipe*, 2000). These extensions involve affordable goods which take into account the limited buying power of local consumers. As a result, RC Lens is being limited to a down- or middle-market brand. For the time being, we believe the team should capitalize on their core customers through a down- or middle-market brand that is coherent with the attributes of the brand before trying to extend to an up-market brand. Otherwise, it could appear to the customers as "fuzzy" positioning (Kotler, Filiatrault, & Turner, 2000).

Another example of building brand equity through brand extension is the Girondins de Bordeaux. The Girondins de Bordeaux (2004) soccer team has four different brands: the game brand (adidas Collection), a sportswear brand sold in superstores (Club Collection), a leisure brand (Girondins Sport Collection), and an upscale brand (Scapulaire Collection). The legitimacy of this extension, coherent with the brand image, enables the Girondins to protect and enhance its brand equity, especially long-term, in the region and eventually in France and Europe.

Olympique de Marseille has externalized its marketing and brand strategies. One of its partners is adidas, which designs and distributes the team jersey and other OM merchandise. For OM, it is a way to leverage the brand through the distribution channel of adidas in France, Europe, and even internationally. Olympique de Marseille capitalizes on the distribution channel of adidas to increase its visibility and leverage its brand (Motion, Leitch, & Brodie, 2003). OM and adidas strengthen and leverage each other's brand (Speed & Thompson, 2000; *Sport Business Group*, 2002). Also, the brand extension of OM remains within the sports arena in order to avoid diluting the brand and spreading resources all over the place.

Another area that is becoming strong for French soccer teams studied is the teams' involvement in their community. Indeed, they are all increasing their activities and involvement in the city or region where they are established. We talked earlier of the LOSC, which sponsors youth soccer teams in the Lille region, and other teams are following suit in order to strengthen the emotional connection with their fans, develop a good citizen image, and move the younger fans along the emotional continuum by getting closer to them (Burton & Howard, 1999).

However, the entertainment experience is still underdeveloped among French soccer teams. Even though a soccer game is mostly a ritual in Europe, the entertainment experience could be upgraded, because fans are potentially both consumers and actors, especially in a post-modern age (Holt, 2002). Being part of the event is a "must" from the standpoint of the social actualization of the fans (Keyes, 1998). The game in itself is the core product over which a team has not a lot of control; the entertainment surrounding the game, before, during, or after the soccer match is an auxiliary feature or an extension (Mullin, Hardy, & Sutton, 2000) that can potentially enhance the overall experience of the fans and the brand equity of the team, and which a team can control.

Also, even though improvements have already been made, some work needs to be done on the websites of French soccer teams, to help leverage the teams' brands and build virtual communities beyond their local market and give fans that do not live near their team's market the opportunity to maintain and increase their affiliation with their club (Mullin, Hardy, & Sutton, 2000; *Sport Business Group*, 2002).

Catalyst factors for Canadian hockey teams. If we now look at the catalyst factors that Canadian teams use, there is strong emphasis on the entertainment experience taking place in arenas which are the representation of the teams' brands:

> "We want the fans to have the best entertainment experience of their life" (Montréal Canadiens and Toronto Maple Leafs vice presidents, Marketing).

> "From the moment they enter the arena, the fans must live a special experience and feel a unique ambience" (Vancouver Canucks vice president, Marketing).

Sharing the experience with other fans helps stimulate, increase, and nurture the sense of belonging of the fans to the team, and contributes to leveraging the sports team's brand (Underwood, Bond, & Baer, 2001). Going to a game becomes an experience we enjoy ourselves and with other fans, whose experience can influence our own (Desbordes, 2000; Holt, 1995).

This being said, we should point out that the entertainment experience needs to complement what happens on the ice, not replace it. The entertainment at a game should be seen as an auxiliary feature that triggers the emotions fans live, helping combine the intangible benefits (essentially the emotions lived at the arena and the pride to be associated with the team) with the tangible dimensions of the product (result of the game, merchandising, draws during the game, area for family and kids to play outside or inside the stadium, stadium facilities, etc.; Burton & Howard, 1999; Pons & Richelieu, 2004). Keller (1993) refers to the emotional benefits as experiential and symbolic benefits, whereas the tangible dimensions are called functional benefits.

Furthermore, a focus seems to be put on merchandising, as all four teams have introduced different lines of products for five segments—babies, children, teenagers, men, and women—as brand extension can enhance the brand image and goodwill of consumers (*Sport Business Group*, 2002). Successful brand management implies leveraging brand equity to profitable ends, and brand extension provides a way to capitalize on brand equity (Dawar & Anderson, 1994).

However, we suspect Canadian managers too often equate merchandising actions with a brand strategy, which is a perspective that can lead to incoherent marketing initiatives. Examples are the bright orange and yellow caps with a black logo of the Montréal Canadiens, sold in the team boutique at the arena, when the official colors of the team are red, white, and blue and so much emphasis is put on tradition, history, and an obsessive willingness not to alter the logo or colors of the team jersey.

As for the game jersey, older franchises stick to tradition, allowing for only minor changes, while newer teams change their logos and colors regularly, as they try to position the product and establish the brand (Aaker, 1994; Burton & Howard, 1999). On one end of the spectrum, the Vancouver Canucks have had four logos and changed their set of colors three times in 34 years. At the other end, the Montréal Canadiens' logo has not changed since 1932 and the colors have been blue, white, and red since 1911:

> "The Montréal Canadiens is a strong recognized brand, which embeds history and tradition. Hockey greats have worn the Canadiens jersey with this logo on their chest; changing it would be a sacrilege!" (Montréal Canadiens vice president, Marketing).

However, fans want novelty and are eager to spend on their favourite team (*Sport Business Group*, 2002). The Maple Leafs incorporate regular minor changes to their jersey, in addition to using a historic design on their third jersey. Models of former jerseys are widely available in the Toronto area for fans who want to show their blue and white pride. Since a sport is an intangible and experiential product, buying, displaying, or wearing a product such as a team jersey allows fans to extend the emotional experience beyond the sport arena (Mullin, Hardy, & Sutton, 2000). It also helps increase the attachment and identification of fans to the team (Burton & Howard, 1999).

In another area, all the managers interviewed said that players' management is not a marketing tool: "We just want to win games in acquiring players!" (Montréal and Toronto managers).

But nuances exist: having a star on its roster or a local player who has a certain reputation and who has established himself on the field can help draw fan support and generate loyalty to the team (Bobby, 2002). In other words, there is a transfer of sympathy from the player to the team for which he is playing. These local players are also more inclined to be recognized by the community and become involved locally. For instance, French Canadian players are very important to the Montréal Canadiens hockey team: star francophone players are central figures in the Montréal Canadiens marketing campaign.

Constraints and "Moderating" Variables

Constraining factors are variables that can stop or prevent a team from leveraging its brand. Constraining factors can be seen as obstacles in a team's pursuit to establish its brand. "Moderating" variables can help a team build and reinforce its brand equity, as much as they can hurt the team's brand equity or restrain its expansion. We refer to them as "moderating" variables because of i) the relative lack of control teams have on these variables and ii) the impact on brand equity that is both generally difficult to assess for sports teams and ambivalent (Richelieu, 2004; see Table 3).

Constraints and "moderating" variables for French soccer teams. All French soccer teams studied have gone through some financial problems, one of which (Marseille) is still working its way out of trouble. The reality is that financial stability is key before allocating resources to brand strategy and marketing actions (Bobby, 2002; Mullin, Hardy, & Sutton, 2000). The main challenge French soccer teams face are their modest resources either at the national (LOSC, RC Lens) or European level (Bordeaux, Marseille). This reality is definitely a hurdle in moving the team across the brand equity pipeline (Figure 2).

In another area, winning is important because the fans need hope in order to become emotionally involved with the team (Bobby, 2002; Waltner, 2000). A manager of Lille Olympique Sporting Club told us, "If you relegate in Second Division, that could well be the point of no return, as fans might start supporting another team, never to come back to us." But winning also increases the value of the brand, from a financial and marketing perspective. And in this regard, the style of play should be congruent with the identity of the brand (Sport Business Group, 2002). For instance, Girondins de Bordeaux has a tradition of an elegant style of play which fits well with the image of the city and the team of Bordeaux.

Constraints and "moderating" variables for Canadian hockey teams. The constraints Canadian teams face are mainly twofold. First, from an economic point of view, skyrocketing salaries now swallow 75% of their gross revenues. Furthermore, there are factors that are unique to the Canadian context: Canadian teams are "importing" players in U.S. dollars, their revenues are in Canadian dollars, which has lost value toward the U.S. dollar in the last 10 years, they face a heavy tax burden, and their markets are much smaller than those of the majority of U.S. teams. As a matter of fact, the managers of all four teams interviewed agree that the economic model of the NHL needs to be corrected at the end of the actual collective agreement in September 2004. Already 26 out of the 30 NHL teams are in the red (NHL, 2004). Hence, it becomes difficult for Canadian teams to allocate resources to branding when they are fighting for their survival.

Second, the NHL controls the marketing and branding of the teams beyond a 150 km radius. This policy imposed on the teams discourages their commercial initiatives, as it is often not profitable enough for a Canadian team to launch local marketing actions because of the relatively small size of their market. Furthermore, it makes smaller market teams suffocate within their local market, as the revenues they can generate from ticket sale, sponsors, and TV rights are limited because of the size of the market.

Truly, the NHL wants to safeguard the integrity and homogeneity of its brand: centralization provides homogeneity and strengthens the overall quality of the league itself (Mullin, Hardy, & Sutton, 2000), any team being as strong as the league it is part of. Moreover, the coherence and integrity of the brand is essential in order to attract and keep customers (Aaker, 1994; Kapferer, 2001), especially for the NHL, which has lost fans after the 1995 lock-out and which is on the verge of another labour dispute in 2004. But the realities of the 30 markets that compose the NHL are very different, and the league is as strong as its weakest link. The NHL cannot expect to leverage its brand at the expense of teams' brands.

Discussion

The eight cases studied present various approaches in developing a sport team brand equity. These differences come from different identities and positioning, catalysts that teams capitalize on, the constraints they face, and different stages teams have reached in developing their brand equity (Figure 2). Furthermore, we should not forget the fact that two countries and two sports are involved in our study.

The LOSC case illustrates the challenges in building a brand which cannot rely on a strong identity yet whose history is too distant to capitalize on (Mazur, 2002). Moreover, the development of the brand is potentially weakened by the uncertainty surrounding the team. In fact, even though LOSC has existed for nearly 60 years, the team really started building its brand equity in 2000, thanks to good performance on the field in France. The strategic construction of the brand they initiated was a critical first step in building and leveraging a young brand which still lacks credibility against the more established soccer brands in France (Bordeaux, Lyon, Marseille, and Paris Saint-Germain, for instance; Gladden, Milne, & Sutton, 1998). The LOSC brand is an emerging brand which needs to increase its regional presence and reinforce its national image. Its potential is good, but the team will have to overcome some hurdles, such as ensuring more consistency on the field and finalizing the new stadium project.

The RC Lens case underlines that the development of the brand image of a team strongly depends on the roots and social characteristics of the local community (De Chernatony, 2001; Kapferer, 2001). RC Lens remains a regional brand, which carries values that are consistent with the popular dimension of the region. As Serge Dore, the general manager mentioned, "What is possible in the region is not necessarily feasible in Lyon or Bordeaux, where the customers are more 'bourgeois.' In the northern part of France, when people buy a Lens product, they feel like they provide the club with additional financial means" (L'Équipe, 2000). If the team continues to perform well at the French and European level, a national positioning of the brand could be done without alienating local fans, respecting in this regard the family spirit and the historic values of the RC Lens. That is why the club could start by expanding its brand in French regions where the people share similar values as those in the Lens region, such as in industrial zones.

The case of Girondins de Bordeaux is interesting. The club is a regional brand from the south western part of France, but it also has the potential to become a national brand because of its glory days in the

1980s, during which time the team was considered a reference in France. In this regard, Girondins de Bordeaux can capitalize on a rich history and a good record on the field to build and leverage its brand. In fact, constant good performances on the field could help the team generate a national interest, which would be reinforced by an up-market positioning and values such as prestige (Future Brand, 2002). The Girondins de Bordeaux brand could very well become a national brand if the team regularly ranks among the top three teams in France, combined with a solid performance at the continental level. But the managers are realistic. As the marketing director of the club mentioned, "In Europe, there are two types of clubs: those that take part in the Champions League and the others. That is why, right now, Bordeaux can only pretend to be a regional and national brand."

Olympique de Marseille underlines that a team with a rich and glorious past can capitalize on its record in order to remain a national brand and try to leverage its potential at the continental and international level: telling the story helps emphasize the values of a company in the eyes of the customers (Mazur, 2002; Muniz & O'Guinn, 2003; Travis & Branson, 2000). Externalising the merchandising of the team by using complementary partners is a strategy which aims at reinforcing the visibility and the presence of the brand, while capitalizing on the reputation and distribution channel of partners at a low cost. Through co-branding, especially with adidas, OM is able to generate more value for its brand (Motion, Leitch, & Brodie, 2003). In France, OM is already a strong established brand, which can rely on the loyalty of its fans. However, the team will have to perform again at the highest level in European competitions in order to increase its notoriety and visibility beyond France, coupled with sound management.

On the Canadian side, the case of the Montréal Canadiens shows that no matter how strong a brand is, poor performances on the field and bad management can potentially dilute its potency. For a long time, the team took its success on the ice and at the gates for granted. Now, the team is just an average team in the NHL and people can even stay home and have access to entertainment options. Furthermore, if the idea of capturing young customers and moving them along the emotional continuum is interesting, it poses the risk that the team will alienate other segments by focusing too heavily on young customers and the entertainment dimension at the arena, not to mention that young customers' loyalty is fragile at best (Ebenkamp, 2002). The Montréal Canadiens need to instil a clear brand personality (Aaker, 1997). This personality can only exist if there is coherence between the strategic vision of managers and the perception of their fans. Right now, the team relies too heavily on the history and tradition of the club, which are not enhanced by the actual team performance on the ice.

Like the LOSC in France, the Ottawa Senators' past successes are too old (early 1900s) to capitalize on. It is a local brand that has the potential to become a regional then a national brand with more exposure on national television. But right now, the Ottawa Senators still need to strengthen their brand locally by building their fan base. In this regard, their grassroots programs within the Ottawa region community are key to building and leveraging the Ottawa Senators brand, especially among young customers who were born with the team. Furthermore, the club has been a Stanley Cup contender for the last few years. Thus, the Senators can capitalize on their success on the ice in order to strengthen their visibility and the emotional connection with the fans in the Ottawa region, Ontario, and eventually across Canada (Mullin, Hardy, & Sutton, 2000). The Ottawa Senators have initiated good marketing actions, like the introduction of a third jersey, which displays a Canadian symbol on the shoulders and which could appeal to fans nationally.

The Toronto Maple Leafs possess a strong, historic brand which transcends the performance on the ice. The Maple Leafs own a brand they can leverage through merchandising, and also through broadcasting. The recent launch of Leafs TV could give the team the means for its ambitions, and also bring a better balance between what the people who attend games and those who watch the games on TV pay (Mullin, Hardy, & Sutton, 2000). Moreover, an unclear picture of the lines of products offered could lead to an overextension of the brand (Bottomley & Doyle, 1996): in the 2003 team catalogue, the merchandise is displayed in such a way that BBQ sauce sits next to caps and bobbleheads! Furthermore, the Maple Leafs have to comply with the policy of the NHL, which limits team branding within a radius of 150 km and prevents the Maple Leafs from building a global brand: "We could be the Real Madrid of hockey, but not the way the NHL operates today" (Maple Leafs vice president, Marketing).

The Vancouver Canucks are a relatively young franchise without a successful record to report yet. It is a local and regional brand, which could develop some pockets of virtual community (Muniz & O'Guinn, 2001) outside Canada, such as in Sweden, thanks to the Internet. Indeed, the team has several Swedish players on its roster, who can act like anchor players in order to promote the brand overseas (Aaker, 1997; Mullin, Hardy, & Sutton, 2000). Strong efforts have recently been made to clarify the identity and positioning of the team. The team emphasizes attributes of the brand that strike a chord among Vancouver fans. In order to become a regional and even national brand, the team will have to capitalize on a clear identity and positioning. More exposure on national television could help too. The small market of 1.5 million people, characterized by small and medium enterprises, is a constraint that is amplified by the 150 km radius policy of the NHL. In the mid- to long-run, this could pose a threat to the franchise.

Conclusion

In this paper, we have looked at the situation of four French soccer teams and four Canadian hockey teams. If French soccer teams have a brand strategy, it is not the case for Canadian hockey teams, with the exception of the Toronto Maple Leafs. Consequently, marketing actions undertaken by Canadian teams are rarely in line with the definition of a solid identity and clear positioning that would help teams in their quest for long-term commercial viability.

Truly, we could underline some weaknesses in Canadian hockey teams' actions that sports teams in general should avoid: i) considering that merchandising actions equate with a brand strategy; ii) focusing on generating quick short-term revenues by initiating merchandising actions that are not consistent with the identity and positioning of the sports teams; iii) initiating promotional actions without a clear purpose to strengthen the identity and positioning of the sports team; and iv) believing that winning is a marketing tool that can replace a brand strategy and coherent marketing actions. In fact, successful organizations develop a brand strategy that is part of integrated marketing, where the focus is on creating value for both the company and the customers (Kotler, Filiatrault, & Turner, 2000).

We must say that the environment plays a major role, as the mode of operation of the league determines the growth potential of the brand equity of a sports team. Truly, the decentralized approach of the French soccer league opens the door to huge discrepancies between the most dynamic teams and the others. But it seems to encourage French soccer teams to initiate marketing actions in order to compete against other European brands.

In the NHL, the mode of operation discourages even those who have the means of their ambitions to initiate marketing actions. It also confines small market teams to their very limited market, condemning them to remain local or, at best, regional brands. The NHL should take into consideration the realities, specificities, and needs of the 30 markets and help each team thrive depending on the size of the market (Canadian teams) and the importance the game of hockey has in some less natural markets (Miami, Nashville, Phoenix, etc.). This applies to all sports leagues: a brand needs visibility in order to enter the consideration set of the consumer and have a chance to be bought (Kotler, Filiatrault, & Turner, 2000), and also to transcend its original market (Keller, 1993).

That is why we believe the mindset could be switched from building a fan base to building a team's brand community that transcends gender, age, social classes, and geographical boundaries (McAlexander, Schouten, & Koenig, 2002; Muniz & O'Guinn, 2003). Sports teams need to find ways to combine the intangible benefits (essentially the emotions lived at the arena and the pride to be associated with the team) with the tangible dimensions of the product (result of the game, merchandising, draws during the game, area for family and kids to play outside or inside the stadium, facilities at the stadium, etc.; Burton & Howard, 1999). Hence, the brand truly becomes a unifying, coherent, and holistic offering which enables a team to instil trust and develop customers' loyalty toward its products (De Chernatony, 2001).

This should help the most dynamic teams and work toward ensuring the long-term viability of their franchise. In return, this could benefit the league, which, in North America, aims at maximizing the economic profit for the league as a whole (Li, Hofacre, & Mahony, 2001).

Building a brand is not a miracle remedy or a panacea. Nonetheless, we believe that it is part of the equation in order to help sports teams gain some financial stability and viability, especially for smaller market teams, in both North America and Europe. Indeed, strong brands are able to generate trust and loyalty from their customers and reinforce the emotional and personal relationships with their fans (De Chernatony, 2001; Kapferer, 2001). Consequently, teams can make their fans live the brand and thus generate revenues even beyond the sports arena, especially during less successful times (Bobby, 2002; Gladden, Milne, & Sutton, 1998).

If financial resources and winning are necessary in order to build and leverage a brand, they are not enough in building brand equity. It is also how you spend your money that matters (Future Brand, 2002; Gladden, Milne, & Sutton, 1998) and how you take advantage of winning in order to increase fans' attachment and loyalty to the team, among others through the sale of team merchandise (Mullin, Hardy, & Sutton, 2000; Sport Business Group, 2002). Ideally, a team should build enough of a strong brand to protect itself from the contingencies of on-field performances. Furthermore, history and tradition can be a double-edge sword for teams that go through a rebuilding process. If the actual product on the field or on the ice is not congruent with what the team used to stand for and poor performance extends in time, fans can start distancing themselves from the team and the brand (i.e., Montréal Canadiens).

At the next stage of our research, we will look more closely at the different types of sports teams' fans, the attributes of the sports team brand they are looking for when they are in contact with the team, as well as the most appropriate marketing actions teams could undertake in order to satisfy the needs of their different segments. We should also study the synergies that exist between the brand strategies of sports teams, the policies of the league and the merchandising actions of licensees, and how these synergies could be improved in order to better help teams leverage their brand.

Finally, the weaknesses of the study are intertwined with its exploratory nature. First, because of time and resource constraints, we worked with eight teams. These teams have similarities but do represent realities of their own, which in a way limits the external validity of our research. Second, we looked at the situation of French soccer and Canadian hockey teams. Some could argue that the comparison is questionable because two different sports, two different environments, and two different modes of operation of the respective league are involved, not to mention that the global appeal of soccer and hockey are each very different. But we believe this comparison provides some useful findings in the context of an exploratory research. Third, because of resource constraints, one or two managers were interviewed, which could affect the validity of the results. However, we believe the risk was reduced in part by the different sources of information we consulted (Perrien, Chéron, & Zins, 1986).

References

Aaker, D. A. (1994). *Le management du capital-marque: analyser, développer et exploiter la valeur des marques.* Paris: Dalloz.

Aaker, J. L. (1997). Dimensions of brand personality. *Journal of Marketing Research, 34*(3), 347-356.

Barwise, P., Higson, C., Likierman, A., & Marsh, P. (1989). *Accounting for brands.* London: London Business School and the Institute for Chartered Accountants in England and Wales.

Bedbury, S., & Fenichell, S. (2002). *A new brand world.* New York: Viking Press.

Bobby, D. (2002, April). Can a sports club be a brand? *Sport Business International,* Retreived September 1, 2002, from http://www.wolff-olins.com/sportsclub.htm.

Bolotny, F. (2002, November-December). Quel modèle économique pour le football français? *LFP Magazine.* Retrieved December 1, 2002, from http://www.footpro.fr/magazineLFP/pdf/n4.pdf.

Bottomley, P. A., & Doyle, J. R. (1996). The formation of attitudes towards brand extensions: Testing and generalising Aaker and Keller's model. *International Journal of Research in Marketing, 13,* 365-377.

Bousch, D. M., & Loken, B. (1991, February). A process tracing study of brand extension evaluations. *Journal of Marketing Research, 28,* 16-28.

Burton, R., & Howard, D. (1999). Professional sports leagues: Marketing mix mayhem. *Marketing Management, 8*(1), 36-46.

Cavusgil, S. T., & Zou, S. (1994). Marketing strategy-performance relationship: An investigation of the empirical link in export market ventures. *Journal of Marketing, 58*(1), 1-21.

Chaudhuri, A., & Holbrook, M. B. (2001). The chain of effects from brand trust and brand affect to brand performance: The role of brand loyalty. *Journal of Marketing, 65*(2), 81-93.

Dawar, N., & Anderson, P. F. (1994). The effects of order and direction on multiple brand extensions. *Journal of Business Research, 30,* 119-129.

De Chernatony, L. (2001). A model for strategically building brands. *Brand Management, 9*(1), 32-44.

Desbordes, M. (2000). *Gestion du sport.* Paris: Vigot.

Desbordes, M., Ohl, F., & Tribou, G. (2001). *Marketing du sport,* 2nd edition. Paris: Economica.

Ebenkamp, B. (2002). Youth shall be served. *Brandweek, 43*(25), 20-25.

Eisenhardt, K. M. (1989). Building theory from case study research. *Academy of Management Review, 14*(4), 532-550.

Future Brand. (2002). Winning isn't everything. It's how you build the brand that counts. Retrieved September 1, 2002, from http://futurebrand.com.

Girondins de Bordeaux. (2004). Retrieved March 1, 2004, from http://www.girondins.com.

Gladden, J. M., Milne, G. R., & Sutton, W. A. (1998). A conceptual framework for evaluating brand equity in Division I college athletics. *Journal of Sport Management, 12*(1), 1-19.

Glasgow Celtic. (2004). Retrieved March 1, 2004, from http://superstore.celticfc.net.

Gustafson, R. (2001, April 5). Product brands look set to gain new advantage. *Marketing,* 20.

Holbrook, M. B., & Hirschman, E. C. (1982). The experiential aspects of consumption: Consumer fantasies, feelings, fun. *Journal of Consumer Research, 9*(2), 132-140.

Holt, D. B. (1995). How consumers consume: A typology of consumption practices. *Journal of Consumer Research, 22*(1), 1-16.

Holt, D. B. (2002). Why do brands cause trouble? A dialectical theory of consumer culture and branding. *Journal of Consumer Research, 29*(1), 70-90.

Kapferer, J. N. (1998). *Les marques, capital de l'entreprise: créer et développer des marques fortes* (3rd éd.). Paris: Éditions d'Organisation.

Kapferer, J. N. (2001). Is there really no hope for local brands? *Brand Management, 9*(3), 163-170.

Kashani, K. (1995). Comment créer une marque puissante? *Les Échos.* Retrieved February 1, 2003, from http://www.lesechos.fr.

Keller, K. L. (1993). Conceptualizing, measuring, and managing customer-based brand equity. *Journal of Marketing, 57*(1), 1-22.

Keller, K. L. (2003). Brand synthesis: The multidimensionality of brand knowledge. *Journal of Consumer Research, 29*(4), 595-600.

Keyes, C. L. M. (1998). Social well-being. *Social Psychology Quarterly, 61*(2), 121-140.

Kotler, P., Filiatrault, P., & Turner, R. E. (2000). *Le management du marketing.* Boucherville, FR: Gaëtan Morin éditeur.

La Voix du Nord (2001). Retrieved December 1, 2002, from http://www.lavoixdunord.com/vdn/journal/plus/sport/foot/losc/0817mag2.shtml.

L'Équipe (2000). Retrieved December 1, 2002, from http://www.lequipe.fr/Football/Lens_Modernite.html.

Levitt, T. (1981). Marketing intangible products and product intangibles. *Harvard Business Review,* 94-102.

Li, M., Hofacre, S., & Mahony, D. (2001). *Economics of sport.* Morgantown, WV: Fitness Information Technology.

Lofland, J., & Lofland, L. H. (1995). *Analyzing social settings.* Belmont, CA: Wadsworth.

LOSC (2004). Retrieved March 1, 2004, from http://www.losc.fr.

Matear, S. M., Gray, B. J., & Irving, G. P. (2000). What makes a good export channel relationship? *Asia Pacific Journal of Management, 17*(3), 539-559.

Mazur, L. (2002, March 28) Innovation and branding make a powerful mix. *Marketing,* 16.

McAlexander, J. H., Schouten, J. W., & Koenig, H. F. (2002). Building brand community. *Journal of Marketing, 66*(1), 38-54.

Montréal Canadiens (2004). Retrieved March 1, 2004, from http://www.canadiens.com.

Moore, E. S., Wilkie, W. L., & Lutz, R. J. (2002). Passing the torch: Intergenerational influences as a source of brand equity. *Journal of Marketing, 66*(2), 17-37.

Motion, J., Leitch, S., & Brodie, R. J. (2003). Equity in corporate co-branding: The case of Adidas and the All Blacks. *European Journal of Marketing, 37*(7-8), 1080-1118.

Mullin, B. J., Hardy, S., & Sutton, W. A. (2000). *Sport marketing*, 2nd edition, Champaign, IL: Human Kinetics.

Muniz, A. M., & O'Guinn, T. C. (2003). Brand community. *Journal of Consumer Research, 27*(4), 412-432.

NHL (2004). Retrieved March 1, 2004, from http://www.nhl.com.

Olympique de Marseille. (2004). Retrieved March 1, 2004, from http://www.olympiquedemarseille.com.

Ottawa Senators. (2004). Retrieved March 1, 2004, from http://www.ottawasenators.com.

Patton, M. (1980). *Qualitative evaluation methods*. London: Sage.

Pellemans, P. (1999). *Recherche qualitative en marketing: Perspective psychoscopique*. Bruxelles: De Boeck Université.

Perrien, J., Chéron, E. J., & Zins, M. (1986). *Recherche en marketing: Méthodes et décisions*. Boucherville, FR: Gaëtan Morin éditeur.

Pons, F., & Richelieu, A. (2004). Marketing stratégique du sport: Le cas d'une franchise de la Ligue Nationale de Hockey (LNH). *Revue Française de Gestion, 30*(149).

RC Lens (2004). Retrieved March 1, 2004, from http://www.rclens.fr.

Richelieu, A. (2004). Building the brand equity of professional sports teams. In B. Pitts (Ed.), *Sharing Best Practices in Sport Marketing* (pp. 3-21). Morgantown, WV: Fitness Information Technology.

Rijkenberg, J. (2002). *Concepting—Creating successful brands in a communication-oriented era*. Henley-on-Thames, UK: World Advertising Research Centre.

Shannon, J. (1999, September 9). Battle of world football brands. *Marketing Week*, 22.

Speed, R., & Thompson, P. (2000). Determinants of sports sponsorship response. *Journal of Academy of Marketing Science, 28*(2), 226-238.

Sport Business Group (2002). Maximising revenue from licensing and merchandising. Retrieved September 1, 2002, from http://www.sportsbusiness.com/static/reports_intros/index.adp.

Sunde, L., & Brodie, R. J. (1993). Consumer evaluations of brand extensions: Further empirical results. *International Journal of Research in Marketing, 10*, 47-53.

Toronto Maple Leafs (2004). Retrieved March 1, 2004, from http://www.torontomapleleafs.com.

Travis, D., & Branson, R. (2000). *Emotional branding: How successful brands gain the irrational edge*. Prima Venture.

Underwood, R., Bond, E., & Baer, R. (2001, Winter). Building service brands via social identity: Lessons from the sports marketplace. *Journal of Marketing Theory & Practice*, 1-13.

Vancouver Canucks (2004). Retrieved March 1, 2004, from http://www.canucks.com.

Waltner, C. (2000, August 28). CRM: The new game in town for professional sports. *Informationweek*, 112-116.

Worsley, J. (2001, October 18). Brand loyalty vs. venue loyalty. *Leisure & Hospitality*. Retrieved September 1, 2002, from http://www.henleycentre.com/press/cut_20011022154033-657.phtml.

Case Study: How to Get a Minor League Promotion Major League Publicity

DOUGLAS BLAIS
ERIC C. SCHWARZ

Contributors:
Jeff Eisenberg, General Manager, Manchester Monarch Hockey Club
Todd Marlin, General Manager, Nashua Pride Baseball Club

Introduction

Disco Demolition Night in Chicago, 1979. Jay Buhner Haircut Night/Buhner Buzz in Seattle in 1994, followed two years later by Human Bobblehead Night in Florida. Sausage Races in Milwaukee. These are all some of the exciting promotions brought to fans in professional sports. Fans get to participate, and the teams get national exposure—both good and bad—on ESPN, Fox Sports, and other local, regional, and national broadcasts. According to a study by Boyd and Krehbiel (2003), promotions are effective, raising attendance by an average of 19.6%. However, this average will vary from team to team based on the type of promotion run. Some of the most popular promotions that involve spectator interaction include Shirt Off Their Backs nights, '80 nights, and Cultural Celebrations (King, 2003).

At the minor league level, there are hundreds of great promotions offered every night across the country with little or no publicity outside of the local market. However, on rare occasions, a minor league promotion receives major league publicity. How does this happen? What can other minor league teams do to market their teams and their promotions to a wider audience?

This case study will document the success of "Mullet Night," presented by the Manchester (NH) Monarchs Hockey Club, the AHL affiliate of the Los Angeles Kings. For the past two years, it has been one of the most exciting promotions in minor league hockey and has received national acclaim and coverage on ESPN—especially by former NHL player and coach, Barry Melrose. In addition, this case study will document the success of "Richard Nixon Bobblehead Night," presented by the Nashua (NH) Pride Baseball Club, an independent league team that is a member of the Atlantic League.

Mullet Night

For the past two years, the Manchester Monarchs of the American Hockey League have administered a promotion called "Mullet Night." Prior to offering this promotion in 2003, the front office of the organization contemplated numerous promotions to offer during the season. According to Jeff Eisenberg, general manager of the Manchester Monarchs, "The Monarchs have the same goals for other promotions: sell tickets, add value, and build brand. While the organization may have slightly different goals for individual promotions . . . the ultimate goal is to use promotions to get to a sell-out." The organization's goals is not to have promotions on the dates they call "dog dates"—those dates that will be low capacity due to a game being midweek or on a holiday, or the game is against a non-rival opponent—as the promotion will do little to help attendance. The Monarchs gauge whether a promotion was successful or not by getting a game that was not going to be a sell-out to reach sell-out. The result of this will be that the more sell-outs, the "hotter" the ticket becomes.

According to Eisenberg, the Manchester Monarchs use promotions to "help keep the Monarchs on the minds of the fans," and that the promotions are used so "that the fans always have fun." They do this in a number of ways to maintain their visibility in the public eye. They begin this by being "promotion heavy" during first 20 games, which is traditionally the time of year where fans are not thinking about hockey yet—especially with the Major League Baseball post-season, and the National Football League being in mid-season. As Eisenberg stated, "The goal with every promotion is to 'under promise and over deliver,' as this will enhance the experience of the fans, entice them to come back, and promote the team further through word of mouth."

However, as with all promotions, there tends to be two major concerns. The first is the question, "Can you have too many promotions?" According to Eisenberg, the answer is yes, "because the promotions become less special." This is directly related to the second concern, specifically related to price promotions. According to Eisenberg, "This is a 'slippery slope,' as your numbers will go up short-term, and then down. A perception builds in the market that you can always get discounted tickets, and hence price promotions will begin to devalue the product."

To measure the success of the "Mullet Night" promotion, the Monarchs had three keys benchmarks. The first would be an increase of ticket sales. Second is if the promotion enhanced the game experience. Finally, did the promotion create brand awareness and exposure, both before and after the event? In pre-event planning, the Manchester Monarchs felt that the promotion had a chance of success for a number of reasons. "Mullet Night" was unique, as it had never been done before by anyone. The number of people anticipated to participate in the promotion would be large (5,000 wigs were to be given out). Not only is the hairstyle funny, but it also has a cult following in hockey. Finally, and most importantly, the promotion was geared to "make fun of themselves," hence not taking themselves too seriously.

For a promotion to work, the front office staff of the Manchester Monarchs had to get information out about the event. This was accomplished in a number of ways, including involving the media (including the largest radio and television media outlets in the state) by providing the media with material to "pre-sell." They also promoted a contest for the best mullet, and hyped the event as "a part of the American lifestyle . . ."

The first year, the event was a tremendous success. Why? According to Eisenberg, there were a number of reasons:

- Putting hair on people (5,000) is funny.
- Players wore the hair during warm-ups.
- Kids wore the hair the entire game.
- There was a sub-culture that appeared at the game—people made their own T-shirts, wore fake teeth (ugly green teeth, buck teeth).
- The interviews conducted brought people into it—they became part of it. They took the interviews "seriously" and gave appropriate answers.
- They were able to get Barry Melrose involved, which gave the event credibility—he is a hockey icon, the "hockey guy" on ESPN—this also helped to get in on ESPN.
- "It was still funny in the 3rd period."
- A certain "mood" had been created from the pre-event publicity. "You could feel the excitement."

- Fans were the ones who made the event so successful.
- Security wore mullets.
- Hall-of-Fame made it even more of an event—where famous people who had real-life mullet were "inducted" into the Mullet Hall of Fame.

During the second year, this event was not going to be repeated. According to Eisenberg, this was mainly because it is tough to do events (not giveaways) more than once, as the novelty often wears off. There was a serious concern that having the event a second year would not be as successful. However, with the help of folklore hockey icons "The Hanson Brothers," the event became a success once again. However, there is a serious concern that it is going to be costly to exit (third mullet night), because it is going to be tough to beat the previous two events. Eisenberg stated, "The purpose of having this exit strategy is because there is a finite life to all promotions, and organizations must be conscientious to develop an exit strategy for any promotion once it has run its course, but the promotion must exit in a 'big' way."

In the case of "Mullet Night," all three benchmarks were achieved, and after two years the promotion exited in a "big" way, especially in the area of brand awareness and exposure. The promotion received coverage on ESPN (courtesy of Barry Melrose), CNN, TNN, and Hockey Night in Canada. In addition, over 80 local television and radio affiliates ran the story. Charlie Sherman, the Sport Director for WMUR TV in Manchester, New Hampshire, was critical in getting national exposure. Before the game was complete, Sherman went to the office and edited highlights, uploaded it to the satellite, and sent the corresponding satellite numbers for the networks to download. This allowed all media outlets to download footage and put it on TV. While the first mullet night received a short mention the first year, the second mullet night received approximately four minutes of coverage on ESPN. In expanding their reach nationally, the *Los Angeles Times* (the home city of the parent organization, the Los Angeles Kings) ran an article on the second page of the sports section that discussed the event. According to Eisenberg, "It was great to have the exposure in Los Angeles with the parent company, as it adds credibility to the Monarchs' organization." From a local perspective, this exposure was well received and accepted by sponsors and fans. The ticket was the "hottest" ticket in town, with season ticket holders being "proud" to have a ticket to the game. The post-game coverage added to the "allure" of the event.

Richard Nixon Bobblehead Night

A promotion conducted by the Nashua Pride Baseball Club, an independent baseball team playing in the Atlantic League, was Richard Nixon Bobblehead Night. According to Todd Marlin, general manager of the Nashua Pride Baseball Club, the "Watergate Day" promotion on the 35th anniversary of Watergate (June 17, 2004) came about as the front office was planning promotions for the upcoming 2004 season in November of 2003. "I found a calendar with almost every possible holiday and days of significance," said Marlin. As they went through the June month matching dates with home games we would have, they noticed that we had a game in conjunction with the anniversary of Watergate. A discussion ensued to think of a few things the organization could do that could make a night out of it. Their primary promotional tool was the Richard Nixon bobblehead, which was given to the first 1,000 fans through the gates. The dolls have Richard Nixon in a suit with his arms giving the "peace" sign.

As the planning process evolved, the Pride decided that they should incorporate some of the notable events that happened during that infamous night. The organization came up with shredding tickets as fans entered the game, blocked off the PA booth so nobody could see in, and had Ken Cail (the PA announcer) speak in a monotone, just as Deep Throat did. In addition, the Pride placed "bugs" under seats and winners were given prizes. Additionally, during the third inning, there was no PA, music, or scoreboard for 18 1/2 minutes. It was later described as a "sinister force" that had intervened and caused the mechanical problems. Marlin said, "It took some people a minute to get it, but once they did, they all got a good laugh out of it."

Overall the promotion was great, and the organization got very good regional coverage, including two of the three Boston stations, all the New Hampshire television stations, and play and mentions on most New Hampshire radio stations. More importantly, the Nashua Pride received national coverage on

CBS Nightly News radio, as well as on Major League Baseball (MLB) Radio. The Nashua Pride were also featured in a number of sport industry trade magazines, including the *SportBusiness Journal* and the *Team Marketing Report*.

Conclusion

According to Rick Orienza, director of promotions and advertising for the Pittsburgh Pirates, "No question, it's getting harder to find items that get people excited. We've found that we need to do more than just give things away to get people in for promotions. We try to create a sense of an event. You have to do something that gets people's attention and adds to their experience" (King, 2002b). Given that one of the fundamental requirements of successful marketing is that marketing managers understand exactly what drives consumers to purchase their product, it is imperative that sport marketers discover exactly what motivates fans to attend their events (Bernthal & Graham, 2003). The hurdle for clubs has been finding items that play to fans' appetites without exceeding sponsor budgets (King, 2002a). At the same time, teams are looking to market their teams and their promotions to a wider audience. The promotional concepts developed by the Manchester Monarchs with their Mullet Night and the Nashua Pride with their Richard Nixon Bobblehead Night show that with a little creativity, they can have a successful event and get a minor league promotion major league publicity.

References

Bernthal, M. J., & Graham, P. J. (2003, September 1). The effect of sport setting on fan attendance motivation. The case of minor league vs. collegiate baseball. *Journal of Sport Behavior, 26*(3), 223-239.

Boyd, T., & Krehbiel T. (2003). Promotion timing in Major League Baseball and the stacking effects of factors that increase game attractive. *Sport Marketing Quarterly, 12*(3), 173-183.

Eisenberg, J. (Speaker). (2004). Interview with Doug Blais. (personal interview).

King, B. (2003, October 20). Theme nights, events boost lagging giveaway promotions. *SportBusiness Journal, 6*(26), 43.

King, B. (2002a, November 2). Signed-ball giveaway latest promo idea. *SportsBusiness Journal, 5*(28), 1, 67.

King, B. (2002b, October 21). Bobbleheads still most dependable MLB promo? Nod yes. *SportsBusiness Journal, 5*(26), 1, 40-41.

Marlin, T. (Speaker). (2004). Interview with Eric Schwarz. (email correspondences).

Gender as a Determinant of the Relative Merits of Celebrity Sports Figures in Magazine Advertising

MELISSA ST. JAMES
JAMES E. SWARTZ

Abstract

The authors examine the usage of female vs. male sports figures as endorsers in magazine advertising. Previous literature indicates an increase in the number of female athletes awarded endorsement contracts as well as an increase in the dollar amount of these contracts.

Prior research has shown that female endorsers are more credible than male endorsers and therefore female sports figures may act as role models for women of all ages, perhaps even more than their male counterparts. Studies have shown that female athletes can have a positive impact particularly on young people's self-image and self-identification.

This pilot study examines magazine advertisements for a female sports figure endorsing a sports-related product paired with a male sports figure endorsing a sports-related product, as well as a female sports figure endorsing a non-sports related product paired with a male sports figure endorsing a non-sports related product. If female endorsers are indeed more credible than male endorsers, it can be expected that both the female endorsement advertisements will fare better than the male endorsement advertisements on the advertising effectiveness measure.

Introduction

The fastest growing segment of celebrity endorsement advertising is in the sports area. According to *Sports Marketing News*, over $500 million is attributed to sports celebrities' endorsement contracts (Shani &

Sandler, 1991). Since the 1996 Olympic Games, women have been offered endorsement contracts notable in both their number and dollar amount. However, females still lag far behind male athletes in both areas. This paper combines a look at celebrity endorsements and the rationales for their effectiveness and a summary of a study performed for this research endeavor, examining the effectiveness of female vs. male sports figure endorsement advertisements, with both sports-related and non-sports-related products. Conclusions and recommendations for future research are also included.

Literature Review

Celebrity Endorsers

The use of celebrity endorsers in advertising dates back to the 1800s, and its impact on advertising effectiveness has been a source of much debate and research. Some researchers have found that celebrity endorsers are likeable and attractive, serve as an attention-getting device and aid in recall (Kamins, 1990). However, others have found that, although attention and recall are important, credibility and believability are the keys to favorable attitude formation and purchase intention. The problem is that credibility and believability do not necessarily follow from the favorable impressions resulting from likeability and attractiveness (Kamins, Brand, Hoeke, & Moe, 1989).

The use of celebrity endorsers in advertising is aimed at increasing message *persuasiveness*. The goal of a persuasive message is to cause a person to adopt the attitude advocated by the communicator through the formation of desirable attitudes toward an innovation, idea, or product. A celebrity endorser has been defined as an individual who is known to the public (e.g., an actor, a sports figure, an entertainer) for his or her achievements in areas other than that of the product class endorsed (Friedman & Friedman, 1979). Examples include Jerry Seinfeld pitching American Express or Julia Louis-Dryfus promoting hair color. Each is known for being an actor/comedian, not a financial advisor or hairdresser. In fact, this definition can be expanded to include those celebrities who endorse products from their area of expertise or fame (i.e., Michael Jordan endorsing athletic shoes) (St. James, 2004).

Celebrity endorsements are, however, expensive and risky. Michael Jordan would not even consider an endorsement contract for less than $10 million. And one has only to look at the O. J. Simpson (Hertz Rental Car) and Madonna (Pepsi) history in advertising to know that situations involving celebrities are tenuous. If advertisers are to be successful in the use of celebrities, the more knowledge they have of why and when celebrities are successful endorsers, the more likely they are to choose carefully and to create successful associations. And the more likely they are to be able to justify the expense.

For example, consumers can be affected by qualities the celebrity brings to the endorsement process, such as the celebrity's attractiveness and perceived image, or credibility, defined by researchers as a combination of expertise, trustworthiness, and attractiveness (Ohanian, 1991). To better interpret the endorsement process, this paper will rely primarily on Grant McCracken's 1989 study proposing a meaning transfer model as an approach to studying celebrity endorsement effectiveness.

McCracken's theory will be discussed in detail later in the paper; however, in essence it states that the celebrity is endowed with certain cultural meanings that are passed from the celebrity to the product, and in turn to the consumer—thus ensuring the celebrity endorser's effectiveness in the persuasion process.

Reasons for the Effectiveness of Celebrity Endorsers

Michael Kamins (1989) illustrated that the use of celebrity endorsers is effective because of the identification process, one of three social influence processes identified by Herbert Kelman (1961) through which an individual may adopt an attitude advocated by a communicator—in this case, the celebrity endorser. Of the three processes—compliance, identification, and internalization—identification and, to a lesser extent, internalization have been shown to be important to the study of celebrity endorsers in advertising.

Compliance, when a person is influenced by someone advocating a position or product in the hope of getting a favorable reaction from the communicator, is not applicable to celebrity endorser advertising because there is essentially no interaction between the consumer and the celebrity endorser (Kamins, 1989). In other words, the consumer has little or no chance of being acknowledged by the celebrity endorser for having purchased the product.

Identification, however, has been strongly linked to the effectiveness of celebrity endorsements in advertising in part because it is related to the attractiveness and likeability of the celebrity endorser. Identification relies on the receiver adopting the attitude of the endorser because they want to emulate or be like the endorser (Kamins, 1989). For example, the "I want to be like Mike" campaign appealed to those who wanted to emulate Michael Jordan. A 1996 study looked at identification as a mediator of celebrity effects and also found support for using a celebrity the audience can identify with to increase the likelihood of achieving lasting attitude or behavior change (Basil, 1996).

Internalization, the third process discussed by Kelman, is the process whereby the receiver believes the communicator is honest and sincere and also believes that the communicator wants the receiver to adopt the communicator's attitude because that attitude is consistent with his or her own value system. This process is not strongly linked to celebrity endorsement advertising because celebrities are sometimes seen as "doing it only for the money" and the believability of the ad becomes questionable. However, in combination with identification, internalization can be a means of encouraging self-enhancement and attitude change. Internalization can therefore be a valid self-presentation management tool only if the attitude of the communicator is in fact consistent with the consumer's own values.

Match-Up Theory

Kamins' follow up study, "An Investigation into the Match-Up Hypothesis in Celebrity Advertising: When Beauty May be Only Skin Deep" (1990), addresses the above mentioned believability issue by testing the hypothesis that attractiveness of a celebrity endorser may enhance attitudes and purchase intentions only when the images of the product and the celebrity "match-up." Since self-presentation and impression management rely on the idea of individuals striving to promote an image of themselves in other's eyes, both the image of the product and the image of the celebrity must be such that the consumer wants to be identified with that product in some way. Presenting oneself as associated with the celebrity by purchasing the endorsed product is a way of identifying with the celebrity, using the product as a bridge for incorporating the attributes identified with the celebrity into one's own self-presentation.

Kamins showed support for using an attractive celebrity endorser for an attractiveness-related product to enhance attitudes and endorser credibility. The study also illustrated support for the converse, that use of an attractive celebrity for an attractiveness-unrelated product had no effect on attitude and credibility measures as compared to the use of an unattractive celebrity endorser for the attractiveness-unrelated product. Kamins cites Kahle and Homer's 1985 study as evidence of research supporting the assertion that a physically attractive source aids attitude change toward products, issues, and advertising-based evaluations.

Both the Kamins and the 1985 Kahle and Homer report link the "match-up" hypothesis to social adaptation theory. This theory states that the adaptive significance of information will determine impact. With regard to attractive celebrity endorsers, this theory implies that the consumer may believe that using the endorsed product will enhance their own physical appearance like it did (at least in the mind of the consumer) for the celebrity endorser.

A study by Lockwood and Kunda entitled "Superstars and Me: Predicting the Impact of Role Models on the Self" also supports this "match-up" theory and examined specifically self-enhancement and self-presentation. The authors proposed that only relevant superstars provoked self-enhancement and inspiration. They found that if an individual feels the success of the role model was attainable, the star provoked self-enhancement, but self-view was only affected if the star's domain was relevant to the individual (Lockwood & Kunda, 1997).

Credibility of the Celebrity Endorser

When discussing credibility it has been shown by several researchers that more often than not a highly credible source is more effective, produces more positive attitudes toward the product or position endorsed, and results in more behavioral changes than a less credible source (Buhr et. al., 1987). Self-enhancement theory would dictate that the individual wants to be thought of well by others and would therefore be influenced more by a credible source because they want a positive image association. If the celebrity turns out to be a fraud or a suspected criminal (i.e., O. J. Simpson), then the association becomes negative and the individual would gain nothing from identifying with the celebrity. In fact, the self-view might suffer because the individual now is associated with a negative personality figure. If you have been wearing "O. J." shoes for the past five years and O. J. is now a suspected murderer, you have used his image to self-enhance and now must contend with the possibility of negative fallout from others—they may not "think well" of you anymore.

Previous literature has identified three major dimensions of source credibility: expertise, trustworthiness, and attractiveness (Kahle & Homer, 1985; Maddux & Rogers, 1980; Ohanian, 1991). Expertise is defined by Ohanian as "the knowledge that the communicator seems to possess to support the claims made in the advertisements." Trustworthiness has root in the consumers' confidence that the communicator is honest and objective in providing information in the advertisement. Inclusion of attractiveness of the source as a component of source credibility has direct ties to the use of celebrities as endorsers (Ohanian, 1991). These are all positive traits in a celebrity that one may want to emulate or incorporate into one's self-presentation. It must be noted that adolescents are also susceptible, however, to influence from celebrities in ways that can produce adverse effects. Atkin and Block (1983) have shown that celebrity endorsements of alcohol products are particularly effective with teenagers. The celebrity figure is seen by the teenagers as trustworthy and more competent than ordinary spokespersons. Also, Stanton et al. (1996) found that the influence of a celebrity on teenagers' smoking habits increased in late adolescence. The teenagers felt the celebrity wouldn't endorse a product harmful to them.

Meaning Transfer Model

The final study examined here is a slight departure from the previous works. Grant McCracken, in a 1989 study entitled "Who is the Celebrity Endorser? Cultural foundations of the Endorsement Process," proposes an alternative meaning transfer model. In effect, McCracken's theory is that the celebrity is endowed with certain cultural meanings which are passed from the celebrity to the product and in turn to the consumer—thus ensuring the celebrity endorser's effectiveness in the persuasion process. McCracken's criticism of previous models is predominately that "they do not capture everything at issue in the endorsement process" (McCracken, 1989).

The cultural meanings a celebrity brings to the endorsement of a product are varied. McCracken lists attributes such as status, class, age, personality, gender, and lifestyle types as a few. The idea is that in order for a celebrity to be successful in the endorsement process, a transfer of these meanings or qualities must take place between the celebrity and the product, and ultimately between the product and the consumer. The example cited of James Garner endorsing Mazda cars shows that Garner's inherent qualities—maturity, confidence, good humor, and "Americaness"—in essence "made the properties of the car" (McCracken, 1989).

The general transfer of meaning in advertising is when advertisers position their product. This means that the advertiser (or manufacturer) identifies the cultural meanings they want their product to embody. BMW and Jaguar are positioned to appeal to a certain target market based on status, sophistication, high income level, and exclusivity—cultural meanings that consumers can then associate with the product. It is up to the advertiser to choose the appropriate methods of conveying these meanings—choosing media, executional elements of the advertisement, and placement in appropriate locations—in a way that facilitates meaning transfer.

The cultural meanings embodied in celebrities have power that unknown actors or spokespersons cannot match (McCracken, 1989). Celebrities' visibility and longevity work in their favor—we have come to associate certain meanings with them because we have seen them in movies, or on the athletic field, or on the stage, displaying these qualities time and time again. Robert Mitchum *was* toughness because we saw him portray it over and over again, and that became his cultural meaning association.

Impression management and self presentation through incorporating or taking on the cultural meanings associated with the celebrity is a means of identification. As mentioned above, the celebrity has fashioned an image through his or her career and endowed the product with this cultural meaning through association and the endorsement process.

Now, how does the consumer take on these cultural meanings? Simply buying or using the product is not enough—the consumers must make the qualities their own. The idea is that we are all finding meanings in our possessions and using these meanings to create selves (McCracken, 1989). Celebrities personify this process; they have succeeded in creating a persona endowed with cultural meanings we now associate with the celebrity. The public nature of the celebrity-created self makes the celebrity inspirational to the consumer (McCracken, 1989). Consumers emulate celebrities through the meaning transfer process—the product endorsed by the celebrity becomes a concrete method of creating an enhanced self for the consumer. Not only does the celebrity provide the image we want to attain and the blueprint, but, in effect, they are providing the bricks and the mortar with the product endorsement. Adams-Price and Greene (1990) found that adolescent boys in particular formed identificatory attachments, a type of secondary attachment in which adolescents expressed a desire to be the attachment object, to celebrity figures and that these relationships were important in the development of their social identity. These secondary attachments serve as a means of incorporating characteristics attributed to the celebrity into the teenagers' self concept.

Study on the Use of Sports Figures in Print Advertising

This current study examined attitude toward the advertisements shown in Appendix A. Each advertisement features a celebrity athlete endorsing a product, detailed as follows:

- A female athlete (Martina Hingis for Yonex tennis racquets) endorsing a sports related product (implying expert condition).
- A male celebrity athlete (Andre Agasse for Penn tennis balls) endorsing a sports related product (implying expert condition).
- A female celebrity athlete (Anna Kournikova for Omega watches) endorsing a non-sports related product.
- A male celebrity athlete (Pete Sampras for Movado watches) endorsing a non-sports related product.

In order to assess attitude toward the advertisements, respondents were asked to complete the following scale items after being asked to "Please indicate how you feel about the advertisement above by placing an X at the appropriate point on the following scales":

1. Pleasant ___:___:___:___:___:___:___ Unpleasant
2. Fun to see ___:___:___:___:___:___:___ Not fun to see
3. Enjoyable ___:___:___:___:___:___:___ Not enjoyable
4. Important ___:___:___:___:___:___:___ Not important
5. Interesting ___:___:___:___:___:___:___ Not interesting
6. Informative ___:___:___:___:___:___:___ Not informative
7. Entertaining ___:___:___:___:___:___:___ Not entertaining
8. Useful ___:___:___:___:___:___:___ Not useful
9. Not Boring ___:___:___:___:___:___:___ Boring
10. Makes me curious ___:___:___:___:___:___:___ Does not make me curious

In addition, respondents rated the celebrity athlete on Ohanian's credibility scale by completing the statement "I find the celebrity/athlete pictured in the advertisement to be" using the following scale items:

1.	Attractive	___:___:___:___:___:___	Unattractive
2.	Classy	___:___:___:___:___:___	Not classy
3.	Beautiful	___:___:___:___:___:___	Ugly
4.	Elegant	___:___:___:___:___:___	Plain
5.	Sexy	___:___:___:___:___:___	Not Sexy
6.	Dependable	___:___:___:___:___:___	Undependable
7.	Honest	___:___:___:___:___:___	Dishonest
8.	Reliable	___:___:___:___:___:___	Unreliable
9.	Sincere	___:___:___:___:___:___	Insincere
10.	Trustworthy	___:___:___:___:___:___	Untrustworthy
11.	Expert	___:___:___:___:___:___	Not an Expert
12.	Experienced	___:___:___:___:___:___	Inexperienced
13.	Knowledgeable	___:___:___:___:___:___	Unknowledgeable
14.	Qualified	___:___:___:___:___:___	Unqualified
15.	Skilled	___:___:___:___:___:___	Unskilled

The scales used in the study were examined using the Cronbach alpha reliability procedure (Cronbach, 1951). Nunnally (1979) suggests Cronbach's alpha of .7 as an acceptable level of agreement. The following table shows the Cronbach alpha scores for each of the scales used in the study, indicating acceptable levels.

Table 1: Scale Reliability – Cronbach Alpha		
Scale	**Cronbach**	**Scale Items**
Attitude toward Advertisement "Please indicate how you feel about the advertisement above by placing an X at the appropriate point on the following scales:"	.912	• Pleasant/Unpleasant • Fun to see/Not fun to see • Enjoyable/Not enjoyable • Important/Not important • Interesting/Not interesting • Informative/Not informative • Entertaining/Not entertaining • Useful/Not useful • Not Boring/Boring • Makes me curious/Does not make me curious
Attractiveness	.919	• Attractive/Unattractive • Classy/Not classy • Beautiful/Ugly • Elegant/Plain • Sexy/Not Sexy
Trustworthiness	.924	• Dependable/Undependable • Honest/Dishonest • Reliable/Unreliable • Sincere/Insincere • Trustworthy/Untrustworthy
Expertise	.915	• Expert/Not an Expert • Experienced/Inexperienced • Knowledgeable/Unknowledgeable • Qualified/Unqualified • Skilled/Unskilled

The descriptive statistics for the sample are shown below in Table 2. Age groups were listed on the survey instrument as 18–23, 24–29, and 29–34.

Table 2: Age				
	Frequency	Percent	Valid Percent	Cumulative Percent
Valid 0	1	.4	.4	.4
1	177	66.3	66.3	66.7
2	67	25.1	25.1	91.8
3	22	8.2	8.2	100.0
Total	267	100.0	100.0	

Gender (descriptive statistics shown in Table 3 below) was coded as Male = 1 and Female = 2.

Table 3: Gender				
	Frequency	Percent	Valid Percent	Cumulative Percent
Valid 1	135	50.6	50.6	50.6
2	132	49.4	49.4	100.0
Total	267	100.0	100.0	

Table 4 shows the ethnic makeup of the sample. Using the U.S. Census Bureau categories, ethnicities were coded as

1. White
2. Spanish/Hispanic/Latino
3. Black, African American or Negro
4. Native Hawaiian
5. Guamanian or Chamorro
6. American Indian or Alaska Native
7. Samoan
8. Other Pacific Islander_____(please specify)
9. Asian Indian
10. Chinese
11. Filipino
12. Japanese
13. Korean
14. Vietnamese
15. Other Asian _____(please specify)
16. Some other race _____(please specify)

Table 4:		Ethnicity			
		Frequency	Percent	Valid Percent	Cumulative Percent
Valid	1	75	28.1	28.1	28.1
	2	44	16.5	16.5	44.6
	3	16	6.0	6.0	50.6
	4	1	.4	.4	50.9
	6	1	.4	.4	51.3
	9	12	4.5	4.5	55.8
	10	41	15.4	15.4	71.2
	11	17	6.4	6.4	77.5
	12	5	1.9	1.9	79.4
	13	10	3.7	3.7	83.1
	14	16	6.0	6.0	89.1
	15	5	1.9	1.9	91.0
	16	24	9.0	9.0	100.0
	Total	267	100.0	100.0	

It is expected that, as in previous research, female endorsers will be more effective than male endorsers. Also, it is expected that age, gender, and ethnicity of the respondents will have an impact on their evaluations of the advertisements. The expert condition should also have an impact on the evaluations of the advertisements in this study, supporting prior research showing expertise as a determinant of advertising effectiveness in celebrity endorsement advertising. The primary questions addressed in this research study are as follows:

Are male sports figures more effective than female sports figures (as endorsers) in magazine advertisements?

Do the age, gender, and ethnicity of a respondent affect attitude toward the ad for an endorsement advertisement featuring a female sports figure vs. one featuring a male sports figure?

Therefore, the hypotheses tested in this pilot study are as follows:

H1: Female sports figures as endorsers will be more effective (measured by attitude toward the advertisement) than male sports figure endorsers, regardless of the product category (expert condition).

H2: The advertisement featuring the expert condition will be more effective (measured by attitude toward the advertisement) than the advertisement featuring the non-expert condition, regardless of the gender of the endorser.

Table 5:	Descriptive Statistics											
	N	Range	Minimum	Maximum	Mean		Std.	Variance	Skewness		Kurtosis	
	Statistic	Statistic	Statistic	Statistic	Statistic	Std. Error	Statistic	Statistic	Statistic	Std. Error	Statistic	Std. Error
AADAK	267	6.0	1.0	7.0	4.233	.078	1.2685	1.609	-.163	.149	-.391	.297
AADPS	267	5.8	1.0	6.8	3.695	.078	1.2806	1.640	-.125	.149	-.558	.297
AADMH	267	7.0	.0	7.0	4.349	.073	1.1902	1.417	-.616	.149	.706	.297
AADAA	267	6.0	1.0	7.0	4.126	.079	1.2939	1.674	-.377	.149	-.153	.297
Valid N (listwise)	267											

H3: Respondents' age, gender, and ethnicity will have an impact on attitude toward the advertisement in an advertisement featuring a sports figure as endorser.

Table 5 on the previous page shows, upon examination of the means for the attitude toward the advertisements in the study, that the endorsement advertisements using a female sports figure were rated more favorably than the endorsement advertisements showing a male sports figure. This supports H1 in that both the Anna Kournikova (non-sports related product) and the Martina Hingis (sports related product) advertisements were rated higher than the Pete Sampras (non-sports related product) and the Andre Agassi (sports related product) advertisements.

The figure above also shows that H2 is supported since both of the advertisements featuring the implied expert condition (those featuring the sports-related product) were rated higher than the two advertisements featuring the non-sports related products, which imply no expert condition, regardless of the gender of the sports figure featured in the advertisement.

The further results of our investigation are shown in Table 6 below. As shown, upon examination of the MANOVA results, age and gender of the respondent appear to have a significant effect on the overall evaluations of the advertisements while ethnicity does not. This, in part, supports H3.

Table 6: Results: Multivariate Tests		
Effect		**Sig.**
Intercept	Pillai's Trace	.000
	Wilks' Lambda	.000
	Hotelling's Trace	.000
	Roy's Largest Root	.000
AGEGR	Pillai's Trace	.039
	Wilks' Lambda	.039
	Hotelling's Trace	.039
	Roy's Largest Root	.039
ETHNICIT	Pillai's Trace	.245
	Wilks' Lambda	.245
	Hotelling's Trace	.245
	Roy's Largest Root	.245
GENDER	Pillai's Trace	.000
	Wilks' Lambda	.000
	Hotelling's Trace	.000
	Roy's Largest Root	.000

a Computed using alpha = .05
b Exact statistic
c Design: Intercept+AGEGR+ETHNICIT+GENDER

However, upon examination of the ANOVA results (Table 7 below), it can be seen that age of the respondent only had a significant impact on the attitude toward the advertisement for the ad featuring Martina Hingis, which paired a female celebrity athlete with a sports related product.

Table 7: ANOVA – Age		Sum of Squares	df	Mean Square	F	Sig.
AADAK* AGEGR	Between Groups (Combined)	3.456	3	1.52	.713	.545
	Within Groups	424.591	263	1.614		
	Total	428.047	266			
AADPS* AGEGR	Between Groups (Combined)	5.268	3	1.756	1.072	.362
	Within Groups	430.936	263	1.639		
	Total	436.204	266			
ADMH* AGEGR	Between Groups (Combined)	13.633	3	4.544	3.291	.021
	Within Groups	363.174	263	1.381		
	Total	376.807	266			
AADAA* AGEGR	Between Groups (Combined)	1.151	3	.384	.227	.887
	Within Groups	444.165	263	1.689		
	Total	445.316	266			

Gender of the respondent had a significant impact on both the Anna Kournikova and the Pete Sampras ads, which featured a female sports celebrity paired with a non-sports related product and a male sports celebrity paired with a non-sports related product, respectively (see Table 8 below).

Table 8: ANOVA – Gender		Sum of Squares	df	Mean Square	F	Sig.
AADAK* GENDER	Between Groups (Combined)	50.232	1	50.232	35.233	.000
	Within Groups	377.815	265	1.426		
	Total	428.047	266			
AADPS* GENDER	Between Groups (Combined)	8.952	1	8.952	5.552	.019
	Within Groups	427.252	265	1.612		
	Total	436.204	266			
ADMH* GENDER	Between Groups (Combined)	.007	1	.007	.005	.945
	Within Groups	376.800	265	1.422		
	Total	376.807	266			
AADAA* GENDER	Between Groups (Combined)	1.224	1	1.224	.731	.393
	Within Groups	444.092	265	1.676		
	Total	445.316	266			

Finally, as shown in Table 9, ethnicity of the respondent—even though all four pictured celebrities are Caucasian—did not have a significant impact on the attitude toward the ad in any of the four cases.

Table 9: ANOVA – Ethnicity		Sum of Squares	df	Mean Square	F	Sig.
AADAK* ETHNICIT	Between Groups (Combined)	27.382	12	2.282	1.447	.145
	Within Groups	400.664	254	1.577		
	Total	428.047	266			
AADPS* ETHNICIT	Between Groups (Combined)	28.025	12	2.335	1.453	.142
	Within Groups	408.178	254	1.607		
	Total	436.204	266			
ADMH* ETHNICIT	Between Groups (Combined)	15.386	12	1.282	.901	.546
	Within Groups	361.421	254	1.423		
	Total	376.807	266			
AADAA* ETHNICIT	Between Groups (Combined)	24.354	12	2.030	1.225	.266
	Within Groups	420.962	254	1.657		
	Total	445.316	266			

It is important to note that the attractiveness, trustworthiness, and expertise variables (as rated by the respondents) have a significant impact on the attitude toward the advertisements in each case. This is an indication that we must delve further into the match-up of the celebrity and the product in order to assure a successful advertising pairing (see subsequent tables).

Table 10: ANOVA[b] - Anna Kournikova Advertisement

Model	Sum of Squares	df	Mean Square	F	Sig.
1 Regression	197.168	3	65.723	74.867	.000[a]
Residual	230.878	263	.878		
Total	428.047	266			

a Predictors: (Constant), EXAK, ATTAK, TRAK
b Dependent Variable: AADAK

Table 11: ANOVA[b] - Pete Sampras Advertisement

Model	Sum of Squares	df	Mean Square	F	Sig.
1 Regression	212.424	3	70.808	83.218	.000[a]
Residual	223.780	263	.851		
Total	436.204	266			

a Predictors: (Constant), EXPS, ATTPS, TRPS
b Dependent Variable: AADPS

Table 12: ANOVA[b] - Martina Hingis Advertisement

Model		Sum of Squares	df	Mean Square	F	Sig.
1	Regression	162.766	3	54.255	66.665	.000[a]
	Residual	214.041	263	.814		
	Total	376.807	266			

a Predictors: (Constant), EXMH, ATTMH, TRMH
b Dependent Variable: AADMH

Table 13: ANOVA - Andre Aggasi Advertisement

Model		Sum of Squares	df	Mean Square	F	Sig.
1	Regression	229.825	3	76.608	93.498	.000[a]
	Residual	215.492	263	.819		
	Total	445.316	266			

a Predictors (Constant), EXAA, ATTAA, TRAA
b Dependent Variable: AADAA

As a final note, although not a major hypothesis in this study, the respondents' attitude toward celebrity endorsements in general was assessed using a one-item scale as follows:

Overall, how do you feel about celebrity endorsement advertisements?

I love them ___:___:___:___:___:___:___ I hate them

In the analysis, it was found that those with a favorable attitude toward celebrity endorsement advertisements and those with a non-favorable attitude did vary in their evaluations of all of the featured advertisements in the study, as shown in the table below.

Table 14: ANOVA – Attitude Toward Celebrity Endorsement Advertisements

		Sum of Squares	df	Mean Square	F	Sig.
AADAK* ATTCEAD	Between Groups (Combined)	82.118	7	11.731	8.783	.000
	Within Groups	345.929	259	1.336		
	Total	428.047	266			
AADPS* ATTCEAD	Between Groups (Combined)	60.733	7	8.676	5.985	.000
	Within Groups	375.471	259	1.450		
	Total	436.204	266			
ADMH* ATTCEAD	Between Groups (Combined)	47.729	7	6.818	5.366	.000
	Within Groups	329.078	259	1.271		
	Total	376.807	266			
AADAA* ATTCEAD	Between Groups (Combined)	36.901	7	5.272	3.343	.002
	Within Groups	408.416	259	1.577		
	Total	445.316	266			

Conclusions and Recommendations

The research examined in the literature review above showed that forming associations with celebrities through the endorsement process is a means by which consumers can manage their image through adoption of cultural meanings associated with the celebrity. In striving to maintain positive self-views, self-presentation plays a large role. In "striving to promote the perception that others think well of" you, celebrity endorsers play a role in supplying the cultural meanings upon which we as consumers can draw. They have done the legwork and tested the personas and qualities in the public eye, allowing us to absorb the positive aspects in order to present ourselves in a positive light. McCracken is correct when stating that a celebrity and his or her meaning to consumers is "highly complex." Perhaps it is not attractiveness or credibility alone that makes successful endorsers and therefore the source models alone do not capture the endorsement processes entirely.

This current study has shown some positive effects related to age, gender, and ethnicity (of the respondents) as well as differences in the overall evaluations of the female vs. male endorsement advertisements. The study examined four different advertisements in which four very different sports figures appeared. Future research can further pinpoint effects by employing created advertisements using the same celebrity for both product categories. In this current study, the sports figures chosen for the expert versus non-expert condition (whether or not the product in the advertisement was sports-related or not) differed significantly on other measures such as attractiveness and trustworthiness. In other words, there were significant differences in the means of the pairs of sports figures; the two expert condition sports figure endorsement advertisements differed significantly from each other, as did the two non-expert condition advertisements. However, the three main hypotheses were supported, with the exception of the case of ethnicity contained in H3.

Future research should delve deeper into the area of what makes a celebrity meaningful to consumers and the method of matching celebrities to appropriate products. An instrument to determine meaning and attributes that contribute to the effectiveness of celebrity endorsers must be devised that encompasses more than the existing instruments. Further, the examination of the impact of female endorsers, both celebrity and non-celebrity alike, must be examined in order to fully appreciate the impact.

References

Adams-Price, C., & Greene, A. L. (1990). Secondary attachments and adolescent self-concept. *Sex Roles, 22*(3-4), 187-198.

Atkin, C., & Block, M. (1983, February/March). *Journal of Advertising Research, 23*(1), 57-61.

Basil, M. D. (1996, Fall). Identification as a mediator of celebrity effects. *Journal of Broadcasting and Electronic Media, 40*(4), 478-495.

Buhr, T. A., Simpson, T. L., & Pryor, B. (1987). Celebrity endorsers' expertise and perceptions of attractiveness, likeability, and familiarity. *Psychological Reports, 60*, 1307-1309.

Friedman, H., & Friedman, L. (1979). Endorser effectiveness by product type. *Journal of Advertising Research, 19*(5), 63-71.

Goldman, K. (1995, 12 October). Women endorsers more credible than men, a survey suggests. *Wall Street Journal*, Print Media Edition: Eastern edition.

Kahle, L. R., & Homer, P. M. (1985, March). Physical attractiveness of the celebrity endorser: A social adaptation perspective. *Journal of Consumer Research, 11*, 54-961.

Kamins, M. A. (1989, June/July). Celebrity and noncelebrity advertising in a two-sided context. *Journal of Advertising Research*, 34-42.

Kamins, M. A. (1990). An investigation into the "match-up" hypothesis in celebrity advertising: When beauty may be only skin deep. *Journal of Advertising, 19*(1), 4-13.

Kamins, M. A., Brand, M. J., Hoeke, S. A., & Moe, J. C. (1989). Two-sided versus one-sided celebrity endorsements: The impact on advertising effectiveness and credibility. *Journal of Advertising, 18*(2), 4-10.

Kelman, H. C. (1961, Winter). Processes of opinion change. *Public Opinion Quarterly, 25*, 57-78.

Kover, A. J., Goldberg, S. M., & James, W. L. (1995, November/December). Creativity vs. effectiveness? An integrating classification for advertising. *Journal of Advertising Research, 35*(6), 29-38.

Lockwood, P., & Kunda, Z. (1997, July). Superstars and me: Predicting the impact of role models on the self. *Journal of Personality and Social Psychology, 73*(1), 91-103.

Maddux, J. E., & Rogers, R. W. (1980, August). Effects of source expertness, physical attractiveness, and supporting arguments on persuasion: A case of brains over beauty. *Journal of Personality and Social Psychology, 39*, 235-244.

McCracken, G. (1989, December). Who is the celebrity endorser? Cultural foundations of the endorsement process. *Journal of Consumer Research, 16*, 310-321.

Norman, N. M., & Tedeschi, J. T. (1989). Self-presentation, reasoned action, and adolescent decisions to smoke cigarettes. *Journal of Applied Social Psychology, 19*(7), 543-558.

Ohanian, R. (1991, February/March). The impact of celebrity spokespersons' perceived image on consumers' intention to purchase. *Journal of Advertising Research*, 46-54.

Perreault, Jr., W. D., & Leigh, L. E. (1989). Reliability of nominal data based on qualitative judgments. *Journal of Marketing Research, 26*(2), 135-48.

Sellers, P. (1989, 8 May). The ABCs of marketing to kids. *Fortune, 119*(10), 114-120.

Shani, D., & Sandler, D. (1991). *Marketing News, 25*(6), 8.

Solomon, M. R. (1983, December). The role of products as social stimuli: A symbolic interactionism perspective. *Journal of Consumer Research, 10*, 319-329.

Stanton, W. R., Currie, G. D., Oei, T. P. S., & Silva, P. A. (1996). A developmental approach to influences on adolescents' smoking and quitting. *Journal of Applied Developmental Psychology, 17*, 307-319.

Sullivan, R. (2001, 3 September). For women: A golden age. *Time, 158*(9), 62, 2p, 2c.

A Case Study of the SARS Epidemic and the Toronto Blue Jays

DAVID SYNOWKA
SCOTT BRANVOLD
SUSAN HOFACRE

Abstract

Severe acute respiratory syndrome (SARS), a new and contagious disease, migrated from Asia to Toronto during the spring of 2003. The World Health Organization (WHO) issued an international travel advisory to Toronto during the last week of April resulting in significant declines to the city's international tourism and entertainment industry revenues. This case study discusses how the city and Toronto Blue Jays baseball organization were impacted by and responded to this crisis. In today's world, governments and other organizations need to plan for the possibility of catastrophic events using the tools of risk assessment with scenario planning, and to utilize a recognition, prioritization, and mobilization strategy. The Blue Jays organization reacted to the crisis with aggressive marketing to reduce the impact and worked with other Toronto tourism and event agencies to build local morale and attendance.

Introduction

Imagine all is right with the world and there is great optimism that the upcoming sporting event or season will bring happiness and entertainment to scores of fans. Then within a short period of time, an unexpected act of nature or man beyond the control of the organization has the potential to disrupt the event, creating loss of organizational revenues and image. But the reality is that the potential for crisis extends beyond your own organizational boundaries. The questions are what can you do and how do you react when it happens?

Crisis events are possibilities organizations need to acknowledge, address, and plan for in order to minimize damages and enable recovery. Recent examples of crisis events are the September 2001 terrorist attacks on the World Trade Center and Washington, DC, the anthrax attacks via the postal system to media and governmental agencies, and the 1989 World Series San Francisco earthquake. Organizations attempt to minimize exposure and maximize response by having risk management plans, as well as by creating structured planned marketing and public relations responses to maintain public credibility.

Often one cannot measure the effectiveness of a crisis response until the crisis has passed for days, weeks, months, and even years following the event. Immediate priorities for risk managers are first to protect the lives, health, and safety of employees and customers by effectively meeting their needs following the event. Second is the consideration of associated economic impacts of the event, including the direct and indirect expense costs, the loss of current and short-term revenue, and the preservation of jobs. In turn, managers face the challenge of returning a business back to operation and handling potentially huge complicated fiscal losses. A final priority will be the organization's image and credibility status during recovery (Veysey, 2003). Today an organization cannot effectively operate or react to a major crisis without building coalitions and relationships with governments and related industries.

Crisis and Catastrophe Response Planning

Historically, society has been confronted with crises ranging from terrorist attacks to financial malfeasance to the new emerging diseases. According to a study by Mitroof and Alpasian (2003), the benefit of effective crisis management planning by companies is a reduction in the number and scope of crises, resulting in better financial returns on assets, a longer organizational life span, and a higher public perception of corporate image.

Watkins and Bazerman (2003) state that all organizations are vulnerable to "predictable surprises," so companies should be proactive in minimizing their risk. Their recommended approach is employing a process of recognition, prioritization, and mobilization (RPM) as a central element of risk management planning and response.

According to the authors, psychological, organizational, and political vulnerabilities are barriers for companies that hinder an effective RPM strategy. Table 1 summarizes the key elements of these organizational barriers.

Table 1: Barriers to Effective Crisis Management (From Watkins & Bazerman, 2003)		
Psychological	**Organizational**	**Political**
Assumption that things are better than they are	Organizational complexity fragments & distorts key information data	Organizational power structure may overvalue interests of favored groups
Supports evidence for preconceptions & discount facts that do not agree with preconceptions	Data may be withheld and upper management receives incomplete & filtered information	Not in touch with governmental systems
Lack of attention as to what others are doing externally & internally	Organizational silos disperses responsibility & dilutes decision making authority	Lack of building broad consensus with governments and industry stakeholders
Emphasis on maintaining status quo	Lack of prospective results in issues being unrecognized or not prioritized	Internal organizational politics
Lack of personal experience with problem situation		

Being oblivious to emerging threats affects the most experienced leaders. There are really no surprises—warnings are often visible but ignored or given a cursory examination and consideration. Failure to prioritize occurs when a potential crisis is recognized but is not deemed sufficient to be given immediate attention. Finally, even when a crisis is recognized and given a strong priority, there can be lapses in mobilizing an effective response.

A critical part of RPM is the prediction of catastrophes, where two techniques can be used. These are risk assessment and scenario planning and are defined in Table 2 (Kennedy et. al., 2003).

Table 2: Summary of Risk Assessment and Scenario Planning Techniques (From Kennedy et. al., 2003)	
Risk Assessment	**Scenario Planning**
Systematic process of examining probabilities of future events	Is a strategy tool
Examines various outcomes focusing on benefits and cost estimates	Have qualified, knowledgeable individuals internal & external from the organization
Combines objective and subjective evaluations	Review strategies, research external trends, identification of critical business components, & potential trouble areas
Assists with alternative crisis responses and establishing priorities	Identify possible scenarios within established time frame
	Design preventive/preparatory responses
	Incorporate business continuity planning, medium term operational planning along with a strategic horizon plan
	Schedule an annual planning exercise
	Review and modify policy to address changes with internal & external organizational environments

The modern media and mass communications network from 24/7 international satellite news to the Internet creates a new challenge. Not only is the immediacy of breaking stories a concern for organizations and governments in addressing problems and issues, but it increasingly necessitates a timely factual and credible response. Additionally, the Internet is an unregulated medium plagued by the dissemination of false information, rumors, myths, and exaggeration of facts.

With catastrophic events, the organization's communications and quality of relationships with media, employees, customers, local government, and other stakeholders are essential with disaster recovery efforts. Coalition building is crucial in mobilizing an effective, creditable response to a crisis event and to sustain and build morale with implementing a recovery.

SARS and Toronto

In the spring of 2003, a mysterious infectious disease with a high mortality rate originated in Asia. Severe Acute Respiratory Syndrome (SARS) created worldwide panic as well as devastated national, regional, and local businesses and economies. SARS was a virus appearing to be as contagious as the flu, with a high mortality rate and no effective antiviral drugs to combat it.

One of the impacts of the SARS virus was a ripple effect through the tourism industries and international business communities in Hong Kong and China. In Asia, sport was not immune to the SARS epidemic, with the relocation of the 2004 Women's World Cup from China to the United States.

Through the modern air transportation system, the disease quickly migrated to a number of other countries. The first cases of SARS in Toronto, Canada, were first recorded and announced on March 14, 2003. A week later, health care workers in a Toronto Hospital exhibited SARS symptoms, which attracted international attention.

On April 23, 2003, the World Health Organization (WHO) announced a travel advisory for Toronto with the reporting of 132 probable SARS cases resulting in 12 deaths (Shipley, 2003). On April 30, the advisory was lifted, but the damage had been done.

Several weeks after the travel advisory, a second wave of infections and deaths in late May again brought notoriety to the city. At the end of June, SARS finally waned in Canada with 251 probable cases and 43 deaths, with most cases and all deaths being in Toronto. On July 2, 2003, WHO removed Toronto from the designation of a SARS impacted area and a week later the U.S. Centers for Disease Control and Prevention lifted its travel alert (Naylor, Chantler, & Griffiths, 2004).

Impact of SARS

In Toronto, tourism generates $3.4 billion annually and is the city's second leading industry. SARS significantly impacted this area of the city's economy. Attractions such as the Toronto Zoo reported attendance declines ranging from 40 to 60%. From March 2 to May 31, 2003, the Toronto tourism industry estimated losses of $190 million in revenue due to the SARS outbreak (Daniels, 2003). Business travel was down by 20%, with restaurants reporting 20 to 30% declines. Hotel occupancy decreased by 30% in April and May compared with the same period in 2002. Approximately 800 bus tours, along with five trade shows, were canceled with two being postponed and one other being moved to Montreal (Harris, 2003). Thousands of Toronto tourism employees were impacted by either losing jobs or having their hours cut. The 2003 economic impact of SARS was projected to be a $1 billion dollar (Cdn) loss to Toronto's gross domestic product, with tourism, transportation, and retail being the most affected sectors (Krauss 2003).

Toronto's Recovery Strategy

By early summer, it was apparent that external visitors were not coming to Toronto. A local campaign, "Toronto: You Belong Here," was focused at the population within a two-hour radius of the city. The strategy was to have locals become tourists within their own community. Events were heavily advertised and promoted by the local media. These included Caribana (the largest cultural festival on the continent), the Molson Indy, and a "Concert for Toronto" that included performers such as Neil Young, Sarah McLaughlin, and the Rolling Stones. These events met previous and expected attendance figures. An estimated one million copies of "Your Official Toronto Playbook" (including discount coupons for local entertainment destinations) were distributed by retail outlets, at local events, shopping malls, and at various attractions (Daniels, 2003). In early fall of 2003, Tourism Toronto received $10.7 million (USD) from the Ontario government to subsidize marketing efforts in order to recover and revitalize the tourism industry in the business, convention, and international sectors (Green, 2003).

The Toronto Blue Jays and SARS

The Toronto Blue Jays organization was impacted by the SARS epidemic at the beginning of the 2003 season. Part of the franchise revenues is dependent on the tourism trade from group sales in United States border towns and cities, along with convention visitors to the city. The Blue Jays' season was beginning when SARS began making its mark, and a nine-game home stand was scheduled to be held after the WHO's travel advisory to Toronto. Major League Baseball (MLB) reacted by issuing precautions to visiting teams, such as not signing autographs, not mingling with large crowds, not to visit hospitals, and avoiding the use of public transportation (Shipley, 2003). Two days following the WHO travel advisory, the first home game against the Royals drew an estimated 16,500 fans, which was the largest crowd since opening day. There was an estimate that cancellation of group sales may have totaled up to 30,000 tickets by mid July, and this did not include the loss of "walk-up" fans (Rodgers' Communications sees decline, 2003). Paul Godfrey, President of the Blue Jays, stated the team had $3million (Cdn) in loss revenue largely related with a 15% decline from U.S. fans by mid-August (Blue Jays challenged, 2003).

The Blue Jays realized the priorities of the SARS crisis extended beyond the economic impact on the organization to tourism-related industries along with the image and the morale of the city. The Blue Jays organization embarked on a strategy to demonstrate that SARS was not a threat to game attendees. The team started a policy of having five to six players signing autographs prior to every game. The Blue Jays' parent company, Rogers Inc., purchased the inventory of tickets for a May game against the Texas Rangers and sold them for $1 (Cdn) or .69 (USD) each. The result of the promotion had tickets being sold at 2,000 per hour with an announced attendance of 48,097. The cost of the promotion to Rogers Inc. was estimated to be $484,000 ($USD). In the weeks to follow, there were other discounted promotions with several $2 ticket nights (Fidelzeid, 2003).

The organization worked with other entertainment events to build attendance. Blue Jay tickets were packaged as "Its Time for a Little T.O." and included hotel accommodations, restaurant dinners, and theatre events for $125 (Cdn) (Bray, 2003). Another promotional package was "Steal a Base, See a Race and Experience WWE SmackDown In Your Face," which included a ticket to a Blue Jays game, the Toronto Indy, and the WWE event at the Air Canada Center, which was priced at $69 (Cdn) (Sports Fans get 3fer deal, 2003). The Blue Jays also helped by having one of their best records in June that helped to drive attendance and morale.

A financial review of the 2003 season and the impact of SARS revealed that even though the 2003 attendance increased by 162,000 over the previous season, the revenue per ticket generated had decreased. The bottom line for the 2003 season revealed an improvement over the 2002 season. This was largely attributed to lower payroll costs by $18 million (USD), along with a rise of the Canadian dollar over the U.S. dollar that had a net foreign exchange of $5,000,000 (USD) for the Blue Jays as well as Rogers assuming full ownership for the 2004 year (Blue Jays trim losses, 2004).

In looking at the recovery from the 2003 SARS episode, for the 2004 April-June period, the team reported a loss of $7.3 (Cdn) million as compared to $14.2 million (Cdn) loss for the same quarter in 2003. Blue Jays management credits the improved financial report due to lowering the team payroll, the MLB revenue sharing structure as well as the increased value of the Canadian dollar with the USD. As of July 2004, the revenue per ticket is up due to the elimination of two tickets for one and other discounts, but attendance has declined by 13%, especially with "walk-up" crowds. However, the organization reports the attendance decline is related to team performance (Lackner, 2004).

In Retrospect

According to Piovesan (2003), when the WHO issued the Toronto travel advisory, Toronto officials either took a defensive stance or remained silent. Government officials were viewed as outraged with the advisory and argued this action should be rescinded by the WHO. Also, officials responded that a $10 million marketing campaign was a key to addressing this issue. The international media continued reporting of new deaths and new cases globally connected to the city as well as Toronto being the SARS center outside of Asia. Few reported on the positive measures implemented to protect tourists and citizens. Instead, the media focused on Toronto's public surprise and outrage.

Psychologically, Toronto city officials lost the media battle and their credibility, resulting in an economic decline for the tourism industry and its employees. Organizationally and politically, this was a first-time modern major crisis event for Toronto's public officials. They did not anticipate or study past events such as the initial reaction of Chinese officials to SARS, the outbreak of foot and mouth disease, mad cow disease in Europe, or the September 11, 2001 events; and, in turn, they failed to understand or respond to new age global media.

Using the RPM approach, the Toronto Blue Jays organization reacted quickly to the SARS outbreak with Paul Rodgers, President of the Toronto Blue Jays, and Bob Rodgers, CEO of Rodgers Communications (parent company), taking high public profiles and leadership positions in establishing a strategic response. Both recognized the consequences the news of the SARS epidemic would have on MLB and understood the Toronto SARS infections were not widespread within the general public. The organization decided to employ a strong marketing and promotional campaign to increase morale in the community by offering discounted tickets along with utilizing the sport media to change the perceived "plague city" image to one that was still quite healthy and an attractive destination. Finally, the Blue Jays responded by encouraging close player contact to the public, aggressively discounting their product to gain media attention, and building relationships with hotel, restaurant, and tourism promotions to package significantly discounted products to increase tourism trade, image, and morale.

Conclusion

The WHO international travel advisory significantly impacted Toronto's tourism and image. Events such as September 11, 2001, and the SARS situation need to be studied and be part of risk management assessment and scenario planning tools for governments and businesses to coordinate efforts to minimize losses and enact a quick effective recovery. The Toronto Blue Jays organization played a part in rebuilding city image and community morale. Public relations and marketing strategies are an essential component of recovery efforts, and sport is a vehicle that may be able to make important contributions.

Realistically, the Toronto's SARS crisis did not reach the kind of high magnitude painted by the international media. But what if SARS had been more contagious? What if cases numbered in the tens of thousands and deaths in thousands? In today's world, catastrophic events can devastate community, regional, and national economies. Sports and other related industries should realize the potential for the period of disruption of operations and incorporate an RPM approach.

References

Blue Jays challenged by the dollar (2003). *ESPN.com: Sport Business*. Retrieved August 19, 2003, from http://sports.espn.go.com/espn/sportsbusiness.

Blue Jays trim losses (2004). *Toronto Globe and Mail*. Retrieved February 4, 2004, from http://www.theglobeandmail.com.

Bray, D. (2003). Marketing after SARS. *Marketing Magazine, 108*(27), 15.

Daniels, C. (2003, 1 September). Toronto looks into tourism recovery after SARS scares. *Prweek, 6*(34), 19.

Erwin, S. (2004, 5 February). Blue Jays still lost money in 2003 but a lot less of it. *Toronto Star*, p. E 2.

Fidelzeid, G. (2003). Blue Jays have just the ticket for SARS fears. *Prweek, 6*(18), 24.

Game sells out after $1 tickets special in wake of SARS (2003). *ESPN.com: Baseball*. Retrieved April 29, 2003, from http://sports.espn.go.com/mlb/.

Green, C. (2003). City reaches down deep to recover from SARS & other issues. *Meeting News, 28*(4), 20.

Harris, C. (2003). The cost of SARS. *Canadian Underwater, 70*(6), 16-18.

Jays show signs of improving . . . on balance sheet (2004, 22 July). *Toronto Star*, p. 1.

Kennedy, P., Perrottet, C., & Thomas, C. (2003). Scenario planning after 9/11: Managing the impact of a catastrophic event, *Strategy and Leadership, 31*(1), 4-13.

Krauss, C. (2003, 27 July). SARS abates in Toronto, but tourism still lags. *New York Times*, p. 5:3.

Lackner, C. (2004) Jay's book value in a slump. Retrieved July, 22, 2004, from http://www.theglobeandmail.com.

Mitroff, I., & Alpasian, M. C. (2003). Preparing for evil. *Harvard Business Review, 81*(4), 109-115.

Naylor, C. D., Chantler, C., & Griffiths, S. (2004.) Learning from SARS in Hong Kong and Toronto. *JAMA, 291*(20), 283-87.

Piovesan, R. (2003). Toronto's pr bungle on SARS. *Marketing Magazine, 18*(18), 7.

Prewitt, M. (2003). Toronto struggles back as SARS warning lifted. *Nation's Restaurant News, 37*(19), 8.

Rogers' Jays losses decline (2003, July 17). *Toronto Globe and Mail.* Retrieved July, 17, 2003, from http://www.theglobeandmail.com.

Sandomir, R. (2003, 24 April). The SARS epidemic: BASEBALL; Health officials tell visiting major league teams to take precautions in Toronto. *New York Times,* p. 12:1.

SARS devastates restaurants in Toronto (2003). *Restaurant Business, 102*(9), 12.

Shipley, A. (2003, 23 April). MLB to issue teams SARS precautions. *The Washington Post,* p. D 1.

Shipley, A. (2003, 25 April). The discomfort of home; MLB teams deal with SARS fears as Blue Jays head to Toronto after road trip. *The Washington Post,* p. D 1.

Sports Fans get 3fer deal. (2003, 9-15 June). *Street and Smith's SportsBusiness Journal, 6*(7), 40.

Veysey, S. (2003). Studying disasters can aid response plan. *Business Insurance, 37*(16) 24-5.

Watkins, M., & Bazerman, M. (2003). Predictable surprises: The disasters you should have seen coming. *Harvard Business Review, 81*(3), 72-80.

Editor Biography

Brenda G. Pitts is currently a professor and the Director of Sport Management and the Director of the Sport Business Research Center at Georgia State University in Atlanta, Georgia. She is distinguished as the Dr. Earle F. Zeigler Scholar of 2000, one of the first Research Fellows of the North American Society for Sport Management in 2001, and the 2004 Dr. Garth Paton Distinguished Service Award. Dr. Pitts is author or coauthor of four sport marketing textbooks and numerous publications and presentations, and is published in scholarly journals such as the *Journal of Sport Management, Sport Marketing Quarterly, Journal of Vacation Marketing, International Journal of Sports Marketing and Sponsorship,* and *International Journal of Sport Management.*

Author Biographies

Kevin Ayers is an associate professor of sport management at Western Carolina University, where he teaches financial aspects of sport and sport marketing.

Stephen L. Baglione has been a part of the Saint Leo University faculty for eight years. He has expertise in the field of marketing research and is a past recipient of Research of the Year in business (second) and teaching. He is active in the American Marketing Association and is a faculty advisor.

Balbir Bal has been a part of the Saint Leo University faculty for five years. He has expertise in the field of computer science (robot programming). He is currently a student advisor.

Dennis L. Bechtol is an assistant professor at Northwood University, Florida campus. Dr. Bechtol previously taught strategic management, marketing, and organizational leadership in the Graduate School of Management and Technology at the University of Maryland. He most recently taught sport finance, sport marketing, sport leadership, and sport sponsorship and public relations in the graduate sport management program at the University of Texas. He has also taught undergraduate and graduate courses at George Mason University, Northern Virginia Community College, and the University of New Mexico. Dr. Bechtol is a member of the North American Society of Sport Management, the National Association for Sport and Physical Education, and the National Association of Assembly Managers.

Douglas Blais is the program chair of sport management at Southern New Hampshire University and a section editor of the *Sport Marketing Quarterly*.

Scott Branvold is a professor of sport management at Robert Morris University in Pittsburgh, Pennsylvania. He has numerous publications and teaches a number of graduate and undergraduate courses in sport management and sport marketing.

Corey Braun works for West Wayne Advertising in Atlanta, Georgia.

Jan Charbonneau is a lecturer in the Department of Marketing at Massey University, New Zealand. Her academic interests include cross-cultural gender and ethnic portrayal in advertising, legislating online marketing to children, and use of technology in teaching and celebrity/athlete endorsements.

Mei-Yen Chen is an instructor at the National College of Physical Education and Sports, Taiwan.

Steve Chen recently became a faculty member of the United States Sports Academy in Spring of 2004. He earned his D.S.M. from the Academy, his M.S. from Cal State University Fullerton, and his B.A. from UCLA. Before studying at the Academy, Dr. Chen was involved in basketball as a student manager and graduate assistant at Division-I schools and as a coach for two professional teams in Taiwan. Chen is currently an assistant professor of the Sport Management Department at the Academy and serves as the co-editor of the *Sport Coaching Journal*.

Ta-tsung Chiou is a member of the United States Sports Academy.

Vincent Couvelaere is a graduate of Université Laval, where he was a research assistant in sport marketing. He is currently employed at Total France in Paris.

R. Brian Crow is currently in his fourth year as an associate professor of sport management at Slippery Rock University. He is presently the President of the North American Society for Sport Management (NASSM). Prior to this election, Crow was NASSM's Business Office Manager for two years and a Member-at-Large on the Executive Council. Crow recently ended his three-year tenure as Editor-in-Chief of the *Sport Marketing Quarterly*. In 2005, Crow started a sport marketing and fan consultation company, GameDay Consulting, LLC, a firm specializing in the training, certification, and monitoring of GameDay employees at sport venues. Current clients include the Buffalo Bills. Dr. Crow currently is an educational consultant for Nike Grassroots Basketball and the Nike All-America basketball camp, and served as a strategy consultant for SOKOL USA. Crow has done research for the Nokia Sugar Bowl, the Black Sports Agents Association, and the Mississippi Sea Wolves (ECHL).

Vassilis Dalakas is an assistant professor of marketing at Northern Kentucky University, Highland Heights. Previously he taught at the Campbell School of Business at Berry College. He earned his Ph.D. in marketing from the University of Oregon in 1999. His research interests include consumer behavior, sponsorship, sports marketing, consumer socialization, and cross-cultural marketing. His research has been published in the *Journal of Business Research*, the *Journal of Consumer Psychology*, the *Journal of Consumer Marketing*, *Sport Marketing Quarterly*, the *Journal of Euro-Marketing*, and several conference proceedings.

Kathryn Dobie is an associate professor of logistics in the Department of Business Administration at North Carolina A&T State University in Greensboro.

Dan Drane is an assistant professor and coordinator of the Coaching and Sport Administration Department at the University of Southern Mississippi in Hattiesburg. His research interests include accessible golf, sport celebrity endorsements, service-learning, youth sports, social and economic impact of sports, golf and the environment, gambling in sport, and purchasing in sport organizations.

Ron Garland is an associate professor in the Department of Marketing at the University of Waikato, Hamilton, New Zealand. His research interests include sport marketing, market research methodology, services marketing in general, and bank marketing in particular. He has published several chapters on sport marketing in sport management texts as well as general marketing issues in a variety of journals, including the *European Journal of Marketing*, *Journal of Marketing Theory and Practice*, *International Journal of Bank Marketing*, *Journal of Financial Services Marketing*, and *Tourism Management*.

James Grant is a professor at the American University of Sharjah in Washington, D. C.

Joe Fernandez works for Chick-Fil-A in Atlanta, Georgia.

John A. Fortunato is an assistant professor in the department of advertising at the University of Texas at Austin. Dr. Fortunato is the author of *The Ultimate Assist: The Relationship and Broadcast Strategies of the NBA and Television Networks*. He received his Ph. D. from Rutgers University.

Daniel C. Funk is an assistant professor in the sport management program at the University of Texas at Austin. Dr. Funk earned a Ph.D. in sport management at The Ohio State University with an emphasis in consumer behavior. His primary research interests include understanding the psychology behind sport consumption in the sport market place. Dr. Funk has published scholarly work in scientific journals including *Leisure Sciences*, *Sport Marketing Quarterly*, *Sport Management Review*, *Journal of Sport Management*, *International Journal of Sports Marketing and Sponsorship*, and *International Journal of Sport Management*. He has worked on various national and international projects examining consumer involvement with professional sport teams and leisure activities.

Stewart Gillman has been a part of Saint Leo University faculty since January 2000. He has expertise in the field of sport management, marketing, and psychology/sociology of sport. He is a part of the Sport Marketing Association and North America Society of Sport Management. He is also assisting in beginning a Sport Management/Golf Course Management Association for the university campus.

Susan Hofacre was the director of the sport management program and a professor of sport management at Robert Morris College in Pittsburgh, Pennsylvania. Upon her passing in January of 2005, the National Association of Collegiate Directors of Athletics (NACDA) named Dr. Hofacre the 2005 NCAA Division I-AA / I-AAA Northeast region's General Sports TURF Systems Athletic Director of the Year.

Maria Hopwood is a professor and course leader for the public relations program at the University of Teesside, UK.

Erin P. Hughes is programs director of the Resident's Interhall Congress at the University of Arkansas.

Heikki Karjaluoto is a professor in the Department of Marketing at the University of Oulu, Finland.

Manne Kesti is a professor in the Department of Marketing at the University of Oulu, Finland.

Eunyi Kim is a visiting assistant professor at Texas A&M University in College Station, Texas. She has published in *Journalism and Mass Communication Quarterly* and has presented research papers at meetings of the International Communication Association and Midwest Political Science Conference and elsewhere.

Timo Koivumäki is a professor in the Department of Marketing at the University of Oulu, Finland.

Andrea Lansford works for Big Time Products in Rome, Georgia.

Soonhwan Lee is an assistant professor of sport management at College Misericordia in Pennsylvania. He received his B.A. from Myong Ji University, his M.S. from Illinois State University, and his D.S.M. from the United States Sports Academy.

Chia-ying (Doris) Lu is an assistant professor in the Sport Management Department at National Taiwan College of Physical Education. After she earned her doctoral degree from Flordia State University, she went back to Taiwan to work in an academic environment and help prepare individuals to work in the sport industry. Her primary areas of research interest are sport marketing, sport management, and consumer behavior.

Carol Lucas is the marketing research manager for the Georgia World Congress Authority and the Georgia Dome.

Melissa Johnson Morgan is a senior lecturer in the Marketing and Tourism Department of the University of Southern Queensland's Faculty of Business in Australia. Up until December of 2002 she was an assistant professor of marketing at the A.B. Freeman School of Business at Tulane University in New Orleans. Her research focuses on the experiential consumption of sport and she has developed a unique phenomenon sampling methodology. Her other research interests include extreme sport consumption communities, sport tourism, and sport governance effectiveness.

Eric J. Newman is an assistant professor in the Department of Marketing at California State University. He has worked in the travel industry including the Carlson Network and Delta Airlines and has also worked in the computer industry with Zenith Data Systems and Computer Consultants. He also worked in sports marketing including sports arena and hockey franchise development for Center Ice Consultants and in the restaurant field for the Omni Corporation. Dr. Newman has been a Marketing/Advertising club advisor for many years and is the current CSUSB Marketing Club advisor. His student clubs have won numerous awards including top placements at the AAF College World Series and have traveled around the country. Dr. Newman's current research is in the area of Internet marketing.

Jaime Orejan is an assistant professor of Leisure and Sport Management at Elon University. His research interests include management and organization—particularly football (soccer)—marketing/management, international sport governance and international education, and sport history (football).

Sung-Bae Park is an instructor at the University of Northern Colorado as well as the president of the Korean Student Organization on campus.

Dennis Phillips has been a college professor and administrator for 24 years, the past 13 at the University of Southern Mississippi. He is currently the associate director of the School of Human Performance and Recreation at USM. He has also been the graduate coordinator for the School of HP & R, a college assistant athletic director at Springfield College, and assistant director of marketing and special events for the Volleyball Hall of Fame. He has been the president of the Mississippi State AAHPERD organization, chair of both the Athletic Council and Sport Management Councils of the Southern District of AAHPERD, and on the Executive Boards of the National Council on Accreditation of Coaching Education (NCACE) and The Sport Law and Recreation Association (SLRA). Dr. Phillips has been an active member and presenter at the North American Society of Sport Management (NASSM) and SLRA for many years, and has been a reviewer of both organizations' presentation proposals. He has written two chapters in Law for Recreation and Sport Managers, one chapter on Legal Issues of Hazing in Sport, and is co-author of the book *Profiles of Sport Industry Professionals*. He currently serves on the Governor's Commission on Physical Activity and Sport in Mississippi.

Mark Pritchard is an assistant professor in the College of Public Programs at Arizona State University. He received his B.S., M.S., and Ph.D. in leisure studies and services from the University of Oregon in Eugene. His academic interests include research in recreation and travel settings, consumer marketing studies, and the psychology at work in commitment and loyalty.

André Richelieu is a marketing professor at Université Laval, Québec, Canada. In 2002, he completed his Ph.D. at the joint doctoral program in administration in Montréal. His research interests focus on i) the development of brand equity by professional sports teams and how they leverage their brand; ii) the internationalization of the firm and the institutional levers that firms can use in order to enter foreign markets. Prior to his academic career, Richelieu worked in the business industry, spending, among others, over two years in Romania. He has lived in or visited 40 countries.

Annu Ristola is a professor in the Department of Marketing at the University of Oulu, Finland.

Jari Salo is a professor in the Department of Marketing at the University of Oulu, Finland.

Eric C. Schwarz is an assistant professor of sport management at Daniel Webster College (N.H.) and coordinator for the sport management program. In addition to his teaching duties, he is also faculty advisor for the Daniel Webster College Society for Sport Management, and oversees all sport management practica and internships. He has served as assistant director of facility scheduling and event management at SUNY Stony Brook, as assistant director of student life for intramurals and recreation at SUNY Oswego, and as director of campus recreation services and adjunct faculty at Drew University (N.J.). He also started the East Coast Sports Academy, a company that offered summer camps, year-round clinics, and individual and team training programs for children of all ages.

Melissa St. James is an assistant professor of marketing in the College of Business, Administration, and Public Policy at California State University, Dominguez Hills. She received her Ph.D. in marketing from The George Washington University and her research has led to six published works. For two and a half years she was a full-time lecturer at CSU San Bernardino, as well as a professor at the University of San Diego and The George Washington University.

Jane Summers is the head of the Marketing and Tourism Department in the Faculty of Business at the University of Southern Queensland in Australia. Her teaching and research interests are in the areas of consumer behaviour, e-marketing and sport marketing. Her specific interest in sport marketing has evolved due to the call from both practioners and academics for more research in this area and for a greater understanding particularly of consumer behaviour and attitudes in relation to sport consumption. She is also currently researching the international applicability of some of these consumption related issues.

James E. Swartz teaches courses in promotions management and entertainment marketing at California State Polytechnic University. His published work has appeared in the *Journal of Advertising Research*, the *Journal of Integrated Marketing Communication, Public Relations Review, Public Opinion Quarterly*, and the *Journal of Advertising*, and he has presented more than 50 refereed papers at conferences such as IBA, ICA, AAA, FBD, PCA, AEJMC, and MEA. He has been named an Eisenhower Fellow at the Smithsonian, a research fellow at the Center for Strategic and International Studies, and an IAT postdoctoral fellow at the University of Texas-Austin.

David Synowka is a professor of sport management and director of sport administration at Robert Morris University in Pittsburgh, Pennsylvania, where he has resided for over 25 years. Apart from being an integral part of both the Sport Management and the NCAA Division I Athletics Programs, he was the head athletic trainer from 1978-1987 and developed the sport medicine facilities and service at the institution.

Michael Volkov is an associate lecturer in marketing and touring at the University of Southern Queensland. He has numerous publications and is a Fellow of the Academy of Marketing Science, an Associate Fellow of the Academy of World Business, a Member of the Market Research Society of Australia, and a Member of the Australian Institute of Management. His research interests include consumer behavior, marketing communication, sport marketing, e-marketing, and public policy.

Alvin Williams is Chair of the Department of Management and Marketing and a professor of marketing at the University of Southern Mississippi in Hattiesburg, Mississippi. He has published articles in various journals including *International Journal of Purchasing and Materials Management, Industrial Marketing Management, Journal of Personal Selling and Sales Management, Psychology and Marketing, Journal of Marketing Education*, and *Journal of Marketing Theory and Practice*. He has received various outstanding service awards from the National Association of Purchasing Management and is on the editorial boards of several journals.

James Zarick is an associate professor at High Point University in High Point, North Carolina.

Mark Zhang is a doctoral assistant at the United States Sports Academy. He currently teaches undergraduate courses in sport management.